Bodies of Reform

America and the Long 19th Century

GENERAL EDITORS
David Kazanjian, Elizabeth McHenry, and Priscilla Wald

Bodies of Reform

*The Rhetoric of Character
in Gilded Age America*

James B. Salazar

NEW YORK UNIVERSITY PRESS

New York and London

NEW YORK UNIVERSITY PRESS
New York and London
www.nyupress.org

LIBRARY OF CONGRESS CATALOGING-IN-PUBLICATION DATA
Salazar, James B.
Bodies of reform : the rhetoric of character in Gilded Age America /
James B. Salazar.
   p.   cm.—(America and the long 19th century)
Includes bibliographical references and index.
ISBN 978-0-8147-4130-6 (cl : alk. paper)
ISBN 978-0-8147-4131-3 (pbk. : alk. paper)
ISBN 978-0-8147-4132-0 (e-book : alk. paper)
1. American fiction—19th century—History and criticism.   2. Character
in literature.   3. Characters and characteristics in literature.   4. National
characteristics, American, in literature.   5. Character—Political
aspects—United States—History—19h century.   6. Rhetoric—Political
aspects—United States—History—19th century.   7. Political culture—
United States—History—19th century.   8. Politics and literature—United
States—History—19th century.   I. Title.
PS374.C43S36   2010
823'.809353—dc22   2010019202

New York University Press books are printed on acid-free paper,
and their binding materials are chosen for strength and durability.
We strive to use environmentally responsible suppliers and materials to the
greatest extent possible in publishing our books.

Manufactured in the United States of America
c 10 9 8 7 6 5 4 3 2 1
p 10 9 8 7 6 5 4 3 2 1

A book in the American Literatures Initiative (ALI), a collaborative
publishing project of NYU Press, Fordham University Press, Rutgers
University Press, Temple University Press, and the University of Virginia
Press. The Initiative is supported by The Andrew W. Mellon Foundation.
For more information, please visit www.americanliteratures.org.

Contents

Acknowledgments

Character has proven to be a strangely cumbersome, yet also intangible, topic of study. Pivotal in so many diverse texts and discourses of the nineteenth century and yet the express subject of so few, character seemed to be both everywhere and nowhere, easy to see yet difficult to understand. Fortunately, I have had the guidance and inspiration of many supportive friends, colleagues, and teachers in developing this study. I would first like to thank my colleagues at Temple University for their generous support as I worked on the final stages of the manuscript. I am particularly grateful to Miles Orvell, who unflinchingly gave much time and energy to reading entire drafts of the manuscript and who helped guide the project to its final completion with excellent advice on direction and scope. Discussions with Peter Logan on the discourse of fetishism in the nineteenth century, and his useful feedback on chapter drafts, have also helped me to keep the historical and theoretical ambitions of this project in balance. Steve Newman, Dan O'Hara, Eli Goldblatt, Shannon Miller, Sue Wells, and Larry Venuti have also provided many useful comments and insights on the project at many stages, and fellow Americanists Kate Henry, Michael Kaufmann, and Oliver Gaycken have exposed me to new archives and perspectives on the nineteenth century that have enriched the book immensely. Jena Osman, Sue-Im Lee, Suzanne Gauch, Rachel Blau DuPlessis, Patricia Melzer, and Lisa Rhodes have also provided the kind of intellectual community that has been invaluable to the development of my ideas on the project and to keeping my sanity through its completion. Thanks as well to Carolyn Karcher for her support and guidance on bringing the work to publication.

Beyond Temple, a number of people have supported my work in many incalculable and all too painfully calculable ways. Gillian Harkins and Edlie Wong have been unfailing friends and indispensable readers of the manuscript over the long course of its development, and I owe them a very special thanks. David Kazanjian has encouraged the project at many critical moments as well. Participants in the Haverford Faculty Working Group in American Studies have also provided excellent feedback on the project and stimulated my thinking in many ways, particularly Tina Zwarg, Homay King, Bethany Schneider, Jean Lutes, and Heather Hicks. Special thanks to Gus Stadler and Susan Ryan for their incisive readings of the manuscript and astute suggestions toward revision. Detailed discussions with Christopher Lukasik, Mark Feldman, Corey Capers, Howard Horowitz, and Christopher Diller on different aspects of the book have also been immensely valuable. And Masha Raskolnikov, Dale Carrico, and Catherine Zimmer have been sustaining interlocutors from the very beginning and good friends throughout.

A number of scholars have helped give the project its shape at some of its earlier stages, particularly Nancy Ruttenburg, Stephen Best, Stephen Hartnett, Felipe Gutterriez, Charles Altieri, and Trane Devore. Jill Bergman, Debra Bernardi, and John Bryant have provided much editorial guidance on particular chapters, and Bill Brown has been a gracious supporter of the project in its early stages and reader of some very early sections. Carole Blair helped clarify the importance of classical and modern rhetorical theory to the aims of the project as well. I am particularly grateful to Judith Butler, Donald McQuade, Sam Otter, and Shannon Jackson, who helped give shape and inspiration to the project in its formative stage. I owe a particular debt of gratitude to Judith Butler, who has been a generous reader and an unflagging supporter of the project throughout its development, and who seemed to know exactly when to put up the guard rails and when to let me roam. Donald McQuade has helped shape the contours of the project as a whole and guided me through the intricacies of my own writing, and for that I am very thankful. Without Samuel Otter this project would be a very different, lesser thing. Sam has enabled me to see the project more clearly against the broader landscape of nineteenth-century U.S. literature and culture and has given me advice on particular chapters and the arrangement as a whole that have been absolutely indispensable. Shannon Jackson's knowledge of the archive and ability to see thematic and conceptual connections between the chapters have been enormously helpful, and to her I owe many thanks. I am also enormously grateful to Michael Rogin, who in early readings and conversations helped to give shape to the project and whose own work has been such a guide to my own. He'll always be sorely missed.

A number of institutions have supported the development of *Bodies of Reform*. Summer Research Awards and a Faculty Study Leave from Temple University helped me to complete much of the research and writing of the final manuscript, and a Junior Faculty Grant from the Office of the Vice President for Research and Graduate Studies at Temple enabled me to conduct research on physical culture at the New York Public Library. A fellowship from the Center for the Humanities at Temple University helped me to refine different aspects of the final chapters, as did the discussions of the project with other members of the fellowship group, particularly Hillary Dick, Richard Immerman, and Elizabeth Varon. Early work on the project was also completed with the assistance of a University of California Dissertation-Year Fellowship. Thanks to the Dartmouth College American Studies Summer Institute, where I presented on portions of the manuscript, and to Elizabeth Maddock Dillon for her comments and Donald Pease for his support. Eric Zinner and Ciara McLaughlin at NYU Press have also been invaluable guides through the intricacies of the publishing process. Thank you to the graduate students in my seminars on the rhetoric of character, fetishism and the imagination, and the nineteenth-century child for stimulating my thinking in so many ways and to Nicole Cesare for her excellent assistance editing portions of the manuscript. And I'm grateful as well to the New York Public Library, University of Delaware Special Collections, Harry Ransom Humanities Research Center at the University of Texas at Austin, Connecticut Historical Society, Colonial Williamsburg Foundation, and University of Illinois at Chicago Library Special Collections for their help tracking down difficult sources. Portions of chapter 1 have been previously published as "Philanthropic Taste: Race and Character in Melville's *The Confidence-Man*" in the journal *Leviathan: A Journal of Melville Studies*, and portions of chapter 5 have been previously published as the essay chapter "Character's Conduct: The Democratic Habits of Jane Addams's 'Charitable Effort,'" in *Our Sisters' Keepers: Nineteenth-Century Benevolence Literature by American Women*, ed. Jill Bergman and Debra Bernardi (Tuscaloosa: University of Alabama Press, 2005). Thank you to Wiley-Blackwell, publishers of *Leviathan*, and the University of Alabama Press for permission to use this material.

Finally, I'd like to thank Amze Emmons, Josephine Park, and James Ker for their sharp wit, fine meals, and scholarly acumen and Betty, Jim, and Mac Holton for their sustaining support through some of the toughest stages of completion. Special thanks to my ever patient and supportive family for their unwavering love and faith in what I do even though it takes so incredibly long to get it done. And my deep and abiding gratitude goes to Adalaine Holton, who has been a vital and patient companion on this strange road. Her wise counsel on everything from sentence construction to overlooked sources to conceptual nuance have been essential to this book's completion.

Introduction

"The Grandest Thing in the World"

> My first assertion is one that I think you will grant—that everyone in this room is a judge of character. Indeed it would be impossible to live for a year without disaster unless one practiced character-reading and had some skill in the art. Our marriages, our friendships depend on it; our business largely depends on it; every day questions arise which can only be solved by its help. And now I will hazard a second assertion, which is more disputable perhaps, to the effect that on or about December, 1910, human character changed.
>
> —Virginia Woolf, "Mr. Bennett and Mrs. Brown"[1]

> When I was a young man, we talked much of character. . . . It is typical of our time that insistence on character today in the country has almost ceased. Freud and others have stressed the unconscious factors of our personality so that today we do not advise youth about their development of character; we watch and count their actions with almost helpless disassociation from thought of advice.
>
> —W.E.B. Du Bois, "My Character," in *The Autobiography of W. E. B. Du Bois*[2]

Bodies of Reform studies what was perhaps *the* most coveted object of nineteenth-century American culture, that curiously formable yet often equally formidable stuff called character. So much more than simply the bundle of traits that distinguish and define an individual's identity, character was to many nineteenth-century Americans, as Orison Swett Marden somewhat gleefully put it, "the grandest thing in the world."[3] The impact of the concept of character on the culture of the nineteenth century is hard to miss, its influence difficult to overstate. A pervasive and defining keyword across a range of nineteenth-century political, literary, philosophical, scientific, and pedagogical discourses, character was a concept that mediated understandings of the most fundamental relationships between individuals and their bodies, bodies and civil society, and civil society and the state. Conceived at the intersection of literature and politics, the concept of character connected the literary work of novelists to the ideological work of cultural nationalists in the nineteenth century and played a pivotal role in the articulation of national, racial, and gender identities in the United States. Character was a central category as well in the broader liberal tradition out of which the United States emerged and has long been a key term for imagining the reach of the public over the private sphere as well as the reach of the nation over and into the citizen. Indeed, it is difficult to imagine another concept that has done so much hard and politically charged work throughout the history of the United States. From the patricians of the early republic to post-Reconstruction racial scientists, from fin de siècle progressivist social reformers to postwar sociologists, character has had a very long and checkered career articulating national identity in the United States.[4] It is thus surprising that, at a time in which postnational critiques of the intersections of race, gender, and class in the ideological construction of "American character" have so invigorated U.S. literary and cultural studies, few have asked why "character" itself emerged as such a privileged mediator of national identity and public culture in the United States.[5]

Bodies of Reform closes this gap in U.S. literary and historical studies by charting the development of character as a central object of literary representation and social reform in the fictional genres, reform movements, and political cultures of the United States from approximately 1850 to 1920. The book's first aim is to make visible a unique archive in which the cultural practices of reading and representing character can be seen to operate in relation to the character-building strategies of social reformers by reading novelists such as Herman Melville, Mark Twain, Pauline Hopkins, and Charlotte Perkins Gilman in relation to a diverse range of historical documents also concerned with the formation and representation of character, including child-rearing guides, muscle-building magazines, police gazettes, libel and naturalization law, benevolent society publications, psychology textbooks, Scout handbooks, and success manuals. In these readings, I delineate the ideological formulation of what I call the "rhetoric of character" by elucidating the various yet interconnected meanings of character across this diverse range of political, popular, scientific, and literary discourses. More importantly, I examine the practices of individual and collective embodiment through which such meanings were used to negotiate the structural relations and symbolic practices that organized literary culture and national life toward the end of the nineteenth century. In so doing, *Bodies of Reform* revises our understanding of this familiar, influential, yet surprisingly underexamined category of nineteenth-century literary and political practice by resituating the study of character within a broader cultural politics of embodiment, a politics that shaped the most important debates over the cultural meaning, social mobility, and political authority of the raced and gendered body in this tumultuous period of American history. Such a perspective hopes to make visible the critical role the rhetoric of character played in redefining the legal and cultural meanings of citizenship and personhood in the shifting economic order and expanding imperial enterprises of the United States as it expanded the domestic and international reach of state power in the first decades of the twentieth century.

In recovering character's importance to the politics of embodiment that shaped the literature and culture of the late nineteenth century, a period usually associated with character's cultural and ideological decline, *Bodies of Reform* offers a critical revision of traditional scholarly perspectives on the rhetoric of character. The rhetoric of character has been commonly understood as a theory of self-formation, cultivated by the novel form, whose ideological function was to inculcate those forms of economic agency and social discrimination essential to the formation and regulation of a liberal, democratic public sphere in the United States. As many scholars have argued, this regulatory model naturalized forms of social, political, and economic exclusion by obscuring the role of the body—particularly the white male body—in defining the universal, disembodied "character" of the democratic citizen-subject.[6] Character has come to be identified with an interior, private self whose social and civic value is measured by its subjection of, and liberation from, the impulses and social particularity of the physical body. The history of character has thus been emplotted within a narrative of decline in the second half of the nineteenth century. In this narrative, character's increasing obsolescence as a cultural and regulatory ideal is ascribed both to the gradual recovery of the body as a site of political contestation in, for example, the abolitionist and women's rights movements and to the emergence of the mass-mediated, consumer culture of modern industrial capitalism in its "Gilded Age," a culture increasingly regulated through the elicitation and organization of a theatrical, expressively embodied "personality" rather than through the internalized self-restraint of "character."[7]

Bodies of Reform challenges this period-defining myth in U.S. literary and cultural history by arguing that such stories of character's devaluation in the social and visual economies of the Gilded Age, like the laments over character's presumed decline, are what enable and extend its cultural work and regulatory function. I develop this argument by first elucidating the performative logic of embodiment and disembodiment through which character had long carried out its cultural work. I then trace the influential role that this logic of embodiment played in the cultural transformations said to cause character's demise. My aim is to make visible the centrality of the rhetoric of character to the disciplinary forms and regimes of cultural representation that defined the culture of modern commodity capitalism in terms of a democratized vision of middle-class character. But I also aim to make visible the "eccentric characters" who haunt both the center and the margins of the liberal democratic imaginary, by charting the destabilizing effects of the cultural identification of character with white masculinity, as well as the alternate forms of political agency such instabilities make possible, particularly for those who are most vulnerable to its discriminatory function.[8]

Bodies of Reform thus makes visible the central role that the rhetoric of character played in both sustaining *and* challenging the forms of racial and gender discrimination, economic inequality, and cultural imperialism that dominated the concerns of late nineteenth-century novelists, social reformers, and cultural nationalists alike. The rhetoric of character destabilized the conventional signifiers of race and gender by detaching the materiality of race and gender from the indexicality of the physiological body and lodging it in the performative acts of character, acts through which character settled as lived experience and social fact. And yet, while this meant that the signifying traits of race and gender could be rewritten, through character building, as the self-authored traits of the well-formed, "successful" character, the rhetoric of character also provided an expanded and more flexible hermeneutics of the body, gesture, and visage that could be more effectively used to defend the discriminatory classifications of race, class, and gender by racial scientists, cultural nationalists, educators, and policymakers. The promise *and* peril of the rhetoric of character that emerged at the end of the nineteenth century was that it provided a powerful resource for challenging the social and legal delimitations of race and gender while also articulating a newly elaborated and delimiting taxonomy of race, class, and gender "types." Character's broad and frequently contradictory appeal to a diverse range of writers and

reformers, such as William Dean Howells, P.T. Barnum, Anna Julia Cooper, Luther Standing Bear, W.E.B. Du Bois, G. Stanley Hall, John Dewey,
and Theodore Roosevelt, thus lay, I argue, in its promise not only to make
legible the social and economic forces of a rapidly developing nation but
also to provide a seemingly concrete mechanism for managing, challenging, or transforming those forces.[9]

What I argue in the chapters that follow is that the reversibility of the
relationship between the sign and referent of character was what made the
rhetoric of character such a powerful instrument of social control *and* of
self-empowerment in nineteenth- and early twentieth-century U.S. culture. Character's cultural importance is most often located in its value
as a referential origin and grounding substance to the shifting cultural
signs, performed identities, and manufactured values of the "society of
the spectacle" that has come to define late modern capitalism.[10] As its etymological origins suggest, however, character has long been conceived as
a "substance" that is not only indistinguishable from but also the product of those forms of manufactured symbolic value that it presumably
challenges. The essential properties of character have been defined, at
least since the ancient Greeks, in terms of a unique conjunction of textual meaning, monetary value, and manufactured form. The Greek word
χαρακτηρ (*kharakter*), for example, was originally defined as "a mark engraved or impressed, the impress or stamp on coins and seals" and was
metaphorically extended to include "the mark impressed (as it were) on
a person or thing, a distinctive mark, characteristic, character."[11] Drawing on this original conception of *character* as simultaneously a product
of publication, minting, and manufacture, Noah Webster similarly defines *character* in his first *American Dictionary of the English Language*
(1828) as "a mark or figure made by stamping or impression, as on coins"
or "a mark or figure made with a pen or style, on paper, or other material used to contain writing," a definition that also included "the peculiar
qualities, impressed by nature or habit on a person, which distinguish him
from others."[12] Rather than referring to an originary essence or origin,
character thus refers, as J. Hillis Miller has argued, to the act of figura-
tion itself, the act of inscription through which meaningless materiality
is transmuted into linguistic form and commercial value.[13] Like the mass-
produced characters embossed on coins or the reproducible alphabetic
characters struck on the publisher's metal "types," character names the
transmutation of material substance into both linguistic form and commercial value. Character has thus come to name a process identified not

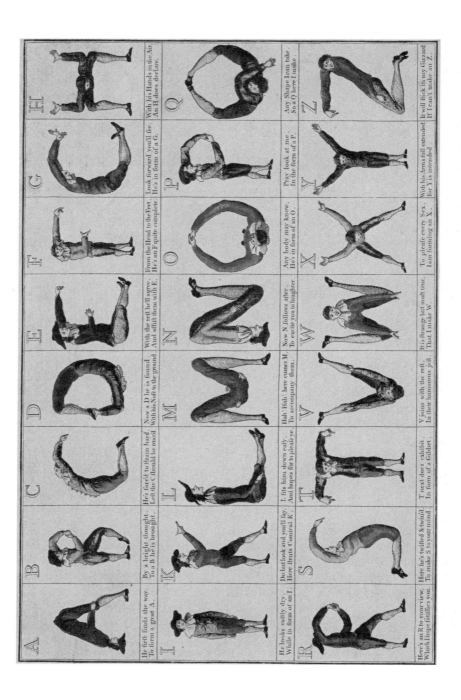

only with the production of the commodity form and the published text but also with the impression of identity on the mind itself, a mind whose original state, as John Locke famously put it, was most like that of a sheet of "white paper, void of all characters."[14]

Bodies of Reform thus studies those principles, practices, and institutions of reform—those "bodies of reform"—that sought to render the body as the site of character's appearance and intelligibility. It studies, in other words, those practices of reform and representation that sought to derive from the mute materiality of the body the elemental characters that were essential to the social and symbolic language of the public sphere. Character's unique constitution in these many nineteenth-century bodies of reform—and the vexed politics they occasion—is perhaps most succinctly illustrated in two images drawn from opposite ends of the nineteenth century. The first image (fig. 1) is of a figurative alphabet, *The Comical Hotch-Potch, or The Alphabet Turn'd Posture Master,* an alphabet that taught children the different characters of the alphabet not simply by repeating the rhyming phrase that sounds them out but also by forming these characters out of their very bodies, just as little "Demi," one of the first March grandchildren in Alcott's *Little Women,* "learned his letters with his grandfather, who invented a new mode of teaching the alphabet by forming the letters with his arms and legs,— thus uniting gymnastics for head and heels."[15] The alphabet thus makes visible the ways that children were encouraged to imagine the formation of character as a process of reforming their bodies into the socially intelligible "characters" that comprised the orthographic and grammatical elements of a larger social language. The second image (fig. 2) is from the cover of *The Chicago Times Portfolio of Midway Types,* a souvenir booklet of photographs of the ethnological exhibits at the Chicago World's Columbian Exposition of 1893. Visually citing in the figurative characters of the word *type* the photographs of different ethnic and racial types within the portfolio, the cover illustration represents and distinguishes each ethnic "type" by giving it the form of a distinct letter—from the Asiatic "E" to the Pacific Islander "P" to the Turkish "S"—thus offering not only initial examples of the character "types" displayed within but also a statement of the theory of character itself in its visual conflation

Fig. 1 (opposite page). "The Comical Hotch-Potch, or The Alphabet Turn'd Posture Master," created by Carrington Bowles, 1782. (The Colonial Williamsburg Foundation)

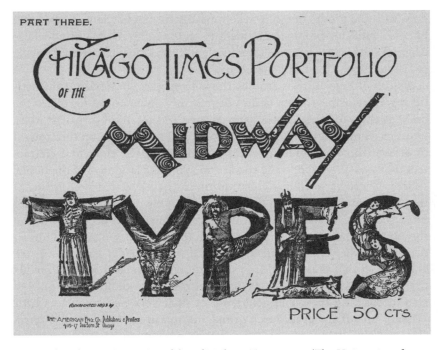

Fig. 2. *The Chicago Times Portfolio of Midway Types*, 1893. (The University of
Delaware Library, Newark, Delaware)

of the different definitions of character.[16] Rather than figuring the body
as the vehicle for the formation of the child's character and expressive
capacities, in this image the body is constrained within the particular
characters of delimited ethnic and racial "types." Thus, these two images together foreground the possibilities and the dangers of character's
grounding in the signifying capacities of the body.

My study thus centers on the Gilded Age because the problem of false
appearances and counterfeit values that such a name suggests, I argue,
is central to the disciplinary and cultural work of the rhetoric of character. Character is commonly invoked—both then and now—as antithetical to, and protection against, the seductive displays and superficial social performances said to govern the mass culture of modern consumer
capitalism.[17] Grounding ballast in the shifting winds of a mass-mediated
culture, orienting compass in the circulating seas of commodity fetishism, the substance formed through character building promised a kind of

authenticity and self-possession that could liberate one from the corrupting influence of social conventions, seductive commodities, and dissembling others. Taking my cue, however, from Ben Halleck, who wryly notes, in William Dean Howells's *A Modern Instance*, that "character is a superstition, a wretched fetish," I argue that character was the most gilded of objects in a mesmerizingly Gilded Age and thus read the late nineteenth century not as the period of character's decline but rather the period in which character's own spectacular constitution was recognized and remobilized as a critical instrument of social reform and literary representation.[18] Thus understanding the fetishistic logic that had long governed the rhetoric of character is, in my view, essential to understanding the culture of spectacle and commodity capitalism taken to define this period in U.S. history.

Which is not to say that character was not *perceived* to be in decline by writers of the Gilded Age. Indeed, it was the common lament over character's perceived decline that most animated the character-building activity of the period. As Brook Thomas has put it, "the perceived disappearance of character actually created a nostalgia for it."[19] Many of the character-building movements of the Gilded Age, such as the Boy Scouts of America, were explicitly conceived as responses to the decline in character— and therefore questionable gender—of America's youth brought about by urban industrial capitalism. In showing how character was an object of such intense interest precisely because of its own unavailability, precisely because it was in essence always at the brink of its own decline, my project thus aims to make visible the ways that the rhetoric of character continues to operate through the very lament of its decline and disappearance and aims to point the way to understanding the continued legacy of the rhetoric of character today.

The Culture of Character

The concept of character has had a somewhat ghostly presence in studies of nineteenth-century U.S. literature and culture, both ever-present and yet never quite seen. Studying the unique traits and defining features of the "American character" has of course been a favorite activity of writers and intellectuals from J. Hector St. John de Crèvecoeur and James Fenimore Cooper to Sarah Josepha Buell Hale and Alexis de Tocqueville to Walt Whitman and Henry James.[20] With the cold-war rise of American

Studies as a discipline in the mid-twentieth century, the "pursuit of the American character" took on renewed prominence as a field of academic study, but largely as an assumed object rather than as a historically constructed category.[21] Although early works by Constance Rourke, David Riesman, and Christopher Lasch began to reflect, albeit obliquely, on the genealogical origins and ideological function of the concept of character in American culture, Karen Halttunen's *Confidence Men and Painted Women* (1982) and Warren Susman's brief but influential essay in *Culture as History* (1984) were perhaps the first studies to assess critically the concept of character within a broad historical framework. And yet, though scholars have since considered the cultural significance of character in works largely devoted to other topics, character, as Alan Trachtenberg once pointed out, still "has not received the critical attention that it deserves."[22]

My study takes its initial bearings from Warren Susman's argument that nineteenth-century American culture was "a culture of character."[23] Susman's claim that "a popular vision of the self defined by the word 'character' became fundamental in sustaining and even in shaping the significant forms of the culture" is based on his observation that "such a concept filled two important functions. It proposed a method for both mastery and development of the self. But it also provided a method of presenting the self to society."[24] Susman's distinction between character's formation and its appearance—a distinction reflected in Noah Webster's 1828 dictionary entry on character—makes clear the two seemingly distinct definitions of character and the kinds of cultural processes these different meanings governed. Character was, on the one hand, defined simply as that unique combination of particular traits or "qualities" that differentiated the identity of one individual from another. On the other hand, character was defined as the material product of a process of self-mastery and self-formation and thus the achievement of those esteemed and exemplary individuals who were thereby distinguished as "possessors" of character. Character was, in other words, both a descriptive and an evaluative term, a term that designated both difference and distinction. It differentiated the particular identity of individuals from one another but was also that which ranked individuals within a hierarchical scale of social value legitimated by the attribution of "merit."

My aim in this study, however, is not simply to trace these two different meanings of character, these two sides of character's semantic coin, in the cultural and political discourses of the period. Rather, I examine the two distinct yet interrelated sets of cultural practices this semantic split shaped and inspired—practices of "character building" and of "character representation"—and the critical role these practices *together* played in shaping the political culture, literary forms, and social and economic practices of late nineteenth- and early twentieth-century American culture. My aim is thus to sketch a kind of cultural history of character by focusing on what I call the rhetoric of character, a formulation that is meant to foreground the importance to character's cultural work in the nineteenth century of both individual, collective, and institutional practices of self and social reform, on the one hand, and literary, social, and political forms of reading and representation, on the other. Character was not only a theory or concept of the self; it was also a way of performing and practicing the self. And so in focusing on the rhetorical dimensions of character's cultural work, I mean to delineate character's meaning within a diverse range of cultural discourses but also to elucidate the many personal and social practices those meanings shaped and inspired. What such a focus makes visible is the formal contradictions and expressive incongruities that many character-builders, such as Edwin Whipple, recognized and affirmed as an inherent feature of character's irreducible rhetoricality: "Men communicate themselves when they produce from their vital activity, it follows that their productions will never square with the abstract opinions of the understanding, but present a concrete, organic whole, compounded of truth and error, evil and good, exactly answering to the natures whence they proceed."[25] My emphasis on the rhetorical dimensions of character is also meant to underscore the longstanding place of the concept of character—or *ethos*—within the classical rhetorical tradition itself by reading the rhetoric of character, and the many published manuals and guides to building, reading, and representing character, as taking up the cultural work of the classical rhetoric manual whose death at the hands of late nineteenth-century modernity has perhaps been too prematurely announced.[26] I read the rhetoric of character as not just a defining "discourse" of the nineteenth century, in other words, but an important yet unrecognized chapter in the history of rhetoric itself.

I take this semantic distinction between building and representing as my point of departure because it also points the way toward a broader genealogy of the rhetoric of character, a genealogy that makes visible the multiplicity of its origins and the diversity of practices it inspired and governed. What follows are some introductory remarks toward such a genealogy that will I hope help to clarify the subject as well as the method of this study. It is a genealogy that aspires neither to completeness nor com-prehensiveness. Its purpose, like the subsequent chapters, is not to chart a single genealogical arc of development in the history of character but rather to point to some of the many origins of the rhetoric of character and to the overlapping "residual" and "emergent" historical forms, to borrow Raymond Williams's terms, that it takes in the nineteenth century. The rhetoric of character has a complex history rooted in an array of cultural traditions, social practices, and specialized discourses, including natu-ral science, moral philosophy, liberal political theory, Protestant theol-ogy, legal argumentation, portraiture, drama, the literary sketch, and the modern novel. It is thus a history with many overlapping and diverging strands, some bound up with the history of specific institutions or special-ized academic and professional disciplines, others more loosely evolving in the more popular practices and discourses of the public sphere. *Char-acter* was a term that also meant and did many things; it was at times a topic of debate and disagreement and at times an assumed term, at times a practice of critical revelation and at times a practice of ideological erasure. So while it is a central assumption of this study that, as one educator put it in 1914, "sometimes there is more history in a word than in the written an-nals," I follow Raymond Williams in treating character as a "key word in which both continuity and discontinuity, and also deep conflicts of value and belief, are . . . engaged."[27] The task of this study is thus to attend to the ways that the rhetoric of character provides a site for the extension and operation of power but also for exceeding, undoing, or challenging the reach of power. As Amanda Anderson has put it, "any genealogy of character should, of course, acknowledge the ways in which the concept functions to create and enforce social distinctions. But like other complex cultural forms, the category of character is neither exhausted nor fully de-fined by its complicity, in various writings or historical transformations, with exclusivity and power."[28] In the overview that follows, I provide an initial sense of these complex functions by charting some of the points of intersection and divergence between the two most important, and over-lapping, strands within the broader history of character in the nineteenth century—those of character building and character representation.

Building Character, Building Nation

This book considers, in the first instance, the discourses and practices of character building common to so many of the diverse projects of social re- form and nation building across the nineteenth century. Character's emer- gence as a key term in the nationalist discourse of the late eighteenth and early nineteenth centuries derived from its ability to name the underlying substance or material of the nation itself, a substance that, as scholars such as Gillian Brown, Karen Sánchez-Eppler, and Caroline Levander have un- derscored, was often modeled on the figure of the malleable or "impres- sionable" child.[29] Indeed, as its root, *natio* (or "to be born"), indicates, the concept of the nation, as Levander puts it, "derives from the idea of the child, and the concept of the nation continues to be understood within the founding context that the child provides."[30] Character thus emerged in the early national period as a concept that linked the pedagogical discourses of child rearing to political debates over the formation of a democratic society in order to articulate what Homi Bhabha has referred to as the "nationalist pedagogy" of the self-governing citizen-subject.[31] Legislators and educators in the early national period founded the project of produc- ing a unified citizenry bound by a common national identity and capable of self-governance on the project of "building character" in the nation's youth. Early education reformers such as Benjamin Rush, Noah Webster, and Horace Mann, for example, argued for the establishment of a national school system on the grounds that, as Webster puts it, "the education of youth is, in all governments, an object of the first consequence. The im- pressions received in early life usually form the characters of individuals, a union of which forms the general character of a nation."[32] Conversely, popular authors of child-rearing manuals, such as Lydia Maria Child, would emphasize the nationalist implications of their domestic treatises by arguing that "the safety and prosperity of our republic" hinges on the capacity of "American Mothers" to shape the "future dispositions and characters" of their "young babes," a capacity commonly ascribed to the mother's ability, as Fanny Fern puts it in *Ruth Hall*, to "inscribe, indelibly, on that blank page, characters to be read by the light of eternity."[33]

As a term that sutured together the categories of child and citizen, char- acter was the subject of a diverse range of popular texts and discourses in the early national period. The many child-rearing guides, pedagogical treatises, and character-building manuals produced in increasing num- bers in the three decades before the Civil War by authors such as Child,

John Todd, Amos Bronson Alcott, Catherine Beecher, Rufus Clark, and Henry Ward Beecher became prominent cultural sites for the articulation of "biopolitical narratives" of national identity, narratives in which the development of individual character and national character were conceived as not simply reflective or "analogical" measures of one another but rather as inextricably bound together in their very formation.[34] These manuals sought to guide the nation's youth through a process of character building founded on a regimen of self-discipline, emulatory and sympathetic identification, and the cultivation of good habits whose purpose was to protect against the broad array of "influences" that might conspire to "stamp" the youthful character. The aim of character building was thus not simply to inculcate a set of good traits while extirpating potentially bad traits but rather to build up, by mastering and consolidating the loose assemblage of traits into a coherent, self-possessed "orientation," a strength, solidity, or energy of character that would provide a shield against the external *and* internal influences that could impinge on one's liberty. Such a well-formed character was thus "liberated" from the undue influence of, and dependency on, other people, as well as from the instinctual drives and overwhelming passions that enslaved one to the body and from the particularized interests that arose from the body's contingency of origins and experiences.

As guides as well to the formation of self-governing and independent citizens, these character-building manuals imagined the child not simply as the "plastic" material on which the particular traits, values, or customs of an indigenous national type might be "impressed" but also as the kind of self-founding, antigenealogical national subject who—as embodied by Thomas Paine's figure of the parentless child in *Common Sense*—was defined by the term *character* itself.[35] In the early formulations of nationalist discourse that developed across a range of print genres, citizenship was thus formally equated with the cultivation of the forms of self-governance and socially calibrated self-interest that distinguished "having" character from merely "being" a particular type of character in the republican framework. This form of "good moral character" was thus enshrined by the Alien and Sedition Acts of 1795 as a formal requirement of acquired citizenship status and is still employed today to deny citizenship applications or to deport "resident aliens" from the United States.[36] Character building has thus been seen as a resolution to the problem of "self-governance" that plagued both the citizen and the state in liberal democracy— the problem of how to maximize liberty while also maintaining the social order—by internalizing the regulatory function of state institutions so that, as Christopher Castiglia concisely puts it, "citizens became administrators . . . of themselves."[37]

The rhetoric of character that was developed in early nationalist discourse became foundational in many of the reform movements of the nineteenth century as well.[38] Social reformers focused not only on the "formation" of the waxen, malleable character of the impressionable child but also on the "re-formation" or strengthening of the insufficiently formed adolescent or adult character, particularly in the latter part of the century. Offering protection from the fate of individuals such as the title character in Walt Whitman's early novel *Franklin Evans, or The Inebriate* (1842) or of Vandover in Frank Norris's *Vandover and the Brute* (1914), whose congenitally formless and "pliable character" ultimately leads to degeneracy and brutish insanity, temperance reformers throughout the century saw character building as the primary technique for fortifying the will's capacity to resist not only the temptations of strong drink but also the temptations of consumer culture and its "addictive" popular and literary entertainments.[39] Organizations such as the YMCA and YWCA and the "muscular Christianity" movement more broadly focused their attention on rehabilitating the character of the nation's youth through the development of physical strength and the "hardening" of their bodies.[40] Physical-culture activists such as Charlotte Perkins Gilman and Jane Addams more radically saw in muscle building the promise of a transformation in the very meaning and experience of gender. Such an emphasis on bodybuilding was also pivotal to the projects of nation building pursued by late nineteenth- and early twentieth-century character-building "agencies" such as the Boy Scouts of America, which received explicit congressional sanction for its efforts to "inculcate character" and thereby "insure good citizenship" in the nation's youth. As one champion of the Scouting movement, Theodore Roosevelt, proverbially put it, "character is the decisive factor in the life of an individual and of nations alike."[41]

The appeal of the concept of character to many social reformers was that it recognized and even critiqued the structural role that environment or "influence" played in the formation and degradation of character. And yet, the overwhelming emphasis on character as the primary instrument and agent for transforming the very social, political, and economic conditions that produced it functioned to reinscribe the power embedded in those structural conditions as the misrecognized "power" of character itself. Such a conceptualization of character thus frequently aligned it with that unique form of material value that seemed magically endowed with the power of self-creation—the power of capital itself. Character was thus most commonly described by the midcentury in terms of the common catchphrase "character is capital." The term *capital* was not simply a metaphor used to describe the benefits of character building but rather was a theoretical declaration of character's ontological status as itself a fetishized form of value that, like capital, was generated through its own "mysterious self-generating circular movement."[42] Charity and benevolence-society workers, in their "friendly visits" to the poor, for example, frequently sought to distribute to the poor not cash but the more ameliorative "coin of character" through the sterling example of their own exemplary middle-class character. This paradoxical formulation of character as a form of capital found more troubling expression not only in texts such as William Wells Brown's 1853 novel *Clotel*, which depicts "a Southern auction, at which the bones, muscles, sinews, blood, and nerves of a young lady of sixteen were sold for five hundred dollars; her moral character for two hundred," but also in the accounting books of midcentury credit agencies, which similarly began appraising character's value as capital in their reports to banks by classifying the character of loan applicants with evaluative designations such as "A number 1" or "second-rate."[43]

Building up one's fund of character's "capital" was promoted in the "self-help" literature of Benjamin Franklin and later of Horatio Alger, P.T. Barnum, and Booker T. Washington, as well as in the massive number of best-selling "success manuals" published after the 1870s (manuals with such titles as *Capital for Working Boys: Chapters on Character Building*), as the key to economic and professional "success."[44] Character was prized in these manuals as above all a kind of "accumulating fund—constantly increasing in value, and daily acquiring to itself fresh accessions of stability and worth."[45] By century's end, these visions of character were also frequently criticized by figures ranging from W.E.B. Du Bois to Henry James for their ultimate devolution into a defense of "money-getting," practices that threatened to impoverish the more enduring and "richer" character derived from the pursuit of "culture."[46] Drawing on these many diverse associations of "success" and social value with the possession of character, writers and activists ranging from Frederick Douglass to Luther Standing Bear, José Martí, and Charles Chesnutt nonetheless embraced, in different ways, the broader value of character building as a central component of the struggle for civil rights, political recognition, and economic opportunity in the nineteenth century.[47] As Douglass succinctly put it, "'there is gold in the earth, but we must dig it'—so with character."[48]

The Private Properties of Published Character

As these identifications of character with capital suggest, character's value did not derive from the properties inherent within individuals themselves but rather was constituted in the social, cultural, and economic exchanges in which they circulated. Nineteenth-century character builders thus recognized in practice what in theory they often disavowed, namely, that the public self constituted through acts of social and self-representation was just as important as the private self formed by acts and institutions of character building. Indeed, what made character into an object of such profound cultural anxiety throughout the nineteenth century, I argue, was the constitutive dependency of the private self formed through character building on the public self circulating in, and legitimated by, the field of representation. I thus read the extensive discourse on the *formation* of character in relation to an equally diverse range of writings devoted to the *representation* of character.

The practices and discourses of character representation have a history that both is distinct from the history of character building and yet also intersects and overlaps with it in many important ways. This is nowhere more apparent than in the history of one of the most significant cultural forms of character representation, that of "reputation"—or what Noah Webster's *American Dictionary* would define as "character by report."[49] Reputation's importance as a representational form has its origins in a number of legal and political conundrums posed by its socially constituted character. Although often dismissed either as a superficial and frequently unreliable social measure of a person's "real" character or as a relic of the antiquated culture of "status," reputation came to be seen as a democratizing force in the "culture of contract" that marked the emergence of modern democratic capitalism.[50] Rather than the artificial social value or cultural capital predetermined by one's inherited status within a relatively fixed social hierarchy, reputation was refigured in the republican discourse of the late eighteenth and early nineteenth centuries as the measure and reflection of the inner character that constituted a person's true "merit," a character revealed in the particular assessments of one's public acts and expressions that accrued in the form of quasi-biographical social narratives and letters of reference.[51]

This revalorization of reputation as a democratic measure of social value is indicative of the broader representational dilemma that the concept of character both produced and promised to resolve. Like the Calvinist theologians of the colonial period, who vested political authority in the "invisible" character of an "elect" that was, however, only indirectly discernable through the unreliable expressions of its "visible" character, nineteenth-century Americans defined character within an expressivist theory of the self wherein the public signs or representations of character were taken to have an indexical, yet frequently illegible, relationship to the private, inner self that was their source and origin.[52] Such a relationship was frequently expressed in terms of the commonplace—here expressed in the words of Abraham Lincoln—that "character is like a tree and reputation like its shadow. The shadow is what we think of it; the tree is the real thing."[53] The problem plaguing this representational logic, as Walter Benjamin has observed, is that character is presumed to be "apprehended only through signs, not in itself" and hence necessarily entailed its own unverifiability.[54] Because character was ultimately knowable only through the manners, behavior, and bodily indicators through which it appeared, it was vulnerable not only to errors of interpretation but also to the misrepresentations of the skilled manipulator of signs, making character into the site of a profound hermeneutic anxiety.

It was the project of character building, however, that promised to resolve the problem of character's unverifiability. In its formulation as an element of liberal ideology, character came to name not just the unique traits that distinguish and identify an individual in the public sphere; it was more importantly the term that distinguished the person who has taken possession of those traits through a process of self-formation. "Character" denoted not simply who one "is" but also what one "has," or, to be more precise, character denoted the product of "having" what one "is." Thus, in John Stuart Mill's formulation of the liberal concept of character, "a person whose desires and impulses are his own—are the expression of his own nature, as it has been developed and modified by his own culture, is said to have a character."[55] In the motivational psychology of character builders, character named the ideal of a vertically integrated and self-possessed will, a will that was no longer determined by the automatic impulses of animal instinct, the dumb repetitions of routinized habit, or the predetermined behavioral scripts of social conventions, and thus whose actions could be taken as an authentic manifestation of its own determinate intentions. Such an individual who was seen to "have" character was thus one who reliably *was* just what he or she *appeared* to be.

Because having character meant taking possession of the motivational mechanism of action and appearance itself, one proved one "had" character, in this retroactively circular logic of character, simply by forcefully and "distinctly" making one's appearance through acts of will in the public sphere. As Webster puts it in his dictionary entry on character, "we say a character is not formed, when the person has not acquired stable and distinctive [i.e., distinguishable] qualities."[56] "Integrity" and "honesty" were thus the conventional indicators of such an ideal character not because they were socially useful or morally idealized traits but because they named the structural integration and transparency of expression that was achieved through the will's calibration of action and intention. Character marked in its ideal form, in other words, not just the reliable origin of social identity but the securing of the relationship of referentiality itself. What legitimated reputation in the public sphere was thus that its appearance was itself taken as the sign of the well-formed character, of having undergone the labor of self-negation and universalizing abstraction that was the aim of early character building, a form of disembodied, impersonal authorship or "publication," as Michael Warner terms it, that legitimates one's participation in the public sphere simply by one's predetermined presence in it.[57]

The rhetoric of character thus promoted a democratic vision of self-governance and upward mobility that legitimated and secured existing social hierarchies through the very gesture of overcoming them. Persons of character were recognized as authentic, as reliable expressions of their inner character, not because that character has been verified outside the field of its appearance but rather because of the way that they clearly and distinctly appeared in the public sphere itself, an appearance that was itself culturally conditioned by the regulatory, embodied social grammar of race, class, and gender. Thus while character was defined in terms of its liberation from, or negation of, the particularity of the body's passions and instincts as well as its socially determined meanings, it was a designation that was "available only to those participants whose social role allows such self-negation (that is, to persons defined by whiteness, maleness, and capital)."[58] Thus an individual's legibility within the public sphere retroactively corroborated a process of character formation as the origins of that legibility, thereby rewriting the terms of race, class, and gender difference not simply in terms of different kinds of character "types" but as differences in the coherency and legibility of character, a difference marked, for example, in such culturally prominent tropes as the "inscrutability" of the Asian, the "dissembling" of the African, or the "masquerade" of women.[59] The referential distinction between the "real" substance of inner character and the representations through which it appeared, moreover, functioned to occlude its regulatory function by disavowing the role of cultural representations and social norms in constituting what comes to count as character. Thus the rhetoric of character performed its regulatory work by, on the one hand, legitimating and securing existing social hierarchies as the meritocratic product of character building while also subjecting those persons excluded from the public sphere, on the other hand, to an unending process of self-discipline on the unrealizable promise of upward mobility and social and legal equality.

Reputation thus acquired by the nineteenth century an important yet peculiar legal status. Reputation was defined, as Webster puts is, as "a valuable species of property or right," a property right that E.L. Godkin similarly defends in his 1890 essay as "The Rights of the Citizen to His Own Reputation."[60] The paradox of reputation, however, was that it was situated within a domain of legal protections afforded not to the classical liberal subject invested with certain inalienable rights but rather to a form of legal personhood that confounds the distinction between person and property. Such an ambiguous status is reflected, for example, in the development of nineteenth-century copyright law, which, on the one hand, sees literary characters as simply textual artifacts owned, like the text they are indissociable from, the author who produced them, but also, on the other hand, recognizes literary characters as independent entities who might wander away from their authorial owners and take on new lives in other works.[61] By the end of the nineteenth century, a similar paradox is reflected in Samuel Warren and Louis Brandeis's landmark argument for the modern "right to privacy," which describes public representations or reproductions of one's character not as an externalized possession vulnerable to theft but as an "injurable" extension of the human body.[62]

It was, however, in the broader tradition of defamation law that these paradoxes within liberal conceptions of character were most pronounced. Although defamation—whether in the spoken form of *slander* or the published form of *libel*—is now largely adjudicated in, and viewed as, a private, civil dispute between two individuals, the legal protections afforded to character in defamation law were originally conceived in terms of the criminal act of "seditious libel" codified in English common-law tradition in the seventeenth century and thus originally defined as "crimes against the state and society."[63] Reputation was legally recognized in and protected by defamation law as a material form of personal property of which one could be "robbed." And yet reputation was not, as Cheryl Harris has famously argued, a demarcated thing, "alienable" from its owner and hence exchangeable for other goods in the way that other forms of property were.[64] Reputation was, rather, something that, like capital itself, was inherently capable of creating value and therefore something to which an individual had the legal "right of use and enjoyment." Reputation thus named a kind of second, supplemental self with a rather ambiguous and frequently contested jurisprudential and ontological status. Reputation was a commodity form that, as inalienable, distinguished its owner from other forms of human property in that it could not be owned or possessed by another. And yet, reputation was a possession that also dispossessed its owner by remaining forever out of reach in the disseminated representations in the public sphere.

Reclaiming the Question of Character

The antebellum period has commonly been described as a period in which the ideological assumptions and representational forms that governed character's regulatory function in the early national period were increasingly undermined by a particular set of political, economic, and social transformations, transformations that rapidly accelerated in the decades following the Civil War. Most importantly, this period was one in which the discriminatory effects of character's implicit yet disavowed identification of citizenship with the presumptive body of white masculinity were increasingly called into question by social reformers and in particular by abolitionists and women's rights activists, who made character into the contested site of what Bruce Burgett has termed a "politics of the body."[65] As Karen Sánchez-Eppler has put it,

> Assumptions of a metaphorical and fleshless political identity were disrupted and unmasked through the convergence of two rhetorics of social protest: the abolitionist concern with claiming personhood for the racially distinct and physically owned slave body, and the feminist concern with

claiming personhood for the sexually distinct and domestically circumscribed female body.[66]

More broadly speaking, the antebellum period has also been described as
a period in which a consumption-oriented mass culture, increasingly organized around the conspicuous desires, affective sentiments, and embodied
performances of a salaried middle class, began to eclipse the more local-
ized, production-oriented economy centered on the thrift and hard work
of the property-owning bourgeoisie of the early national period. It was this
second "transformation of the public sphere," to borrow Habermas's language, that rendered obsolete the regulatory value of the rhetoric of character and its "repressive" modes of social control.[67]

The middle decades of the nineteenth century have thus commonly
been described as a period that inaugurated what Karen Halttunen refers
to as the "decline of the character-ethic," as the epistemological and representational assumptions behind the rhetoric of character were increasingly called into question and its modes of public validation simultaneously undermined.[68] While I similarly read this period as one in which
character's reliance on, and reproduction of, existing social hierarchies
and their cultural expressions was called into question, such a critique did
not simply reject or abandon the rhetoric of character but rather was part
of a broader and more diverse appropriation of the rhetoric of character,
as a practice and discourse of embodiment, in the culture and politics
of the Gilded Age. Rather than reading these transformations as marking a historical shift from an "inner-directed" paradigm of *character* to
an "other-directed" paradigm of *personality,* I read them within a broader
and more diverse genealogy of character, one that makes visible the public
forms of embodied publication that had not only long governed character's cultural work but that continued to play a pivotal, yet shifting, role
in shaping and negotiating the deceptively "gilded" cultural forms said to
bring about character's demise.[69]

Abolitionists and women's rights activists, for example, challenged the
discriminatory work of the rhetoric of character not by simply exposing
and repudiating its mystifications and reifications of the body's particularity but rather by reappropriating that power to refigure and revalidate
the cultural meaning and lived experience of the raced and gendered
body. Abolitionists such as Frederick Douglass, for example, critiqued
the racializing assumptions behind the rhetoric of character through an
evaluative decoupling of character from whiteness, particularly in the

last edition of his autobiography, which is organized more as an episodic series of sketches, such as the chapter "A Slaveholder's Character," of the varying characters of his different slave masters.[70] Rather than repudiating the rhetoric of character altogether, however, Douglass famously lays claim to its legitimating logic both by establishing himself through these readings as "a good judge of character" and by establishing in classical terms the development of his own exemplary character, first through the acquisition of literacy and finally by publicly demonstrating an unshakeable resolve in his fight with the overseer Covey.

Indeed, in demonstrating how "the hardships and dangers involved in the struggle [for freedom] give strength and toughness to the character," Douglass establishes the fugitive slave as model for the kind of exemplary character that is formed only in the crucible of adversity.[71] Douglass thus articulates the discourse of adversity that was enshrined in many character-building manuals as "a special asset available only to those lucky enough to have been born into poverty or difficulty."[72] We might thus see figures such as Douglass as making visible and reappropriating the paradoxical logic of "dehumanization" central to the forms of egalitarian exchangeability and universalizing self-negation that constituted the exemplary character of the liberal citizen-subject. As Helen Jun has put it, "this paradox, in which the systematic dehumanization of racialized populations is the condition of their entry into the 'civilized world' to become modern subjects of democratic freedom, is the contradiction endemic to the project of modernity itself."[73]

Women's rights activists of the early nineteenth century similarly challenged the role of character in sustaining yet obscuring the presumptive masculinity of citizenship. Women were paradoxically figured within the rhetoric of character as primary formers of a character that, in theory, they did not themselves possess. While it was commonly held that "human character, in all its interests and relations and destinies, is committed to woman, and she can make it, shape it, mould it, and stamp it just as she pleases," women were not usually seen as *having* the attributes of character they were entrusted with instilling, since *having character* was invariably to evoke masculine-coded attributes associated with willing in the public sphere.[74] The forms of sympathetic understanding, or of what Richard Brodhead calls "disciplinary intimacy," that presumably qualified women as stewards of character, in other words, were often difficult to square mimetically with the self-reliant qualities that marked the possessor of true character itself.[75]

And yet, while many women's rights activists embraced the celebrated and principal role of mother and wife as the maker of character within the family—and thereby endorsed the presumption that such a role derived not from a woman's possession of character proper but rather from her more circumscribed possession of a specifically *feminine* character or "virtue"—others more radically laid claim to the universalizing rhetoric of character itself. In *Woman in the Nineteenth Century*, for example, Margaret Fuller argues that "the only efficient remedy [to social problems] must come from individual character," and so true social reform is foreclosed by the theoretical and practical exclusion of women from the benefits of character, for "bad institutions . . . prevent individuals from forming good character, therefore we must remove them."[76] Thus Fuller, like many women's rights advocates, claimed not only that "the standard of character is the same for both sexes" but that such a standard encompassed those particular attributes of both masculinity and femininity that only together gave shape to the "whole character."[77]

The formal and social dynamics that made the rhetoric of character so appealing as a strategy of embodied publication can perhaps best be seen in the rise of one of the most popular movements of the nineteenth century: phrenology. The emergence of phrenology as a popular practice of reading and representing character in the 1840s and 1850s was in many ways a response to the historical transformations of the antebellum era that made traditional indicators of character such as reputation both practically unreliable and ideologically suspect. As the traditional representational forms of locally accumulated reputation became unreliable or irrelevant in the far-flung and expanding commercial, communication, and transportation networks through which an increasingly diverse, and anonymous, population of regional and global migrants flowed and transacted, a new hermeneutics of character emerged that was reliant on the character discernable at a glance, on the capacity incisively and immediately to "read" the character of strangers in the shape, movements, and gestures of the physical body.[78] Although most well known for their practice of reading character in the bumps on one's head, phrenologists developed a range of character-reading strategies that scrutinized many different aspects of the body, from its skeletal proportions and muscular development to its colors and textures to its most subtle gestures and expressive energies. Although this emphasis on the body has often been critiqued as a form of biological determinism, phrenology's popularity in the United States was grounded in its recognition of the physiological body as not merely an archival index of fixed character traits but more importantly as a powerful mechanism for transforming and rewriting one's "inherited" or biological character.

Phrenologists such as Orson Squire Fowler and Samuel Wells, who re-packaged and popularized the theories and methods of earlier European physiognomists in the United States, as well as an increasing number of social reformers, saw character reading not simply as an instrument of so-cial surveillance but more importantly as a guide to "self-improvement."[79] These methods of self-improvement, moreover, repudiated the traditional emphasis on moral, introspective reflection and focused instead on ex-trospective practices of reading, representing, and performing the body as the mode of character's formation. Or as one later manual writer put it, "every human body shall register personal history, publishing a man's deeds. . . . [T]he fleshy pages of to-day show forth the soul's deeds of yes-terday."[80] Character was fundamentally formed, in other words, through the regulation and manipulation of its embodied modes of public appear-ance. Like Blaise Pascal, whose "wonderful formula," as Louis Althusser famously summarizes, "says more or less: 'Kneel down, move your lips in prayer, and you will believe,'" character builders similarly saw character not simply as the origin and cause of its public expressions but also as a product of those expressions, as a product of those public performances that had the power to materialize the character they signified.[81] As Samuel Wells put it, "Temporary expressions have a tendency, by means of fre-quent repetition, to become permanent. A scowl or a frown constantly recurring, finally assumes the character of our essential traits. . . . By con-tinually assuming a particular character, we may, in the end, make it our own; and the expression at first put on at will can not be so easily put off."[82] Falsely signifying that one had character was thus the first and most important step in the formation of character itself. The problem of false appearances that character building was meant in theory to overcome, in other words, turned out to be in practice essential to the most significant methods of character building.

The example of phrenology thus shows how early social reformers, in their critical appropriations of the rhetoric of character, did not simply critique and condemn the cultural scripts and bodily signs that deter-mined what counts as the well-formed character, but embraced strategies of bodily performance and interpretation as an inherent principle of char-acter building. What made character an object of such profound cultural fascination was thus the fact that its inner or private reality was not simply dependent on those strategies of self and social representation that comprised its public character but rather was an interiority that was inextricable from and only known through its publication in and as the expropriated properties of the body's public legibility. Indeed, this reversal of the relationship of sign and referent, I argue, was what had long constituted character's powerful appeal not only in the Gilded Age's culture of attractions but also within the republican culture of the early national period against which it is defined. Even in such classical models of character formation such as that depicted in John Locke's early treatise on education, for example, it is the child's ability to externalize and socially mediate its relationship to itself through the "reputation" it perceives in the faces of others that is critical to the reflexive interiority that is the hallmark of the liberal character.[83] The dramaturgical, externalizing dimensions of the citizen were similarly recognized in the standard legal formulation, "assuming the character of the citizen," that was regularly used in naturalization law and international treaties to emphasize, in contrast to the "inalienable" rights recognized in and protected by the Constitution, the more contingent "clothing" of citizenship that, for example, could be stripped from Dred Scott and all persons of African descent in the famous *Dred Scott v. Sandford* case of 1856.[84]

Although phrenology quickly waned as a popular movement after the 1850s, the underlying physiognomic premise out of which it grew—that character could be read in the physical form and details of the body and could also literally be re-formed through the performances and representations of the body—continued to shape many of the most important literary, scientific, and social practices well into the late nineteenth and early twentieth centuries. Character-reading manuals such as *How to Study Strangers* (1895), *Character Analysis by the Observational Method* (1915), and *Character Analysis: How to Read People at Sight* (1923), as well as more general treatises such as *The Philosophy of Character* (1924), *Character and the Conduct of Life* (1927), and *Physique and Character* (1925) remained popular well into the twentieth century even as they incorporated statistical methods, modern psychology, and a more commercial, market-oriented framework.[85] Photography also emerged as a particularly valued technology of character reading, as photographers such as Thomas Eakins and Francis Galton sought to exploit photography's power to fix and capture otherwise indiscernible aspects of the visual field, and in particular aspects of character in the visible body, which the naked eye had difficulty detecting.[86] By the end of the nineteenth century, the field of "characterology" emerged as a distinct "scientific" discipline that combined the principles of physiognomy with the documentary power of photography and archival metrics of criminology in a comprehensive "science" of character "types," a science that also played a significant role in the development of the emerging "social sciences" of sociology and anthropology.[87] Sociologists, anthropologists, ethnologists, and criminologists thus together developed increasingly sophisticated interpretive methods for discerning and categorizing character types, methods that were important as well in the "civilizing missions" of U.S. imperialists and the projects of social engineering that marked the advent of the Progressive era. These interpretive methods, in their delineation of character from the subtle signs of the body's form, manners, and behaviors, also provided a theoretical foundation for the system of "racial science" that was increasingly influential in the discriminatory legal codes, social practices, and policy debates of the late nineteenth and early twentieth centuries. These methods also underwrote the production of racialized character types as major consumer and entertainment commodities in, for example, the ethnological displays of world fairs, expositions, midways, and carnivals.[88] The rhetoric of character thus played a key role in structuring and underwriting the emerging modes of surveillance, technologies of seeing, and archiving imperatives that have been identified by scholars such as Michel Foucault, Jonathan Crary, and Alan Sekula with modernity itself.[89]

Learning One's Letters

The arena of cultural production in which reading and representing character has figured most prominently is of course that of literary fiction, and it is in the history of the novel form that the overlapping histories of the rhetoric of character come most plainly into view. The nineteenth-century novel has been described not only as a print genre where readers encountered a new range of fascinating and often quite moving characters but also as a place where the character of readers themselves were transformed as they learned from their novels the social and psychological workings of character itself. The establishment of the novel as a popular yet controversial commodity in the early to mid-nineteenth century has in particular been tied to the role novelistic character was imagined to play in the building of character itself. As Jane Tompkins has famously argued, the popularity and cultural significance of novels in the first half of the nineteenth century derived not from their aesthetic appeal as "objects of interpretation and appraisal" or from their mimetic capacity to reproduce actual historical events or personages but rather from their didactic value as "agents of cultural formation."[90] And one of the most important aspects of the "cultural work" performed by early novels, as Glenn Hendler has more recently argued, was the work they performed as "agents of character formation."[91]

Indeed, the broader story of "the rise of the novel" form itself has been described at least since Ian Watt in terms of the novel's role in the formation of the "modern individual," an individual whose ability to distinguish and mediate the relationship between the private and public has come to define what it means to have character itself.[92] Frequently drawing in particular on Jürgen Habermas's genealogy of the public sphere and Benedict Anderson's theory of "imagined communities," more recent histories of the novel in the United States often imagine the two poles of literary and readerly character as forming an identificatory axis around which the modern nation was forged.[93] By experiencing the private thoughts and feelings that lie behind the public lives of fictional characters, these accounts argue, readers cultivated a sense of their own private interiority, as distinct from, yet oriented toward, the social forms and economic transactions of the public sphere. Or as Mr. Bhaer counsels the aspiring writer Jo March in Louis May Alcott's *Little Women*, "the study of character in this book will help you read it in the world, and paint it with your pen."[94] Such an articulation of the public and the private in novels thus not only facilitated the formation of a democratic public sphere in which public affairs could be deliberated on independently of the machinery of the state, but novelistic characters also provided an emblematic site of sympathetic identification and "shared feeling" around which a national "imagined community" could be formed.

Essential to the formation of the "modern individual" within such a model was the realist imperative of novelistic representation to construe the privacy and particularity of individualized characters.[95] How exactly that particularity was best conveyed, of course, was a matter of great debate, and critics such as Watt locate the genesis of the novel in the resolution of the conflict between "internal and external characterization" and in particular in the novel's ability to absorb the traditional typological form of the character sketch within an expanded narrative strategy of character depiction.[96] As Deidre Shauna Lynch has argued, however, this account of the novel has resulted in a hierarchizing critical distinction between "flat" characters, who exhibit the conventional traits and predictable behavior of generic social "types," and "round" characters, who exhibit the cognitive and emotional depth, reflective agency, and behavioral complexity of the fully realized individual.[97] Such a distinction between flat and round character has, more importantly, shaped a historical narrative of the development of novelistic genre in the United States that, like the claims of prominent realists of the time, figures the formal innovations of realism and its ability to characterize the complexities and particularities of fully rounded characters as the logical culmination of the novel form in the late nineteenth century.[98] As Amy Kaplan has put it, "'character-painting,' not 'story-telling,' is the hallmark of realism."[99] Conventionally defined by the compositional methods associated with late nineteenth-century authors such as Mark Twain, William Dean Howells, and Henry James, realism's concern with the regional and cultural specificities, social negotiations, and psychological complexity of character is often figured as a reaction against the unusual or fantastic characters of romance and sensationalism and, more importantly, the stock character types and conventional narrative formulas of the popular sentimental genre.[100] As Howells's put it, "it is one of the hard conditions of romance that its personages . . . can rarely be characters with a living growth, but are apt to be types, limited to the expression of one principle, simple, elemental, lacking the God-given complexity of motive which we find in all human beings we know."[101] Many realists thus sought to portray the particularities of the individual "specimen," as Isabel Archer fondly terms it in James's *Portrait of a Lady*, rather than the generalities of the abstract "type," a strategy that for Howells meant not "heap[ing] up facts" but rather presenting every fact as an indication of character, for "nothing [is] insignificant; all tells for destiny and character."[102]

Such a history of the novel form in the United States—one first promoted by realists themselves—thus replicates, in its account of the emergence of the individualized, realist character over the typological characters of earlier fictional forms, the broader humanist story of character's historical emergence as a challenge to the reductive, dehumanizing discourse of social types, whether it be in the antiquated culture of status or its modern recapitulation as the standardized and mass-produced "stereotypes" of commodity capitalism. Realists frequently defended their strategies of characterization, for example, not simply in terms of their aesthetic superiority as representational forms but because of their power to revise and reorient the traditional character-building function of the novel form around a properly "aesthetic" reading experience. Rather than the exciting plots, fantastic narratives, and moving characters of sentimental, sensational, and romance fiction, whose "addictive" yet superficial properties were identified by many realists, as Nancy Glazener has detailed, with the "addictive consumerism" of "a profit-driven culture industry that benefited from the public's dependency on vicarious emotions and excitements," realists frequently emphasized the plain wholesomeness of their literary fare and the deeper aesthetic nourishment of their more complexly drawn characters.[103] Rather than appealing to the base pleasures and imitative modes of sympathetic identification, realists thus sought to appeal to the more elevating, interpretive faculties of aesthetic judgment as a way of cultivating character.

Such a historical narrative positions realism as a final fleshing out of the complex interiority of character, a method of characterization that has been either celebrated for its ability to challenge the racial, gender, and class "stereotypes" through which the rhetoric of character had long sustained its discriminatory work, or condemned as a liberal fantasy whose function is to obscure the disciplinary work of modern commodity capitalism. In late twentieth-century literary studies, as Deidre Shauna Lynch has argued, the latter view has tended to prevail, as the plentitude associated with the realist character has been viewed by critics, particularly those influenced by structuralist semiotics, Althusserian Marxism, and Lacanian psychoanalysis, as a textual effect that enables readers to "misrecognize themselves as free subjects" by identifying with an autonomous liberal subject despite their subjection within the modern capitalist order.[104] Such an identification of literary character with the realist plenitude of the self-constituted subject has thus resulted in an overall disinterest in character as a category of analysis because of a more general "skepticism toward the self-authorizing subject."[105] While such a skepticism animates many of my own concerns in this study, however, I also aim to make visible the ways that character was conceived as a historically contingent, formally incomplete, and performatively constituted mode of subjectivity whose political efficacy was seen to lie in its ability to decompose or disembody the fixed identity categories that governed the public sphere. In so doing, I look beyond the conventional Foucauldian framework that sees such performances of embodiment as necessarily bound up with or captured by the disciplinary aims of a culture of surveillance while also resisting the liberatory rhetoric so often associated with character. I also hope to make clear not only the importance of the category of character in literary history but also its continued relevance to the concerns of contemporary literary and critical theory. As Amanda Anderson has put it,

> [A]s concepts allied above all with habitual practice and self-cultivation, character and ethos need not evoke or consolidate mystified notions of autonomy or individuality. Indeed, these concepts might be seen as fully pertinent to a theoretical field obsessively occupied with naming and delineating the subjective effects and potentialities of its more general, transubjective claims. The subjective forms that currently prevail in literary and cultural studies—identity, hybridity, performativity, and so on—all imagine various ways in which one might enact, own, or modify one's relation to the impersonal determinants of individual identity.[106]

Thus while my study is concerned in part with the ways that late nineteenth-century realism—in its many diverse forms—was used both to extend and also to challenge the cultural work traditionally performed by the rhetoric of character, my aim is also to look at the many diverse and hybrid literary forms obscured by the critical and historical emphasis on realism in the late nineteenth century and at the public forms of embodied self-publication they figure. Rather than documentations of character's interiority and singularity, I read late nineteenth- and early twentieth-century literary texts as explorations of character's origin in the social practices, cultural representations, and embodied performances of the public sphere, as texts fascinated with the public forms through which individuals could glimpse "the reflection of themselves, the photographs of their own characters."[107] My emphasis on a politics of embodiment is thus meant to push beyond culturalist approaches to the body that consider it simply as an instrument of self-expression and cultural inscription. Instead, my project illuminates the ways that character was understood as a form of embodiment that was produced by its expressive forms and that was itself a form of culture rather than the pliant recipient of the impressions made by culture. Like recent work that challenges the dominance of "privacy" as a central category of literary analysis, I consider the public forms of character that were explored in literary texts, as Stacey Margolis has put it, as "not a tool of social discipline but, surprisingly, a kind of heuristic device, a way of placing oneself in relation to the world" that recognized the partial, compromised forms of agency that were possible beyond the discourse of self-determination and the narcissism of the self-founding subject.[108] Thus, for devoted readers of character, such as the protagonist in S. Weir Mitchell's novel *Characteristics,* the study of character yields knowledge not of one's inner life but rather of the destiny of one's public "conduct": "My favorite amusement was to recall men I had known, and to construct for them in my mind characters out of what I had seen or heard of them under the varying conditions of camp, battle, or wounds. This would lead me to anticipate what their future lives would be and how in certain crises of existence they might act. I did this also for myself over and over, until it seemed to me that I could be sure of my precise conduct under any and almost every variety of circumstances."[109] Late nineteenth-century fiction thus functioned, I argue, not simply as the cultural site for the mimetic reproduction of a national or conventionally middle-class character but as the place where one learned the signs of character's social legibility, where one learned which kinds of signs, which kinds of behaviors and social expressions counted as the reliable indicators of character itself. The "question of character" raised by these texts, in other words, was not the mimetic question of how best to reproduce human character in literary language but rather the social question of what counts as the appearance of character itself.

Each of the five chapters of *Bodies of Reform* is organized around readings of literary texts that critically reflect on one of the five main elements of the rhetoric of character—performance, habit, inheritance, exercise, and emulation—in relation to various popular, political, and legal discourses on character. In so doing, my study focuses on the specific literary and social practices that together determine the conditions of legibility through which a person comes to count as a well-formed character, while also bringing into view a more diverse range of cultural discourses on character formation. Although literary texts play a pivotal role, to varying degrees, in the chapters, my aim is not to privilege literary discourse as the most significant or influential cultural articulation of the rhetoric of character. Literary texts were, however, important cultural locations in which the formal dimensions of character's public constitution could be critically examined through considerations of, and debates over, questions of genre and strategies of literary representation, debates that were often inflected as well in the more explicit commentary on the concept of character in the thematic concerns and representational content of the texts. I thus read the formal dilemmas of literary representation and debates over genre and literary form as moments within a broader debate over the structuring role played by the rhetoric of character in the politics of the public sphere.

Chapter 1 explores the racializing dynamics of the rhetoric of character in Herman Melville's last completed novel, *The Confidence-Man* (1857). Situated within the uncertainties of value produced in the wake of westward expansion and its dislocations of social and commercial exchange, Melville's text, I argue, conflates rather than confirms the distinction between personality and character by charting the logical and historical entailment of the abstract equality of the democratic citizen in the exchangeability of the commodity form. Moreover, *The Confidence-Man* interrogates, in its formal strategies of characterization, how racial fictions are transmuted into historical "facts" by the exegetical drive to read properly and to authenticate the performed traits of character. My reading of *The Confidence-Man* thus pays particular attention to the formal and literary strategies through which Melville fleshes out his mysterious characters, formal strategies that make visible the broader cultural and institutional strategies that I explore in more detail in subsequent chapters. Although *The Confidence-Man* is a text published before the Gilded Age, it nonetheless anticipates and encompasses in its literary form the cultural dynamics mediated by the rhetoric of character in the Gilded Age. Melville thus shows how racial character is a textual, interpretive effect of the philanthropy that sustains the confidence man's own oddly self-reliant character, and he anticipates how the philanthropic democratization of character in the late nineteenth century installs and endorses an imperial allegory of racial difference.

Chapter 2 explores the pedagogy of "habit" through a reading of Mark Twain's imperial allegory of national founding, *A Connecticut Yankee in King Arthur's Court* (1889). My analysis turns on the figure of the young page Clarence, who is the exemplary product of the "man-factories" founded to manufacture Yankee men out of Arthurian boys. In his portrait of such a figure, I argue, Twain turns his critical gaze back on the paradoxical figure of masculine identification on which he himself had established his literary reputation: the character of the eternally arrested boy. By tracing the novel's formal inversion of the realist modes of readerly identification that defined the "bad boy" literary genre of the 1870s and 1880s, I demonstrate how Twain mimics and models in the allegorical structure of the novel itself the institutional practices of "boyology" that were taking shape at the moment of *A Connecticut Yankee*'s publication. In aligning these practices with the Yankee's own brand of cultural imperialism, Twain's novel implicates such character-building agencies as the Boy Scouts of America—and the forms of homosocial chumminess, "Indian"

identification, and military training around which they were organized—
in the ideology of "Americanization" that increasingly dominated debates
over racial segregation, Native American sovereignty, immigration policy, and overseas expansion in the 1890s. I then trace the cultural work
of such character-building agencies to the broader discourse of habit as
it was developed in the pragmatist psychology of William James, as well
as in one of the most popular nonfiction genres of the period, the success
manual. The ideological function of the complex pedagogy of will training and self-habituation articulated in such works, I argue, is to obscure
the reification of class difference through a democratization of middle-
class character.

Chapter 3 challenges conventional visual studies approaches to race
and gender through an analysis of the historicizing function of muscle
building in literary naturalism and the physical-culture movement of the
late nineteenth century. The chapter begins with a consideration of Sojourner Truth's famous baring of her muscular arm as a sign of her exemplary character and goes on to ask what kind of political promise was
lodged in the transformations of muscle building. I pursue this question
first through an account of the emergence of muscle as an emblem of national fitness in a variety of educational, phrenological, sociological, and
political writings of the period and of its deeper roots in the rhetoric of
character. I then turn to the spectacular display of muscular bodies and
the rise of bodybuilding contests in the *National Police Gazette* and in the
broader physical-culture media, focusing in particular on the ways that
the muscular body destabilized the visual economy of gender and sexuality. Finally, I examine the writings of Charlotte Perkins Gilman, who was
a physical-culture advocate and avid body builder, and the problematic
role that muscle building plays in her utopian feminist politics and racial
nationalism. My overarching aim in contrasting the visual economy of
the *Gazette* with the narratives of Gilman is to look beyond the classifica-
tory and disciplinary functions through which modernity's visual culture
of surveillance is frequently interpreted. I do this by reading the practices
of muscle building not as a commodification of the body but rather as a
rehistoricization of the body, a rehistoricization that transforms the body
into the visible and kinesthetic record of its own reflexive exercise.

Chapter 4 considers the vexed role that the rhetoric of character played
in articulating the physiognomic taxonomies of racial science but also in
mobilizing challenges to the corporeal schemas of racial character and
the policies of segregation and disenfranchisement they legitimated. The

chapter begins by studying the development of the rhetoric of character in both abolitionist discourse and in postbellum discourses of racial uplift in terms of its promise to reinscribe the racialized body with the socially legitimating signs of gender and class. The rest of the chapter is then devoted to a reading of Pauline Hopkins's novel *Contending Forces* (1900) and her response to Reconstruction and post-Reconstruction-era debates over the role of character building in projects of racial uplift. In its portrait of the critical agency of the heroine Sappho Clark's "sterling character" and queer sexuality, Hopkins's novel, I argue, offers a critical rejoinder to both the scientific discourses of racial character and the liberationist discourse of the representative man by forwarding, in her transnational, intergenerational tale, a diasporic theory of character formation that centers on the labor of history, rather than the mechanism of inheritance, in the constitution of political agency and social critique.

Finally, chapter 5 takes up the problems of emulation and exemplification in the reform of character by examining Jane Addams's critique and rearticulation of the character-forming effects of the class contact experienced in traditional charity work. In challenging the gendered assumptions of women's work as philanthropic "stewards of character" and exemplars of middle-class character, Addams was able to capitalize on the power of the charity relation as a scene of interclass and interethnic contact while also extricating it from its emulatory function of character building and from the assimilationist practices of "Americanization" being enacted on Native American reservations and boarding schools and in the overseas territories of the United States after the Spanish-American War. Addams also stages her critique, forwarded in such works as *Democracy and Social Ethics*, through a complex refiguring of the literary dimension of her own autobiographical character in *Twenty Years at Hull-House*. In striking a performative middle ground between an understanding of character as either social inscription or radical self-determination, Addams makes a counterhierarchical notion of interclass and interethnic identification essential to a "Progressive" realization of a pluralist, democratic civic sphere.

1

Philanthropic Taste

Race and Character in Herman Melville's The Confidence-Man

All the nice and subtle questions concerning personal identity can never possibly be decided, and are to be regarded rather as grammatical than as philosophical difficulties.

—David Hume, *A Treatise on Human Nature*[1]

To interpret someone's character (handwriting) is to interpret his character (physiognomy) is to interpret his character (personality) is to interpret his character (some characteristic text he has written), in a perpetual round of figure for figure. To read character is to read character is to read character is to read character.

—J. Hillis Miller, *Ariadne's Thread*[2]

My study begins with Herman Melville's 1857 novel *The Confidence-Man: His Masquerade*, a text that seems to announce—and perhaps to mourn—the closing of the era of character. Set on the riverboat *Fidèle* as it travels up the Mississippi River one April Fool's Day, *The Confidence-Man* portrays a series of swindles perpetrated by one singular, and quite "original," confidence man. The confidence man—in Melville's text but also as a well-known social type—is named for his signature method of assuming an identity and then garnering the confidence of strangers in order to extract money from them—in *The Confidence-Man* in the form of donations to bogus charities, purchases of counterfeit stock or worthless patent medicine, investments in pyramid schemes, or a simple loan from one trusting, even if newfound, friend to another. The emergence of the confidence man in literature, popular periodicals, and advice manuals of the

1850s has been seen as marking a breakdown of character as a regulatory principle within the social and economic exchanges and far-flung market culture in America's expanding empire of the mid-nineteenth century.[3] Melville's portrait of the facility and ease with which the confidence man is able to pass off his counterfeit character has thus been seen as a particularly sustained diagnosis of not only a new and troublingly deceptive social type but a more troubling crisis of confidence in the concept of character itself.

Generations of critics have sought to understand the original character of the confidence man himself, therefore, by analyzing how that character is made possible by the uniquely American civic space figured by the Mississippi riverboat *Fidèle,* on which the peculiar events of this April Fool's Day take place. Ships have, for Melville, always borne more than their manifests declare, and the "faithful" *Fidèle* is no exception: it is burdened with no less a task than representing the diverse characters and attenuated exchanges of America's expanding empire. And what most defines this civic space, Melville insists in the opening pages of the text, is the dizzying "strangeness" of its social and economic exchanges. What most defines this "ship of fools" is that it is, at bottom, a ship that, "though always full of strangers, . . . continually, in some degree, adds to, or replaces them with strangers still more strange."[4] The "strangeness" of the *Fidèle* has thus been understood as describing a broader crisis of character, as the familiar, stratified relations of republican society were being transformed by the new attenuations and mediations of improved long-distance transportation and communication, the representations of a rapidly growing journalistic media, and the social dislocations of urbanization, industrialization, and mass migration.[5] As strangers increasingly interacting across regional, cultural, and racial divides, individuals could no longer make recourse to the sedimented reputation of familiar members of a local community and thus grew increasingly reliant on the ability to read at a glance the character of strangers. The "strangeness" of late antebellum society thus made confidence between strangers an increasingly necessary, yet precarious, condition of economic and social exchange.

The Confidence-Man thus charts the promise and peril of this reliance on the legibility of character at a time when the terms of that legibility were themselves increasingly unreliable. Rather than simply portraying the social implications of this crisis of character, however, Melville interrogates the cultural work performed by the rhetoric of character, this chapter argues, by restaging its formal logic in the textual and interpretive dynamics produced by the novel itself. Melville's broader fascination with the concept of character is evident in many of his literary works, from the identity-altering tattoos of *Typee* to the physiognomic taxonomies of *Moby-Dick* to the phrenological fascinations of *Billy Budd*. But in *The Confidence-Man*, Melville explores the cultural work performed by the rhetoric of character by aligning that work with the operations of literary characterization itself. This is most apparent in the novel's three metafictional chapters (14, 33, 44), in which the narrator, in unexpected and seemingly candid asides to the reader, explicitly defends what seem to be improbable moments in the text by reflecting on the improbabilities, inconsistencies, and impenetrabilities common both to the act of literary characterization and to the social constitution of character. More significantly, Melville draws on the conventions of literary representation to foreground and to examine critically the interpretative conditions necessary for character's appearance as a social object. Melville does this by predicating the coherency of his narrative on the presumption that there is a single, masterful character behind the many disguises and "characters" of the confidence man, while also studiously failing to confirm such an assumption. In aligning the manipulative intentions of the confidence man with the depth of literary character to which Melville continually points but never reveals, *The Confidence-Man* thus raises, I argue, the question of character's fictional construction, a construction as important to the novel form as to the liberal agency such a form was imagined to inspire.[6]

The confidence man's unmatched ability to capitalize on any situation and turn it to his profit has led many critics to describe him not as a national "threat" but as an extreme, even parodic, embodiment of the self-interest and enterprising pluck that were being identified with the "American character" as the individualistic ideals of liberalism were eclipsing the earlier republican ethos of civic virtue. Or as one critic of *The Confidence-Man* has more flatly declared, "Americans have always been, in one sense or another, confidence men."[7] The seemingly infinite malleability of the confidence man's character similarly evokes, as a form of self-negation, the universal perspective and formal equality that define the character of the modern citizen. But what is most striking about *The Confidence-Man* is that it also figures the confidence man's strategic agency in terms of an ability to read other characters within the novel, characters who are much more cursorily sketched. By organizing each of the chapters of the first half around the contrast between the impenetrability—and superior strategic agency—of the confidence man, and the all-too-transparent character of his many victims, Melville frames the novel around a contrast between two distinct genres of literary characterization: the character sketch and the romance novel.[8] We thus perceive the transparency of the various characters sketched in the early chapters, while also seeing such a transparency appropriated by a confidence man whose inner motives and intentions must be assumed by the reader yet can never ultimately be confirmed or revealed. Rather than integrating these two generic forms into the conventional narrative form of the modern novel, however, Melville separates and juxtaposes them in order to foreground the dynamic that drives the broader rhetoric of character itself. Melville emphasizes, in other words, the dependency of the liberal agency figured by the confidence man—his capacities for character reading and the universality embodied in his ever-changing character—on the production and consumption of a stream of completely legible character types.

In delineating the literary dynamics of Melville's novel, this chapter ultimately aims to make visible the racializing effects of the confidence man's spectacular self-constitution as both a social agent and a literary character. In the opening pages of the novel, Melville portrays the *Fidèle* and the many characters it conveys as representative of the demographic diversity of the Jacksonian era:

> [On it] there was not lack of variety. Natives of all sorts, and foreigners; men of business and men of pleasure. . . . Fine ladies in slippers, and moccasined squaws; Northern speculators and Eastern philosophers; English, Irish, German, Scotch, Danes; Santa Fé traders in striped blankets . . . Quakers in full drab, and United States soldiers in full regimentals; slaves, black, mulatto, quadroon; modish young Spanish Creoles, and old-fashioned French Jews; Mormons and Papists . . . grinning negroes, and Sioux chiefs solemn as high-priests. (9)

The opening description of the *Fidèle* establishes it as a public space defined by its ethnic and racial diversity, a place where "there was no lack of variety, . . . a piebald parliament, an Anacharsis Cloots congress of all kinds of that multiform pilgrim species, man" (10). What such a framing suggests is that the agency of the impenetrably deep and supremely self-interested confidence man finds its expression among and in contrast to individuals defined by the particularities of race and ethnicity. We might thus read *The Confidence-Man* as an allegorization of the relationship of the liberal agency of the confidence man to the particularities of race and ethnicity that exclude individuals from the privileges of that agency; we might read it, in other words, as an allegorization of the "distinctly modern, epistemological *interdependence* of universalism and particularism" through which, as David Kazanjian and others have argued, the privileges of citizenship are distributed in the United States.[9]

But what is most conspicuous about this insistence on the diversity of the riverboat *Fidèle* is that none of the novel's characters end up representing that diversity. What is most conspicuous about Melville's invocation of the category of race is that it presumes to mark everything *on board* that "ship of fools" and yet fails to be the distinguishing mark of its particular passengers. "Black Guinea" of course walks its diegetic decks, but he only serves to foreground the unreliability of racial marking altogether. His minstrel performances are suspected to be those of a "white masquerading as a black" (31). What has often been viewed as one of Melville's most satirically cutting works of social critique, in other words, seems at first glance less an interrogation of Jacksonian pluralism than a kind of self-enclosed game in which white men genially conspire to out-charm one another.[10]

Such a refusal to make racial difference the distinguishing feature of what Melville otherwise insists is a "piebald parliament" of diverse character types might announce a repudiation of the concept of race and its visual economies of social classification. It might, if such a refusal did not belie the persistent reliance on the figure of race in the central dilemmas of the novel. In a novel perhaps most famous for its indecipherability, questions of race and ethnicity emerge most conspicuously at moments of possible thematic and formal resolution. Racial attitudes not only define the two central figures of the novel (the Indian-hating "misanthrope" and the "philanthropic" "taster of races"), but nested stories of racial encounter are often positioned as temptingly rare allegorical explanations of characters or clarifications of narrative or philosophical ambiguities.[11] Of those interpolated tales, the story of the Indian-hater, Colonel John Moredock, has provoked perhaps the greatest critical debate. At least since Elizabeth Foster's landmark reading of the novel, the task of exegetically disentangling the "inverted allegory" of the Indian-hater has been a key critical strategy of making sense of Melville's conceptual and literary sleights of hand or, conversely, of proving the insistent irresolvability of the novel.[12]

The story of the Indian-hater is reported by a "stranger" (later identified as Charlie Noble) to the self-described "philanthropist" and cosmopolitan "taster of races," Frank Goodman, who dominates the second half of the novel as the final and culminating apotheosis of the confidence man. After overhearing a discussion between Goodman and his misanthropic counterpart, Pitch, the eavesdropping Charlie approaches the philanthropist to warn him of the dubious character of this "Missouri bachelor." His warning takes shape as the story told to him by his father's friend, the Judge James Hall (which he recalls "almost word for word") of Colonel Moredock in particular and the "metaphysics" of Indian-hating in general. The story wraps up the episodic structure of the first half and inaugurates the new representational games of the second with its own tempting but questionable offer—an offer to puncture analogically the dissimulative surface of narration with an "explanatory" fable. The fable is most immediately offered as an explanation of the misanthropic character of Pitch, an explanation that also allegorically aligns the confidence man with the duplicity of the "Indian race." This duplicity of character is what the misanthrope is said to "hate," and the story has long been read simply as an allegory of the misanthropic critique of the confidence man's duplicity, the racial dimensions often factored out as "mere" allegorical bearer.[13]

The story of the Indian-hater thus seems to confirm the conventional narrative of character's historical decline by contrasting the performative mastery of social conventions that define the confidence man's charismatic "personality" with the skeptical social misanthropy of the self-reliant "character." While such a misanthropic character promises to defend against and even "exterminate" the corrupting influence of the confidence man, it is one that ultimately fades away and yields to the cultural dominance of the confidence man. And yet, the Indian-hater story troubles this historical narrative as much as it seems to affirm it. For although the confidence man emerges at the end of the novel the unvanquished master of circumstance, the story of the Indian-hater documents this ascendancy of the confidence man in much more ambivalent terms.

First, the misanthropic Indian-hater seeks to wipe out duplicity in and as the figure of the "Indian." But the "authenticity" and sincerity that he offers in exchange are ultimately revealed as an avowed kind of genocidal sincerity. The nostalgic call for a return to the individualistic ideals of the self-reliant character that it might be said to make is thus shown to be one with spectacularly catastrophic and genocidal consequences. The story leaves us with the dilemma of having to choose, in other words, between the genocidal sincerity of the misanthrope and the "philanthropic" exploitations of the confidence man. Furthermore, the story offers a highly problematic figure to represent the ascendance of the philanthropic character. While the Indian-hater is represented as a historically anti-quated and disappearing figure in the story, the "Indian character" of the confidence man seems equally endangered as an enduring cultural icon and more importantly as a historical reality given the Native American's violent removal from, or containment on, the nation's frontiers. What then are we to make of the seemingly empty gesture here of explanation, an explanation that only installs the dilemma of having to choose between a genocidal but "reliable" character and a "philanthropic" yet relentlessly exploitative one? More importantly, if the pivotal story of the Indian-hater is not itself the story of the confidence man's ascendance, then how does the dilemma it produces provide the means for the ascendance of the phil-anthropic character? If we accept that the novel thematizes the dilemma of having to rely on a social assessment of character that can nonetheless never be secured, then what are we to make of such a conspicuous use of race to resolve this representational dilemma? How is race figured here as a consequence of the simultaneously literary and social problems of rep-resentation posed by the rhetoric of character itself? Why does the novel offer a story of racialization to resolve the problems of reliable character, and what might it mean if this apparent resolution turns out itself to be a kind of confidence game?

My aim, in pointing to the dilemma posed by the "explanation" of the Indian-hater story, is not to contest the pivotal significance that the In-dian-hater story has in the thematic and formal texture of Melville's novel or the allegorical force of its proffered resolution. Indeed, I argue that the story of the Indian-hater does resolve the central dialectical relation of the novel, the relation between the philanthropic character of the confi-dence man and the character of his one abiding foil, the misanthrope. But it does so only in order to show the costs of such a resolution. The failure of the explanation to explain is not simply another example of the text's tautological web of self-canceling "moot points," as William Ramsey care-fully argues, but rather is a failure that shifts attention to the racializing consequences of such a drive to interpret the inscrutable text of charac-ter itself.[14] The interpretive inference that a racially unmarked, uniquely self-reliant and consolidated agent lies behind the polymorphous masks of the confidence man, like the unmasking of the misanthrope's self-reli-ant character, this chapter demonstrates, requires the endorsement of an imperial allegory of racial difference and the interpretive consolidation of racialized characters. *The Confidence-Man* thus models in the revelations and occlusions of its literary form the cultural work performed by the rhetoric of character itself.

Philanthropy's Gift: A Federal Taste for Race

The opening chapter of *The Confidence-Man*, "A Mute Goes Aboard a Boat on the Mississippi," introduces us to the textual nature and characteristic posture of the book's title character, even if we are unsure whether we are meeting that character himself. The scene opens as "a man in cream-colours" who "was, in the extremest sense of the word, a stranger" (3) steps on board the riverboat *Fidèle*. What is less clear, however, is whether this stranger also steps squarely into the role of the protagonist. After boarding the *Fidèle*, this figure of "fair," "flaxen," "creamy" whiteness stands beside a posted placard warning of the "recent" arrival "from the East" of "a mysterious impostor, . . . quite an original genius in his vocation" (3). What has often confused readers of the novel is whether this scene introduces the confidence man in the figure of the mute or, rather, through the warning of the placard.[15] With what might now be called a cinematic astuteness, the opening scene uses the movements of the mute to direct both the growing crowd's and the reader's gaze to the posted placard in order to establish that placard as a written caption for the mute's otherwise speechless character:

> Stared at, but unsaluted, with the air of one neither courting nor shunning regard, but evenly pursuing the path of duty, lead it through solitudes or cities, he [the mute] held on his way along the lower deck until he chanced to come to a placard near the captain's office, offering a reward for the capture of a mysterious impostor, supposed to have recently arrived from the East—quite an original genius in his vocation, as would appear, though wherein his originality consisted was not clearly given; but what purported to be a careful description of his person followed. (3)

The choice presented by this scene between the mute and the imposter described by the placard, however, is a false one. The opening scene does not simply present the first "game" of the confidence man or telegraph his imminent arrival but rather demonstrates in the juxtaposition of placard and mute the spectacular epistemology of those games. The mute, like the confidence men who will follow him, fixes the crowd's gaze on the very spectacle of confidence and character, on to its "advertisement," only in order to transact his deceptions within its covering glare. Time after time the confidence man makes questions of confidence—of trust in the veracity of character—the central topic of conversation, only in order to elicit that confidence from his interlocutor. Such conversations are as apparently unrelated to the confidence man himself as the poster is to the mute, for the content of these discussions is rarely recognized as revealing signs of the man himself but rather is taken as words unrelated to his otherwise "mute" identity. Like the mute beside the placard, in other words, the confidence man obscures his identity by placing it just beside himself, by making his speech something that does not reflect or reference his own character.

When the mute finally "speaks" by writing on the "small slate" that he carries around, he tells the crowd more than they are able to hear: he tells them that the essence of his confidence game is best described in terms of "charity," a "Charity [that] thinketh no evil" (4). The phrase the mute writes on his slate seems an ironic defense of the figure of the confidence man, a tongue-in-cheek effort to contain the caustic effects on interpersonal confidence that such a warning might instill. But the mute's action does more than that: it also names the very syntax that connects the figure of the mute to the words of the warning, the logic by which the game of confidence will proceed, the logic of "philanthropy." As the crowd grows increasingly hostile toward what they take to be his "pertinacity," the mute's slate becomes his "shield" as he passes through the crowd, all the while rewriting a string of Pauline maxims, from "Charity suffereth long, and is kind" to "Charity endureth all things" to "Charity believeth all things" to "Charity never faileth." The phrases not only semantically portend the fate of the individuals in the crowd, who will mistakenly extend a charitable hand to the confidence man, but they also identify the increasingly jostled and hemmed-in mute with the "suffering" and "enduring" charity that, despite the failing confidence of the crowd in the mute's innocence, itself does not "faileth." While the crowd attends to the meaning of these phrases, they do not notice that what matters here is how he rewrites them, for just as "[t]he word charity, as originally traced, remained throughout uneffaced, not unlike the left-hand numeral of a printed date, otherwise left for convenience in blank" (5), so too will the figure of the "philanthropist" remain as the only stable subject in the confidence man's parade of masquerades. In identifying himself with the unchanging subject of these various phrases, the mute demonstrates the very powers of predication that will empower the confidence man. His power will lie in the ability to qualify his identity with a range of different characters, predications that will take as their only stable grammatical "subject," like the sentences on the slate itself, the figure and identity of the charitable "philanthropist."

The confidence man's character is defined throughout the first half of the novel by just such a "philanthropic" relation to his fellow passengers. While the moniker "philanthropist" as an abstract character type emerges in the pivotal chapter beginning the second half of the novel—a chapter tellingly titled "A Philanthropist Undertakes to Convert a Misanthrope, but Does Not Get Beyond Confuting Him"—the term also refers to one of his early masquerades as a charity worker for the Seminole Indian Widow and Orphan Asylum. Melville's portrait of the agent's imperial aspiration to establish a charity system that extends across the globe, of course, points to and satirizes the forms of colonial violence that will be carried out in the name of a character-building "civilizing mission" in the late nineteenth century. But it also prefigures the central strategy of the confidence game. "Philanthropy" names the confidence man's own signature strategy of unquestionably extending his confidence to strangers in order to set the unique logic of the confidence game in motion. True to the story of William Thompson, the historical source of the confidence man, who would ask to keep a person's gold watch for a day as proof that the person had "confidence" in a well-intentioned stranger, our confidence man obligates his victim through his own unsolicited, charitable offer of friendly confidence.[16] In making his own "gift" of confidence to the strangers he encounters, he lays claim to a reciprocal obligation to match that confidence and makes cash the token pledge by which that confidence is proven. As he says to the Widow in the Ladies Saloon, "you have confidence? Prove it. Let me have twenty dollars" (44). The confidence man does not seek out the (unearned) confidence of the other in order then to execute an economic transaction under the legitimating ruse of a false character. Rather, he makes economic transactions the legitimating sign of social confidence; he makes cash the token pledge by which his victims "prove" their confidence in his character. As he so brazenly puts it (perhaps too brazenly, given that it does not succeed here) to Charlie Noble, "Yes . . . you are going to loan me fifty dollars. I could almost wish I was in need of more, only for your sake. Yes, my dear Charlie, for your sake; that you might the better prove your noble kindliness, my dear Charlie" (179).

The philanthropy of the confidence man's character, however, is explicitly defined by his signature "love" of ethnic difference, a love that he claims derives from his "cosmopolitan" nature. The philanthropist and "cosmopolitan" Frank Goodman appears in the second half of the novel as the last in the confidence man's parade of masquerades. But the difference here is that Frank's turns out to be no disguise at all. He seems to be the unmediated embodiment of the confidence man "himself"; he appears in bearing and dress the distillation of the confidence man's "motley" and mutable character. His remarkable appearance, as described in chapter 24, seems less a disguise than an overt performance of his capacity for disguise. His suit is a confusion of ethnic types and national costumes, a sartorial summation of his mimetic capacity for masquerade:

> This ungentle mention of the toucan was not improbably suggested by the parti-hued, and rather plumagy aspect of the stranger, no bigot it would seem, but a liberalist, in dress. . . . In short, the stranger sported a vesture barred with various hues, that of the cochineal predominating, in style participating of the High-land plaid, Emir's robe, and French blouse . . . [and adorned with] a sort of Indian belt, confining the redundant vesture; the other [hand] held, by its long bright cherry-stem, a Nuremberg pipe in blast, its great porcelain bowl painted in miniature with linked crests and arms of interlinked nations—a florid show. (131–132)

This "stranger" seems to bear his identity on his sleeve, as he announces to his fellow passengers, in a language they cannot quite comprehend, that the man behind the masks is simply a collection of those masks. The relentlessly skeptical Pitch, of course, recognizes that Frank's citational fashion is less the expression of an inner character than the dissimulating mark of what he calls an "African pantomime." When the suspicious Pitch asks who this stranger is (insisting that he is not who he seems), the "stranger" responds by offering not his name but rather the explanation that he is "[a] cosmopolitan, a catholic man; who, being such, ties himself to no narrow tailor or teacher, but federates, in heart as in costume, something of the various gallantries of men under various suns" (132).[17]

The cosmopolitan initially describes this "federating" power of his character in terms of the humanist ethic of sympathy that is, he proclaims, the "principle of a true citizen of the world," a principle represented by "fraternal and fusing feeling" of the traveler, to whom "[n]o man is a stranger." This universalized "philanthropic" love of "humanity," however, quickly devolves into a kind of fetish for racial difference:

Served up à la Pole, or à la Moor, à la Ladrone, or à la Yankee, that good
dish, man, still delights me; or rather is man a wine I never weary of com-
paring and sipping; wherefore am I a pledged cosmopolitan, a sort of Lon-
don-Dock-Vault connoisseur, going about from Teheran to Natchitoches, a
taster of races; in all his vintages, smacking my lips over this racy creature,
man. (133)

The philanthropist's grounding of his cosmopolitan capacity for disguise
in a "taste for race" draws on two distinct "idioms of race" common to the
nineteenth century: that of material "type" and that of "common descent."[18]
His intoxicating consumption of racially marked characters relishes in
what it takes to be the material properties that define and distinguish racial types.[19] But "taste" is not simply the sensual registration of material
qualities; it is the connoisseur's capacity to delineate and articulate what
counts as the "distinguishing" characteristics, to distinguish what counts
as the vintage "character" of race itself. The cosmopolitan's analogy of race
to wine is moreover no arbitrary one, for etymologically "raciness" refers
specifically to the taste of wine or, more importantly, to the taste imparted
to a wine by the particular soil from which it comes.[20] In enjoying that
"racy creature, man," the cosmopolitan invokes the idiom of race as descent in his determination of "vintage," in his determination of origin from
perceived properties. This capacity for construing the signifying marks of
the body and making them into the expressions of origin—this taste for
race—is thus the ground of the hermeneutic capacity that empowers his
mastery of character. It names his capacity to provide referential origins
for perceived qualities; it names his capacity to ground the unreliability of
character and to "federate" these differences within his own domesticating,
philanthropic character. The cosmopolitan, in his taste for racial difference,
is one who "incorporates" that difference as the domesticated, democratic
pluralism of his own altruistic character.[21]

This fetishizing capacity to consolidate his own character through a
cosmopolitan taste for race is the mimetic force that also sets the entire
novel in motion. For the "cosmopolitanism" of the confidence man also
names the *narrative* "federation" of his various characters through the racial "performance" of "Black Guinea." The "Black Guinea" of chapter 3,
who follows quickly on the heels of the extraordinarily "white," nearly col-
orless mute, is perhaps most famous for the list he provides of what turns
out to be the many avatars of the confidence man. The list that appears
in this chapter, conspicuously titled "In Which a Variety of Characters

Appear," has been long used for divining Melville's intentions and compositional reconsiderations. Less has been said, however, about the way the list legitimates the future avatars through its self-forecasting logic.[22] Guinea, "a grotesque negro cripple" (10), is found performing his awkward tambourine show on the decks of the *Fidèle* while catching copper pennies in his mouth. Intruding on this "game of charity," the "limping, gimlet-eyed, sour-faced person" (12) of the wooden-legged cynic appears on the scene and begins "to croak out something about his deformity being a sham, got up for financial purposes." And not only is the Guinea's bodily deformity a forgery, the cynic goes on to contend, but so too are that body's racial signifiers, for "he maintain[s] that Guinea was some white scoundrel, betwisted and painted up for a decoy" (31). When questioned as a fraud by this "misanthropic" cynic, Guinea produces a list of "character references" as the only kind of "documentary proof" (13) that he can offer to secure the "confidence" of the increasingly suspicious crowd, a list that seems to describe many of the future disguises of the confidence man. Guinea's appeal to these various "characters" who will attest to his identity is meant to verify his own character through an appeal to the self-evident character of these various "gentlemen." Their "reputable" character would presumably provide a legitimating referent for his own questionable one.[23]

And yet his citation of this referential logic inverts its legitimating power: Guinea's questionable character ends up legitimating the confidence man's various characters through a referential short-circuit. For when indeed these avatars are later encountered by the "dupes" of subsequent chapters, they are of course recognizable as the Guinea's benefactors, that recognizability translating into a kind of substance of character, as they bear the truth of Guinea's claim to their existence. Mr. Roberts, the country merchant and the next in a long line of victims, thus "trusts" the "stranger" John Ringman: "[T]hough I have not the pleasure of personally knowing you, yet I am pretty sure I have at least *heard* of you, and recently too, quite recently. A poor negro aboard here referred to you, among others, for a character, I think" (18). The Guinea's questionable character is able to validate and verify the future characters of the confidence man, making them into recognizable bearers of attestation despite the fact that no referent attests directly to their reliability, to their own character. Their reputation does not ground their ability to be the "reference" of another's character but rather is a reputation "made" in the very gesture of attestation itself. They are reliable, in other words, because they attest; they do not attest because they are reliable.

A Guinea is also a common British coin, and the confidence man evoc-atively trades on the value of race as such a transcendental signified guar-anteeing the value of his character through relations of social exchange. As such a currency, he is able to give the fiction of value to the various ex-changeable "characters" of the confidence man, a value constituted in the marketplace of reputation yet mis-taken, like the monetary value of com-modities, as an expression of their "true" character. What Melville adds to this rather classic story of character's social constitution, however, is that its power to materialize the substance of character as referential origin hinges on the fungibility of racial identification, on the "problem" of ra-cial passing and its exposure of the unreliability and ultimately arbitrary nature of racial signifiers. And yet, while this masquerade foregrounds the arbitrary and thereby fictional nature of race's "materiality," it does so only in order to renaturalize the materiality of race in the process. If the confidence man's future avatars are to be trusted, they must retrospec-tively confirm the Guinea's racial identity. They must confirm that the questionable marks fetishistically poured over by the crowd, "the knotted black fleece" and "good-natured . . . black face" (10), are indeed the legiti-mate signs of race.[24]

The singular identity and underlying character of the confidence man across his many masquerades is thus a presumption that turns on the naturalization of race's material character, a presumption that Melville replicates as the condition of the confidence man's coherency as a literary character. The assumption behind most readings of *The Confidence-Man* is of course that there is a single scheming character behind the various masks of the confidence man. The structure of the text insists on such a reading. The full title of the novel, *The Confi-dence-Man: His Masquerade,* suggests such a singular agent in its use of the possessive "his," as does the interrelated structure of many of his cons and the consistency of their methods. But the novel with equal care calls into question the presumption that all of the cons are the work of a single agent.[25] Melville's narrator never actually takes us be-hind the scenes to confirm the identity of the confidence man, nor do the many portraits of characters' inner thoughts reveal the duplicitous strategizing of a confidence man. Two different avatars, moreover, of-ten engage the same person in immediate succession and with little notable change in appearance other than a new set of clothes and yet are not recognized as the same man. Similarly, the length of time be-tween two avatars' appearance (which Melville deliberately measures out by tracing the continuous action or thoughts of one character from one chapter to the next) often provides little if any opportunity for the "costume change" we presumably witness. By simultaneously insisting on and then undermining a reading that would locate a single agent behind the various performances of the confidence man, Melville underscores the necessarily hypothetical nature of his "true," inner character. This is not to say that Melville is simply demonstrating that there is no "true" origin to character, that character exists only in the unreliable play of appearances and the economies of social exchange. By making a single confidence man the inevitable, though uncon-firmable, protagonist of the narrative, Melville delineates the forms through which such an intentional agent is elicited as a hypothesis and as only a hypothesis within the rhetoric of character, and the racializ-ing work such an elicitation performs.

The Bitter Cure: Misanthropy's Rage for Self-Reliance

The skeptical figure of the "misanthrope"—and the self-reliant philosophy he espouses—is positioned throughout *The Confidence-Man* as the one possible antidote to the philanthropist's dissembling drug of confidence and the only real challenge to the racializing logic that empowers the emergent philanthropic character. Indeed, when the philanthropist makes his appearance by stepping on board the *Fidèle*, it is a ship that seems to be already policed by the misanthropic character. The novel thus appears to be structured around this dialectical armature that binds these two fig-ures of the misanthrope and the philanthropist together. What begins as a rhetorical antagonism between the avatars of the philanthropist and the various skeptics who challenge his methods—the "No Trust" barber Wil-liam Cream, the wooden-legged cynic, the "Invalid Titan" of chapter 17, and the Missouri bachelor Pitch—becomes in chapter 24 a struggle be-tween two abstracted character types—the "misanthrope" and the "phi-lanthropist"—and finally ends as two competing philosophies of character and character formation in the encounters with the "transcendentalist" Mark Winsome and his pragmatic disciple, Egbert. At the center of this parade of misanthropes and philanthropists stands the nested figure of the Indian-hater, who explains the misanthropic attitude and marks the transition from the first half's clash of characters to the second half's clash of philosophies, a transition also marked by the change in tenor from warnings of the dangers of blind trust to an interrogation of the dangers of skeptical mistrust.

The cynic's misanthropic challenge to the performances of the confidence man is ultimately explained through the example of the backwoodsman Pitch. In the conversation between Pitch and the Philosophical Intelligence Officer, a conversation that echoes in many ways Lorenzo Dow's 1813 dialogue *Cosmopolite Interrogated, or, a Dialogue between the Curious and Singular*, the clash of these two characters is portrayed as a clash of rhetorical principles.[26] The misanthrope challenges the seductive and disarmingly persuasive discourse of the confidence man with a form of rhetorical intransigency grounded in the unmediated integrity of his character. In scene after scene, the confidence man calibrates his character to that of his victim and proceeds with his con by philanthropically seeking the dialogic consensus and confidence necessary to deliberative rhetoric. Pitch protects himself from this rhetorical trap through a misanthropic refusal of the philanthropic gesture of deliberative rhetoric. As he himself sums it up in the credo of his name, "My name is Pitch; I stick to what I say" (117). Pitch makes this statement both as a rebuff to the Philosophical Intelligence Officer and as a statement of his reiterative, monological relation to language as they take up the question of character in terms of the virtues and vices of the orphan boys sent to the frontier to work for men such as Pitch. Pitch's rejoinder here is a refusal to debate his claim and to seek democratic consensus, for debate inevitably entails compromise and a consideration of alternative positions. His claim—in this typically overdetermined case the claim that "[a]ll boys are rascals, and so are all men"—is a statement representative of his "fifteen years' experience," not a "metaphysical" principle about character that he wishes to defend argumentatively (126). Pitch's "sticky" language is used not so much to defend as to repeat his claim about the immutability and innate depravity of character. As a statement it is simply an "expression" of his experience, and as a statement there is nothing to do but reiteratively "stick" to it when challenged by the Officer's theoretical argument that "a youth of one character can be transformed into a man of the opposite character" (124).

Language is for Pitch nothing more than a medium for expressing the content of his character, never a reflexive mode of its formation, and hence a seemingly unassailable barrier to the persuasive strategies of the confidence man. He is not simply hostile to the more "rhetorical" of the confidence man's strategies, but he even refuses debate altogether. Pitch will challenge the Philosophical Intelligence Officer's fallacious connections with, "But is analogy argument? You are a punster" (124). And yet when the confidence man offers to "just enter into a little argument," he is cut off by Pitch's "No more little arguments for me. Had too many little arguments to-day" (136). Pitch has little use for language and, it turns out, even less for argument. His laconic challenge repudiates the terms of democratic deliberation itself, as he dismisses the entreaties of the Officer with, "Ah, you are a talking man—what I call a wordy man. You talk, talk" (125).

Pitch is no stickler for principle, for in him "instincts prevail . . . over precepts" (145). And yet Pitch's insistence that language can only express, never transform, character also reveals the inconsistency and mutability of his character. Pitch sticks to what he says once he has said it, but that does not mean that he will always say the same thing. What matters to Pitch is the veracity of the statement, its fidelity to the instinctual, willing core of his character, not its dogmatic consistency to an avowed set of beliefs. His language does not index the principles of a fixed ethical or metaphysical system but rather the varying state of his desire. As Mark Winsome later puts it, echoing Emerson's plaint that "[a] foolish consistency is the hobgoblin of little minds," "I seldom care to be consistent" (193).[27] Unlike the confidence man, who in the mastery of language's various dialogic forms articulates the fiction of a strategic, coherent character, the misanthrope retreats from civil deliberation in order to preserve the integrity of his instincts and will, yet only to reveal his varying character. As Toni Morrison more ironically notes of her character Soaphead in *The Bluest Eye*, "he found misanthropy an excellent means of developing character."[28] Both the misanthrope and the philanthropist end up being defined by their "mastery" of character, which they nonetheless secure through very different means. While the misanthrope clings to a vision of character beyond the reach of society and of language itself, the philanthropist asserts a rhetorical, performative model of character whose guiding principle is that "life is a pic-nic *en costume*; one must take a part, assume a character, stand ready in a sensible way to play the fool" (133). His capacity to read the character of his victim and adapt any of his many assumable characters in response to it is the ground of his own ironic iteration of "self-reliance."

Genealogy's Fetish: Hating the Indian-Hater

In restaging the challenge of the misanthrope to the philanthropist in terms of the frontiersman's genocidal pursuit of the "duplicitous Indian," the Indian-hater story and its explanation of the misanthropic character is positioned as the allegorical key to the novel itself. Charlie Noble's recounting of Judge Hall's story suggests from the start that incidents in the story are "less advanced as truths of the Indians than as examples of the backwoodsman's impression of them" (146). His story is offered, in other words, as a genealogy of the racist "impressions" that conspire to instill the Indian-hating attitude in an otherwise noble mind: it is a geneaology of racism itself.[29] First of all, the story explicitly discounts a historical explanation of Moredock's genocidal rage as simply one turn in an overall cycle of frontier violence, a cycle driven by the violent encroachments and displacements of westward expansion into Native American territories. As Foster and others document, Melville "carefully omits . . . the extenuating explanations of Indian rapine as revenge for white injustice" from his retelling of the story, going to great lengths to edit these references out of his source document, James Hall's 1835 *Sketches of History, Life, and Manners, in the West.*[30] The story, in other words, "explains" the "Indian savagery" that incites Moredock's rage not as itself a response to the violences of American expansion, or as an innate aspect of the "Indian race," but rather as an "impression" formed by the backwoodsman about the Indian's duplicitous character. Moredock's attitude is said to be eventually triggered by the traumatic experience of his family's death at the hands of an aggrieved band of Indians, but this event is only the last of a series of equally traumatizing racial fictions. "The character of the Western frontiersman," as Helen Hunt Jackson similarly describes it in the 1884 novel *Ramona*, was thus "a singular accumulation of such strata,—the training and beliefs of his earliest days overlain by successions of unrelated and violent experiences, like geological deposits."[31]

Second, the Judge's story begins with the "metaphysics" of Indian-hating produced by the "backwoods education" of not just the biographical Moredock but the frontiersman in general. It is an education largely consisting of myths and stories of the dangerously "unreliable" Indian character, of "histories of Indian lying, Indian theft, Indian double-dealing, Indian fraud and perfidy" (146). The implication is that the backwoodsman is conditioned to hate the Indian as these stereotypes are pedagogically and prejudicially inculcated in the young unbiased mind.[32] But the story also undermines this simple reading of racist conditioning in its equivocation on the innocence of the unbiased mind. Melville suggests that such an unbiased mind is the ground on which such racist ideas take root when he precedes this educational story of the backwoodsman with a description of his characteristic type, a description that figures—even caricatures—the character of self-reliance (144). This self-reliant figure of solitude, whose "untutored sagacity" and suspicion of social "precepts" make him "one who less hearkens to what others may say about things, than looks for himself, to see what are things themselves" (144), is positioned in the narrative sequence as the recipient of this racist education. And yet it is unclear how such a person who looks to the "things themselves" would fall prey to the tall tales of the forest chroniclers. Indeed, while narratively positioned as the recipient of this education, this self-reliant character type is also positioned, in the developmental logic, as the product of that education, for it is the type of man that eventually develops from the boy who receives that education.

The story thus shows that the self-reliant character seemingly immune to and untouched by racist representations is the very product of those representations. Self-reliance is not an ideal, racially unmarked expression of character's achievement of self-identification but rather a fiction produced by the logic of empire itself. More importantly, the self-reliant character is defined by the Indian-hater story not only as a product of America's imperial expansion but also as a character who erases his racist origins through the violence he enacts on the frontier. In this sense the backwoodsman can himself reappear to America not as the product of its racist pedagogy but as the civilizing ideal of a race-transcending form of liberated self-sufficiency, an ideal that defines what it means to have character:

> Though held in a sort a barbarian, the backwoodsman would seem to America what Alexander was to Asia—captain in the vanguard of conquering civilization. What ever the nation's growing opulence, does it not lackey his heels? . . . The tide of emigration, let it roll as it will, never overwhelms the backwoodsman into itself; he rides upon advance, as the Polynesian upon the comb of the surf. (145)

The syntax of this oft-discussed imperial analogy, however, is perhaps more revealing than it at first appears. The Indian-hater "seems" to America what Alexander "was" to Asia; that is, the Indian-hater appears as the bearer of civilized society in his advancements into the territories of the analogically "Asiatic" Native American. And yet the fact that he is "held in a sort a barbarian" would also seem to analogize America to Asia, an Asia that presumably does not recognize the civilizing benefits of this barbarian from the West. America would in that case be not the agent but the object of its own civilizing mission. The Indian-hater does not civilize the society that he conquers but the society for which he conquers. But America sees the Indian-hater as barbarian because, as frontiersman, he has turned his back on civil society in his relentless push into the "solitude" of the west and not because he is somehow bringing the civilization of the frontier to America. How then does the Indian-hater's movement *away* from American society civilize it? How, more importantly, does his violence civilize the nation that both witnesses it and yet misrecognizes it?

A third genealogy of racism is suggested by the other figures in Melville's complex, imperial analogy. Like "Moses in the Exodus, or the Emperor Julian in Gaul" (145), the Indian-hater leads America into the "empty" wilderness, or rather into a wilderness emptied by his movement into it. The "emptiness" of the frontier was commonly cited to explain the "exceptional" role of the United States in the progress of world history by later historians such as Frederick Jackson Turner, who saw in that emptiness the opportunity for an "Americanizing" encounter with "the primitive," and by Malthusian sociologists such as William Graham Sumner, who saw in it relief from the "pressure in the oldest countries" of overpopulation that produced social inequality.[33] In Melville's Malthusian reformulation of the pursuit of what Thomas Jefferson referred to as "empire for liberty," the "tide of emigration" washes out across the frontier seeking to disperse the inequities of the "old world" through an absorption of the underutilized resources of the "new world."[34] But Melville is doing more than reiterating the Malthusian justification of territorial appropriation. The purpose of the backwoodsman is not to guarantee "the nation's growing opulence or power" in his pursuit of untouched resources, for such an "opulence and power" is merely the product of the opportunism that "lackeys his heels." The purpose of the backwoodsman rather is to be untouched by the wave and yet remain the figure of its leading edge. The backwoodsman secures the empire for liberty and equality but does so by securing the purity and survival of the "race" itself in his flight from the "overwhelming" tides of immigration, a purity preserved by the image of his own self-reliant character. The backwoodsman is the embodiment of what the wave presumably seeks and guarantees, not simple opulence and power but the liberty and equality promised by colonial expansion. The backwoodsman thus safeguards the whiteness of character itself as the privileged mark of the rights-bearing citizen of the civilized republic.[35]

What the Indian-hater demonstrates is that the material marks of race are not so much the projected discriminations of an otherwise racially disavowing character but a body of social fictions that not only sustain that character but sustain it by materializing race in its wake. Not only does the Indian-hater's pursuit naturalize "a race which he believes to be red from a cause akin to that which makes some tribes of garden insects green" (146), but he "exterminates" the record of this naturalization of race with the image of his own self-reliant character. The real danger arises when the backwoodsman adds his "private passion" to these social fictions of the "community," for "we have then the stock out of which is formed . . . the Indian-hater *par excellence*" (149). The Indian-hater par excellence, in his pursuit of the solitary life of exterminating a race, also exterminates himself as an object of representation in his total withdrawal from social contact: "How evident that in strict speech there can be no biography of an Indian-hater *par excellence,* any more than one of a swordfish, or other deep sea denizen; or, which is still less imaginable, one of a dead man. The career of the Indian-hater *par excellence* has the impenetrability of the fate of a lost steamer. . . . [It] shall never become news" (150). While the Indian-hater story, on its surface, warns of the genocidal, exterminating dangers of a man raised on a "metaphysics" of Indian-hating, the story also suggests that the even greater danger of the Indian-hater "*par excellence*" is that, as the instantiation of what Homi Bhabha calls nationalism's "narcissism of self-generation," he paradoxically exterminates the very traces of his own formation in order to appear as the self-reliant, solitary "vanguard" of the civilizing mission.[36]

In adumbrating the logic of "empire for liberty," the chapters on Indian-hating tell a story of the realization of "community" mythologies as the material marks of race, a story that recognizes how the "civilizing mission" of American settler colonialism operates under the national fiction of the self-reliant character. And yet the most salient feature of this critique of racial representation is that it subsequently falls prey to Melville's own characteristic dissembling, a dissembling that, I contend, is exactly its point. As the narrative progresses, the Indian-hater story is framed as just another pawn in the game of confidence, as the "boon companions" Charlie and Frank make discussing the story the basis of their quickening confidence. Indeed the story becomes the referential touchstone for the entire second half of the novel. The story, though told by Charlie in order to "warn" Frank of the misanthropic Pitch, is quickly appropriated by Frank as he turns a discussion of the misanthrope into the occasion for more drinking and convivial bonding, and hence the basis for Frank's confidence-pitch to Charlie. Although this request for a loan "between friends" is rebuffed by Charlie, this failure is nonetheless itself put to use in the subsequent philosophical debate with the transcendentalist Mark Winsome and, more pointedly, is interrogated in the dramatic reenactment with Winsome's "disciple" Egbert, where Egbert "plays" Charlie, and Frank "plays" the "character" of himself.

The story and the novel as a whole show to what uses a "metaphysics" can be put, and here the "federating" philanthropist uses the story to dislodge the "colonizing" misanthrope as a model of self-reliant character and to redefine the terms of character itself. Frank's appropriation of the Indian-hater story as the instrument of his final confidence game, and the perseverance of the confidence man at the text's end, have thus been read as documenting the triumph of what we might call, following Warren Susman, the spectacular theatrics of a socially constituted "personality" over the socially disavowing, self-reliant "character" as a cultural ideal, a triumph achieved, moreover, through the exposure of character's own duplicitous cultural formation.[37] Karen Halttunen's landmark reading of the figure of the confidence man, for example, locates such a figure within a historical narrative that charts the rise and fall of what she refers to as "the character-ethic."[38] With the emergence of a "new corporate context" in which "personality skills, such as that subtle quality called charm, were more useful to the ambitious youth than the qualities of industry, sobriety, and frugality," Halttunen argues, "executive ability or management— the art of manipulating others to do what you wanted them to do—was far more valuable than the ascetic self-discipline of an earlier era."[39] What is interesting about Halttunen's account, and about such narratives of character's decline more generally, however, is that they also demonstrate the historical and conceptual interdependency of character and personality. Personality is portrayed as the mode of subjectivity emblematic of late modern commodity capitalism and yet is also figured in these accounts as the much more ancient origin of and antecedent to the concept of character as well.

In Halttunen's broader genealogy of the confidence man, for example, the "character-ethic" emerges in response to the performative dangers of the confidence man, a danger against which "young men were urged to defend themselves through character formation. . . . [B]y exercising self-possession, self-government, and, above all, self-reliance, he placed himself beyond evil influences and became a law unto himself."[40] Indeed, not only did the confidence man incite the very character ideal that he would also subsequently supplant, his performative personality was the product of a contradiction or conflict internal to the rhetoric of character itself: a conflict between the need to cultivate self-reliance as well as the forms of reputation that required one to attend to one's "standing in the eyes of others ... [and] please an audience of strangers."[41] Thus despite Halttunen's insistence on a narrative of character's decline, she describes the concepts of character and personality as both diachronically related and synchronically fused, as constituting a kind of ongoing historical dialectic in which character continually emerges as the resolving term: "The concept of character represented an effort to reconcile two different views of human nature: the premodern concept of soul, which focused on man's inner spiritual being as he confronted God alone, and the modern concept of personality, which turned attention to man's external standing before other men."[42]

Such a dialectic can be seen as well in the treatment of character by writers such as Ralph Waldo Emerson. Emerson is perhaps best known for the account of the socially disavowing, "noncomformist," "concentrated" character of "self-reliance" that he presents in his famous essay "Self-Reliance" (1841). But in the essay "Character" that he published in 1844, he presents a vision of character, elements of which can be seen as well in "Self-Reliance," not in terms of the "self-sufficingness" that can resist all influence but in terms of the outward-directed, "animating" force of personality that influences others "directly by presence, and without means" like the mesmeric force of "magnetism."[43] Rather than an inward-turning form of self-mastery, such a "character wants room" for the "exhibition of character" and expansively "encloses the world, as the patriot does his country, as a material basis for his character, and a theatre for action."[44] Such a dialectical concept of character is evident as well in the character-building manuals of the period, which frequently portray the principles of "personality" not as antithetical to but as incorporated within the structure of "character." The self-reliance that is so often taken as character's ideal, for example, is directly challenged by early character builders such as Rufus Clark, who defends "philanthropy" against the "universal misanthropy" that is "poisoning the minds of the young and blasting the immortal hopes of thousands": "The experiment of obtaining lasting happiness under the law of selfishness has been a failure.... It indicates that the moral faculties are deranged, —that there is insanity in the heart, if not the intellect.... [T]he age in which we live has claims upon your philanthropy."[45] P.T. Barnum similarly begins his character-building manual,

Fig. 3. P.T. Barnum, *Dollars and Sense; or, How to Get On: The Whole Secret in a Nutshell* (New York: Henry S. Allen, 1890), 18–19.

Dollars and Sense, with a distinction between the "grumblers" and the "optimists" who constitute the "two different classes" of the world: "One class naturally looks on the bright side of life, and the other upon the dark side."[46]

Whereas Barnum favors the more plucky attitude of the optimist, Booker T. Washington calls for a balance, in his book *Character Building,* of both "the dark side and the bright side, the discouraging side and the encouraging side" if one is to form character properly.[47] Edwin Whipple similarly locates within the character of "characteristic men" elements of both character and personality in *Character and Characteristic Men* (1866) but warns against the "consuming" nature of enigmatic personalities such as Emerson describes: "we must keep them at such a distance as to save our own personality from being insensibly merged into theirs. They are dangerous guests if they eat you, but celestial visitants if you can contrive to eat even a portion of them."[48]

Thus what we see in the dialectic formed by the misanthrope and the philanthropist are the ways that the discourse of character is structured around the disavowal of its own performative personality. Rather than sequential terms in an overarching history of the subject's cultural forms, character and personality each describe overlapping and interrelated cultural ideals that together negotiate the relationship between the forms of independence and interdependence that constitute the self. The framing of the Indian-hater story tells us, more importantly, that the ascendance

of the philanthropic character is achieved through the philanthropic gesture of reforming the misanthrope through a genealogical account of its
origins. When Charlie finishes recounting his story, Frank sets out immediately to secure the genealogical reading of it. Frank secures this reading
of the story, paradoxically enough, by seeming to dispute it. Frank's initial
response to the Indian-hater story is to defend Pitch against the defama-
tory explanation of his misanthropic character:

> "Charity, charity!" exclaimed the cosmopolitan. . . . "God forbid that my
> eccentric friend should be what you hint. You do not know him, or but
> imperfectly. His outside deceived you; at first it came near deceiving even
> me. But I seized a chance, when, owing to indignation against some wrong,
> he laid himself a little open; I seized that lucky chance, I say, to inspect
> his heart, and found it an inviting oyster in a forbidding shell. His outside
> is but put on. Ashamed of his own goodness, he treats mankind as those
> strange old uncles in romances do their nephew—snapping at them all the
> time and yet loving them as the apple of their eye." (156)

Frank defends Pitch by claiming that inside he is not really a misanthrope
but rather a philanthropist who "hide[s] under a surly air a philanthropic
heart" (176). Of course it had also been the point of the Indian-hater story
to trace genealogically the cultural origins of Pitch's misanthropic attitude,
an attitude he then mistakes for his self-made character. What the story
"explained" was the fiction of self-reliance and its role as a kind of mask
for the colonizing work it performs. Hence Frank's claim that Pitch's self-
reliant misanthropy is a put-on does not challenge Charlie's story: it challenges an oversimplified reading of it. And by insisting on such a reading of
Pitch as a "surly philanthropist," Frank takes exegetical control of Charlie's
story and secures the meaning and implications of the story as a genealogy
of America's colonizing racism.

   In saying the misanthrope is a "surly philanthropist," Frank shows that
all claims to such an authentic character are themselves a kind of philanthropic confidence game. As we know from the fetishized character of the
philanthropist himself, such an essential "heart" of philanthropy is really
no heart at all. The heart of philanthropy is, as the confidence games of the
first half underscore again and again, the most insidious form of misanthropy, namely, that of the "genial misanthrope." Frank's claim, however,
extends beyond the example of Pitch. Not only does Frank's interpretation

of the story construe Pitch as a kind of philanthropist, but the interpretive conversion itself demonstrates the more general "progress of genialization" for which Frank is the avowed spokesman:

> And so, thanks to geniality, the misanthrope, reclaimed from his boorish address, will take on refinement and softness—to so genial a degree, indeed, that it may possibly fall out that the misanthrope of the coming century will be almost as popular as, I am sincerely sorry to say, some philanthropists of the present time would seem not to be. (177)

The dialectically fused figure of the "genial misanthrope," a figure already represented by the deceptive geniality of the confidence man, thus becomes the productive figure of the "coming century's" aspirations to "progressive" reform. The "modern" (175) age of "geniality" that Frank and Charlie here together announce does not simply counteract misanthropy but absorbs and rearticulates its social functions. Charlie agrees with Frank that "[g]eniality has invaded each department and profession. We have genial senators, genial authors, genial lecturers, genial doctors, genial clergymen, genial surgeons, and the next thing we shall have is genial hangmen" (175). But it is Frank who spells out what this "invasion" of geniality really means: "'As to the last-named sort of person [the hangman],' said the cosmopolitan, 'I trust that the advancing spirit of geniality will at last enable us to dispense with him'" (175). The philanthropist promises, in this astonishing thesis of the regulatory power of his brand of civility, to replace the legal violences of the hangman with the civilizing violences of a federating "all-fusing" geniality. What the philanthropist promises is to rearticulate the social violences of the "century to come" (177) as the mediated violence of the confidence game itself.

This transition from the "colonizing" character of the misanthrope to the "federating" character of the philanthropist, which the novel is said to interrogate, is one in which the racializing discourses of colonial expansion are not so much exposed and eliminated as they are translated into the new powerfully representative vernacular of a spectacularly self-constituting, philanthropic character, a vernacular that will dominate the culture of the Gilded Age and the reformist aspirations of Progressivism itself.[49] In showing how the confidence man is constituted as an "original character" because of his "philanthropic" orientation to racial difference, because of his fetishizing "taste for race," Melville powerfully shows how even the political unmasking of America's imperial past and its racial fictions is itself a kind of confidence game that risks occluding an ongoing aesthetics of racial difference operating through the presumably neutral determinations of the essential content of character. The promise of character to replace the delimitations of race, in other words, is paradoxically one that can only make character into the greatest of racializing rhetorics.

2

Character Is Capital

Manufacturing Habit in Mark Twain's Character Factory

Character is Habit Crystallized.
— Frances Willard, *What Frances E. Willard Said*[1]

Under the guidance of the later biological and psychological science,
human nature will have to be restated in terms of habit.
— Thornstein Veblen, *The Theory of the Leisure Class*[2]

The prominence of the confidence man and his many avatars as
an object of concern in the fiction, popular periodicals, and advice literature of the mid-nineteenth century was not simply a reaction to the threat
he posed as a new social type but rather expressed the broader ambiva-
lences many people had toward the performative dimensions and imperial
implications of the iconic national character he announced and installed.
Figures such as Benjamin Franklin, whose famous *Autobiography* was published in 1818, were increasingly canonized as "representative characters"
not necessarily because of their introspective self-reliance, moral discipline, and self-transparency but rather because of their capacity for a kind
of dramatic self-*fashioning* highly attuned to the subtleties and norms of
social convention. For Franklin, such a capacity was best summarized in
the *Autobiography* in his references to himself as a kind of textual or print
character whose identity, like the "errata" printed to correct the errors in a
publication, could also be "revised" and reissued in the political and social
theaters of the public sphere. The "character" of Thomas Jefferson was similarly described, in works such as John Quincy and Charles Francis Adams's
Life of John Adams, in terms of the "duplicity" and "indirection" that hung

around his public life like "a vapor."[3] Even George Washington, seemingly the most stalwart and steady of the founding fathers, was well known for dutifully recopying as a young man a book of manners and etiquette that, as historian Gordon Wood has pointed out, he followed with a "purposefulness" that "awed his contemporaries . . . [and] that gave his behavior a copybook character. . . . Washington was obsessed with having things in fashion and was fastidious about his appearance to the world. . . . Indeed, he always thought of life as 'the Stage' on which one was a 'Character' making a mark."[4]

In the years leading up to the publication of Melville's *The Confidence-Man*, such a national character was increasingly represented by the regional figure of the frontier merchant or "Yankee character," a character who, like the American "Jonathan" in Lowell's *The Biglow Papers* (1848), was defined as a kind of "angular hybrid with its hitherto unheard-of combinations of 'mystic-practicalism,' 'calculating-fanaticism,' and 'sour-faced-humor.'"[5] Such a hybrid figure merged not only the "self-reliance" of the frontiersman but also the worldly cunning of the "cosmopolite" into a composite figure that became, in the words of Sheila Post-Lauria, "the dominant symbol, not just of the American confidence man, but of American national character."[6] A complex historical amalgam that fused narratives of New England origins with the "manifest destiny" of frontier settlement, the Yankee character emerged in the post–Civil War period as a contested emblem of the expansionist aims and industrializing agenda of American entrepreneurialism. And of the many spectacles that emerged within the carnivalesque commodifications of the postbellum period, such an enterprising character has proven to be one of the most riveting and enduring fetishes of economic and political authority in American culture.

With the publication in 1873 of *The Gilded Age: A Tale of Today*, Mark Twain and his coauthor, Charles Dudley Warner, gave name to an era increasingly fascinated and repelled by the aura of false appearances and counterfeit value. But while Twain and Warner negatively defined this formative era in American culture by the excesses of capitalist speculation and endemic political corruption, it was not until *A Connecticut Yankee in King Arthur's Court* that Twain critically reflected on that most enduring and fascinating counterfeit of the Gilded Age marketplace, the counterfeit of the philanthropic character. Organized around the exemplary character of the man of pluck and enterprise, *A Connecticut Yankee in King Arthur's Court* sends the charismatic jack-of-all-trades and master of invention,

Hank Morgan, back in time to "prove" sardonically the superiority of his "capablest" character not only over the hollow, "humbug," authority of King Arthur's court but also over the false valuations of Gilded Age authority such an aristocracy represents. Twain's story thus takes us through the checkered but comic career of Hank Morgan's "civilizing mission," from his ascendancy to the position as "the boss" through the spectacular fetishization of his own magical character to the modernization of the kingdom's economic, political, and social institutions. We witness more troublingly the increasingly autocratic relish with which Morgan pursues his agenda of progressive reform, and in particular the devastating ending of the novel, when Morgan realizes his new "republic" amid a sea of corpses after having turned his "modern" technologies against twenty-five thousand of the kingdom's subjects.

Although the historical "contrast" and at times polemicizing point of view give the novel its strikingly satiric edge, critics of *A Connecticut Yankee* have long had difficulty discerning exactly which way that satiric edge is meant to cut.[7] Is the novel a defense of the democratic and technological reforms for which the Yankee stands, as Howells and others have argued, or is it a critical indictment of the displaced and imperial violences inaugurated by those reforms, as argued by more recent critics such as John Carlos Rowe?[8] The many contradictions in the novel's form and critical concerns have not helped to resolve these debates, and indeed what has proven most confounding is the Yankee's own highly questionable character. What I want to suggest, however, is that the Yankee's own incoherent character is not simply a formal obstacle to the interpretation of Twain's text but rather embodies and exposes the contradictions that structure the broader cultural narratives of character building itself. For the philanthropic project that Morgan comes to represent is premised on the political promise of character itself, and not, as many critics suggest, on the promise and pleasures of ameliorating products or modern political rights.

Morgan's classic agenda of progressive reform turns not on the technological and legal transformations he so spectacularly enacts but rather on the equally spectacular semiotic challenge his character poses to these unsubstantiated signifiers of feudal power. It is by making his exemplary character the new measure of cultural authority that Morgan promises to sweep away once and for all the fetishistic "reverence for rank and title" that so enslaves King Arthur's subjects.[9] In portraying Morgan as the reformer of the false valuations and representational forms that animate and enable aristocratic power—the same power that, as critics ranging from Marx to Veblen have argued, animates the commodity form—Twain evokes not only the reformist power of the enterprising "Yankee" character but also the power of demystification identified with realist literary practice. Not only does Morgan promise to remake the character of the Arthurian people; he models that making on the realist practice and promise of literary characterization—and on the remaking of himself into the central character of his own literary narrative. Not only does Morgan promise to make "real" characters out of the Arthurian people, in other words, but he also promises to make them into "realistic" characters, into characters invested with the demystifying and documentary power of realism itself. Twain thus figures in his Connecticut Yankee, as Michael Davitt Bell puts it, the allegorical equivalent and "fictional embodiment of the 'realist,' a 'real' man of practical attainments, who disdains literary falsehood and who therefore, to recall Howells's terms, champions 'democracy in literature' in its struggle against the 'aristocratic spirit' embedded in 'pride of taste.'"[10]

The ambivalence with which Twain portrays the Connecticut Yankee and his civilizing mission reflects an ambivalence not only toward the ideology of character the Yankee represents but also toward the social and political promise vested in the practice of literary realism. More importantly, *A Connecticut Yankee in King Arthur's Court* critically reflects, this chapter argues, on a particular kind of character that emerged in the decades following the Civil War as an idealized object of identification among both literary realists and social reformers—the character of the eternally arrested, adolescent boy. Twain's literary fame in large measure was established on the basis of his novelistic explorations of the "bad boy" character in such works as *The Adventures of Tom Sawyer* (1876) and *The Adventures of Huckleberry Finn* (1885), a character type that was also the subject of early novels by many prominent realists, including William Dean Howells and Charles Dudley Warner. Twain's fantastic portrait of the imperial mission of a globe-spanning time traveler in *A Connecticut Yankee in King Arthur's Court*, however, has commonly been seen as marking a broader shift in his literary career away from the boyish subjects as well as from the realist form of his earlier boy books. Not a particular favorite of children in the late nineteenth and early twentieth centuries, and seemingly lacking in boys as central characters, *A Connecticut Yankee* has been read by many critics as marking the beginning of Twain's darker and increasingly pessimistic final period, a period in which he turns away from the nostalgic culture of boyhood to more explicitly "topical"—and increasingly polemical—interrogations of modern technology, political economy, and imperial expansion.[11]

Rather than turning from the culture and character of boyhood to the darker realities of imperial expansion, however, I argue in this chapter that Twain's novel critical reflects on the character-building function of the bad-boy figure and the imperial implications of its civilizing mission. Although no longer centered on an actual boy, *A Connecticut Yankee* nonetheless tells the story of an incorrigibly boyish but now fully grown adventurer who is eager to translate his boyish pluck into real "bossing" authority by re-creating "America" among the "white Indians" of feudal England. And in founding this history-eclipsing mission on the transformation of a kingdom of "boyish" subjects into a nation of manly characters, as well as on Morgan's own formative identification with the boyish subjects that he ultimately tries to destroy, Twain does not shift away from the ideological concerns of his earlier boy books but rather uses the novel's allegorical structure to reflect more critically on them. Twain's time-travel narrative allegorically traps his central character within a circuit of identification with the boyish knights and knightly boys of Camelot, I argue, in order to restage and interrogate the logic of readerly identification and imaginative impersonation that made the bad-boy novel such a valued instrument of character building and model of realist representation in the early decades following the Civil War.

I pursue this argument by considering the cultural work that character building performs not only through the spectacularly violent failures of its civilizing mission but also through the uniquely destabilizing effects of its one seeming "success": the training of the young page Clarence and "the darling fifty-two." Clarence, whom Morgan befriends in the opening scenes of the novel, is the first and exemplary product of the "man-factories" Morgan builds to manufacture Yankee men out of Arthurian boys. First lieutenant and beloved aide to the newly enshrined Yankee "boss," Clarence and the elite corps of fifty-two young boys he helps to train are not just essential co-conspirators in the Yankee's project to transform medieval England into a modern, industrial democracy; they are the vision and exemplars of what are to be its first "citizens." And as the first citizens of the new republic, Clarence and the boys are testaments to the upward mobility made possible in a republic founded on the merits of character rather than on the "unearned supremacy" (69) of inherited rank and title.

But while they are stamped in the entrepreneurial image of their mentor and boss, Clarence and the boys turn out to confound the logic of identification and reproduction on which such a meritocracy of character depends. As the representative of the fully realized character of the Yankee's new society, the figure of Clarence and the "darling fifty-two! As pretty as girls, too" (430) seem less an embodiment of the presumptively masculine quality of that character than a subtle but no less insistent challenge to it. For while Clarence and the boys represent the successful manufacture of Arthurian boys into Yankee men, Twain marshals his realist's eye for detail in his characterizations of Clarence and the boys to call into question the symbolic role they are narratively positioned to take.

Although these details, and Morgan's charged investment in narrating them, have drawn critics' attention to what has been called the "feminized" qualities of Clarence and the boys, such a reading too easily succumbs to the rhetoric of character that it endeavors to explain. For although it might be tempting to situate Clarence and the boys within a historical narrative of character's decline and the "crisis of masculinity" anxiously associated with such a decline, I argue that Clarence and the boys testify more to the decidedly gender-confounding logic internal to the rhetoric of character itself. The failure of Clarence and the boys to exhibit the terms of a masculinity they are narratively positioned to represent just might tell of a "failure" essential to the pedagogy of character building itself.

Twain's novel thus not only offers a critical interrogation of the promise of character as an object and instrument of reform; it also makes visible the social and historical dynamics that fueled the broader explosion of interest in character building in the decades following the Civil War. In the pages that follow, I thus read Twain's novel as a critical intervention in the rhetoric of character mobilized in the decades following the Civil War around the figure of the eternally arrested boy—a nostalgic figure Twain had himself long been invested in defending—and in the kinds of cultural work that such a figure made possible. First, I trace the novel's critical inversion of the realist modes of readerly identification and narrative interpellation that defined the bad-boy literary genre on which Twain had established his literary reputation. In this critical inversion, Twain mimics and models—in the allegorical structure of the novel itself—the institutional practices of "boyology" that began to take shape around the time of *A Connecticut Yankee*'s publication, as well as the realist modes of characterization that informed those practices. In figuring through Morgan's world-historical project the forms of homosocial "chumminess," "Indian" identification, and technomilitary training that were to become a staple feature of such "character-building agencies" as the Boy Scouts of America, Twain explores the imperial implications and cultural origins of such institutions. Twain's use of the time-traveling narrative, I argue, formally interrogates the evolutionary narratives of developmental arrest that these institutions used to link the formation of the child's character to the civilizing of racialized peoples around the globe. More importantly, I consider as well the "theory of habit" that underlay these imperial pedagogies by examining their role in structuring the Yankee's own methods of character building as well as the methods of one of the most prominent genres of character building in the late nineteenth century, the genre of the "success manual." Like the Yankee's own vexed declaration that "training is everything," habit was paradoxically figured in these manuals as both the obstacle to and instrument of character building. I thus read the success manual as part of a broader theory of habit that extended across a range of scientific, literary, and philosophical discourses, a theory that figured character as both the disciplinary product of, as well as liberation from, the automations and mechanizations of modern industrial capitalism.

The Nationscape of Adolescence

Mark Twain is perhaps the most famous exponent of novelistic boyhood in the United States. Not only are young boys the central characters and primary narrators of many of his greatest novels and short stories, but Twain's own signature wit and narrative voice are, as Bill Brown has argued, "the most significant narratological preservation of the child" in American literature.[12] Twain's place in the canon of American literature was established largely on the basis of his most famous boy books, books that also contributed to the canonization of the adolescent boy himself as an emblematic figure of American literary nationalism.[13] Twain's fascination with the culture and agency of the adolescent boy has commonly been understood in terms of his power to figure forms of resistance to, and critical perspectives on, the character-building methods employed, as

Huck Finn complains, to "sivilize" the unruly character of boys. Twain's literary elaboration of the bad-boy character is thus indicative of growing tensions within the rhetoric of character in the 1870s and 1880s, tensions rooted in a revaluation of the child as the subject of character building in both literary and cultural practice. Although the child and in particular the adolescent boy had long been figured as most precariously in need of character building, the adolescent boy emerged in the 1870s and 1880s, as T.J. Jackson Lears and others have argued, as a new and paradoxical figure of the ideally formed character itself: "the innocent child was a vision of psychic wholeness, a 'simple, genuine self' in a world where selfhood had become problematic and sincerity seemed obsolete."[14] Figured in terms of a romantic primitivism that associated the child with a kind of adamic innocence, the bad boy offered a vision of character whose emotional spontaneity and expressive innocence offered a refreshing alternative to the homogenizing conformity and artifice that not only was associated with the emerging consumer practices of modern "adult" life but that was also increasingly identified with the traditional forms of character building promoted in early conduct manuals, domestic fiction, and Sunday-school literature. As subjects in need of character building but also skeptical toward the reified conventions of character building, bad boys, as Roberta Trites has put it, had "the potential to participate in a culture as reformers or as people in need of reform."[15]

Twain's interest in the bad-boy figure grew out of a longstanding fascination with, and antipathy toward, the rhetoric of character and the methods of character building promoted in conduct manuals, child-rearing guides, religious primers and textbooks, phrenological manuals, and domestic fiction. Although critical of many of the conventionalities of character building, Twain's nonetheless maintained a fascination with the concept of character throughout his career, a fascination driven by his interest in the inscrutability of the boy. As Colonel Sellers puts it in *The American Claimant*, "I really consider that one of the main things that has enabled me to master the difficult science of character-reading was the livid interest I always felt in that boy and the baffling inscrutabilities of his ways and inspirations."[16]

In two early short stories, "The Story of the Bad Little Boy" (1865) and the "The Story of the Good Little Boy" (1870), Twain's critical perspective on the rhetoric of character began to focus in particular on the character-building function of children's literature, a process premised on the child's readerly identification with the exemplary character of the "good boy" or "good girl." In the years leading up to the publication of *A Connecticut Yankee*, Twain continued to satirize the didactic prescriptions and moralizing tone of popular etiquette and child-rearing manuals, didactic fiction, and Sunday-school primers of the antebellum period.[17] So numerous were Twain's parodies of these character-building methods that they have more recently been collected and reprinted as mock etiquette and advice manuals for children.[18] Twain even began writing, although never completed, his own "burlesque etiquette manual" at the urging of William Dean Howells.[19] For Twain, the greatest danger of traditional character building, as he summarizes in one of his mock character-building sermons, was the homogenizing threat that its mass-produced types posed to the individuality and authenticity of character that it was supposed to cultivate: "Build your character thoughtfully and pains-takingly upon these precepts; and by and by, when you have got it built, you will be surprised and gratified to see how nicely and sharply it resembles everybody else's."[20]

Twain's fascination with the rhetoric of character also extended to the practices of reading and representation it promoted and their emphasis on the signifying power of the body. Of particular interest—and repeated ridicule—throughout his life was the popular "science" of phrenology and its methods of character detection. Twain had been, as a young boy, an avid reader of Weavers's *Lectures on Mental Science According to the Philosophy of Phrenology* and had his own character read by phrenologists on numerous occasions. References to these experiences and to traveling phrenologists frequently appear with quite comic effect in Twain's fictional and autobiographical writings. But Twain also explored more seriously the broader impact of the physiognomic logic of character "detection" on legal culture and racial ideology in his later novel *Puddn'head Wilson* and in shorter works such as "The Secret History of Eddypus."[21] And although Twain regularly mocked the indexical promise of phrenology to read character in the form and features of the body, the "concepts and language of phrenology," as Cathy Boeckmann and others have argued, continued to inform Twain's own practice of literary characterization as well as his highly crafted self-construction as a public persona throughout his life.[22]

Twain's interest in the bad boy was also a reflection of the increased prominence of the bad boy as a new character ideal in the decades following the Civil War. During this period, a new genre of fiction, devoted to the adventures and exploits of the bad boy, emerged as critical rejoinder to the character-building function of children's literature and domestic fiction and the advice manuals on which they patterned themselves.[23]

Typically traced back to Thomas Bailey Aldrich's *The Story of a Bad Boy* (1869), and popularized by authors such as Charles Dudley Warner, William Dean Howells, and most famously by Twain himself, the bad-boy genre took aim at the moral and narrative dichotomy of the "good boy" and the "bad boy" around which earlier authors of children's literature such as Samuel Goodrich, Jacob Abbott, and Horatio Alger, Jr., had structured their immensely popular stories.[24] The goal of the bad-boy author, as Aldrich rather bitingly put it, was "to draw a line at the start between his hero—a natural, actual boy—and that unwholesome and altogether improbable little prig which had hitherto been held up as an example to the young."[25] Bad-boy book authors thus defended their works as an explicitly realist corrective to the ideologically distorted image of boyhood in juvenile literature and domestic fiction. Told from the adult perspective of a "former boy" who narratively reinhabits the feelings, attitudes, and perspectives of his own boyhood past, the quasi-autobiographical bad-boy book was imagined by its authors to provide a faithful and true depiction of events and experiences of boyhood from the perspective of the boy himself.[26]

The ostensible "badness" of the boy was figured in these books not as the sign of moral failing or a malformed character but rather of the confidence, self-possession, and inventiveness on which the boy's forming masculine character would find its surest footing. The bad-boy book thus focused on the adventures, exploits, and general mischief of boys who, unlike their good-boy counterparts, lived beyond or in open defiance of the moral prescriptions and repressive dictates of traditional character building. The bad boy thus figured an alternate process of character building, one premised on an imaginative, unmediated engagement with nature as well as on the socializing dynamics of the naturally formed culture of the boyhood "gang." The formative world of the bad-boy character was one located beyond the feminizing space of the home and prescriptive pedagogy of the school in the many outdoor spaces that, like Delorac's Island in Howells's *Boy's Town*, take the boy "beyond the bounds of civilization."[27] What these natural spaces afforded the bad boy, however, was not simply an escape from the civilizing conventions of modern society but rather the character-building opportunity imaginatively to re-create civilization anew, like Twain's enterprising Yankee, in the social clubs, diverse forms of economic exchange, cultural rituals, and public performances of boy culture.

The cultural appeal of the bad-boy genre was that it modeled a new character ideal and thereby offered itself as a new instrument of character-building identification, particularly to urban children seen as increasingly alienated from such a healthy, natural world of boyish activity. And yet, while the bad-boy authors frequently promoted their characters as alternate models of character building for children, the collapse of the positions of character, narrator, author, and reader within the nostalgic perspective of the adult, "ex-boy" author also seems to foreclose the child's place within the circuit of readerly identification. Although ostensibly addressed to a child reader, in other words, the bad-boy genre was structured in terms of nostalgic appeal to the "antimodernist" sentiments of an adult audience who found therapeutic escape from the fracturing effects, numbing experiences, and diminished opportunities of modern corporate capitalism in the idyllic worlds of a boyhood past. Thus rather than tracing the lives of the young heroes into adulthood in order to demonstrate the fruits of character building to a child reader, as Alger and Alcott do, bad-boy books largely abandon the developmental narrative and consequentialist moralizing that had defined didactic fiction in order to indulge the therapeutic fantasies of their adult readers. Oriented around a relatively fixed period of time and episodic in narrative development, the bad-boy book, as Bill Brown has argued, essentially "spatializes" boyhood by replacing its developmental chronology with a sequence of episodes that chart the different synchronic spaces of boy culture. The bad-boy book thus constructs in the many spaces and dynamics of boyhood culture, as Brown puts it, a therapeutic vision of an idealized American past untouched by "the crises of war and . . . political, demographic, and socioeconomic upheaval. . . . Boyhood thus becomes a site where a residual America can be preserved, where the exceptionalist vision can be projected, where nationhood can be embodied outside history."[28]

What is unusual about the bad-boy genre, however, is not simply that it appealed to such an adult reader but that it also made such an appeal, as Glenn Hendler and others have argued, by nonetheless structuring its address to the identificatory position of the child reader.[29] Although Twain, for example, originally conceived of *The Adventures of Tom Sawyer* as "*not a boy's book, at all. It will only be read by adults. It is only written for adults,*" he was convinced by Howells nonetheless to "address adult readers by pretending to write for children."[30] Twain thus recast *Tom Sawyer* in the generic form of the boy book in order to enhance its appeal to an adult male audience eager to reinhabit the readerly position of the boy. Other authors of the bad-boy book similarly structured their texts in terms of such an address to an adult male reader who, like the narrator himself, not only takes pleasure in the nostalgic reconstruction of a boyhood past but also takes pleasure in being addressed as a boy reader, a boy reader, moreover, who is thereby asked to form a character-building identification with the boyish characters about whom he reads. Thus in a formal application of Howells's belief that "an adult audience could be constituted through an overt address to boys," the bad-boy book inverts the conventional sentimental dynamic of identification by, as Hendler puts it, "interpellating readers as men by addressing them as boys. The genre . . . stages and restages a crisis of masculinity, offering as a pleasurable point of identification a figure who apparently puts into question culturally valorized masculine ideals like individuality, autonomy, and self-possession."[31] In making the forming character of the bad boy an object of identification for adult men, the bad-boy genre inverts the character-building teleology of narrative itself. Rather than providing a narrative of character development for an impressionable young reader, the bad-boy genre imagined the bad-boy character as a restorative object of identification for the culturally precarious masculinity of adult men. We might thus think of the traits of character attributed to the bad boy not so much as the object of identification for the formative boy reader but rather as providing what David Macleod calls "a simulacrum of manliness" through which men sought to reconstruct the masculinity their own adult life had seemingly imperiled.[32]

For bad-boy authors such as Thomas Bailey Aldrich, Charles Dudley Warner, William Dean Howells, and of course Twain himself, the most important aspect of the bad boy's character-restoring power was his atavistic possession of a naturally inherent "savagery," for, as Warner famously puts it in *Being a Boy* (1878), "Every boy who is good for anything is a natural savage. . . . He has the primal, vigorous instincts and impulses of the African savage, without any of the vices inherited from a civilization long ago decayed."[33] The identification of the bad boy with the racialized figure of the primitive savage was part of a broader ideological shift in the cultural meaning and function of character building in the United States. Central to this shift was the revalorization of "savagery" as an essential element of, rather than the antithesis to, the well-formed "masculine" character. This revalorization of the discourse of savagery has conventionally been understood as marking the emergence of new economic ideals of aggressive competition, self-reliance, and public self-promotion in the emerging corporate capitalism and consumer culture of the late nineteenth century, a culture in which the restrained, deferential traits of republican "manhood" no longer guaranteed economic prosperity, cultural authority, or political power.[34] The bad-boy character provided, in other words, a figurative escape into the pastoral, imaginative life of a premodern, anticapitalist world, while also embodying the enterprising and unsentimental agency of the capitalist himself. Thus not only did reviewers of *Tom Sawyer*, for example, celebrate Twain's "ability to recreate 'that wild village life which has schooled many a man to self-reliance and energy,'" but later critics such as Frank Norris more derisively saw in the bad-boy character so common to "Child Stories for Adults" the narrow self-interest and fetishistic thinking of the capitalist himself: "Do you know who he is? He is the average American business man before he grew up."[35]

For bad-boy authors such as William Dean Howells, moreover, the glory-seeking, competitive, self-reliant savagery of the bad boy embodied not the eclipsing of ethical responsibility by the dictates of self-interest but rather a democratic regrounding of ethics in the recognition of character's "merit" rather than on the artificial forms of social distinction that produce, according to Howells, those "social cruelties which are the modern expression of the savage spirit otherwise repressed by civilization." These artificial social distinctions, he goes on to argue, "were unknown among the boys. Savages they were, but not that kind of savages. They valued a boy for his character and prowess, and it did not matter in the least that he was ragged and dirty."[36]

What made the bad-boy character such a restorative emulatory ideal was not simply the unmediated relationship to nature that its "savagery" presumably enabled but also the training it provided in the fetishistic thinking that threatened masculine character in the first place. Such a training came in the form of the bad boy's imaginative engagement with and incorporation of the fantastic literary characters portrayed in their favorite books, an ability to animate the world with imaginary characters that defined the "fetishism" associated with primitive societies.[37] Perhaps most famously displayed by Tom Sawyer, a character defined by his seemingly endless knowledge and obsessive reenactments of fantastic scenes from children's adventure books, such fantastic characters populate the everyday world of the bad boy, who, as Thomas Aldrich notes, "religiously believing every word he read, . . . no more doubt[s] the reality of Sinbad the Sailor, or the Knight of the Sorrowful Countenance, than he [does] the existence of his own grandfather."[38] Evincing a savage "fondness for display" and "passion for ornament that," as Charles Dudley Warner puts it, "induces the African . . . to decorate himself with tufts of hair, and to tattoo his body," the bad boy performatively reenacts these many scenes and characters from his books in a picturesque display of his own character.[39] The bad-boy character is formed through a socially mediated, performative incorporation of the many romantic characters about whom he reads, a process that, as Hendler points out, ultimately constitutes "what little interiority his character possesses."[40] Rather than consolidating in the unified interiority of the liberal subject, however, the character composed of such "inward" multiplicity is one whose ultimate resolution into a singularly integrated character, Howells suggests, is by no means guaranteed:

> Every boy is two or three boys, or twenty or thirty different kinds of boys in one; he is all the time living many lives and forming many characters; but it is a good thing if he can keep one life and one character when he gets to be a man. He may turn out to be like an onion when he is grown up, and be nothing but hulls, that you keep peeling off, one after another, till you think you have got down to the heart, at last, and then you have got down to nothing.[41]

What is central to the formation of the bad-boy character is thus not simply his unmediated, grounding relationship to the natural worlds beyond the artificial social and economic forms of modern civilization but also his incorporation of the many romantic characters he reads about in books, characters who texture and decenter the boy's inward world with their proliferating multiplicity.

The Bad Boy Grows Up

Although Twain continued to write boy books late into his career, his literary exploration of the adolescent boy as an idealized object of identification seems to come to an end with the publication of *A Connecticut Yankee in King Arthur's Court*, a book that largely abandons the realist form, child characters, and thematic concerns of his most successful boy books. And yet, although *A Connecticut Yankee* does not assume the conventional form of the bad-boy genre, it is a novel fundamentally structured by the concerns of the bad-boy genre. Indeed, *A Connecticut Yankee in King Arthur's Court*, I argue, does not turn away from the bad-boy genre but rather takes up that genre as the subject of its allegorical perspective in order to examine the formal and identificatory dynamics of its broader cultural work. The most obvious trace of the bad-boy genre in *A Connecticut Yankee* is of course the character of Hank Morgan himself, whose unreliable and self-aggrandizing narrative style, love of the "picturesque," and glory in getting up a good "effect" evoke for many readers the imaginative style of Twain's boy narrators, as have his destructive, unchecked savage tendencies toward the novel's end. Twain's time-traveling narrative, moreover, realizes the imaginative dreams of the bad boy by returning Morgan to the mythical, adventurous fictional world that bad boys such as Tom Sawyer and Tom Bailey so eagerly read about in their books. The boyishness of Hank Morgan, moreover, is what ultimately defines his exemplary character, a character that finds its fullest expression in the economic agency he realizes as the kingdom's first and only "Boss." As Martha Banta has put it, Morgan "proves to be a boy to the core" in that he is a character in whom "boss-dom enfolds boy-ness and vice versa."[42] And yet the transformation of such a boy in *A Connecticut Yankee* into the violent, yet ultimately impotent, instrument of such "civilizing" and character-building forces—both in the form of Hank Morgan and also in the form of his corps of young boy lieutenants—suggests that boys, both good and bad, had for Twain suddenly become something more of a problem.

Although the "unruly" character of the boy had long been seen by Twain and others as a touchstone for the kind of "authentic" character formed outside the prescriptive conventions of character building, by century's end this unruliness was becoming identified with a "boy problem" of increasing public concern.[43] As one "Treatise on Boy Training" put it, "Wherever there is a boy there are problems to be solved."[44] In the handbook for what was to become the most successful and self-avowed character-building "agency" in U.S. history, the Boy Scouts of America, Ernest Thompson Seton succinctly expresses the broader cultural anxiety out of which the "boy problem" emerged:

> Every American boy, a hundred years ago, lived either on a farm or in such close touch with farm life that he reaped its benefits. . . . [H]e was physically strong, self-reliant, resourceful, well-developed in body and brain. . . . He was respectful to his superiors, obedient to his parents, and altogether the best material of which a nation could be made.
>
> We have lived to see an unfortunate change. . . . [W]e see a very different type of youth in the country to-day. . . .
>
> *Degeneracy* is the word.

> To combat the system that has turned such a large proportion of our ro-
> bust, manly, self-reliant boyhood into a lot of flat-chested cigarette-smokers,
> with shaky nerves and doubtful vitality, I began the Woodcraft movement in
> America.[45]

Seton's lament at the "decline of character" was typical in that it focused on
the decline of the particularly masculine attributes of that character, attributes that were being undermined by the urban-industrial "system" emerging during the Gilded Age. While Seton's concern was specifically with the
corrosive *effects* of this new system of urbanization and "the consequent
specialization of industry" on young boys, he (like many other reformers
of the time) also identified that system with the unruly character of the
boy itself. Boys had become a problem, in other words, in that their unruly
and precocious character was coming to define a nation increasingly seen
as experiencing the growing pains of its own awkward adolescence. The
task facing the nation was, in the eyes of many social reformers, to contain through character building the adolescent precocity seen to endan-
ger the nation's development as an industrializing capitalist state. Building character in young boys thus emerged in the Gilded Age as a kind of
national panacea for managing not only the devastating, capricious cycles
of the boom-bust laissez-faire economy but also the "gang" mentality of
corrupt legislative and judicial authorities and the seductive attractions of
the emerging urban consumer marketplace—as well as for uplifting and
assimilating the "adolescent races" considered to be under the nation's pa-
ternal charge. Thus whereas Emerson celebrated the "nonchalance of boys"
as "the healthy attitude of human nature" in his essay "Self-Reliance," that
nonchalance by the end of the century became more indicative of a boy
problem of increasing national concern.[46]

In Twain's portrait of the boyish exploits of a savagely picturesque
Connecticut Yankee, he seems to reflect critically on the bad-boy genre by
turning his satirical eye toward the adult male reader who seeks to restore
his character through an identification with the bad boy. Twain's use of
the time-travel narrative in particular frames the entire novel in terms of
just such a restoration by positioning Morgan's ascent to his position as
the boss as a recovery of the masculine authority he was unable to sustain
in his former life. As the emblematic man of pluck and enterprise, Hank
Morgan had risen to the position of the boss in his former life because of
his uniquely capable Yankee character, a character that also made him a
master over other men:

I am an American . . . a Yankee of the Yankees—and practical; yes, and nearly barren of sentiment, I suppose—or poetry, in other words. . . . I went over to the great Colt arms-factory and learned my real trade; learned all there was to it; learned to make everything: guns, revolvers, cannon, boilers, engines, all sorts of labor-saving machinery. Why, I could make anything a body wanted—anything in the world, it didn't make any difference what; and if there wasn't any quick, new-fangled way to make a thing, I could invent one—and do it as easy as rolling off a log. I became head superintendent; had a couple of thousand men under me. Well, a man like that, is a man that is full of fight—that goes without saying. With a couple of thousand rough men under one, one has plenty of that sort of amusement. I had, anyway. At last I met my match, and I got my dose. (4–5)

Morgan's rise to factory boss is one that is legitimated in terms of neither the early capitalist authority of the artisanal, master craftsman nor the bureaucratic rank of an emerging corporate capitalism. A man inherently "full of fight," Morgan settles conflicts and workshop disputes not with persuasive words, superior skills, or appeals to the trappings of rank but through the sheer physical violence of his own embodied will. Meeting his "match" in a workshop brawl with one of his subordinates, however, Morgan is knocked back in time from the Colt rifle arms factory of nineteenth-century America to King Arthur's kingdom by a skull-splitting blow to the head. Morgan's failure to maintain his position as a threatening superintendent is what sends him back in time, yet only to restore that lost authority as the now virtually unassailable boss. The entire generic conceit of Twain's time-travel narrative is thus defined by its project to restore—and seemingly repeat—the violent authority of this fallen boss.

Twain's choice of medieval England as the destination for his time-traveling Yankee seems to be driven by his desire to set up the most striking contrast between modernity and its medieval origins. But in sending Morgan back to the medieval period, a setting Twain makes clear in his preface is based more on the mythologized romances of Malory than on historical fact, Twain does not seek out the blank slate of a precapitalist past on which to reconstitute the institutions of modern democratic capitalism but rather transports Morgan to the medieval fantasy world that was the imaginative home of the bad boy himself. As Joseph Kett and others have demonstrated, the chivalric ethic and emulatory social practices of medieval culture emerged in the late nineteenth century as a common framework for understanding the culture of childhood and as a popular fantasy world among children themselves.[47] Stories of medieval knights were not only favorite reading among boys, but the chivalric code of the medieval knight was invoked by many character builders, as the fascinatino with chivalry in the *Boy Scouts Handbook,* boyology manuals such as *The Knights of the Holy Grail: A Solution of the Boy Problem,* and boy's clubs such as the Order of the Knights of King Arthur suggests, in order to understand and direct the shifting identifications of the adolescent boy.[48] Twain's choice of a medieval setting, in other words, situates Morgan not in historical time but rather in the textual space of the bad-boy reader, who in his journey back in time to the mythical world of boyhood adventure seeks to restore his lost masculinity not only by identifying with the boy but more importantly by imagining himself as the adventurous fictional character with whom the bad boy identifies.

Just as Twain transforms Morgan into the protagonist of the bad boy's favorite adventure books, so too does Morgan imagine himself to be the character-building object of identification for the boyish knights of Camelot. Morgan's self-construction as an object of identification, and the civilizing mission he constructs around it, substitutes for, and enables him to disavow, his own need to maintain his masculine character through his precarious identification with boys. Twain thus takes up the readerly logic of the bad-boy book as the subject matter of his "historical" allegory, an allegory that identifies character builders as driven by the insecurities over their own masculine character. More importantly, Twain indicts the violences of late nineteenth-century "cultures of U.S. imperialism" as emerging from the collapse of the identificatory circuits that drive character building.[49] For while Morgan imagines himself to be the model character with whom the "savage" and "childlike" Arthurians should identify, he cannot escape from *his own* identification with the boyish competitions and "savage" theatrics of the Arthurians themselves. It is this tautological circuit of identification that launches but also ultimately undercuts his character-building mission, thus producing the spectacular violence of the novel's end.

Morgan establishes himself as the boss, for example, by using his bad-boy skills at "getting up a good effect" to perform a series of "miracles" that endow his character with the kind of spectacular, magical, mystifying power that he had set out to challenge.[50] The folly of Morgan's strategy, therefore, is that in his effort to disabuse the people of their penchant for pomp, he fails to deliver the sobering substance of character. His character, it turns out, is itself constituted as a mere fiction of referential origins, and thus when he finally destroys the embodied representatives of aristocratic power in the culminating "Battle of the Sand Belt," he leaves quite literally nothing in its place but his own fictionalized character. The narrative consequence of his killing is that he himself disappears, as Merlin puts him to sleep with a spell and sends him forward in time to the century from which he came, leaving nothing behind but the *story* of his fabulous and ultimately failed career. He becomes, in other words, simply the central narrating character of his own fantastic story, a story that Clarence, who finishes its final chapter, tucks away with the Yankee's sleeping body to accompany him back to the nineteenth century. Morgan is thus transformed by his failure from a "person" within the diegetic reality of the novel into the literary character of his own autobiographical manuscript, a manuscript that is "now" being read in the frame tale by an admiring "M.T." The ultimate irony is thus that the failure of Morgan to become a "real" object of identification for the bad boys of King Arthur's kingdom is what transforms him into the central character of a fantastic medieval adventure that actually became treasured reading for many adolescent boys in the United States. This parodic use of the genre of historical romance enables Twain to expose the identificatory relays and ideological fantasies that sustain the "realism" of the bad-boy genre and, more importantly, to make visible the role of the bad-boy figure in establishing the character-building institution as one of the most significant late nineteenth-century instruments of Americanization and imperial expansion.[51]

We might thus understand the publication of *A Connecticut Yankee* in 1889 as response to or anticipation of the character-building agendas of what Kenneth Kidd has described as "institutional boyology."[52] In the decade immediately following the publication of *A Connecticut Yankee*, a new set of specialized, philanthropic organizations emerged that sought to translate the formative practices, social interactions, and imaginative world portrayed in bad-boy literature into large-scale institutions and federal "agencies" of character building. Youth organizations such as the Young Men's Christian Association, the Boy's Brigade, the Sons of Daniel Boone, the Order of the Knights of King Arthur, the Woodcraft Indians, and, most significantly, the Boy Scouts of America, were founded by a new group of professional, largely male, self-described "boyologists" who worked in tandem with a group of educators, psychologists, sociologists, comparative anthropologists, and criminologists who together composed the "child study" movement.[53]

These "boy workers" or "boyologists," as Henry William Gibson called

them, imagined their "agencies"—which combined elements of both the
modern corporate franchise and the government bureau—to augment
and complete the work of character building that is only partially and often indirectly carried out in traditional institutions such as the home, the
school, and the church.[54] Particularly important to the development of these
institutions of character building, and to the eventual decline of the bad-
boy genre, as Kidd argues, was their appropriation of the literary forms of
readerly identification and character development modeled by the bad-boy
genre. The boy workers who ran these institutions, for example, imagined
themselves as similar to avuncular ex-boy narrators, whose intimate knowledge of "the influences that formed his [the boy's] character" enabled them
to replace the "disciplinary intimacy" of the domestic scene with the far
more edifying homosocial "chumminess" of the institutional boy worker.[55]
Youth organizations thus turned to the wilderness camp or playing field
as an isolated space within which to foster new forms of voluntary kinship
in an all-male social world guided by the charismatic leader. The intimacy
formed in this culture of "chumship" cultivated rather than repressed the
play instinct, love of imaginative storytelling, and socializing gang mentality of boyhood culture and established the camp leader as the source of an
edifying "contagion of character" that circulated between himself and the
boys as well as among the boys themselves.[56]

Twain's *A Connecticut Yankee* similarly focuses on one "unsentimental" yet very chummy character builder, whose technological, commercial,
and cultural institutions are geared toward transforming a kingdom of
boyish subjects into a nation of manly citizens. Finding himself "a man
among children" (67) upon his arrival in Camelot, Morgan sets out to become the greatest of boy workers, one who, in creating in world-historical
terms the cultural and institutional conditions for character building,
hopes thereby to refound the American nation from his vantage point in
the feudal past. And although Morgan fails to transform his kingdom of
metaphorical children into a nation of historical men, he nonetheless suc-
ceeds in creating a troop of fifty-two young boys of the most "capablest"
character and sincere chumminess, a troop with whom he encamps to
Merlin's cave to re-create in the wilds there the foundations of the new
American republic.

Twain's critical indictment of such an avowed boy worker, who also
enlists young boys in his genocidal project of cultural imperialism, thus
does not simply tell the "other side" of the bad-boy story by fleshing out
in the form of Hank Morgan the new disciplinary formations established

to subdue the bad boy's defiant character but also implicates the critical stance of the bad boy in the institutional practices that were fast becoming the vehicle of the nation's imperial expansion. In order to understand the kinds of cultural work such a character performs, Twain thus turns his attention in *A Connecticut Yankee* to those forms of "training" Morgan institutes to sustain the savage circuit of his character-building mission.

The Character-Building Factory

While Hank Morgan initially leverages many of his reformist bets on the mimetic power of his own spectacular character, he also covers those bets by establishing an array of institutions whose ultimate purpose, like the boyological organization, is to train these Arthurian boys into proper Yankee men. As critics have long pointed out, the concept of training plays a particularly prominent yet peculiar role in Twain's narrative, functioning as both an impediment to Morgan's reforms as well as a defining instrument of his character-building mission. Throughout *A Connecticut Yankee,* for example, Morgan refers to the Arthurians in terms of a chain of interlinked metaphors that range from "boys," "children," and "infants" to "white Indians" and "savages" to "animals," "rabbits," and "insects." Morgan uses these terms to describe what he sees as the intransigent, mechanical, unconscious nature of their cultural training and inherited habits. Chained as they are to animal instinct and imitation, the Arthurians are reduced by their habits, in Morgan's eyes, to the status of mere "creatures of habit."

From Morgan's earliest encounters with the king's court to the final Battle of the Sand Belt, the biggest obstacles he encounters to his reforms, for example, are neither technological nor particularly political; the biggest obstacles he encounters, and indeed the obstacles that eventually do him in, are the "inherited ideas" or "habits" of the people:

> Inherited ideas are a curious thing, and interesting to observe and examine. I had mine, the king and his people had theirs. In both cases they flowed in ruts worn deep by time and habit, and the man who should have proposed to divert them by reason and argument would have had a long contract on his hands. (65)

Morgan might recognize here that his nineteenth-century ideas are as

equally "inherited" as those of the "king and his people," but the candor of
his historicist equanimity is quickly belied as he goes on to mock the exegetical shortcomings of one particularly troubling "inherited idea":

> For instance, those people had inherited the idea that all men without title
> and a long pedigree, whether they had great natural gifts and acquirements
> or hadn't, were creatures of no more consideration than so many animals,
> bugs, insects; whereas I had inherited the idea that human daws who can
> consent to masquerade in the peacock-shams of inherited dignities and un-
> earned titles, are of no good but to be laughed at. (65)

As Morgan continually laments, the most dangerous "inherited idea" of
the Arthurians is their inability to distinguish between the "style" of aristocratic pretension and the "substance" of capable character. What the Arthurians suffer from is their own fetishizing fixation on the "masquerade"
of feudal power, and what Morgan promises is to break the spell of these
empty signifiers of power by rooting them firmly in their proper referential ground, by rooting them in, in other words, the legitimating ground of
character.

Morgan's reformist task is thus to lend a realist substance to what is
ultimately their romantic folly by waging exegetical war on the empty signifiers of feudal power. Morgan first wages this war by focusing on dispel-
ling the ideas themselves by establishing in his secret "civilization-nurs-
eries" an "admirable system of graded schools" (81). But while he might
be a "giant among pigmies, a man among children, a master intelligence
among intellectual moles" (67), Morgan and his educational system prove
to be no match for the entrenched habits of thought he encounters in, for
example, the vindictive queen Morgan LeFay: "It was useless to argue with
her. Arguments have no chance against petrified training; they wear it
as little as the waves wear a cliff. And her training was everybody's. The
brightest intellect in the land would not have been able to see that her position was defective" (155). Indeed, when the knights with the backing of
the Church eventually declare war on Morgan, Clarence makes clear the
failure of his efforts to enlighten the nation:

> "Save your breath—we haven't sixty faithful left!"
> "What are you saying? Our schools, our colleges, our vast workshops,
> our—"

"When those knights come, those establishments will empty themselves and go over to the enemy. Did you think you had educated the superstition out of those people?"

"I certainly did think it."

"Well, then, you may unthink it." (418)

The danger of inherited ideas is thus that, although figured as merely so many accumulated habits, they take on the material reality of the body itself in that "[o]ld habit of mind is one of the toughest things to get away from in the world. It transmits itself like physical form and feature" (210).

Morgan's paradoxical response to the unconscious and intransigent training of habit is to make recourse to the very same mechanical processes that define the dehumanizing nature of habit by establishing a system of "man-factories" as central instrument of his character-building mission. As Morgan boasts, "It's a Factory where I'm going to turn groping and grubbing automata into *men*" (157). Morgan imagines the mechanized routines and repetitive motions of the factory as a vehicle of character building and method for undoing the "savage training" of cultural inheritance. And yet, what remains unclear is how exactly the factory will be able to transform the machine-like, animal instincts of the Arthurians into the self-governing character of the modern liberal subject. Twain's investment of Morgan's reformist promise in the mass-produced and standardized products of the factory seems to betray the very independence and individuality of character that he seeks to instill. For while the purpose of the man-factory is to manufacture Arthurian "automata" into Yankee men, factories are the place where we imagine human beings to be reduced to the "automated" functionality of the machine.

Morgan's reliance on the man-factory as the instrument of character building has frequently been read as a sign of Twain's increasingly deterministic worldview, expressed in Morgan's exasperated, ambivalent declaration that "training is everything; training is all there is to a person" (162), as well of his increasing hostility toward the promise of technology as his investments in the impossibly complex Paige typesetting machine nearly bankrupted him. Twain's emphasis on the man-factory, however, foregrounds and critically examines the prominent and paradoxical role that habit was imagined to play as a liberatory practice within character building, a role that came to be figured in terms of the "character factory." As Mark Seltzer and Mark Rosenthal have argued, the factory emerged as an important yet paradoxical model for the national project of charac-ter building in the Gilded Age.[57] The influential founder of the Boy Scout movement in England, Robert Baden-Powell, for example, frequently en-visioned the process of character building in terms of the mechanistic flows of the modern factory: "Our business is not merely to keep up smart 'show' troops, but to pass as many boys through our character factory as we possibly can: at the same time, the longer the grind that we can give them the better men they will be in the end."[58] In the United States, the founders of the Boy Scouts of America similarly imagined their organiza-tion as a "citizen-making factory," an argument that was applied as well in the reorganization of the public school system.[59] In order to facilitate a well-rounded and consistent formation of students, for example, public high schools were restructured around the assembly-line principles out-lined in Taylor's *Principles of Scientific Management*, with students pass-ing through a rational series of class periods organized around discretely defined tasks or subjects (mathematics, biology, English, etc.) that were controlled by, like Henry Ford's model factory, a sequence of whistles or bells. Citing President Roosevelt's declaration that "[t]he public schools are the factories of American citizenship," educators such as Marian George similarly argued that "every school should be a character factory," for "the teacher does not want any poor goods sent out from his or her school or citizen factory, and insists on obedience in order that the pupil shall be made into a good citizen. Poor material is as undesirable in citizens as in the goods we buy, and more expensive and worthless."[60]

The Pedagogy of Habit

Twain's his complex portrait of the shifting and frequently contradictory role of training in *A Connecticut Yankee*—embodied by the paradoxical image of the man-factory—reflects on the paradoxical yet formative role that the concept of habit played in the character-building institutions in-spired by the bad-boy genre. Indeed, Twain's focus on the term *habit* to describe not only the mechanical training and standardized, repetitious products of the factory but also the broader influence of cultural inheri-tance as a conservative force in the formation of character points to the broader significance of the concept of habit across a range of scientific, political, and economic discourses. *Habit* emerged in the late nineteenth century as a term used to explain not simply the common forms of virtue and vice but a wide range of natural and cultural phenomena that included, for example, the mechanisms of the economy, the patterns of growth in animals and plants, the dynamics of childhood development, and the forces of cultural inheritance and social influence. Habit emerged as the subject of numerous articles in popular periodicals on such topics as the reading habit, the habits of bees, the habits of good society, and even "the habits of habits."[61] So pervasive was "the philosophy of habit" that social theorists such as Thornstein Veblen were even moved to declare that "[u]nder the guidance of the later biological and psychological science, human nature will have to be restated in terms of habit."[62]

The discourse of habit that emerged in the Gilded Age marked the end of a long reversal of the traditional formulation of the relationship of character to habit. For the Calvinist theologians of the colonial and early national period, habit had long been regarded as simply an expressive indicator of the divine "stamp" given to character. Character, early Puritan theocrats argued, was "an *internal* Thing, [that] can be judged of by others, only from the *outward* Discoveries of it."[63] The "visible character" manifested in habits of conduct was thus considered to be, at best, simply an expression of an inner, "invisible" character that itself remained untouched by changes in or alterations of habit. As Locke's influential formulation put it, "God has stampt certain Characters upon Men's minds, which, like their shapes, may perhaps be a little mended; but can hardly be totally alter'd, and transform'd into the contrary."[64] The association of character with a kind of "stamping" also dates back to the earliest origins of the term. The word χαρακτηρ (*kharakter*), the ancient Greek source for the English word *character*, referred to a self formed as "the mark impressed (as it were) on a person or thing, a distinctive mark, characteristic, character," and thus imagined the self as the product of a repetitive process of inscription like that of "a mark engraved or impressed . . . on coins and seals."[65] Metaphorically linking the numismatic transformation of formless substance into valuable money and the mechanical process of textual reproduction, habit described the iterations and transferences through which character appeared, like the alphabetic types imprinting their form onto paper, as merely the repeated expression of "characters" already firmly stamped.

Over the course of the nineteenth century, however, this expressive relation of habit to character slowly came into question as social reformers, educators, theologians, and moral philosophers turned toward habit as itself an instrument of character building. Benjamin Franklin's brutely mechanical attempts, which so fascinated readers of his *Autobiography*, "to acquire the *Habitude* of all these Virtues," for example, established a model of character building founded more on the daily drilling and mechanical imitation of the visible standards of conduct rather than through introspective reflection, the call of conscience, or the application of moral principles.[66] Such an imitation of virtuous habits did not simply mimic the well-formed and virtuous character, according to Franklin, but more importantly produced it through a recursive logic of reiterative reinscription. Educators, social reformers, and manual writers of the antebellum period, influenced in part by the publication of the first three sections of Franklin's *Autobiography* for the first time in 1818, also increasingly saw character not as divinely "fixed" but rather as an inherently "plastic" substance that hardened by habit into its final shape over the course of a precariously "impressionable" youth. *Habit* thus emerged for self-described character builders of the antebellum period such as John Todd and Rufus Clark, as well as for later character builders eager to apply Lamarck's theory of acquired characteristics, as the blanket term for the "variety of influences and circumstances [that] contribute to the formation of character. . . . *It is the product of many forces, some of which act upon us from without, and others from within*."[67] Habit thus emerged as the primary "instrument," as Clark called it, of character building because of its power to shape and "fix" the material disposition of character while in its youthful, plastic state. As John Todd put it in his influential *Student's Manual* (1835), "The whole character may be said to be comprehended in the term *habit*; so that it is not so far from being true, that 'man is a bundle of habits.'"[68]

This rearticulation of the concept of character in terms of habit found its most significant expression in the enormously popular form of what Judy Hilkey has termed the "success manual."[69] The success manual emerged as a distinct genre in the 1870s within a broader manual tradition that extended back to the early primers, advice books, and character manuals of the 1830s and 1840s. Marketed and sold by the subscription book trade as practical advice on how the aspiring, or more frequently not-so-aspiring, young man might find "success" in an increasingly complicated commercial and urban landscape, success manuals extended the scope of the traditional character-building manual in their orientation toward the child's—and more frequently the young man's—future success as an adult. Avidly read and promoted by boyologists as well, success manuals became one of the best-selling genres of the postbellum period, quickly flooding the market in record-breaking numbers.[70]

Twain, of course, was no stranger to the rhetoric of the success manual; he owned several copies of popular manual author Samuel Smiles's *Thrift* and many other success and character-building manuals.[71] And as one of the very few major novelists to publish books, including *A Connecticut Yankee*, through the subscription book trade, Twain was in all likelihood quite familiar with the many success manuals that were such a profitable and prominent part of the subscription industry. Indeed, the promotional title page of the subscription edition of *A Connecticut Yankee* is cast in the inspirational vernacular so familiar to success-manual readers.[72] More importantly, Twain's portrait of the itinerant Yankee, hawking the character-building power of modernity in this frontier land of chivalrous "Indians," evokes not only the rhetoric of the success manual but the entrepreneurial figure of the success-manual subscription salesman who, as Hilkey describes, sought to spread Northeastern values of civilization and character to frontier families as well as to the exceedingly chivalric culture of the South. The paradox of such an enterprising figure of success, however, was that while he seemingly embodied the values of individuality, originality, and self-determination, the manuals he sold promised to mold such a "self-made" man through a methods of compulsion, imitation, and repetition usually seen as the antithesis of agency itself.

The underlying message of the hundreds, if not thousands, of success manuals published in the second half of the nineteenth century was that habit was at the heart of character building. Although not all, or even most, success manuals devoted specific chapters to the topic of habit, as John Todd did in his early *Student's Manual*, for most manual writers this was a reflection of the pervasive importance of habit as an all-encompassing instrument of character building. Unlike the particular traits or virtues that were the topic of most chapters, habit was discussed throughout as the overarching instrument through which such traits were themselves inculcated. The manuals as a print genre also modeled a process of character building premised not on reasoned argument but rather on the sheer repetitive power of habit, as authors produced massive tomes of largely borrowed, frequently plagiarized, and always formulaic material taken from classical literary, biographical, historical, and philosophical sources, as well as from the manuals of competing authors, while also reissuing their texts in multiple editions, frequently simultaneously by different publishers.[73]

Although habit was portrayed as central to the work of character building, the success manuals displayed a deeply ambivalent attitude toward habit. Habit was figured within success manuals as a dangerously subtle form of repetition that could either consolidate in the form of an energetic and empowered character or solidify into the unbreakable, mechanistic cycles of "addictive" repetition. Habit's contribution to character stemmed, paradoxically enough, from its banality and insignificance as a form of action. For William Matthews, who wrote one of most popular manuals, *Getting On in the World; or, Hints on Success in Life* (1877), as for most success-manual authors, character building was premised not on the power of the heroic deed or lofty principle but rather on, as Mathews put it, "the repetition of things severally insignificant that make up human character."[74] While any individual act, word, or deed was as insignificant as a single snowflake or individual strand of a spider's web, to use the common metphors, and thus easily repeated or prevented, it was the iterative power of habit that solidified these insignificant acts into the solid "snow banks" and binding sinews of character. As Samuel Smiles put it in his enormously popular manual, *Character* (1872), "the best support of character will always be found in habit, which, according as the will is directed rightly or wrongly, as the case may be, will prove either a benignant ruler or a cruel despot."[75]

The danger that habit posed, however, derived as well from the insignificance of these same acts, particularly those seemingly innocent acts that arise from one's natural instincts and so create a sense of pleasure in being satisfied. What makes these "bad habits" bad is not necessarily the particular quality or nature of the individual act but rather their subtle, frequently imperceptible capacity to reify the latent impulses of instinct into an unbreakable cycle of addictive habits, habits that, as Samuel Smiles argues, ultimately "enslave" the youthful character with the "iron chains" of sheer repetition. The highly charged yet common metaphor of slavery was employed by manual writers to point to the forms of bondage that habit's chains of repetition produced, a form of bondage frequently described in terms of its seemingly racializing effects. Rufus Clark, citing the power of habit to "bind the soul as with chains of iron," for example, warns against insignificant acts that become "wicked" through repetition by becoming "a habit that holds [a youth] within its terrible grasp; and it may shortly be as easy for an Ethiopian to change his skin, or a leopard his spots, as for one accustomed to do evil to learn to do well."[76] The discourse of habit, in other words, articulated the distinction between an addictively "fixed" character and a self-possessed character in terms of the categories of racial difference.

What distinguished good habits within this racializing economy of character formation was their power to free youths from the racializing repetitions of habit by training them in forms of self-mastery figured through the discourse of racial domination. For writers such as Samuel Smiles, whose best-selling manuals had an enormous influence on and were recommended reading in the Boy Scouts, resisting the "despotism" of habit was figured as an act of imperial resistance wherein boys "maintain that vigor of mind which is able to contest the empire of habit."[77] In the racialized economy of habit formation, character building was figured as an act of personal and political resistance, or a "putting down" of the threatening tyranny of racializing instincts, a process often described by Smiles and others in traditional terms as the ability "to resist instinctive impulse . . . [through] the exercise of self control."[78]

But while Smiles describes character building in conventional terms as a form of self-control or mastery over instinctual impulse, for him, and for most authors of success manuals, such a mastery was achieved not through the sovereign imposition of rational control but rather through the creation of a set of *new* instincts, instincts whose very purpose was to operate independently of rational reflection and deliberative choice as a kind of supplemental self or "second nature." Key to such a process was the inversion of the enslaving logic of habit: rather than satisfying instinctual desires and thereby instilling an ever-ramifying cycle of addictive pleasure, character was formed by the forced repetition of unpleasant acts, regardless of the particular content of those acts, and the transformation, through such reiterations, of formally painful actions into pleasurable ones. Habit was thus imagined as a kind of pleasure machine because of its power, as Mathews puts it, to "render pleasant things which at first were intensely disagreeable or even painful."[79]

The value of forming good or virtuous habits by taking pleasure in naturally painful acts was not that it enabled one to conform to conventional standards of ethical behavior but rather that it cultivated an artificial set of desires that solidify a new set of instincts, thereby creating a "second nature, which," as Mathews puts it, "is sometimes so powerful as to exterminate the first."[80] This self-destructive formation of such an artificial second nature thus embodies and extinguishes as well the need to repeat, as the history of habit solidifies into what manual writers refer to as an "orientation" or "disposition" to act. Indeed, the sign that a habit has become an aspect of character is when one is freed from the need to repeat, when habit takes the form of a disposition to act in a predictable manner to specific situations or "stimuli." Such a process was thus imagined not just to shape character and thereby "harden" it against the influences of others or of one's own animal instincts but more importantly to "charge" or "energize" character by storing up the cycles of repeated acts as the potentiality of a second nature that, now structured as a "disposition" or "orientation," can finally free itself from the necessity to repeat. Character thus subjected the racializing impulses of animal instinct by becoming a kind of machine whose "vast reserve power" was accumulated, like the repeatedly wound watch or battery charged by the generator's spinning wheels, "by the force of principles that have gathered energy by long and persevering habit."[81] Unlike the addict's withering expenditures of energy in repetitive acts, habit, properly applied, produces energy that can then be applied in a focused manner. Character is thus conceived as a form of suspended, internalized iteration through which the compulsion to repeat is translated into the capacity to act, through which a history of repeated habits becomes a future of predisposed acts. In this sense, the formation of character frees one from the compulsion to repeat but also lays down the course of all future acts, thus realizing the Heraclitan maxim, "character is destiny." The formation of character thus puts into place the only coherent determinant of one's future, thereby robbing, as Walter Benjamin has pointed out, the future of the contingent qualities, uncontrollable directions, and unpredictable conclusion normally taken to define fate: "if a man has character his fate is essentially constant. Admittedly, it also means: he has no fate—a conclusion drawn by the Stoics."[82]

Character's formation as a kind of inner, invisible body charged with the power to act was most commonly described in terms of the notion of "will power," a power also identified with masculinity itself. The technocratic economy of force, power, energy, and influence invoked by success manual writers has frequently been seen as reflecting a new ideal of masculinity rooted in the concept of personality, as opposed to the older republican vision of "manhood" modeled on the inert, stolid force of the hardened character. And yet, despite its different metaphorical valences, the concept of will power remained throughout the nineteenth century the primary force of character that comprises its second nature.[83] More significantly, although this masculinity has been defined in terms of an outwardly forceful yet consolidated form of self-reliance, what is most paradoxical about the success manual's emphasis on the defining force of will power is its melancholic embrace as well of the formative role of "adversity" in eliciting it. As Helen Keller famously put it, "Character cannot

be developed in ease and quiet. Only through experience of trial and suffering can the soul be strengthened, vision cleared, ambition inspired, and
success achieved."[84] The commonplace maxim that "adversity builds character" emerges in success manuals, however, less as a triumphant declaration of self-overcoming than as a melancholic reconciliation to the will's
need to form itself through its own self-negation and cultivation of "pleasurable" pain. The benefits of the will power formed through the experience of adversity, in other words, was not that it guaranteed one's access to
success but rather that it enabled one to withstand, and even to absorb as
energizing power, the pain of adversity and failure.

The cultural function and social stakes of this cultivation of the capacity for pain and of one's sense of imminent failure as a feature of what we
might call, following Jennifer Travis, character's "wounded" masculinity
is perhaps best explained in William James's 1890 treatise *The Principles of
Psychology*.[85] In his chapter "Habit," which, along with the chapter "Will,"
was the most widely read chapter of *The Principles of Psychology*, James
not only describes the psychophysiological foundations of habit, but he
also makes strikingly visible the broader social and political implications
of habit's cultural prominence. James's definition of character in "Habit,"
much like Hank Morgan's description of his own "Yankee" character, relies on a classical association of character with a uniquely masculine capacity for willing in the public sphere:

> A "character," as J.S. Mill says, "is a completely fashioned will"; and will,
> in the sense in which he means it, is an aggregate of tendencies to act in
> a firm and prompt and definite way upon all the principal emergencies of
> life. . . . There is no more contemptible type of human character than that
> of the nerveless sentimentalist and dreamer, who spends his life in a welter-
> ing sea of sensibility and emotion, but who never does a manly concrete
> deed.[86]

In citing John Stuart Mill, James draws on a long moral and legal tradition in which the capacity to will authentically and freely was necessary not
only to the formation of character but, more importantly, to the responsibility of that character before and to the law. As Friedrich Nietzsche famously argued in *Genealogy of Morals*, an argument oddly similar to James
Madison's own in Federalist No. 63, to become a subject responsible before
the law, one must be made to fashion a will, that is, one must be made to
"have" a character.[87]

This classical notion of the self-fashioned will so central to the liberal model of legal rights and culpability, however, had long been vexed by the same paradox that confounds the Connecticut Yankee's own efforts to found a republic of character: how does one fashion an authentic and self-determined will if one's capacity for self-fashioning is only a product of that formation? How is the capacity for authentic, spontaneous invention, in other words, formed by a process of imitation, repetition, and conformity? William James's invocation of this legacy of character building through a precarious habituation of the will was not blind to these thorny philosophical and pedagogical conundrums it inherits. James's point in citing Mill, rather, is not to reiterate the classical dilemmas of character building but rather to resolve them with a physiological account of habitual self-inscription.

All "living creatures . . . are bundles of habits," James triumphantly announces, and "[h]abit has a physical basis," the physical basis of the nerve cell.[88] Taking what has been called Freud's "hydraulic" model of the psyche and "electrifying" it, James's account of habit and character in terms of an economy of internally circulating electrical impulses stimulated by, and discharging into, the surrounding environment gave new empirical heft to the materialist ontology of character building. Habits, in James's view, are simply the result of carving new "channels" or "pathways" into the "plastic" material of the nervous system by the "reflex arc" of repeated actions, thoughts, and behavior. Habit thus becomes, in James's hand, a kind of character-building tool, for through the inscription of "new pathways," the features of character are quite literally written into the body as the material trace of a history of repeated actions and responses.

Although James's account of habit was part of a late nineteenth-century effort to recast the theory of character on a firmer physiological foundation, his account also reveals how such lessons in physiological science functioned more like lessons in moral philosophy. As Allison Winter has argued, the emphasis on physiology in James's psychology is indicative of a broader cultural shift in which the mechanistic principles of habit were coming to replace the traditional regulatory function of sympathy in producing the forms of consensus seen as essential to the workings of democracy: "The reflex arc supplanted 'sympathy' with a network of nerves and nervous influences (akin to electricity) as the causes of 'consensual' phenomena."[89] Thus while James claims that "the philosophy of habit is . . . in the first instance, a chapter in physics," his interest in delineating that chapter is ultimately to outline what he warns are "the *ethical implications of the law of habit*":

> The physiological study of mental conditions is thus the most powerful ally of hortatory ethics. The hell to be endured hereafter, of which theology tells, is not worse than the hell we make for ourselves in this world by habitually fashioning our characters in the wrong way. Could the young but realize how soon they will become mere walking bundles of habits, they would give more heed to their conduct while in the plastic state.[90]

James's address here to "the young" seems to warn them of the importance of forming early on the "good habits" that together constitute a "good character," because once "the character has set like plaster, . . . [it] will never soften again."[91] James's materialist account, however, seems to remove the very quality of willing that was said to define character in the first place. By reducing character down to nothing more than a set of automatic, utterly reflexive firings of the nervous system, James seems to evacuate the notion of character at the same time that he materializes it. Character, it would seem, is not only the set of habitual responses formed in one's youth; it is *nothing more than* that set of habits, with no guarantee that anything like a fully formed agent lies behind the surface of habit. What gets lost in this radically mimetic account of a fully automated character, in other words, is the very capacity for choice, the very "will" and "power of judging" that presumably distinguished character in the first place.

Evoking the economic metaphors and rhetorical fervor of contemporary success manuals, however, James nonetheless goes on to insist on the virtues of this "automating" function of habit because of its power to "capitalize" character into a form of self-generating value:

> The great thing, then, in all education, is to *make our nervous system our ally instead of our enemy*. It is to fund and capitalize our acquisitions, and live at ease upon the interest of the fund. *For this we must make automatic and habitual, as early as possible, as many useful actions as we can. . . .* The more of the details of our daily life we can hand over to the effortless custody of automatism, the more our higher powers of mind will be set free for their own proper work. There is no more miserable human being than one in whom nothing is habitual but indecision, and for whom the lighting of every cigar, the drinking of every cup, the time of rising and going to bed

every day, and the beginning of every bit of work, are subjects of express volitional deliberation.[92]

The virtue or "value" of the well-habituated character is thus not that it has necessarily inculcated a set of good, virtuous, or pragmatic habits, or that it has successfully trained the will, but rather that it has fully and utterly transformed the will into an automated, unconscious reflex of the body. Character building frees "consciousness" from the burden of willing but thereby makes that consciousness into one that, it would seem, can no longer act. Like capital itself, which in the expression of a commodity's value makes invisible or "unconscious" its origins in the laboring body, so too does character become valuable "capital" when it banishes the acting will to the unconscious of habit. James thus sets out to solve the dilemma of character's self-formation by laying out a discipline of "will-training" but ends up burying the will in the deep unconscious of a fully automated and reflexive body. Character, it would seem, is nothing more than the set of inscriptions carved into the body by a will quite literally trying to forget itself.

But what such a will does not forget is the class position into which it was born. As James again goes on to argue with rather disarming alacrity, character building is not the means to upward class mobility, as promised by the success manual, but rather the vehicle for reproducing and policing the social boundaries of class difference. For while character building frees and thereby rarifies the "consciousness" of those "miserable" human beings weighed down by the daily drudgery of lighting their cigars, drinking their drinks, and "rising and going to bed," its primary function for those manual readers most desirous of its upwardly mobile effects is to use that desire to render them unconscious to the unbearability of their own class position:

> Habit is thus the enormous fly-wheel of society, its most precious conservative agent. It alone is what keeps us all within the bounds of ordinance, and saves the children of fortune from the envious uprisings of the poor. It alone prevents the hardest and most repulsive walks of life from being deserted by those brought up to tread therein. It keeps the fisherman and the deck-hand at sea through the winter; it holds the miner in his darkness, and nails the countryman to his logcabin and his lonely farm through all the months of snow; it protects us from invasion by the natives of the desert and the frozen zone. . . . *It keeps the different social strata from mixing.*[93]

A well-habituated character, it turns out, is not what promises to uplift individuals by cultivating their "higher powers" but rather is what resigns them to their "repulsive walks of life," the liberating "effects" of such a habituation seemingly passed on to their social betters. And the "body" that James's leisured but beleaguered cigar smoker must liberate himself from, it also turns out, is the automated body of the working classes. The habituation of character thus not only "liberates" the members of the professional class; it binds them together with its common vernacular of mannered mutual recognition:

> Already at the age of twenty-five you see the professional mannerism settling down on the young commercial traveler, on the young doctor, on the young minister, on the young counselor-at-law. You see the little lines of cleavage running through the character . . . such as vocalization and pronunciation, gesture, motion and address. Hardly ever is a language learned after twenty spoken without a foreign accent; hardly ever can a youth transferred to the society of his betters unlearn the nasality and other vices of speech bred in him by the associations of his growing years. Hardly ever, indeed, no matter how much money there be in his pocket, can he even learn to dress like a gentleman-born.[94]

What the working classes gain in substance from character building, it would seem, the professional classes gain in style. The function of character building, in other words, is to promise and thereby *to fail* to build character and, in the dual function of that failure, "to save the children of fortune from the envious uprisings of the poor . . . and invasion by the natives" by producing differential modes of embodiment that both mark and enact existing hierarchies of class difference. The rhetoric of character thus calls for a profound materialization and automation of the material body not as a universal promise of subject formation but rather as a maintainer of the cultivated manners and social distinctions predicated on the inherited distributions of class.

The differential class function of habit formation was, as we will see in Jane Addams's rearticulation of the traditional charity relation in chapter 5, what enabled the middle class to see itself not simply as possessors of well-formed character but more importantly as philanthropic agents of character building. As Thomas Winter has argued, the late nineteenth-century rhetoric of character structured the class relations of corporate capitalism in terms of a distinction between the "character" of the working classes and the "personality" of the middle class. Such a distinction had a specifically character-building function in that middle-class managers were imagined to use their socially enigmatic personalities to govern workers by eliciting and "facilitating workingmen's self-expression into desirable channels, guiding them on the path toward character."[95] The personality formed in the privacy of the middle-class home thus provided, according to Winter, the basis for character's public appearance, first in that it enabled the delineation and discovery of one's individual identity by "exchanging true expressions of the self for self-revelation from others" through "practices of reciprocal self-disclosure."[96] This private personality provided the basis for what appeared in public as character. More importantly, such a personality could also be used to elicit character from members of the working class who lacked reliable access to such a protected and mutually cultivating domestic space.

James's account of the habituation of character thus reveals and endorses the regulatory work performed by the genre of the success manual and the institutions of character building structured around the inverted logic of readerly identification. In their emphasis on character not as the vehicle to wealth and "money getting" but rather as itself an inherently valuable form of "capital" that provided its own rewards, success manuals promoted a regimen of self-improvement and self-habituation that functioned less to forward individual advancement than to provide moral and intellectual compensation for the increasingly diminished opportunities available within the technocratic, deskilling hierarchies of labor in modern corporate capitalism. Such compensation, as Hilkey points out, came in the form of "symbolic membership" in the middle class by virtue of the effort at building character itself, an argument David Roediger extends as well to include the compensatory "wages of whiteness" extended to the working class.[97] The success manuals thus worked in tandem with an emerging psychological discourse to articulate a new, psychologized vocabulary of class difference whose function was to refigure retroactively the structural inequalities of class as a retributive manifestation of individual differences of character in order to sustain the disciplinary work of character building. The success manuals thus embody and enact in the starkest form the disciplinary work enabled by the rhetoric of character as it was "democratized" to include and empower the working classes in the culture of the Gilded Age. By cultivating a sense of optimistic resolve in the face of adversity, perseverance in the face of failure, and habits of hard work and determination that were their own reward, the rhetoric of character building promoted a vision of character that was more unending process than it was profitable product, a vision of forms of capital that accrued in value so long as they were never cashed in. The rhetoric of character articulated an ideal of masculinity, we might thus say, modeled on the incompletely formed, eternally arrested character of the adolescent boy.

Indian Training

Such a detour through these popular and psychological formulations of the discourse of habit and its power as an instrument of both subjection and liberation enables us to see the kinds of cultural work to which Twain, in his seemingly paradoxical portrait of the Yankee's own failed program of training, is pointing. For what James admits with greater candor than the Yankee himself is the bifurcated social function that the building of character in its very failure performs. Morgan's failure to overcome the "inherited ideas" of the people with his pedagogy of training *is* precisely its point: its failure is indeed its success. For every "dozen trained men" manufactured by his man-factories, "one brilliant expert" is discovered by the "agents" he commissions to "rak[e] the country" for its "brightest young minds" (81). Morgan's meritocracy thus emerges as a kind of fait accompli wherein well-formed characters are "discovered," never "made," by a reflexive logic of mutual recognition, a logic Twain makes clear depends more on political and popular theatrics than on a hermeneutics of depth. Rather than leveling the class hierarchies of aristocratic culture, in other words, Morgan recasts them in Taylorist terms by manufacturing "trained men" for the despotic use of an elite technocratic class of "brilliant experts"—namely "the boss" and his boys.

In the allegorical framework of Twain's novel, therefore, it thus becomes clear that the mechanical thinking and savage love of chivalric display that Morgan laments in the Arthurian character symbolizes an "Indian" character that was in fact the product and identificatory ideal of the character-building institution. Such a valorization of the Indian character is most obvious in character-building organizations such as the Sons of Daniel Boone, the Woodcraft Indians, and the Boy Scouts of America, as well as later groups such as the Camp Fire Girls and Girl Scouts of America, which similarly made identification with the character of the Native American central to their habit-training regimens.

Drawing on the literary tradition of romanticizing "the remarkable

characters that flourished in savage life" that stretched back through the bad-boy book to James Fenimore Cooper, Lydia Maria Child, Catherine Sedgwick, and Washington Irving, organizations such as the Boy Scouts, for example, founded their methods of character building on two distinct but interdependent principles: the ennobling, restorative effects of an identification with Native American character and ritual and the disciplining effects of military drill.[98] Like the fused figure of the Indian-hating misanthrope and philanthropic Indian in Melville's *The Confidence-Man*, these two aspects of character building were fused in the figure of the frontier "scout," a figure who advanced military intelligence and nationalist agendas by adopting "Indian ways." The widespread invocation of the Native American character in these organizations thus exemplifies the historical transition that Twain is concerned to document in *A Connecticut Yankee*, the transition—or rather translation—of the traditional disciplinary role of sympathetic identification associated with the modern novel into the technocratic regimes of habit training so important to the institutions of character building.

As an object of identification, the Indian functions within these organizations as a kind of screen that obscures and enables the differential class function of character building. On the one hand, the Native American provides a displaced locus for middle-class identification with the masculinity of the working class. On the other hand, the identification of working-class boys with the Native American also naturalizes the mechanical forms of training and habituation to which working boys were being subjected, by rendering them in the "picturesque" form of Indian games, rituals, and customs. In the many books Sioux tribal member Charles Eastman (Ohiyesa) wrote on his own Indian "training" for the Boy Scouts and the Camp Fire Girls, for example, he challenged misrepresentations of Native American "woodcraft" as an unmediated, unintentional outgrowth of the Native Americans' "natural," "instinctive" relationship to their environment, a view promoted in particular by Boy Scout cofounder Ernest Thompson Seton in his many idolizing books on Native American culture, such as *The Gospel of the Redman* and *Two Little Savages* (see Figure 4).[99] Just as Eastman himself welcomed "the opportunity of being a minute-man—a Scout!" because of his belief in the power of the "spirit

Fig. 4 (opposite page). Ernest Thompson Seton in Indian costume, 1917. Seton was founder of the Woodcraft Indians and one of the five cofounders of the Boy Scouts of America. (Museum of Canadian Scouting, Scouts Canada)

of the American Indian, the Boy Scout's prototype, to leaven the brilliant selfishness of our modern civilization!" he was also sure to point out that the forms of Indian woodcraft exemplified by the Native American were the accomplishment of disciplined practice and training: "It seems to be a popular idea that all the characteristic skill of the Indian is instinctive and hereditary. This is a mistake. All the stoicism and patience of the Indian are acquired traits, and continual practice alone makes him master of the art of wood-craft."[100]

The "failure" of Morgan's civilizing mission at the end of *A Connecticut Yankee* thus represents Morgan's failure to sustain the fantasy that his "character" is superior to, and identificatory model for, the Arthurian's inferior "Indian" character, a failure on which the character-building institution was predicated. This is perhaps most apparent in Morgan's final, sentimental identification with Arthurian culture, an identification that marks both his imminent death and his rebirth in the timelessness of literary character. So habituated to the culture of Camelot does Morgan become that when he finally returns to nineteenth-century America—the time and place that he supposedly longed to re-create—he is reduced to a state of tragic melancholia. When "M.T." visits Morgan in his room in the "present" at the novel's end and overhears him talking in his sleep, he realizes that Morgan is dreaming that he is back in Camelot, laughing with Sandy over the fact that he had thought himself some sort of strange, time-traveling Yankee, "a creature out of a remote unborn age, centuries hence" (447). Having fought so long to establish the realities of his clear-headed, practical character in the dreamlike world of the mystified Arthurians, Morgan now prefers that dreamy world over his "own," a world in which the memory of his own substantial character appears to him as simply some laughable, insubstantial "notion." The novel closes with Morgan lost in this dreamy state, and yet Twain's initial plan, described in an early sketch of the work, was to end with Morgan's suicide, an ending that underscores the disintegrating effects of the final identification with the culture and character of King Arthur's kingdom.

We might thus understand Morgan's own conflicted identification with a boyish Indian character as Twain's exposure of the ideological erasures performed by character's civilizing mission, as well as an expression of Twain's own ambivalence toward the practices of realist representation implicated in that civilizing mission by its promise of demystification. The tension within Morgan's character that both forwards but also undermines his character-building mission, as he himself admits, is the tension between the principles of efficiency, transparency, and economy that define his exemplary character and his bad-boy love of the "picturesque" and of "getting up a good effect," a love that, Morgan confesses, "is the crying defect of [his] character" (372). Such a distinction between the extravagance of the picturesque and the economy of efficiency, as Cindy Weinstein has pointed out, has also been used to distinguish the documentary fidelity and economy of representation of literary realism from the symbolic and narrative excesses of romance and sentimental literature.[101] Thus while Twain seems to value the realist strategies with which Morgan plans to dispel the mystified forms of aristocratic power, the efficiencies that govern the production of realist character are also aligned with the manufacturing efficiencies of the man-factory, efficiencies used not only to mass produce character but also to destroy masses of the kingdom's subjects in the final Battle of the Sand Belt. Twain's unease thus seems to stem from the connections he sees between the manufacturing efficiencies of the man-factory and the literary economies that make the realist character, two modes of "making character" identified with the character-building mission.

The Yankee in Page Clarence's Court

Twain's interrogation of the rhetoric of character as a practice both of representation and of social reform in *A Connecticut Yankee*, however, charts not just the cultural work its "failures" perform but also the uniquely destabilizing effects of its one seeming "success": the training of the young page Clarence and "the darling fifty-two." Hank Morgan first meets the young page Clarence when, at the beginning of the novel, Morgan is brought into King Arthur's castle for the first time after being found dazed in the countryside by Sir Kay. Convinced that he has been committed to an "insane asylum" after his skull-shattering fight, Morgan begins asking to speak to the "head keeper" among the seemingly mad and gibberish-speaking "patients" of the asylum. And, curiously enough, Morgan finds this light of reason in the form of Clarence, the young page to whom he is referred by the confused and busy cook. Clarence, for his part, has *also* been "seeking" the Yankee, though as Sir Kay's representative page. Morgan and Clarence thus "meet" at the very moment at which they both seek each other out, and it is a scene that stages in visual terms the logic of recognition that will be their long-lasting bond:

"GO 'LONG," I SAID, "YOU AIN'T MORE THAN A PARAGRAPH."

Fig. 5. Twain's play on the double meaning of *page,* which Beard here cites in his caption for the illustration, suggests that Clarence's passage from mere "paragraph" to full-fledged "page" will come about once he has composed within himself an abundance of characters. Mark Twain, *Connecticut Yankee in King Arthur's Court* (New York: C.L. Webster, 1889), 38.

[H]e [the cook] pointed and said yonder was one who was idle enough for my purpose, and was seeking me besides, no doubt. This was an airy slim boy in shrimp-colored tights that made him look like a forked carrot; the rest of his gear was blue silk and dainty laces and ruffles; and he had long yellow curls, and wore a plumed pink satin cap tilted complacently over his ear. By his look, he was good-natured; by his gait, he was satisfied with himself. He was pretty enough to frame. He arrived, looked me over with a smiling and impudent curiosity; said he had come for me, and informed me that he was a page.

"Go 'long," I said, "you ain't more than a paragraph." (15)

Of the very few critics who seriously consider the role of Clarence in the novel, most derive the Yankee's conclusion that Clarence is "pretty enough to frame" (a conclusion that later in the novel is reiterated by the simile "as pretty as girls, too") from the realist detail with which he is rendered by our enamored Yankee narrator. One of the novel's most influential "readers," the illustrator and cofounder of the Boy Scouts of America, Daniel Carter Beard, even took the liberty, in his illustration of Clarence for the first edition of the novel, to conclude similarly from the "dainty ruffles" and "long yellow curls" that Clarence would best be represented by the form and figure of Sarah Bernhardt, the famous French actress.

Beard's static positioning of Clarence, as if before the camera's "framing" gaze, takes its cue from the details of dress and bodily appearance described in the novel. And yet in that depiction of Clarence, the narrative development overtakes these static details as it builds toward the conclusion that Clarence is "pretty enough to frame." What is important about the "plumed pink satin cap" is the way in which it is "tilted complacently over his ear." And what makes him "pretty enough to frame," finally, is that "[b]y his look, he was good-natured; by his gait, he was satisfied with himself." And yet it is these mannered inhabitations *of* the costumed body that render him an image "pretty enough to frame" that are erased from Beard's illustration. His gaze locked straight ahead and his feet planted firmly together, Beard's Clarence has neither look nor gait.

What Beard overlooks is that, in order to become an image within the Yankee's frame, Clarence must become a nascent image of the Yankee himself. What constitutes Clarence as not merely pretty but pretty enough to frame, in other words, is that his own characteristic display of good-natured self-satisfaction mirrors the Boss's own avowed but troubling mix of geniality and self-satisfied arrogance (as do the other members of the

Fig. 6. Mark Twain, *Connecticut Yankee in King Arthur's Court* (New York: C.L. Webster, 1889), 547.

"darling fifty-two"). Clarence is, in other words, the pretty image of the smug geniality that, in its fully developed form, constitutes the "benevolent despotism" that the Boss imagines "would be the absolutely perfect earthly government, if ... the despot [were] the perfectest individual of the human race" (82).

It is from this identificatory recognition that the Yankee's fondness develops and not from what may perhaps eventually become his very "capable" character. Clarence proves in the opening scenes to be more of a "featherhead" whose "foolishness" nearly costs Morgan his life, as his incompetence in telling Morgan the incorrect date (which fouls up his plans for the eclipse) is canceled out only by his equally foolish petitioning of the king to have his planned execution advanced by a day (46). What binds Morgan to Clarence is not that he is capable, or that he is a "featherhead"; it is rather the fact that he is, in the final analysis, a "*mocking* featherhead" (24). It is only when Clarence proves his competence *through* his capacity for irony that he becomes Morgan's avowed "darling" (83–84). When Morgan is first brought before the court as Sir Kay's prisoner, he finds in Clarence a refreshingly cynical voice who mocks Sir Kay's tall tales "with an accent and manner expressive of extravagant derision" (29). Indeed, it is this extravagance that inspires Morgan to found his educational system, as he seeks to educate Clarence up to the point where their shared derision of Sir Dinadan's jokes can find its full expression:

> [O]f course the Scoffer didn't laugh—I mean the boy. No, he scoffed; there wasn't anything he wouldn't scoff at. He said the most of Sir Dinadan's jokes were rotten and the rest were petrified. I said "petrified" was good; as I believed, myself, that the only right way to classify the majestic ages of some of those jokes was by geologic periods. But that neat idea hit the boy in a blank place, for geology hadn't been invented yet. He failed to catch on. However, I made a note of the remark, and calculated to educate the commonwealth up to it if I pulled through. It is no use to throw a good thing away merely because the market isn't ripe yet. (31)

What Morgan sees in Clarence is the capacity for wit and irony that characterizes not only Morgan's own narrating voice but also the satirical point of view from which Morgan makes his progressive political and social critique. And it is a voice uneasily identified with Twain's own, as suggested in the frame tale of the novel, in which we learn that we are not "reading" Twain's story but rather hearing the figure "M.T.," who meets the now-returned Morgan on a tour of Warwick castle, read Morgan's manuscript itself. In placing this reading figure M.T. between Morgan and his readers, Twain makes his own voice a ventriloquized version of Morgan's own: we see Morgan's words only because M.T. is reading them; we hear them only through *his* reading voice.

What Morgan sees in Clarence is thus the literary capacity for satirical "scoffing" that not only governs Twain's compositional practice but also embodies the mutable character that Morgan, like "Mark Twain," struggles to maintain. Clarence embodies for Morgan the ideal character not because he consolidates a particular identity through the cultivation of habit but rather because he embodies the sheer textuality of character itself. As the boyish reproduction of Morgan's character, Clarence's textuality is like the characters that are printed in the first newspaper that Morgan presents like a proud parent to the members of the court. These mesmerized readers, Morgan explains, took this new product of print culture "and gently felt of its texture, caressed its pleasant smooth surface with lingering touch, and scanned the mysterious characters with fascinated eyes" (262). Morgan's description, however, quickly loses itself in the beauty of the characters on the page as he goes on to conflate the wondering faces of the readers with the faces of the tiny alphabetic characters on the printed page:

> These grouped bent heads, these charmed faces, these speaking eyes—how beautiful to me! For was this not my darling, and was not all this mute wonder and interest and homage a most eloquent tribute[?] . . . I knew, then, how a mother feels when women, whether strangers or friends, take her new baby, and close themselves about it with one eager impulse, and bend their heads over it in a tranced adoration. (262)[102]

Just as M.T. discovers upon reading Morgan's manuscript "that it was a palimpsest," Morgan's love of his "darling" Clarence similarly derives from the fact that he proves indeed to be a "page," not a "paragraph," as Morgan playfully chides, on which can be written and rewritten the layered characters of the boy's imaginative characters (7). Or as Morgan puts it when describing his editorial principles, a principle that applies equally to his theory of habit, "the best way to manage—in fact the only sensible way— is to disguise repetitiousness of fact under variety of form: skin your fact, each time, and lay on a new cuticle of words" (259).

Clarence's "scoffing" is the basis of both his meritorious character and his ambiguous gender, something unexpectedly confirmed by Beard's illustration as well. Beard is an important reader of Twain's text not simply because of the polemical power of his illustrations (a power that led to his blacklisting by many publishing houses as an overly "propagandistic" illustrator) but because of his commitments to building a manly character in boys.[103] For not only was Dan Beard also one of, with Ernest Seton, the five cofounders of the Boy Scouts of America, he also said, according to Henry Nash Smith, that "he would like to see a copy of *A Connecticut Yankee* in every household in this country because it would help to bring Americans back to 'the safe, honest, and manly position' outlined for them in the Declaration of Independence."[104] Twain himself, in response to a British editor, similarly argued that he wrote the text specifically for a British audience in order to "pry up the English nation to a little higher level of manhood." But although critics have long assumed, on the basis of Beard's remarks in his autobiography, *Hardly a Man is Now Alive*, that in using Sarah Bernhardt as his model he was simply citing her gender, the discovery by Teona Gneiting of the original photograph on which the illustration was based complicates this story (see figure 7). The image Beard used for Clarence was not simply the image of Sarah Bernhardt; it was the image of Sarah Bernhardt *playing the role* of a boy troubadour in *Le Passant.*[105] Indeed, Bernhardt was herself famous for playing many male roles, such as Prince Charming, Judas, and, most famously, Hamlet.

Hence in using a photograph of Bernhardt playing the character of a young page, Beard construes Clarence not in the terms of a presumptive femininity but rather in terms of a kind of gender role-playing. What Clarence represents to Beard, in other words, is not the fetishized effeminacy of the forming boy but rather the capacity to be a boy ironically as a performed character type. Clarence is not a boy, yet nor is he a girl; he is a *girl playing a boy*, and it is this capacity for assuming and confounding the character of gender that Morgan presumably loves in him. What Beard's rendering of Clarence thus suggests is that Clarence is an exemplary character because, on the one hand, he recognizes and even fulfills the masculinist injunction demanded by the rhetoric of character, and yet, on the other hand, he does so only by drawing attention to the artificiality of that gender identification. What Twain's presentation of Clarence thus suggests is that the gendered injunction of the rhetoric of character is both a necessary and an impossible one, for the logic of character building cannot sustain a discourse of masculinity and yet at the same time cannot do without it.

Fig. 7. "The *Police Gazette*'s Gallery of Footlight Favorites: M'lle Sarah Bernhardt." Reproduction of photograph of Sarah Bernhardt as a boy troubadour in *Le Passant,* published by the *National Police Gazette.* (Harry Ransom Humanities Research Center, The University of Texas at Austin)

Twain's critical interrogation of the rhetoric of character that was articulated in popular genres such as the boy book and success manual as well as in the character-building institutions of the late nineteenth and early twentieth centuries makes visible the ways that class difference was regulated through the displacements, suspensions, and satirical iterations that constitute masculine self-reproduction. Historically produced through the iterations and repetitions of habit, such a masculine character promised liberation from the movement of history itself, a liberation ambivalently embodied by the figure of the eternally arrested boy. The next chapter looks more closely at the self-historicizing dimensions of the rhetoric of character by turning to the reiterative practices of physical training and their promise to materialize character not in the cultivated behaviors, manners, and habits of class and culture but rather in the "physical culture" of the body's muscular materiality. The product of a disciplined history of repetitive acts and willful engagement with physical pain, muscle was increasingly identified as the very stuff of character in the second half of the nineteenth century. Such an identification of character with muscle, I hope to show, inspired a host of character-building practices in public schools, private homes, and urban environments that were modeled on the routines of physical exercise and bodybuilding, and also shaped and inspired practices of character reading that saw in the subtle textures and topography of the physical body a historical archive of an individual's characteristic acts and expressions. Although these practices have commonly been identified with a reconsolidated vision of masculinity at the turn of the century, a muscular masculinity associated as well with the fiction of literary naturalism, I look to the work of Charlotte Perkins Gilman and to the practices and publications of what was known as the physical-culture movement, in order to make visible the ways that muscle building was understood to build a character that challenged rather than reiterated conventional understandings of the gendered and racialized body.

3

Muscle Memory

Building the Body Politic of Character in
Charlotte Perkins Gilman and the
National Police Gazette

Nature has a record of all men's deeds, keeping her accounts on fleshy
tablets. The mind may forget, the body never.
—Newell Hillis, *A Man's Value to Society*
Studies in Self-Culture and Character[1]

In 1851, Sojourner Truth gave a speech to the Akron Women's
Rights Convention that launched her public career and eventually came to
define in many ways her legendary status as feminist icon, staunch abolitionist, and exemplary "self-made" character. The power of the speech,
which has come to be known by the name of its repeated refrain, "Ar'n't
I a Woman?" has often been attributed not only to Truth's unique and sophisticated rhetorical style but also to the equally spectacular presence of
her powerfully formed and muscular body. In Frances Gage's influential
and controversial reconstruction of the 1851 speech, she attempts to re-create the full drama of Truth's performance by reiterating her famous verbal
refrain, "Ar'n't I a woman?" while editorially underscoring the even more
dramatic unveiling of her muscular arm:

> "Well, chillen, whar dar's so much racket dar must be som'ting out o' kil-
> ter. I tink dat, 'twixt de niggers of de South and de women at de Norf, all
> a-talking 'bout rights, de white men will be in a fix pretty soon. But what's
> all this here talking 'bout? Dat man ober dar say dat woman needs to be
> helped into carriages, and lifted over ditches, and to have de best place

eberywhar. Nobody eber helps me into carriages, or ober mud-puddles, or gives me any best place;" and, raising herself to her full height, and her voice to a pitch like rolling thunder, she asked, "And ar'n't I a woman? Look at me. Look at my arm," and she bared her right arm to the shoulder, showing its tremendous muscular power. "I have plowed and planted and gathered into barns, and no man could head me—and ar'n't I a woman? I could work as much and eat as much as a man, (when I could get it,) and bear de lash as well—and ar'n't I a woman? I have borne thirteen chillen, and seen 'em mos' all sold off into slavery, and when I cried out with a mother's grief, none but Jesus heard—and ar'n't I a woman?"[2]

The iconic status of Sojourner Truth's 1851 speech, and its role in establishing Truth, as one reviewer put it after her death in 1883, as "one of the most notable characters in history and one preeminently belonging to America," stems from its evocation of the muscular body as political signifier and in particular from the ability of muscle to constitute Truth as an exemplary and self-made character.[3] Truth's "interesting and decidedly original character" was frequently cited as the source of her political and rhetorical power as commonly as was her powerful physical body, for it was only from a physical frame seemingly "carved out without hand or chisel from the solid mountain mass" that Truth's character, according to Anna Julia Cooper, acquired its critical force.[4]

Truth's speech thus marks an important yet vexed moment in the discourse of character when the muscular body emerged as a controversial site of political agency because of its ability to figure the inherent "equality" of seemingly "different" physiological bodies. Citing examples of her exclusion from and invisibility to the many social rituals of femininity, Truth's speech turns her exclusion into a sign of physical strength, a strength that she not only asserts through her question to be the strength of "a woman" that is equal to any man's but that she also goes on to dramatize through the baring of her own arm, an arm, as Gage editorially underscores, that displays "tremendous muscular power." In juxtaposing her semantically loaded question "Ar'n't I a woman?" against the evocative visual testimony of her muscular arm, Truth thus asks her audience to rethink what femininity might mean such that it can encompass her own maternal body, which bears the history of its racial subjection as the strength of its physical form, a form that, as the speech goes on to assert, represents the new "strength" of the women's movement itself.

In the antebellum context in which Truth's speech first circulated, this deployment of the figure of the slave woman's strength as indicator of the inherent equality of male and female bodies, as well as of the collective strength of the women gathered at such conventions itself, was, as Karen Sánchez-Eppler has argued, a common rhetorical strategy of both the women's rights and antislavery movements.[5] In its more enduring and famous afterlife in the latter half of the nineteenth century, and in feminist and civil rights history more broadly, however, Gage's reconstruction of Truth's speech played an even more problematic role in the postbellum construction of what Nell Irvin Painter has called the "symbolic Sojourner Truth," a quasi-mythological character whose cultural circulation as an "exemplary character" frequently depended on Gage's famous emphasis on Truth's dramatic act of baring her muscular arm. Assessing the critical agency of Truth's deployment of her own muscular body has thus been a notoriously difficult and highly contested task.

What has proven most difficult has been disentangling Truth's own critical voice from the "symbolic Truth" that has long dominated historical scholarship. In part, this difficulty has stemmed from the fact that the purportedly illiterate Truth never wrote down her speeches and turned to white abolitionists and suffragists such as Olive Gilbert and Frances Titus to transcribe and edit the various editions of her autobiography. It is thus unclear the degree to which Truth's own words were shaped by the editorial and political aims of these women.[6] More importantly, the symbolic Sojourner Truth that has come to dominate historical and feminist scholarship has been heavily influenced by the late nineteenth-century reproduction and circulation of Frances Gage's problematic reconstruction of Truth's original "Ar'n't I a Woman" speech. Gage, the chairwoman of the Akron meeting in 1851, published her account of Truth's speech in 1863—some twelve years after it had been delivered—in response to Harriet Beecher Stowe's recently published encomium to Truth titled "The Lybian Sibyl." Gage's account differs from the few contemporaneous reports of Truth's speech that were published in 1851 in two important regards: it attributes to Truth a stereotypically racialized Southern dialect that the native New Yorker and originally Dutch-speaking Truth surely lacked, and it puts pivotal emphasis on Truth's dramatic act of baring her muscular arm.[7] Although the publication of Gage's account during the Civil War helped to make Truth a familiar symbol in mainstream newspapers, it was in the 1870s and 1880s that Gage's account, in its various republications, began to eclipse the work of Truth herself.[8] This suggests that the iconic status of Truth's corporeal politics has more to do with Gilded Age fascinations with the signifying power of the muscular body, which, this chapter argues, emerged as one of the most contested sites of character building in the late nineteenth century.

In addition to the problem of distinguishing between the character constructed by early feminists and Truth's own subversive "performance politics" are the problems raised by the invocation of the muscular female body in the "Ar'n't I a Woman" speech, a strategy that risked reinvoking and participating in the racializing discourses of womanhood that the speech seeks to challenge.[9] Not only does the speech pin Truth's claim to womanhood on her status as the mother of "thirteen chillen," a status systematically delegitimated by the conditions of sexual violence under chattel slavery, but it also makes the recognition of her own agency reliant on the exposure of her own body and its ability to testify in reductively physical terms. Such an assertion of the powerfully muscled body, while intended as an expansion and redefinition of the category of womanhood, also risks conjuring the racialized reduction of the slave woman to an overembodied "primitive other" by potentially figuring Truth as the brutish, masculinized antithesis to an idealized vision of womanhood whose fragility was the sign of its finely tuned sentiment and moral purity. And in such a suggestive unveiling of her own body, Truth risked evoking an excessive sexuality that was used to define African American women and to justify racialized forms of sexual violence throughout the nineteenth century. In choosing Truth's "strong arms" as a feminist salvation, feminists could thus externalize and project the power of their own agency onto the body of Truth in order to preserve the distinctive cultural capital of conventional white femininity.

How then are we to understand Truth's invocation of the muscular body as an assertion of social and political equality, despite the many fetishizing uses to which such an invocation might be put? How might we understand Truth's invocation of the muscular body as a form of what Daphne Brooks calls "subterfuge at the site of subjection," a subterfuge that transforms Truth's own "corporeality into a contested terrain of social and cultural knowledge" even as that corporeality emerges as a historical artifact of late nineteenth-century ideological contestations over the bodily meaning and measure of gender, race, and character?[10] Just as Isabella Baumfree remade herself into the character of "Sojourner Truth" in 1843, might we also understand these late nineteenth-century constructions of her character as the extended authorial effects of Truth herself, who, in writing herself into and through the discourse of character, sought to make her body into just such an historically resonant and contested signifying terrain? What kind of challenge did muscle pose to the racialized and gendered logic of embodiment, and how did it promise to transcend or undo the very physiological and visual taxonomies of which it would seem to be an elemental part? What kind of political promise, in other words, was represented by the muscular body in the late nineteenth-century United States?

Taking Truth's strategic display and mythologized character as my prompt and clue, this chapter examines the cultural alignment of character building and muscle building within a broader cultural politics of muscle that emerged in late nineteenth-century American literature and culture. I delineate this cultural politics of muscle by looking at some examples from the physical-culture movement and then by turning to the literary and political writings of one of the period's most prominent authors and feminist critics, Charlotte Perkins Gilman, who was a committed physical-culture advocate and avid bodybuilder, and to Gilman's vision of muscle as an instrument of character building in her utopian feminist politics and racial nationalism. My goal is to make visible within these texts a vision of muscle building that locates its political promise and cultural significance not in the personal and national sovereignty embodied in the reconsolidated "fitness" of white masculinity but rather in the destabilization and reappropriation of the visual taxonomies of race and gender. Like Twain's account of Hank Morgan's desire to become a literary character through a fantasy of character building, these physical-culture texts similarly explore the ways that physical exercise was imagined to transform and reinscribe the cultural legibility of the physical body by reclaiming its uniquely historical character. Such a transformation, I hope to show, was premised on a belief in muscle's ability not simply to empower and reshape the physical body but to historicize the body; to record and, more importantly, to rewrite the history of the body's movements, actions, and reactions, its labors and its leisure; to rewrite the history written by, in other words, the terms of embodied existence itself.

Building Muscle, Building Character

The final decades of the nineteenth century witnessed an explosion of interest in the practices of physical exercise, organized sports, and athletic displays that collectively came to be known as "physical culture," at the center of which stood the revalorized image of the visibly muscular body. Such a visibly muscular body was prominent in a number of cultural domains ranging from the spectacular displays of sideshow strongmen to the muscular prose and musclebound characters of literary naturalism, from the YMCAs and YWCAs of the muscular Christianity movement to the physical-fitness classes of the public school system. The prominence of such a visibly muscular body marked its emergence in a number of sociological, scientific, literary, and pedagogical discourses as an intense site of ideological contestation in late nineteenth- and early twentieth-century U.S. culture. Although the muscular body had been traditionally associated with the overembodied and thereby dehumanizing corporeality of the working classes and the nation's racial and ethnic minorities, in the latter half of the nineteenth century the muscular body emerged as a powerful new signifier for the "fitness" of a racialized national character. This revalorization of the muscular body has traditionally been ascribed to the appeal of muscle as a regenerative tonic for a nation besieged by the enfeebling effects of modernity and its own "overcivilization." From the fragmentations produced by a division of labor increasingly differentiated into "brain work" and "body work" to the experiential compression of space and time by the new communication, transportation, and labor technologies to the overstimulating saturation of urban consumer culture by sensory and semiotic "attractions," the "civilized" society of what was sardonically referred to as the Gilded Age of U.S. history was increasingly seen by influential reformers such as Theodore Roosevelt, Josiah Strong, George Beard, S. Weir Mitchell, and G. Stanley Hall as a potential threat to the corporeal integrity of the body itself, and in particular to the traditional authority and agency of the white male body.[11]

The revalorization of the muscular body in Gilded Age culture has thus been ascribed to its ability to figure a new ideal of a regenerative national character in the idealized form of the muscular, white male body, a body hardened, expanded, and empowered to withstand not only the enervating demands of modernity but also the "race-diluting" effects of massive immigration and the challenges to traditional white male authority posed by the "New Woman" and the "New Negro."[12] Unlike the earlier corporeal ideal represented for example by James Fenimore Cooper's Natty Bumpoo, whose "person, though muscular, was rather attenuated than full," this new vision of muscular masculinity was one embodied in, as Gail Bederman has argued, "an ideal male body [that] required physical bulk and well-defined muscles."[13] More broadly, muscle provided a rich metaphorical terrain for the articulation of a nationalist narrative of a "body politic" renewed by the definition and hardening of its borders, strengthening of its constitution, and reestablishment of healthy internal hierarchies.

Although this muscular masculinity was formed through the many popular forms of physical exercise, athletic competition, and "strenuous activity," its appeal as a check on the enervating and fragmenting forces of modernity has most commonly been ascribed to its ability to draw on the invigorating strength and virility of the "primitive" body. The figure of the muscular primitive was appealing in part because of its location beyond civilization in both evolutionary time and transnational space, a location that, like the African wilds that restore the noble ancestral vigor of the infant aristocrat Lord Greystoke, in Edgar Rice Burroughs's 1912 novel *Tarzan of the Apes*, promised to save civilization from the dangers of its own degeneracy by restoring the vitality, expressiveness, and sensibilities of the natural body.[14] But this association of muscle with the primitive body also temporalized the ideology of muscle, transforming muscle building into an act of evolutionary time travel, one that returned the individual to a kind of premodern, evolutionarily ancestral body lodged deep within as a kind of vestigial, instinctual self and commonly represented by the figure of the caged beast.

While muscle building was thus conceived as a kind of reflexive process of atavistically recovering the primitive within, it also naturalized a logic of empire that, as Amy Kaplan has argued, privileged engagements with "primitive" peoples and cultures at home and abroad as a therapeutic form of individual and national "exercise."[15] Most famously embodied in Theodore Roosevelt's doctrine of the "strenuous life," this new ideal of national character situated the work of imperial domination—most immediately exercised in the Spanish-American War itself and continued in the more brutal suppressions of nationalist movements in the newly acquired territories—not as extensions of U.S. power but rather as formative of it, as exercises as necessary to the nation's muscular health as the "manly exercises" promoted by educational institutions and the burgeoning physical-culture industry.[16] Not only was contact with primitive societies a vital act of muscle building, but muscle building was also figured by many physical-culture advocates in terms of the character-building effect of civilizing the primitive within. As the article "Muscle-Training" in *The Youth's Companion* advised its readers,

It is easy to find out where the lazy, skulking muscles are. They are like tropical darkies in their disposition. If one does not insist upon their working they will lie down and rest forever. But start them up with any unwonted form of exercise, and what fuss! What a grumbling and aching and limping round! There is nothing for it but to send the blood after them constantly as an overseer, and to keep them at it. When this is done the grumbling and the pain will soon disappear, and the joy which is the reward of honest work everywhere will become the portion of those muscles. They will cheerfully do their part.[17]

The therapeutic effects of muscle building and physical culture more broadly thus extended not only to individuals but to the character of the nation itself, for, as M. V. O'Shea argues in his plea for physical education in public schools, "the character of our physical training will shape in a certain measure the destiny of our nation."[18] Or as Arthur Conan Doyle more dramatically put it in his foreword to the British edition of strongman Eugene Sandow's exercise manual, *The Construction and Reconstruction of the Human Body,* "In the days to come the State will—and should—assert its part ownership in the body of every citizen."[19]

Muscle's association with the expansive power of primitive strength has commonly been viewed as the signifier of an emerging ideal of a physically and sexually aggressive "masculinity" that began to eclipse, around the turn of the century, the older, republican model of "character" premised on the gentlemanly self-restraint and moral bearing of "manliness."[20] This transformation has thus been figured as a kind of return of the repressed, as the return of the primitive drives and instincts that the "manly" force of character had been charged with subduing and redirecting. But what this opposition of masculine muscle to manly character overlooks is the ways that the cultural significance of muscle had long been tied to its association with the manly character to which it is frequently contrasted. This conventional history of masculinity thus obscures the more complicated cultural significance and gendered meaning of muscle in late nineteenth-century U.S. culture, and in particular the ways that muscle destabilized the very gender norms that it is so often taken to inaugurate.

The more limited focus on the evolutionary discourse of primitivism has tended to overlook the more influential—and ultimately destabilizing—role that the discourse of character played in shaping the cultural meaning of the muscular body, as well as in the more personal experience of one's own body in physical exercise and muscle building. Although traditionally identified with one pole of the classical binaries of body and soul, matter and spirit, or "brawns" and "brain," muscle emerged in the nineteenth century as a powerfully polyvalent signifier that challenged and confused such distinctions, and particularly so in its role as one of the primary metaphors for the well-developed character. Not only was character portrayed in early character-building manuals by John Todd and Rufus Clark as a unique kind of "moral muscle," but these manuals also frequently advocated a character-building regimen of "resistance training" modeled explicitly on the physical exercises of muscle building.[21] This daily routine of character building involved repeated exercises in resisting the weighty pull of instincts and habits by performing acts that run counter to one's impulses and inclinations, thereby "toning" the mind and hardening character into a reliable new source of "will power." Many early character builders not only analogized character building and muscle building, however; they also defended physical exercise as itself a primary instrument of character building, for, as one late-century physical-culture advocate put the well-known phrase, "there is character as well as strength in muscle."[22] Todd's devotion of an entire chapter to physical exercise in his influential *Student's Manual* (1835) is indicative of the increasing importance of physical fitness in school curricula as early as the 1820s because of its "character-building" effects.[23] As one of the leading educational journals of the time put it, "We shall give to *physical education* that proportion of our attention which seems due to its importance to form habits and stamp the character."[24]

This is of course not to say that muscle building was not contested in many ways, such as in a *Saturday Evening Post* article titled "Muscles and Brains" (1870), which argued that "the man that cultivates his biceps inordinately, must do so at the expense of his brain," or in cartoons such as "Mr. Slim's Developments in Physical Culture" from *Ballou's Dollar Monthly Magazine* that mocked the expanded size of the muscular body and the pain undergone to produce it.[25] In *The Secret of Character-Building* (1894), John DeMotte argues against muscle's valorization as an indicator of character by demonstrating how "some of the grandest souls have lived in quite rickety tenements."[26] Nonetheless, views such as child psychologist G. Stanley Hall's that "[c]haracter is muscle habits," and "proper muscle-culture" is the "first principle . . . in the education of children" were perhaps more representative of the increased cultural significance of muscle building as a key component of character and nation building.[27]

By the 1850s, "The Muscle Question," as the title of one 1858 article in the *Circular* phrased it, had become an increasingly resonant framework for understanding and addressing broader questions of the physically enfeebling effects of the "modern" reliance on the "iron muscles" of modern machinery as well as the historical dependence on the "muscle" of Southern slavery.[28] These debates over the cultural implications of what one writer referred to as "this age of muscle" were shaped not only by the theories and practices of early character builders, however, but also by the popular rise of one the most influential doctrines of character in the 1840s and 1850s, namely, phrenology. Although phrenology has commonly been understood as a relatively short-lived and highly criticized pseudoscience of the 1840s and 1850s, the underlying premise of phrenology (and of the broader field of physiognomy out of which it grew), that character could be read in the physical form and details of the body, continued to shape some of the most important literary, scientific, and social discourses well into the late nineteenth and early twentieth centuries.[29]

Phrenology has commonly been understood as a "science" that delineated the features of character primarily in the fixed, skeletal structure of the cranium. The phrenological theories condensed and popularized in the United States by Orson Fowler and Samuel Wells, however, lodged the physiological basis of character not in the hard reality of bone but rather in the plastic potentiality of muscle. As physical-culture historian Jan Todd has pointed out, the foundational thesis of phrenology was that the brain was organized in terms of a number of different "faculties" (thirty-seven according to Fowler), each located in distinct masses of muscular brain "fibers."[30] Ruled by the same "law of increase by action and decrease by inaction" that governed muscles, the relative size of these different mental organs thus varied according to how regularly they were used or "exercised," a law of "increase" or "atrophy" that can also be seen, as Fowler points out in his *Self-Culture and Perfection of Character,* in "the hands of sailors and laborers, . . . the feet of dancers and pedestrians, . . . the chests of rowers, the muscles of the laboring classes compared with those of the puny 'upper tens,' the right hand as compared to the left, and, indeed, to every portion of the body."[31]

Phrenology's emphasis on muscle as the material matrix of character served two important functions: it explained how the physiological character of the body functioned as a kind of textual archive of an individual's life, and it also offered up strategies of self-transformation through targeted exercise of weak or atrophied faculties. As Newell Hillis put it in *A*

Man's Value to Society: Studies in Self-Culture and Character (1897), "nature has ordained the body as a system of moral registration. Nature has a record of all men's deeds, keeping her accounts on fleshy tablets. The mind may forget, the body never."[32] The plasticity of muscle—as opposed to the hidden code of blood, the superficial surface of skin, or the fixed durability of bone—not only explained how inherited evolutionary characteristics hardened into the differentiated topography of the body and head; it also explained how a personal history of faculty use and disuse transformed and rewrote those characteristics in the material shape of character. Thus while phrenological methods were frequently employed to delineate a racialized and gendered schema of social and evolutionary types, many phrenologists were more interested in the ways that muscle could be the mechanism of a radical rewriting and "improvement" of inherited character rather than simply an archival index of fixed character traits.[33] Hence, rather than proposing that people live by moral principles applied through introspective acts of self-reflection, phrenologists proposed a performative logic of character building, one premised on acts of readerly extrospection that entailed a careful study of the textured relief and movement of one's own body, followed by a mimetic program of purposive exercises that, in merely imitating certain character traits, created the very material of character itself.

Not only did phrenologists and physiognomists draw on the methods of muscle builders to articulate their process of character building; so too did physical culturalists at century's end embrace phrenology's assertion that muscular development could be the instrument of a radical self-fashioning of character. Indeed the explosion of interest in those self-improvement activities that collectively came to be known as physical culture was in large measure driven by the belief in muscle's unique character-building properties. The language of character building infused debates over the place of team sports and athletic competitions in higher education and over the social value of professional sports, as well as the marketing rhetoric of bicycle manufacturers and promoters of gymnastics, weight lifting, running, and calisthenics, while new institutions of muscular Christianity such as the YMCA promoted competitive exercise and invented team sports such as basketball and volleyball specifically for the purpose of character building.[34]

The appeal of muscle to physiognomists, physical culturalists, and character builders alike was not only that it transformed the body into a unique kind of materially articulated text but more importantly that it provided a medium of self-authorship, one that was imagined literally to rewrite the form and therefore cultural meaning and significance of the physiological body. Muscles were, in other words, what made an individual visible within the gendered, classed, and racialized schemas of social legibility, but they were also the instruments for rewriting the terms of that legibility. This transformation of the accidental body—the body shaped by both evolutionary history and the historical contingencies of modern life and labor—into a material but no less textual character was thus promoted in a burgeoning physical-culture media not simply for its power to shore up an enfeebled white masculinity as the sign of the sovereign liberal subject but also for its more radical democratic promise to override the physiological hierarchies of race, gender, and class. Muscle signified, in other words, not simply the nostalgic reclamation of a historical past but a more wholesale historicization of the body itself.[35] As a signifier of a historically fashioned character, muscle building thus emerged in Gilded Age culture as the vexed site of ideological contestation—offering on the one hand a eugenicist vision of racial fitness through the muscularly developed, racially purified male body and on the other hand a more egalitarian vision of social empowerment for all through bodily transformation. As Michael Budd has put it, "most fitness media tacked a course between the two: veering back and forth from a hysterical rhetoric of biological degeneration to the more euphoric positivism of their own methods that aimed to socially reconstruct the body."[36]

In the sections that follow, I explore the social and political implications of the muscular body as a signifier of character in one of the most important publications in the physical-culture media, the *National Police Gazette,* and in the literary and political writings of one of the period's most important feminist authors, Charlotte Perkins Gilman. My aim is to chart in particular the ways that, rather than affirming a vision of personal and national sovereignty modeled on the material strength of the powerful, white male body, the discourse of muscle destabilized the iconic status of that body. More importantly, in making muscle the new language of character, physical culturalists, social reformers, and literary authors also destabilized the racial and gendered meaning of the physiological body more broadly. As a discourse in which muscle signified not simply the reclamation of a historical past, in other words, but a more radical historicization of the body, the discourse of character thus constituted an important yet vexed arena for challenging the very meaning of race and gender in the late nineteenth- and early twentieth-century United States.

Vanishing Strongmen, Women on Their Muscle:
Archiving Character in the National Police Gazette

The cultural implications of this mechanically produced, abstract muscular character are nowhere more clearly displayed than on the pages of one of the longest running periodicals in U.S. history, the *National Police Gazette*.[37] The *National Police Gazette* rose to prominence in the late 1840s in large part because of the appeal of its illustrated pages and of their thrilling narrative and pictorial portrayals of the spectacular and sordid deeds of actual criminals. By century's end, however, these portraits had given way to lavish images of shirtless muscle builders, prominent athletes, and stage starlets, a seemingly arbitrary transformation that, I suggest, actually charts the shifting and ultimately unstable gender politics of character in late nineteenth-century U.S. culture. The evolution of the *National Police Gazette* in the last three decades of the nineteenth century from the preeminent journal of crime news into, as its masthead proudly declared, "The Leading Illustrated Sporting Journal in America," is an evolution that charts not only the rising importance of muscle in a cultural politics of character but also the role muscle played in destabilizing conventional bodily signifiers of gender and sexuality.

The mission of the early *National Police Gazette* was to submit, in its detailed narratives and woodcut illustrations, the character of criminals to what Shelly Streeby has described as a kind of "panoptic gaze . . . pulling together diverse incidents, crimes, and historical events into a field of visibility for the eye of police power."[38] This was particularly true in its leading series, "The Lives of Felons," but also in its many smaller "notices" of local crimes and trials, which provided detailed descriptions of the criminal character as well as analyses of the motives and causes of criminal acts. As an early prospectus of the *Gazette* described its self-appointed social mission, "The necessity of such an instrument as the *National Police Gazette* to assist the operations of the Police department" stemmed from the fact that the "success of the felon depends mainly upon the ignorance of the community as to his character."[39] The *Gazette* thus sought to dispel this ignorance through the appropriation of the popular "character sketch" form in such regular series as "Glimpses of Gotham" and "City Characters" in order to make visible the various hidden features of the criminal character and of the urban "types" surveyed, for example, in literary texts such as Edgar Allan Poe's "The Man of the Crowd" and popular theatrical productions such as "The Sidewalks of New York" (see figure 8).

The "policing" power of the *Gazette*'s illustrated pages, however, was not entirely aligned in the service of the police, for it frequently turned its gaze toward the police themselves as it also sought, as Guy Reel has pointed out in his history of the *Gazette*, "to right wrongs in the justice system . . . [by] championing equal rights for lower classes, including the public's right to know."[40] In order to fulfill this complex mission, the *Gazette* dedicated itself to the art of character "detection," the goal of which was, as Foucault has famously argued, not simply to identify particular criminals but to delineate the broader and inherent features of the criminal character itself in order to distinguish the congenital "delinquent" from the mere "offender" who has unjustly or temporarily run afoul of the law.[41]

In this sense, the criminological mission of the early *Gazette* might be understood as emerging out of the broader social project of character detection that developed in the United States over the latter half of the nineteenth century. The techniques of identification that initially defined criminology—such as the photographic mug shot and system of anthropometric measurements devised by Alphonse Bertillon, as well as the fingerprinting methods developed by Francis Galton—first arose from the need of police officials to fix reliably or to "arrest" the uncertain identity, and thereby the criminal record, of detained criminals who were eager to "pass" as someone other than themselves.[42] The primary aim of these methods, however, was simply to establish the identity of individual criminals in order to establish a criminal's record as a guide to prosecution and sentencing. As the science of criminology developed in Europe and the United States, however, it quickly turned from the project of individual identification to the classification of character types in order to see the inherent criminal better and thereby also prevent crime. Like more popular methods of character reading from which it borrowed, criminology's promise to expose and thereby neutralize the criminal was only one part of its more ambitious project to make legible and police the social distinctions between the middle class and its racial, class, and ethnic others, particularly in the congested spaces of the modern city, and to provide an axis of distinction between the criminal and the law-abiding body on which various forms of social difference could be projected, mapped, and hierarchically distributed.[43]

The *National Police Gazette*'s fascination with and fetishization of the criminal character made it an important early cultural site for the articulation and mass distribution of what Alan Sekula has called the "social

archive" and a key instrument in the formation of new forms of social, political, and legal discrimination in the nineteenth-century United States.[44] However, in the 1880s and 1890s, the period in which the "characterological" methods of criminology reached their height, the *National Police Gazette* seemed to veer sharply away from its traditional criminological mission. When Richard K. Fox took control of the magazine in 1876, he began a process of transformation that by the mid-1880s had made the *Gazette* into no longer just the leading journal devoted to crime news in the United States but also one of the most prominent sporting journals in the United States. Central to this editorial reorientation of the magazine was the promotion of sporting events of all kinds, including "prizefights, rowing events, aerial jumping, shin-kicking duels, oyster-eating contests, and all manner of other competitions," as well as detailed reporting on and illustrations of the leading stage celebrities, showgirls, and dancers of the day.[45] While ostensibly a radical shift away from its traditional focus on crime, this reorientation of the magazine was in many ways an extension of the sensational appeal of criminal and deviant acts to an even more spectacular combination of crime, sex, celebrity, and sports, a combination that became the successful staple formula of the modern tabloid form.

Central to this shift in editorial emphasis was a distinct transformation of the magazine's visual iconography. As advances in halftone printing enabled the mass reproduction of photographic images in newspapers and magazines, the *Gazette*, like many periodicals, began to incorporate photographs to complement and in some cases replace the traditional woodcut illustrations on which it had traditionally relied. Although these photographs, like those being increasingly employed by criminologists, social scientists, and physiognomists, were commonly used to identify character in the subtle morphology of the physical body, what is surprising about the *Gazette* is that suddenly the most prominently displayed bodies were not those of criminals, deviants, and delinquents but rather the robustly muscled bodies of athletes, weightlifters, boxers, and laborers that were displayed alongside increasingly revealing and sexualized images of the female body. These images, which had long served as visual illustrations of the many stories in the magazine, also grew increasingly detached from

Fig. 8. (opposite page) "The Sidewalks of New York," theatrical poster produced by the Strobridge Litho Company, c. 1899. (Theatrical Poster Collection, Library of Congress Prints and Photographs Division)

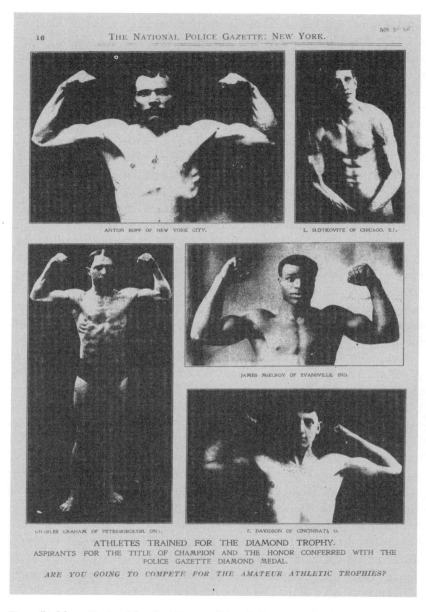

ANTON BOPP OF NEW YORK CITY.   L. SLOTKOVITZ OF CHICAGO, ILL.

JAMES McELROY OF EVANSVILLE, IND.

CHARLES GRAHAM OF PETERBOROUGH, ONT.   F. DAVIDSON OF CINCINNATI, O.

ATHLETES TRAINED FOR THE DIAMOND TROPHY.
ASPIRANTS FOR THE TITLE OF CHAMPION AND THE HONOR CONFERRED WITH THE
POLICE GAZETTE DIAMOND MEDAL.

ARE YOU GOING TO COMPETE FOR THE AMATEUR ATHLETIC TROPHIES?

Fig. 9. "Athletes Trained for the Diamond Trophy," *National Police Gazette* 81, no. 1320 (December 6, 1902): 16.

their illustrative function. Instead of illustrating the many sporting and athletic events on which the magazine was increasingly reporting, these images began to focus on increasingly fetishized and repetitive displays of the flexing muscular male body as well as of the bodies of women who were, as the phrase went, "on their muscle." By 1901 the *Gazette* not only had a regular "physical culture" self-help page, which explained muscle-building exercises illustrated by the accompanying photographs of exemplary physiques, but its "Diamond Medal" contest for "amateur strong men and athletes" and call for "portraits of all big-muscled, well-developed athletes in the country" guaranteed a massive supply of photographs of ordinary muscle builders for its pages.[46]

This reorientation has most commonly been interpreted as a turning of the surveilling, criminological gaze of the *Gazette* back on itself in order to assert explicitly and shore up a vision of masculine authority premised not only on the archiving power of its gaze but on the strength and vitality of the muscular body. As Guy Reel puts it, "When hegemonic masculinities are threatened, the threats can result in masculine 'degradation' and may require a response."[47] Certainly the muscular bodies that populated the pages of the *Gazette* explicitly promoted such a reassuring and normative vision of muscular masculinity, a normativity echoed in such headlines as "Be a Strong Man, Not a Caricature."[48] Competing publications more stridently affirmed such a vision, particularly Bernarr Macfadden's *Physical Culture Magazine,* whose signature maxim, emblazoned on the magazine's cover, promoted such a masculinity in tellingly criminological terms: "Weakness is a crime, don't be a criminal." But while the *Gazette* echoed and frequently affirmed the hyperbolic rhetoric of muscular masculinity, what is most surprising is the way that such a proliferation of muscular men *and* women in the *Gazette* also destabilized the corporeal economy of gender and sexuality as much as it reified a heteronormative binary of gendered bodies. Rather than simply deviant "threats" against which a normative masculinity consolidates itself, the diverse array of gendered forms and sexual identifications detailed in the *Gazette* also constitute important and potential sites of identification that, *as* "provocative," both incite and entice and thereby exceed the containing gaze of the archiving imperative of the character sketch. The problem with reading the *Gazette,* in other words, as simply a response to the many threats posed to the masculinity invested in character by Gilded Age modernity is that the logic of threat and response—so endemic to critical scholarship on the

THE LADIES IDOLIZE SANDOW.

THE STRONG MAN EXHIBITS HIS FORM AT SELECT RECEPTIONS TO THE PRETTY CREATURES.

Fig. 10. "The Ladies Idolize Sandow," *National Police Gazette* 63, no. 856 (January 27, 1894): 1.

formation of gender in the United States at the turn of the century—
tends to obscure the important and frequently subversive cultural work
performed by periodicals such as the *Gazette*. As Shelley Streeby has argued, publications such as the *Gazette* were part of a "culture of sensation" that did not so much reproduce the hegemonic forms and cultural
norms of "a fictive, unified body of the nation-people," as did the "mass
culture" with which the culture of sensation is frequently confused, but
rather existed "in tension with capitalist modernity" and the middle-
class norms through which it reproduces itself.[49] The *National Police Gazette* thus seems, in its own dizzying way, to be surveying and provoking
such a proliferation of forms of gendered and sexual embodiment even
as it attempts to consume and contain them within a consolidated image of masculine spectatorship, and it seems to be using the excessively
signifying power of muscle to do so. In its fascination with muscle we
might thus understand the *Gazette*'s transformation not as an abandon-
ment of the criminological project of character detection but rather as
an exploration and exposure of its inherently destabilizing logic, a destabilization that issues from the archival aspirations of the discourse of
character itself.

This is perhaps most immediately apparent in the *Gazette*'s frequent
decoupling of the aesthetic display of muscle from the performance of
strength, a decoupling that both propelled and vexed the career of the
most famous strongman of the period, Eugene Sandow. Eugene Sandow's
performances in the circuses and exhibitions of Europe often followed the
classic strongman formula of performing spectacular feats of strength,
including lifting seemingly impossible objects such as horses and people
and breaking chains and coins with his bare hands.[50] But what ultimately
distinguished Sandow from other strongmen and fueled his extraordi-
nary popularity, particular in his first trip to the United States in 1893, was
his extraordinarily defined and proportionately balanced musculature,
as well as his spectacular ability to flex his muscles in a rhythmical and
elaborately controlled "muscle dance."[51]

The *Gazette*'s first article on Sandow in 1894, "The Ladies Idolize Sandow," similarly focuses in both the cover illustration and the accompanying text not on his heralded strength but rather on the spectacular nature
of his clearly defined and masterfully controlled muscles. The typically
brief article focuses on the after-hours "performance" Sandow would frequently give to a more elite audience in the intimate space of his parlor
after his stage-show strength exhibitions. After emerging scantily clad and

"in all his physical beauty fresh from the bath," the bared Sandow began his performance with a show of muscle flexing and then an invitation to inspect and verify:

> "Now ladies and gentlemen," says Sandow, "I want you to feel how hard these muscles are . . ." He approaches the first man, takes the outstretched hand and rubs it over the hard muscles of his iron-ribbed chest. An expression of astonishment on the part of the man heightens the expectation of others. Sandow moves along the line, taking hand after hand, until he approaches the first woman in the party. "Never mind," she says timidly. There is a laugh on the part of the men. "Oh, but you must feel it?" insists Sandow: "the muscles are hard as iron, and I want you to convince yourself of the fact." Sandow gently but firmly takes the gloved hand and rubs it over the hardened ridges of muscles. Then he passes on until all have tested the giant's muscles.[52]

What is more surprising than the thinly veiled phallic economy being asserted here is the proliferation rather than containment of its forms. Rather than neatly differentiating the responses of the men and the women along an axis of emulation and desire, both the men and the women are positioned in the narrative as "idolizers" of Sandow who ambiguously shift between relations of desire and identification. Not only are the men ambiguously interested explorers of the ridged muscles, but the women are conversely caught up in a contagion of imitation and identification as they become inspired by the muscle-building fever to transform their own bodies and the very space of domesticity itself: "Of course every man *and woman* after leaving Sandow goes home a firm believer in physical culture. Society is developing muscle at a fearful rate in the secrecy of the boudoir and dressing room. Dumb-bells and tape-measures are growing in demand and Sandow is growing rich."[53] This conflation of the conventionally heterosexual scopic distribution of desire and identification extends to the cover illustration as well, which presumably documents the production of the male body as a newly spectacularized object of an explicitly desiring female gaze but quickly exceeds the expected scopic positions of such a relation. The conspicuously posed female "idolizer" mimics the stance of Sandow as well, as if she too were, in touching his bicep, putting her own on competitive display, a visual iconography that would have undoubtedly also evoked for its readers the very common promotional image of two posed boxing contestants facing each other.

This conflation of gender positions provoked by the display of muscle was also a central feature of the first male physique contests organized by the *Gazette,* Sandow himself, and physical-culture icon Bernarr Macfadden.[54] Origin of both the modern bodybuilding contest as well as of the female "beauty pageant" tradition, these early physique contests not only produced the muscular male body as commodity spectacle but also confounded the gendered positionalities and heterosexual spectator economy thought to govern such displays. In the coverage of Bernarr Macfadden's 1904 physical-culture contest in Madison Square Garden by the *New York Times,* for example, such an excessive display of muscle testifies less to a new vision of muscular masculinity than to an unsettling yet provocative undoing of gender:

> Rarely has there been a site of so much superfluous muscle. It burst out as if it would rend asunder the enfolding skin. That any one of them could have done a hard day's work in a hayfield was doubtful. To the practiced eye of a prizefighter . . . the twenty offered such a temptation for his fists in a grand rally of revenge against fate that he was restrained with difficulty. . . . [Then] the women were brought in. . . . There was a Swedish woman, a well-known artists' model: a black-eyed sylph with muscles of steel, a fighting eye, and a brogue: a chunk of a woman with muscles like those of a man, and many others.[55]

Rather than celebrations of a triumphant masculinity, these displays of muscular bodies were newsworthy because of their unnerving deconsolidation of conventional heterosexual spectatorship. While the woman's chunky yet steely muscles are "like those of a man," they do not thereby foreclose her desirability but rather constitute her as an object of desire who paradoxically exhibits in her masculine muscle the daintiness, grace, and airiness of the mythical "sylph." The muscularity of the men, on the other hand, is the sign of their very failure to fulfill the conditions of labor and violent competition conventionally identified with muscular masculinity, a failure that incites the prizefighter to exact his punishing "revenge."

Although the languid and frequently suggestive nude poses popularized by strongmen such as Sandow and Macfadden and reproduced in bodybuilding contests and physical-culture magazines were often subject to such hostile responses, these images were also the cornerstone of a burgeoning physical-culture industry built on the commodification of male nude bodies for what Thomas Waugh has called "an overtly sexual

Fig. 11. Photograph of vaudeville performer and trapeze artist Charmion (Laverie Vallee née Cooper), c. 1900–1915. (Billy Rose Theatre Division, New York Public Library for the Performing Arts, Astor, Lenox, and Tilden Foundations)

voyeurism" for an audience that was overwhelmingly male.[56] Bodybuilding contests and physical-culture magazines commonly blurred the distinctions between identification and desire as they promoted the visual
pleasures and covert eroticism of male bodies that were, as Waugh demonstrates, "marketed in exactly the same way to the same male gaze in
every medium from mail-order photography and postcards to vaudeville"
as were the female bodies alongside which they were displayed.[57] The classified section of Macfadden's *Physical Culture Magazine* was at times also
the site of ambiguous solicitations of male companionship such as in this
ad: "American bachelor, 48, book lover owning large collection, lover of
nature, devoted to open window sleeping, open-air life and hatless existence; solicits correspondence with young men of athletic build and habit,
fond of literature and wholesome life."[58] We might thus think of Macfadden's own graphic defenses of the "Superb Virility of Manhood" and virulent polemics against "the shoals of painted, perfumed, kohl-eyed, lisp-
ing, mincing youths that at night swarm on Broadway in the Tenderloin
section, or haunt the parks and 5th avenue, ogling every man that passes
and—it is pleasant to relate—occasionally getting a sound thrashing or
an emphatic kicking" as paranoid recognition and disavowal of his own
role in constituting the male body as an object of homoerotic investment
by men across a range of sexual orientations and gender identifications.[59]

Even as muscle building constituted the male body as emblem of the
well-formed character and iconic object of identification and erotic investment, it also transformed masculinity into the site of an intensive self-negation. As muscle became less a sign of the inherent strength or capability
of character and more an aesthetic object in itself, muscle-building techniques shifted from the strict utility of strength training and weightlifting to a more elaborate system of producing visually appealing physiques
modeled on classical statuary. The lifting of heavy weights thus became
something that performers would perform off stage rather than on stage
in order to "pump" their muscles and enhance their visual appeal, the
more important message being not that the body could lift those weights
but that the performer had engaged in a long history of disciplined lifting
to produce such an aesthetically pleasing physical form.

Fasting was perhaps the most extreme version of the common dietary
restrictions that muscle builders used to eliminate the layer of body fat
that might obscure the painstakingly procured muscle definition. Macfadden, for example, ardently promoted prolonged periods of fasting as a way
to combat the "softness" that threatened to obscure the muscular body.[60]

Although other prominent bodybuilders did not necessarily promote fasting to the degree that Macfadden did, most did include in their manuals detailed advice on dieting whose purpose was to enable their readers to re-create the meticulously sculpted bodies of the authors. The well-formed muscular body thus emerged out of a kind of violent, oppositional struggle simultaneously to expand and to shrink the physiological body, the ultimate goal being to make the body turn seemingly inside out by bringing the detailed striations and vascular structure of muscle to the surface such that it begins to represent its visual ideal— the skinless anatomical chart.[61] As fasting advocate (and wife of Boy Scout cofounder Ernest Thompson Seton) Julia Seton emphasized, this radical externalization of the body constituted a process of erasure, self-destruction, and re-creation that also feminized the muscular body as a form of self-adornment and ornamentation, a process through which the material substance of the body is paradoxically transformed into a fashionable article of clothing—a "new flesh suit"—through which one also dons a new character: "When one gets his misfit food body out of the way by fasting, breathing and exercise, he gives the life cells a chance to make him a new flesh suit, and this flesh suit can be of any type that he himself decides."[62] The fascination with muscle in late nineteenth-century American culture can thus not easily be ascribed to its ability to figure a comforting image of masculine strength but rather foregrounds its fleeting, fictive nature, marking not the plenitude of masculinity but rather what Leslie Heywood refers to as a "form of aphanisis or fading of the masculine subject, its slippage in the moment of its constitution. . . . The language of bodybuilding is the language of violence, and the object of that violence is one's own body."[63]

The power of muscle both to build character and to destabilize conventional gender and sexual binaries was perhaps most apparent in its many portraits of women who were "on their muscle."[64] The phrase "on her muscle" most commonly referred to women engaging in physical fights either with other women or with men. In these images, which began appearing in the *Gazette* before Fox began publishing images of the muscular male body, many complex and frequently contradictory forms of female agency are represented. Some women are shown turning their muscle to criminal acts, while others use their muscle to confront or chase criminals of various kinds or even to pursue acts of social reform.[65] The many stories and images of women "on their muscle" confronting "mashers" and "peeping toms," while often explicitly staged within the illustrated frame as objects of visual consumption for a smiling male observer, also frequently portray women using their muscle to confront the very commodifying, masculine gaze that distinguishes the discriminating judge of character. The article and accompanying illustration "On Her Muscle," for example, vividly portrays young Anna O'Keefe knocking out "a youthful specimen of the genus dude" for his degrading advances, and "She Resented an Insult" even more dramatically depicts a young woman dressed as a ballerina nearly bludgeoning to death a man in a monkey costume at Mardi Gras.[66] "A Boston Husband's Punishment" depicts a man who, because he has "objected to his wife's gay card parties," is physically bound by his wife and her friends to a piano and "compelled to be a witness" to their gambling, smoking, and drinking.[67] Here the husband's regulatory gaze itself becomes not the object of explicit violence but rather the instrument of his own subjection, as the man is forced by his wife and her friends to see an act of gender defiance that he does not want to be seen. Such confrontations take place at the editorial level as well, such as in the textual positioning of "The Ladies Idolize Sandow" article within a longer article on "Tom" King, the Female Outlaw, "A Brave but Very Bad Woman."[68] At the center of this story of the transgendered outlaw is a picture of "Tom" King brandishing a whip, an image that no doubt would have evoked the well-publicized and very public whipping Sandow himself received just a few months before by his former assistant, aquatics performer Lurine, the Water Queen.[69] Not only did the publicity surrounding the event expose Sandow's use of fake chains and coins in his act, but he also was beat by strongwoman Katie Brumbach in a lifting competition, a defeat she memorialized, much to Sandow's chagrin, by changing her name to Katie "Sandwina" in mockery of Sandow.

"Vassar Vengeance" tells the story of "Three Plucky College Girls" who, while swimming in the Hudson River one day, spot a man rummaging through their clothes back on shore and even trying some of them on. Going "on their muscle," the three girls chase down the voyeur and thief and proceed to give him a "clubbing that would have made a heeler in a Sixth avenue dive open his eyes, after which they quietly returned to make their toilette."[70] In the illustration of the event, one of the girls in her bathing costume is shown towering over and seemingly lifting the man by his hair, her fist aimed at and ready to pummel the staring eyes of the gruff "tramp" who now wears her clothes. The gaze that these girls punish, moreover, is one that, in witnessing the girls stripping down to athletic swimming attire, is thereby compelled to assume rather than simply

Fig. 12. "Vassar Vengeance: How Three Plucky College Girls Went on Their Muscle," *National Police Gazette* 36, no. 152 (August 21, 1880): 1.

desire the "terrestrial attire" of a conventional femininity that the women themselves have sloughed off. While women are portrayed as the force that disabuses this gender-confused man of his feminizing clothes, in other words, the tramp's masculine restoration is one that transpires not through a repudiation of their threatening agency but rather presumably through an appropriation of it. Not only do the women figure a prototypically athletic, aggressive masculinity the tramp himself cannot seem to maintain; his resumption of such a masculinity can take shape only as the wounded masculinity of the man who has been taught the lesson of his own gender by these muscular women.

Similarly, the article "Belles of Comic Opera Who Will Spend the Summer Developing Muscles—They Have Engaged a Well-Known Athlete to Teach Them How to Punch the Bag and Box" gives a more explicit warning of the disruptions that such a production of muscular femininity will produce:

> Some time this fall, if you should happen to see a party of bronzed, chesty-looking persons, of the gentler sex, striding along The Line, with the heads well up in the air, their shoulders thrown back and their biceps bulging aggressively, pass them by respectfully. If you should happen to be a Johnnie, don't ogle or get gay, for any one of that outfit will be able to put you away with a punch. This is not written as a bit of news, but as a warning. The GAZETTE has always sympathized with unfortunate men, and it doesn't want to see Broadway turned into a battlefield, dominated by Amazons of amazing beauty and wondrous cleverness.[71]

Such images and narratives of women "on their muscle" have most commonly been read as allegorical portraits of the many gendered threats posed by the incursions of the "New Woman"—with her loosened corset, speedy bicycle, and new array of careers—into the traditionally masculine arenas that legitimated character's appearance, as well as the fetishizing containment, in being rendered as an object of consumption for the masculine gaze, of that threat. Certainly for many readers of the *Gazette* these images did indeed offer such a reassuring site of heteronormative, erotic investment. But what is most conspicuous about these scenes is that they are posed as challenges not to the traditional forms of masculine authority and character but rather to the reactionary, containing gaze that is said to be the response to that challenge and constitutive of the visual economy of modern consumer culture. Thus although it would be a mistake to call these representations of women's muscularity a purely *feminist* challenge to forms of gendered violence constituted by the discourse of character more broadly, it would I think equally be a mistake to dismiss them, within either a psychoanalytic or Bakhtinian paradigm, as simply the disarming fetishization of a kind of phallic femininity by a threatened male spectator position or as the carnivalesque thrill of a temporarily inverted social order.[72]

Rather than reading publications such as the *Gazette* as simply the transgressive incitement to a reconsolidated gender binary, we might consider the *Gazette* as an important site in which alternate forms of gendered embodiment were explored and circulated, forms that shaped and informed experiences of gender and sexuality not simply as negative examples of deviant or "inverted" behavior but as more ambiguous forms of alternate sexual lives. As Judith Halberstam has argued, for example, nineteenth-century forms of "female masculinity" should be understood not simply as women acting like or imitating men but rather as alternate, hybrid forms of masculinity that contributed their own stamp to "modern masculinity" itself: "[M]asculine women have played a large part in the construction of modern masculinity . . . [and] have made their own unique contributions to what we call modern masculinity, and these contributions tend to go unnoticed in gender scholarship. . . . [W]hat we recognize as female masculinity is actually a multiplicity of masculinities, indeed a proliferation of masculinities."[73] The adulatory terms through which the story of one woman's many acts of gender passing are told in "Here's a Handsome Girl," for example, chart an ambiguous course between an eroticizing fascination with and an identificatory emulation of her muscular abilities.[74] Detailing her work as a cowboy and a bartender, her ambition to be a prizefighter, and her impressively refined "dudish clothes," the article locates the attractive attributes of her "interesting character" in what we might call, following Judith Butler, her acts of gender insubordination, acts that are celebrated by the *Gazette* but that lead to her repeated arrest by state authorities.[75]

While images of women "on their muscle" are frequently used to portray these forms of female masculinity, more explicit examples of gender passing and of queer sexualities are also frequently explored in the *Gazette*'s many tales of character impersonation. Whereas stories such as "Vassar Girls" and "This Agent Played in Luck" portray men who masquerade as women in order to colonize the private sphere of women with their heterosexual gaze, in the many accounts of women masquerading as men, transgender identifications are frequently used to sustain unconventional sexual relationships that transcend the simple binary of homosexual and heterosexual.[76] "Such a Dilemma," for example, describes a woman "disguised" as a man who marries and brutally dominates another, unsuspecting woman, and "Pretty Female Tramp" tells of a young woman who dresses as a man in order to "tramp" around the country with her male lover.[77] While both these examples position gender masquerade as an artifice used to hide sexual relationships that cannot easily be classified as either homosexual or heterosexual, they also both suggest that such transgendered identifications themselves structured or animated the many forms of queer desire in the relationships. Other stories, however, more explicitly link these forms of female masculinity to lesbian relationships, such as in "They Could Take Care of Themselves," in which a "party of gay girls of New York Bohemian circles declare their independence by dispensing with male escorts during the masquerade ball season, and enjoy a period of pleasure unadulterated by masculine restraint."[78] As one of the girls is quoted as saying, "We come here to enjoy ourselves . . . and we intend to do it our own way." The "queer psychological study" titled "A Female Romeo," on the other hand, tells the more tragic tale of a woman who "would make hot love like a Romeo to her female friends" but who ends up murdering one beloved "friend" after the friend refuses her marriage proposal.[79]

Although these many forms of gender insubordination did indeed pose a threat to conventional understandings of gender and sexuality and were frequently bound up with the commodifying practices of an emerging mass media as well as the target of vicious critique even in the *Gazette,* it would be a mistake to read these diversely gendered forms as simply subsumed within and domesticated by the heterosexual gender binary of a reconsolidated discourse of character. What such a reading all too quickly forecloses is a reading of the alternately embodied forms of character figured within the muscular visual economy of publications such as the *Gazette* and the specific ways such forms circulated within and informed gender norms rather than simply being repudiated and rejected by them. Rather than critically reducing these forms to just so many symbolic threats to the conventional masculinity of character, the question thus raised by the *Gazette* is what kinds of alternately gendered lives might these images, even in their reproduction for a commodifying masculine gaze, also document, and how might we understand them as the product rather than incitement of the rhetoric of character's archiving and muscle-building imperative?

Charlotte Perkins Gilman and the Queer Character of Race

One of the most prominent proponents of muscle building as a politically empowering instrument in the rewriting of gender and sexuality was the author and social theorist Charlotte Perkins Gilman. Gilman's place in the feminist and literary canon has largely been established on the basis of her incisive diagnosis, particularly in her now most celebrated literary work, "The Yellow Wallpaper," of the debilitating forms of gendered embodiment imposed by modern femininity and by the pathologizing medical and scientific perspectives on feminine character. It is thus surprising that, given this attention to the body in Gilman scholarship, relatively little attention has been paid to Gilman's intense and self-avowed "life-long interest in physical culture" and to the formative role muscle building plays in the social philosophy that guides so much of her literary, political, and autobiographical writings.[80]

Gilman's interest in physical culture had begun as early as 1875, when as a schoolgirl she entered into a regular regimen of running, gymnastics, calisthenics, and walking that was only seriously interrupted by her first marriage to Walter Stetson in 1884, an interruption that she suggests also led to her famous "nervous" breakdown. As she recounts in her autobiography, *The Living of Charlotte Perkins Gilman,* Gilman's regimen of physical culture was tied to an explicit project of character building, a project she began at age fifteen in response to the persistently vulnerable, yet potentially liberating, position she and her mother were in when her father left them: "If I was a free agent what was I going to do with my freedom? If I could develop character as I chose, what kind of character was I going to develop? This at fifteen."[81] Lamenting that until this age she had "no character to be specially proud of; impressionable, vacillating, sensitive, uncontrolled, often loafing and lazy," Gilman set out "toward a stronger, nobler character" by borrowing directly from the manifold methods of the character builders.[82] She began to emulate the heroic characters of great men and women, particularly Socrates, followed a daily regimen of self-habituation modeled on Benjamin Franklin's "Art of Virtue," and even implemented a performative approach, such as that espoused by phrenologists, to character building by seeking out a young invalid girl on whom she could "practice" benevolent acts in order to instill a benevolence that she admits she did not initially feel.[83]

Most important to Gilman's efforts to give definitive shape to her character, however, is her simultaneous aim to give definitive shape to her muscular body. The assessment she gives of herself in the opening entry of the journal she began in 1879 centers on what are to her the two most important and interlinked personal facts, the strength of her character and the strength of her muscular body: "Gentle reader, wouldst know me? Verily, here I am. 18 years old. 5 feet, 6½ in. high. Weigh 120 lbs. or thereabouts. Looks, not bad. At times handsome. At others decidedly homely. Health, Perfect. Strength amazing. Character ——. Ah! Gradually outgrowing laziness. Possessing great power over my self."[84] As her commitment to physical culture intensified in her late teens, Gilman also increasingly found in the body shaping and physically empowering methods of physical exercise the secrets to character building as well. It was while pursuing a course of exercise intended to correct her poor posture, for example, that Gilman realized the character-building effects of such a "course of exercises in which small and purely arbitrary decisions were sharply carried out" and their utility for not only shaping her body but also strengthening her "flaccidity of will."[85]

While living in Providence, Gilman became an active proponent of physical culture and was instrumental in the establishment of the Providence Ladies' Sanitary Gymnasium in 1881.[86] Gilman's views on physical fitness, however, and its relation to character building as well as her exercise regimen had already been shaped in large measure by what she referred to as "her bedside Bible, her Atalanta guidebook for the coming race," namely, William Blaikie's popular muscle-building manual *How to Get Strong and How to Stay So* (1879).[87] Blaikie popularized a program of weightlifting that undercut some of the most entrenched assumptions regarding the intersections of masculine strength, race, class, and muscularity.[88] Blaikie, like many character builders and physical-culture reformers of the period, saw in muscle building a critical corrective to the forces of modernity and in particular to the modern division of labor and urban consumer practices that, in his view, were producing what he called the "half-built" bodies of young men *and* women.[89] But rather than a nostalgic call for a return to the healthy country life of an American agrarian past, Blaikie called into question the health benefits of agricultural and working-class labor, repetitive forms of labor that do not produce a proportionately developed body but rather an unbalanced and potentially diseased one.[90] More surprisingly, Blaikie also called into question the vaunted physical superiority of the athlete on the same grounds, noting the disproportionate development of one arm over another by baseball and tennis players, as well as the lack of overall conditioning provided by the halting, episodic nature of many team sports.[91] As Carolyn Thomas De La Peña has put it, "To Blaikie's eyes, the yeoman farmer, symbol of vigorous national health since Jefferson's time, and the athlete, a hero of strength since ancient Greece, were proven weak through the very accomplishments that once validated their strength."[92]

While many physical culturalists focused on restoring an enfeebled white middle class whose bodies were threatened by their relative separation from all forms of physical exertion, reformers such as Blaikie promoted their vision of physical culture among those whose bodies were most punished by the economic and social forms of late nineteenth-century modernity. The way to restore the half-built body thus lay not in the popular forms of "mimetic exercise" that simply imitated the motions of a typical form of labor but rather in exercises that encompassed the totality of labor itself, a totality only reproducible through the use of a system of weightlifting machines modeled largely on those of Dudley Sargent. The muscular body produced through Blaikie's system of pulleys and weights, many of which are still used today, was thus envisioned to be a body that does not hark back to a naturally fit past but rather looks forward to a technological future, a future in which muscle-building machines—and only muscle building machines—will perfect a new, essentially *artificial* body as the physical paragon of health and fitness, a body in which, as health reformer John Harvey Kellogg put it, "[e]very muscle is a living machine."[93] This generic, artificial body was not simply an atavistic recapitulation of some classical or primitive past, nor was it the sign of a history of labor or competitive play; rather it signified the history of its own disciplined self-creation, a reiterative history of simple, otherwise purposeless, repetitious movements whose only aim is to create the idealized image of the devotion to that muscle-building exercise. The generic, mass-producible body promised by Blaikie's system was one that promised, in other words, to recode or overwrite the physiological particularities of the body, particularities that had long defined racialized and gendered forms of exclusion in U.S. law and society in terms of the self-formed character.

For Gilman, the appeal of Blaikie's methods, as she describes them in her autobiography, was their defiance of the conventional assumptions regarding the intersections of masculine strength, race, class, and muscularity and their utopian promise to rebuild all the distorted and "half-built" bodies—particularly women's—produced by the division of labor.[94] Blaikie was one of a growing number of physical culturalists who advocated not only physical exercise but also muscle building and weightlifting for women and girls. In his chapter "Will Daily Physical Exercise for Girls Pay?" for example, Blaikie explicitly defends his program of women's muscle building by directly addressing the concerns that muscle building would rob women's bodies of their "essentially feminine" characteristics, arguing that muscle building remade women's bodies according to the aesthetic proportions and morphology portrayed in classical statuary, thereby restoring the beauty lost in the modern female body.[95] Although Blaikie's vision is frequently understood as simply a more refined version of conventional feminine grace, however, Blaikie goes on to redefine explicitly the terms of feminine grace, in his citation of an address to a local school for girls, in terms of a kind of muscular "squareness":

> As to human form, I might at once appeal to classical models admittedly beautiful, and simply urge that they have a certain *squareness* about them . . . *and this squareness means strength. Any muscle, well developed, is beautiful; muscular lines are lines of beauty everywhere. I have yet to hear admiration of a lady's arm that has not good biceps and triceps* under its coating of feminine adipose; and as to the *forearm,* the most beautiful specimens in flesh and blood that I know of are the forearms of pianistes, *who have muscles of steel from wrist to elbow.*[96]

The "squareness" produced by such "muscles of steel" were not of course valued by all. Early advocates of women's exercise such as Catherine Beecher, Gilman's great-aunt, had promoted the refinement of feminine grace rather than the acquisition of muscle through calisthenics, light gymnastics, "Indian clubs," and dance.[97] Such an approach to women's physical fitness had its roots in the pedagogical theories of Rousseau, who advocated exercise for girls in his famous educational treatise *Emile,* but only for the purpose of making young Sophie more attractive to young Emile, whose purpose in exercising was to increase his sense of autonomy.[98] Many physical culturists objected to exercises that actually increased the size of muscles in women, such as one reviewer of an early calisthenics book who complained that "[a]n arm swollen by physical exertion, a face suffused with the flush of violent effort, may be very becoming in a gentleman; but should we transfer them to a lady they would excite disgust rather than admiration."[99] The danger of such exercise and women's participation in athletics more broadly, according to Blaikie's mentor, Dudley Sargent, was quite simply that it "mannified" the "American woman." Perhaps the most important critic of women's muscularity in the current context was Gilman's first husband, Walter Stetson, who, in newspaper reports of their divorce, makes a point of complaining about "her overzealous pursuit of physical fitness, to the point that 'she became very muscular.'"[100]

For Gilman, the ability of the muscular female body to disrupt the conventional morphology of feminine beauty was precisely its personal and political appeal. While Gilman certainly lauded the benefits in health, grace, and strength acquired through physical exercise, she also emphasized throughout her literary and political writings how such a visibly muscular female body could redefine not just the corporeal semantics of femininity and masculinity but also the economic and political institutions they upheld. One of the most significant explorations of the forms of transgendered embodiment promised by a politics of physical culture can be found in Gilman's largely overlooked short story "If I Were a Man" (1914).[101] Gilman's fantastic tale charts the adventures of "pretty little Mollie Mathewson" as she mysteriously inhabits her husband's body one day and goes out into the world discovering what it is like to experience the world from within the body of a man. As if to underscore her belief in the power of the physical-culture movement to enact social and political change, Gilman published her story in Bernarr Macfadden's *Physical Culture* magazine rather than in her preferred venue of publication at this time, her own journal, the *Forerunner,* and followed it with a companion story the next month titled "If I Were a Woman," which traces the experiences of Mollie's husband, Gerald, as he spends the day in Mollie's body.[102]

In setting "If I Were a Man" almost entirely within Gerald's morning commute, as he walks to and then rides the streetcar to work, Gilman stages the story as a kind of drama of escape from the domestic confines of the home and her emblematic status as "a beautiful instance of what is reverentially called 'a true woman,'" an escape that takes her not only into the social world of men but more importantly into the tactile, somatic, and sensory pleasure of the male body as it moves between the articulated spaces of the public sphere.[103] Mollie's wish, at first glance, might thus be read as embodying a feminist political act, an act in which women lay claim to the full exercise of citizenship rights through a claim to the rights and privileges of men. Her desire to be a man, in other words, might more properly be understood as the desire to have the status *of* a man, to have the freedoms, rights, and entitlements afforded to men, this egalitarian fantasy of disembodied and therefore exchangeable persons being a common trope for articulating modern liberal citizenship itself.

Gilman's story thus might be understood as structured by a politics of disembodiment, one in which the equivalences marked by the exchangeability of bodies promises to free individuals from the social distinctions and legal prescriptions invested in the particularities of the gendered body.[104] For Mollie, such a disembodiment takes the form of the repossession by women of the athletic body, as Gerald in a conversation with other men on the streetcar about the "natural" inferiority of women's "physiology," is prompted by Mollie's consciousness within "him" to defend women's abstract "humanity" in terms of their athletic ability to "play our games."[105] This seeming "civilizing" of Gerald's masculine consciousness by the internal presence of Mollie, however, is one that also seemingly enables Mollie to remain peacefully within his body, for in dislodging the masculine perspective from Gerald's body, it seems that Mollie renders that body one in which she can, for the moment at least, peacefully reside. Gilman's story thus makes the path to humanist disembodiment lie through the reclamation of the athletic body, a reclamation that also kinesthetically reaccustoms Mollie to the world and to the "new and delightful feeling of being *the right size*. Everything fitted now. Her back snugly against the seat-back, her feet comfortably on the floor."[106]

In the story's account of the appropriation of the muscular body, "If I Were a Man" portrays in narrative form the central strategy of Gilman's feminist politics that she articulated in her early social treatise *Women and Economics* (1898), as well as in early novels such as *What Diantha Did* (1909–1910) and *The Crux* (1910) and finally in her feminist utopian novel *Herland* (1915). The target of Gilman's feminist critique in *Women and Economics* (1898) is not only the gendered division of labor but more importantly the "excessive sex-distinction" through which gender difference is itself historically produced, a distinction in which women's economic dependency is maintained through its cultivation as the sexualized traits of a vulnerable, dainty, and ultimately weak femininity.[107]

Gilman's critique of the excessive sex distinction of modern civilization, however, stems not simply from a political concern for the women whose lives are circumscribed by their sexualized status but rather from a more evolutionary concern over the greater harm heterosexual reproduction poses to the "character" of the "race" itself. Gilman's critique of the danger introduced by the *hetero*sexuality structured by gender difference, in other words, is oddly articulated as the threat of "difference" to racial purity itself:

> So we may trace from the sexuo-economic relation of our species not only definite evils in psychic development, bred severally in men and women, and transmitted indifferently to their offspring, but the innate perversion of character resultant from the moral miscegenation of two so diverse souls,—the unfailing shadow and distortion which has darkened and twisted the spirit of man from its beginnings. We have been injured in body and in mind by the too dissimilar traits inherited from our widely separated parents, but nowhere is the injury more apparent than in its ill effects upon the moral nature of the race.[108]

Gilman's evocation of the term *miscegenation* to describe the evolutionary effects of heterosexual reproduction within a conventional framework of gender difference uses one of the most charged images of racial purity to critique the conventional terms of heterosexual reproduction itself. Here the "degenerate" act of "miscegenation," however, is described as the "mixing" of two people not of different races but rather of different genders, the danger of such "mixing" being its production of an "innate perversion of character" within the child. As a perversion of "character," moreover, this "injury" is one that is inherited both "in body and in mind," as the warring and incoherently divergent genders of the child's parents thus become literally inscribed, through the medium of character, as a physically debilitating feature of "the race" itself. Gilman's radical refiguring of the discourse of degeneracy and race suicide thus locates its principle cause not in interracial reproduction or in the nervous "exhaustion" of modern life but rather in the forms of heterosexual reproduction occasioned by "civilized" economic institutions. Moreover, heterosexual sex, although distinguished from racial miscegenation, is nonetheless construed as having its own kinds of racial consequences, Gilman suggests, in the ways that it has "darkened" the white race with its "shadow" and threatened the racial integrity of the nation.[109] The impulse toward the eradication of gender "difference" in sexual relations that underlies Gilman's feminist politics, therefore, as a "humanist" strategy, also ultimately expresses a eugenic logic of racial nationalism.[110]

As a crucial element of her character-building agenda, the program of muscle building thus constitutes the problematic centerpiece of what we might call Gilman's queer racial nationalism in that it restores the reproductive fitness of "the race" through the establishment of a kind of queer sexuality, one premised not so much on the "sameness" of sex but rather on the undoing of gender as a determinate of sexuality altogether. Gilman explores the political limits of such a queer racial nationalism in her early novels *What Diantha Did* and *The Crux,* novels in which young female protagonists test the limits of heteronormativity in the liminal space of the Western frontier and the transformative material of their own muscular bodies. Gilman's first novel, *What Diantha Did,* tells the story of enterprising Diantha, who as a young woman flees the demands of father and fiancé in order to start her own housecleaning business on the West Coast.[111] Central to Gilman's vision of capitalist reform is "Union House," the boarding house Diantha establishes for her workers, an all-women's space that explores the possibilities of life not economically bound to the terms of reproductive heterosexuality. Unlike the utopian female world of *Herland,* however, this space turns out to be a tenuous one. As Union House establishes itself in the town, it comes increasingly under the suspicious gaze of the town's leading residents, particularly Mrs. Thaddler, who "had let fall far and wide her suspicions as to the character of Union House. 'It looks pretty queer to me!' she would say, confidentially. 'All those girls together, and no person to have any authority over them! Not a married woman in the house . . . Pretty queer doings I think."[112] Although the subtle imputation of these "queer doings" is that of prostitution, Gilman very carefully avoids confirming such a reading and instead steadily suggests that the "queer" threat of the girls is their happiness outside the heterosexual narrative altogether.

Although Gilman ultimately restores her protagonist Diantha to the narrative of heterosexual reproduction when her fiancé, Ross, comes to reclaim her, that restoration nonetheless functions also to establish the role of physical culture in the evolutionary improvement of racial character. Uneasy about Diantha's unconventional role as head of a very profitable business venture, Ross is finally convinced of the "wisdom" of Diantha's reengineering of the gender system after himself "proving" the Lamarckian thesis of acquired characteristics in a set of amateur experiments on different "races" of guinea pigs. Ross's experiments focus in particular on the powers of physical exercise to perfect, over the course of "several centuries of guinea-pig time," the overall fitness of his newly created "race" of guinea pigs.[113] These experiments catapult Ross not only to scientific fame but also to the realization, in the closing scene of the novel, that his seemingly "recent" discovery of the evolutionary "truth" of physical culture was in fact the truth that had long guided Diantha's entire life.

Gilman's emphasis on the centrality of physical exercise as the eugenic mechanism of national regeneration is echoed in her second novel, *The Crux*.[114] Although Gilman uses the narrative of heterosexual reproduction to articulate her eugenic vision of racial character in *What Diantha Did,* in *The Crux* the heterosexual narrative is more fully disrupted by the concerns of Gilman's racial nationalism. *The Crux* also tells the story of a young woman, Vivian Lane, who moves out west to Colorado but this time to start a boardinghouse for men with a group of her East Coast friends. The crisis of the story turns on Vivian's courtship with Morton Elder and her eventual discovery of his gonorrhea and syphilis. Even though Morton's "strong, noble character" is said to "grow under [Vivian's] helping hand" to the point that "she grew to feel a sort of ownership in this newly arisen character," Vivian ultimately must reject Morton because of the threat he, and the many "undesirable citizens" like him, pose to the nation's evolutionary stock.[115]

Recoiling from the "crime" that she nearly committed in marrying Morton, Vivian sets out, at the suggestion of her mentor, Dr. Jane Bellair, to perfect her body through a regimen of physical culture by becoming the teacher of "a class of rather delicate children and young girls, in physical culture."[116] This experience, which "had given her a fresh interest in her own body and the use of it," leads to a summer working at a newly founded girls' summer camp, a place where her physical-culture experiences in the wilds of the West lead to her bodily "rebuilding."[117] When she returns to town, it is Vivian's rebuilt body that reintegrates her into the heterosexual economy while also transforming the terms of its desire. As young "candid Percy" remarks to Dr. Hale, the man whom Vivian will eventually marry, "she's the finest woman I ever knew! . . . She's so beautiful and so clever, and so pleasant to everybody. She's *square*—like a man. . . . I'd marry her in a minute if I was good enough."[118]

And yet although *The Crux* seems to end with the eventual restoration of the muscular Vivian Lane to the marriage system, her marriage to the aloof older bachelor Dr. Hale is predicated on the subtle suggestion of his own queer sensibilities. When a group of prominent townsmen reflect on Dr. Hale's domestic life, they approvingly note that it has largely consisted of a "successive relay of boys": "His successive relay of boys, young fellows fresh from the East, coming from year to year and going from year to year as business called them, could and did give good testimony as to the home side of his character."[119] The boys have presumably been sent west from employment agencies to assist Dr. Hale, and yet the continuing discussion, in its syntactical confusion of gender roles, reinforces the more domestic nature of their "business" with Dr. Hale: "It was not in nature that they should speculate about him. As they fell in love and out again with the facility of so many Romeos, they discoursed among themselves as to his misogyny."[120] Although presumably these men turn to reflections on Hale's misogyny in order to understand their own experiences falling in and out of love with various women, the condensation and ambiguity of the passage confuses subjects and objects. Syntactically, these "many Romeos" whose speculations are "not in nature" could just as easily be falling in and out of love with Dr. Hale, or "many Romeos" could even refer to the "relay of boys" whose love for Hale also invites a discussion of his "misogyny" or dislike of women by the other men.

It is in Gilman's more radical, utopian novel *Herland*, however, the fuller implications of such a queer racial nationalism are most radically portrayed.[121] Rather than portraying various independence-seeking muscular women pushing the limits of conventional heterosexuality and the social, economic, and legal institutions that sustain it, *Herland* begins from the reverse point of view by centering on a hidden, all-female society and the question of whether it will, after the intrusion of men from the outside world, rejoin modern civilization in order "to re-establish a bi-sexual state for our people."[122] *Herland* tells the story of three American explorers who, on a scientific expedition in the "savage" territory of some unnamed foreign land, discover on a remote mountain plateau a highly developed society composed entirely of women capable of parthenogenic or "asexual" reproduction. Intrigued by the commercial potential in their first "contact" with this exotic society, the men imagine themselves as colonizers who will quickly be able to subdue this nation of weak women, their civilizing mission frequently read as an allegory of patriarchal domination and in particular of its intrication with modern imperial forms of colonial capitalism. As these men attempt to extend their sexual and economic dominion over this society of women, however, they are repeatedly and resoundingly defeated and are themselves subjected to a very different civilizing process by these powerful "wonder-women."[123] From the men's initial capture by the curiously strong "Amazonian" women to their slow and uneven education in the language, culture, government, and industry of Herland society to their experimental pairing with female partners, *Herland* develops its feminist critique by invoking, yet also reversing, the framework of a kind of gendered civilizing mission. Instead of men embodying the fully civic dimensions of a civilizing authority, Gilman charges women with reforming the incipient and regressive savagery of masculinity, a role that invokes the traditional character-building role of feminine virtue while also rearticulating it within an explicitly imperial framework. The overall narrative trajectory of the novel has thus been read as a feminist rejoinder to the colonizing aspects of patriarchal domination, and in particular of its reliance on liberal forms of private property and a gendered division of labor, but one that, in its national imperative to "tame and train" these captured men, nonetheless retains and affirms its imperial logic.[124]

Gilman's invocation of the imperial logic of the civilizing mission of these muscular women as vehicle of her feminist critique, however, is, as Alys Weinbaum and others have argued, freighted with the racial politics that animated late nineteenth-century forms of U.S. imperialism.[125] This is most apparent in Gilman's choice of geographical setting for the story. Though the location of Herland is never explicitly named, the iconography of Gilman's geographic portrait points to those "remote" areas of eastern Africa approached from the Nile River, where, for example, Pauline Hopkins locates her very different hidden civilization in the novel *Of One Blood*.[126] Gilman's situating of her feminist civilizing mission within—but also literally walled off from—this metaphorical Africa serves a number of important purposes. Most importantly, Gilman identifies the necessary subject of the civilizing mission as the very muscular masculinity that, according to Theodore Roosevelt, Josiah Strong, and others, exercised itself through the "strenuous" exploration and colonization of foreign lands. It is through the very impulse of colonial conquest, in other words, that the men themselves become conquered and civilized, yet by a hidden feminine force that they encounter not in the home but only in that extranational, colonial scene. Thus while evoking the traditional, civilizing role of feminine virtue within the domestic relation, Gilman refigures that role by transposing it outside the borders of the nation while mobilizing it through the muscular bodies of these "Amazonian" women.

The muscular bodies of the Herlandian women are central not only to the civilizing of these particular men but also to the utopian promise of a Herlandian reform of the Western world. What stands out most in the men's initial discovery by three Herlandian women in the opening scene is the women's striking physical form and athletic ability, a form the men initially exoticize as that of fascinating, birdlike, "arboreal" children. But as the men are captured and exposed to the society as a whole, they realize that the "strong trained athletic bodies," shortly cropped hair, and "sturdy forms" of all the women are indicative of their timeless and superior culture, a cultural completeness emblematized by their ageless, androgynous fitness: "They were not young. They were not old. They were not, in the girl sense, beautiful, they were not in the least ferocious. . . . Yet they were not old women. Each was in the full bloom of rosy health, erect, serene, standing sure-footed and light as any pugilist."[127]

The women's physical strength is what is used immediately to overwhelm the men, but over time this physical strength also overwhelms and reshapes, to different degrees, the men's own desire, as well as their sense of their own masculinity, an undoing of gender that drives the romance plot and is the precondition of the restoration of heterosexual reproduction within Herland society. This reconfiguration of desire, however, is also figured as an act of racial subjugation and purification that will civilize the racialized "savagery" of the men. The threat of this masculine savagery is most emblematic in the character of the "brutish" and muscular Terry, who attempts to use physical violence to reestablish "by sheer brute force" his sexual dominance, despite his claim that the men "are not Savages," in the attempted rape of Alima, an act that results in his expulsion from Herland.[128] The greater danger of Terry, however, and of the men more generally, is not the violence of their physical strength, which is easily outmatched by the powerful Herlandian women, but the danger their masculinity, as a form of racial "savagery," poses to the eugenically maintained "Aryan stock" of the Herlandian nation.[129] Rather than mere metaphor for a kind of natural, inner, instinctual strength, the "savagery" idolized in muscular masculinity becomes for Gilman itself a degenerate, dangerously miscegenated racial form, particularly in its espousal of the therapeutic effects of contact with and engrafting of primitive strength onto the civilized body. As Terry laughingly boasts in the song he hums just before the attempted rape, this defiant savagery is something he "learned from the yellow and black," a form of racial contamination of "Terry's character" that can only be undone through an undoing of masculinity itself.[130] Thus the ungendering of these American men, a process to which two of them, Jeff and particularly Van, more successfully submit, is figured by Gilman as simultaneously a process of racial purification that will enable the advanced Herlandian society ultimately to rejoin and uplift the precarious and tottering civilization of the West while also giving it a firmer foothold and "homeland" out in, but not among, the savage nations that surround it. Maintaining that barrier between themselves and the surrounding dark savagery was as crucial to the development of the Herland civilization, in other words, as purging the more embedded savagery of the three men will presumably be to their future development and their reunification with the rest of civilized society.

Charlotte Perkins Gilman's invocation of the power of muscle to reform the character of the nation shows both the critical power of the discourse of character to challenge the cultural codes through which the meaning and experience of the body are regulated and the ways the discourse of character can function to reinforce—even in and through that same critical gesture—the hierarchical distribution and regulation of bodies in the public sphere. Like the muscular iconography of the *National Police Gazette,* whose critical destabilizations of gender and sexuality are largely circumscribed within a visual economy of whiteness, Gilman's work raises important questions about what we might call the intersectional symmetry of race and gender in the discourse of muscle in particular and in the discourse of character more broadly, and it provides an important reminder of the ways that claims to the abstract, disembodied equality described by the "content of character," feminist or otherwise, can also inscribe new forms of exclusion that call for a critical reexamination of the humanist discourse of civil rights more broadly.

The vestment of Sojourner Truth's powerful character in the visual signifiers of her physical strength was thus, as I hope this chapter has shown, a strategy of political and social critique that was freighted with many paradoxes and dangers. For many physical culturalists and social reformers, this lodging of character more fully in the muscular body was meant to underscore character's plastic and reformable nature—and thereby its capacity to transcend the contingent determinations of race, class, and gender. The rhetoric of character thus enabled many physical culturalists, feminists, social scientists, and fiction writers to conceive of the body as a product of personal will rather than a fixed indicator of a gendered identity. And yet, although physiognomic theories of character eschewed many of the surface indicators of race, and in particular the unreliability of what Franz Fanon terms the "epidermal racial schema," these theories also gave a deeper physiological sanction to concepts of racial difference based on even more arbitrary interpretations of the body.[131] Racial scientists, criminologists, ethnologists, and cultural nationalists developed new taxonomies of racial difference, based on a broad array of interpretive, statistical, and visual measures of the body that were used not only to shore up social and political hierarchies of racial difference but also to articulate more firmly the categories of gender and class in terms of a physiognomy of race.

The ability of muscle to refigure the meaning of the racialized body was perhaps most limited by its association with class and labor. Muscle's ability to signify character was premised, as we have seen, on its ability to figure a body mobilized as the agent of its own historicity rather than one that is the merely contingent product of history. The power of muscle to signify character was thus magnified by a body's perceived distance from the historical forces that most fundamentally shaped bodies, that is, by a body's distance in particular from a history of physical labor. Thus although critical gestures such as Sojourner Truth's were meant to make visible the historical legacy of racialized labor in the United States while also testifying to the power of character necessary to overcome the body-destroying aspects of such labor, the critical power to make visible that legacy also undercut its force as a sign of character. While a historical sign of the strength of character necessary to endure and create in conditions of oppressive labor, muscle was often thereby dismissed by the same token as the sign of one's "fitness" for such labor, regardless of whether that fitness was seen as derived from a "primitive" essence or constituted through the experience of subjection itself. In Frederick Douglass's depiction of the "great character" of Madison Washington in his novella *The Heroic Slave* (1852), for example, Douglass uses muscle to represent the power of Washington's undeniable masculinity:

> Glimpses of this great character are all that can now be presented. . . . Madison was of manly form. Tall, symmetrical, round, and strong. In his movements he seemed to combine, with the strength of a lion, a lion's elasticity. His torn sleeves disclosed arms like polished iron. His face was "black, but comely." His eye, lit with emotion, kept guard under a brow as dark and as glossy as the raven's wing. His whole appearance betokened Herculean strength; yet there was nothing savage or forbidding in his aspect.[132]

And yet Douglass also recognizes the fatal circularity of such an appeal to muscle in the *Life and Times of Frederick Douglass* (1893), in which he applauds the power of "the naked iron arm of the negro" as that which will revitalize a moribund, post-Reconstruction-era South while also recognizing that "[t]he standing apology for slavery was based upon a knowledge of this fact."[133]

In order to challenge the interpretative schemas and cultural discourses through which the body was invested with racial meaning in the late nineteenth century, many activists and reformers such as Douglass thus sought to reclaim and redefine the signifiers of class identity through a reappropriation of the self-historicizing function of the rhetoric of character. The rhetoric of character thus emerged in the late nineteenth century, despite its role in articulating racist typologies, as a crucial instrument for challenging the racist representations, structural inequalities, and discriminatory practices of the post-Reconstruction period. Although these critiques frequently focused on the "content of character" rather than the color of skin as a measure of identity and social value, they nonetheless did not detach character from the signifying power of the body but rather focused on reappropriating the class and gender discourses that shaped the racial meaning and significance of the body. The next chapter considers the role of the rhetoric of character in shaping the discourse of what Kevin Gaines has called "racial uplift" in the late nineteenth century by turning to the work of prominent author, editor, and essayist Pauline Hopkins and in particular to her interest in reading and recovering from the body a history that is not bound up with either the "inherited character" of racial science *or* the history-eclipsing assertions of the self-fashioning character. This chapter focuses in particular on the challenges Hopkins's work poses to the conventional discourse of racial uplift itself and its reliance on normative concepts of class and gender to assert and defend a vision of the self-fashioned character. Pauline Hopkins's interest, I argue, is in recovering character as a document in the social history and cultural construction of the body, a history so frequently erased by both the physiological reductions of the racial science and the philanthropic promise of racial uplift.

4

"A Story Written on Her Face"

Pauline Hopkins's Unmaking of the Inherited Character of Race

> Natural history must provide, simultaneously, a certain *designation* and a controlled *derivation*. And just as the theory of structure superimposed articulation and the proposition so that they became one and the same, so the theory of *character* must identify the values that designate and the area in which they are derived. . . . The structure selected to be the locus of pertinent identities and differences is what is termed the *character*.
>
> —Michel Foucault, "Character," in *The Order of Things: An Archaeology of the Human Sciences*[1]

> The concept of character will have to be divested of those features that constitute its erroneous connection to that of fate. This connection is effected by the idea of a network that can be tightened by knowledge at will into a dense fabric, for this is how character appears to superficial observation. Along with the broad underlying traits, the trained eye of the connoisseur of men is supposed to perceive finer and closer connections, until what looked like a net is tightened into cloth.
>
> —Walter Benjamin, "Fate and Character"[2]

In January 1905, the editor of the periodical the *Voice of the Negro* published a series of short "Messages" intended to give advice to its readers on the important question of "the betterment of the race."[3] The short and prescriptive messages, in their effort to encompass the "republic of thought" spanning "both sides of the color line," were solicited from a range of esteemed and "representative white men as well as those of the race." And yet although the editors strove to represent many different "schools of thought," what is most striking about these messages is the common emphasis they place on the role of character in the project of racial uplift. As Rev. H.S. Bradley advocates, "put character above color and principle above pigment cells. Let each individual determine to deserve the good will of the other race."[4] "Character tells, money talks," according to William Hayes Ward, editor of the *New York Independent,* for "after all that can be said the substance of it is *character.* If the white people of the South all had character and the Negroes all had character there would be no trouble."[5] For William H. Council, head of a southern industrial school, the maxim which comes second only to "Hold onto God in all good faith" is "Get character. Get brains. Get dollars. They all count for something in any people."[6] And for Kelly Miller, the foundation of any personal or political action is character, for "[t]he salvation of any overshadowed race will depend upon what they are rather than what they do, upon character more than enterprise, upon endurance rather than endeavor."[7]

The prominence of the rhetoric of character within what has been called the "racial uplift ideology" of the postbellum period was of course not limited to the pages of the *Voice of the Negro.*[8] Getting, having, building, and perhaps most importantly displaying character had been seen by many social reformers as critical to the project of addressing class and racial inequality throughout the nineteenth century, and character was valued as a particularly powerful instrument of reform in the abolitionist movement as well as postemancipation projects of racial uplift.[9] By the time the editor of the *Voice of the Negro* solicited his "Messages" from "representative men" drawn from both sides of the color line, however, the question of character's role in challenging racial inequality in the United States was increasingly dominated by "two different schools of thought," the two schools of thought, that is, that had by that time become prominently identified with W.E.B. Du Bois and Booker T. Washington.[10] The famous debate between these two "representative men" that has dominated understandings of the politics of racial uplift at the turn of the century has usually been understood as a clash driven by their differing educational and political philosophies. But what these opening examples suggest is that this debate is more fundamentally structured by a disagreement over the form and function of character as a vehicle of social reform, a disagreement premised on two different strategies of articulating and asserting class character.

For Booker T. Washington, character was premised on the achievement of an economically defined class status measured in terms of possessions, property, and professional prestige. These material accomplishments signified one's successful ascent up the economic class ladder as a result of character building and thus were seen by Washington and others as an implicit refutation of the cultural stereotypes and discourses of racial inferiority and degeneracy. Washington's vision of character thus echoed and drew in many ways upon the class rhetoric of the success manual. Founded on the belief, as he puts it in his own character-building manual, *Character Building* (1903), that "character is power," Washington promoted a program of character building founded on the socially and personally empowering effects of labor and the industrial values of personal enterprise, thrift, and self-discipline.[11] For W.E.B. Du Bois, character was identified more with a culturally defined class status measured by the cultivated manner and intellect, professional accomplishment, and social, cultural, or political influence that were acquired through higher education and professional training. Such a training not only provided the social and cultural knowledges that were powerful weapons in the struggle for equal rights but also produced a class of talented individuals who embodied in their manner and accomplishments the higher "culture and character" of modern "civilization" that confounded racial stereotypes, while also mediating and enabling the formation of character in the less educated masses.[12] Drawing on an aesthetics of character rooted in republican discourse, Du Bois thus shared with contemporary literary realists a belief in the disclosive power of the "good judge of character," a power he exemplified in his literary writings as well as in his extensive sociological studies of the subtleties of race, class, and gender in the formation of character. In such works as *Health and Physique,* for example, Du Bois mobilizes such an interpretive capacity both to invoke and also to challenge conventional strategies of character detection by employing the poses and conventions of the criminological mug shot, as well as Francis Galton's character-revealing techniques of composite photography, to provide a kind of visual counterarchive of racial character (see figure 13).

Although these two men fundamentally differed in their views on the formative dimensions and signifying aspects of character in the project of racial uplift, differences that can in part be traced to the different character-building traditions on which they drew, they both reappropriated the cultural work of these character-building traditions by focusing on character's power to challenge and refigure the cultural meaning, social status, and political significance of the racialized body in the United States. For

Fig. 13. "Typical Negro-Americans," in W.E.B. Du Bois, *The Health and Physique of the Negro American* (Atlanta: Atlanta University Press, 1906), 5. In a separate section of the book Du Bois provides captions for each of the photographs that briefly delineated the character traits of each of the individuals pictured.

Washington and Du Bois, as well as for writers of character-building and etiquette manuals such as Joseph R. Gay, Elias M. Woods, Silas X. Floyd, Emma Azalia Hackley, and Sarah Estelle Haskin, the appeal to character was much more than a strategy of "self-representation" aimed at correcting the system of stereotypes used to justify the racist formations of the postemancipation era.[13] The acquisition of character was meant to challenge the very epistemological and semiotic foundations of race itself. Such a challenge was grounded in the ability of the rhetoric of character to unmoor the meaning of race from the physiological body and to rearticulate racial identity in terms of the class indicators that signaled the presence or absence of the talents and capabilities of character.

The emphasis on the concept of character in the discourse of racial uplift might thus be understood as part of a broader cultural shift in the late nineteenth century in which, as Cathy Boeckmann has carefully argued, the rhetoric of character was increasingly used to articulate and mediate understandings of racial identity in the United States. The belief in the power of character to replace and redeploy the signs of race was, as Boeckmann demonstrates, paradoxically bound up with the late nineteenth-century development of "racial science" in the emerging social sciences and in particular the theory of "neo-Lamarckian culture-evolution."[14] The most important feature of racial science, Boeckmann argues, was that through it the "language of race" found a new, more pervasively elaborated, and ultimately more unpredictable home in the "language of character." Such a reconceptualization of race in terms of character was a response to an increased destabilization of the category of race and in particular to the unreliability of visual signs as indicators of racial difference toward the end of the nineteenth century. As Boeckmann argues, "the need to locate the supposed essence of racial difference fell upon the concept of inherited racial character—a racial essence that is connected to the features of race but which can also be extricated from them."[15] The concept of character not only provided the semantic and epistemological resources to articulate racial difference in terms of behavioral and cultural traits (rather than fixed bodily marks); it also was able to preserve the logic of kinship, inheritance, and "blood" on which legal and social determinations of race relied. Thus while the discourse of character detached race from the surface features of the visible body through which it had been traditionally construed, it also lodged race more deeply in the body by identifying it with the subtle signs and manners of character.

In Boeckmann's account of the development of racial science, the capacity to reconceive race in terms of inherited character depended on the appropriation of French biologist Jean-Baptiste Lamarck's theory of the inheritability of acquired traits. Though largely discredited in 1904 by August Weissman's theory of chromosomal inheritance, Lamarck's theory had a profound impact on the understanding of race in the United States because it was able to theorize the connections between culture and biology in Darwin's theory of evolution and thereby resolve many of the paradoxes that arose when Darwin's theory was used to explain the evolutionary and historical development of racial difference.[16] Darwin's theory had itself radically challenged the notion of "polygenism," which had emerged as the prevailing theory of racial difference in the first half of the nineteenth century. In the polygenist racial theory of Louis Agassiz and Josiah Nott, for example, racial difference was a reflection of the multiple origins of human creation; the human species was created in multiple and distinct moments of creation, and the original differences of race were preserved and passed on as an inherent and unchanging biological essence.[17] Darwin's evolutionary theory, however, in its account of the physiological development of species over time, challenged such a notion of a static and ultimately unchanging racial essence. Racial "scientists" of the late 1860s and 1870s thus returned to a "monogenetic" account of racial difference premised on the historical malleability of character in relation to its environment. This revised version of the theological monogenism that held that all races descended from Adam and Eve was now able to posit a single origin to the human species while accounting for the differential evolution of "races" over time, with different races being conceived either as the product of different evolutionary trajectories (visualized as different branches on a tree) or, more commonly, as developmental stages on a single evolutionary ladder.

In racial scientists' appropriation of evolutionary theory, however, they adopted the ideas of Lamarck to make one very important modification to Darwin's theory. Lamarck's innovation was to argue that individual traits acquired by a person during his or her lifetime could be passed down as inherited biological traits. Uncomfortable with the mere element of chance as the motor of evolutionary development, most racial scientists in the United States seized on the Lamarckian principle of acquired traits in order to integrate and justify the role of human agency and even individual choice in the mechanism of evolutionary "progress."[18] Evolutionary progress did not have to wait for the chance event of mutation, and the subsequent testing of that mutation by the environment, but rather could be propelled by the attempts of individuals to perfect themselves and thereby "the race" by bringing the sheer force of their will to bear on their own and others' bodies. Racial difference, in this model, could thus be ascribed to the progressive efforts of a particular racial group, and culture could now be seen as the evolutionary medium through which those efforts were made and expressed. The power of Lamarck's theory was that not only could it account for the transmission and inheritance of cultural forms as a kind of racial capital, but it could also envision cultural "achievement" or "civilization" as an evolutionary indicator of racial development. As Joseph Le Conte put it,

> [O]ne of the most important recent modifications of our philosophy of life, forced upon us by the theory of evolution, is the recognition of the fact that a very large part of every man's intellectual and moral capital comes by way of inheritance.... [T]he inherited bank account is continually growing from generation to generation by small additions from individual acquisition. The growing inheritance constitutes the evolution of the race.[19]

Because the concept of character already connoted a process of self-formation in relation to cultural and biological forces, a process that was inscribed into the behavior and comportment of the body itself, it was seized on by racial scientists as the definitive term for this process of racial evolution and inheritance. What character was able to articulate, in the neo-Lamarckian redefinition of evolutionary inheritance, in other words, was the essential *historicity* of race.

The irony of this neo-Lamarckian turn to the concept of character by racial scientists was that it thereby also provided an important weapon for challenging the racist policies and laws that racial science was often developed to justify. In transforming "the question of race into a question of character," racial science recognized the essential historicity of race and thus recognized individuals' capacity to transform or exceed any of the biological or cultural forms through which their racial identity might be defined. This capacity of character both to articulate and yet to destabilize the category of race was what made it such an attractive and powerful weapon for challenging the legal prescriptions, social forms, and cultural representations of racial inequality. The embrace of this substitution of the concept of character for that of race by reformers such as Washington and Du Bois, however, had two important effects. First, these efforts to historicize evolution with character had the effect of dehistoricizing character, of positing character as the medium through which individuals could transcend their inherited traits and characteristics through character building. Thus the embrace of the rhetoric of character as a strategy of racial uplift often had the effect of eclipsing history with the power of self-determination. Second, these appropriations of the rhetoric of character also inherited its broader disciplinary implications and strategies. Thus the use of the rhetoric of character to challenge racial hierarchies was often premised on an implied or explicit endorsement of class and gender hierarchies.

One can see this latter danger, for example, in the work of José Martí, the famous Cuban revolutionary who worked as a journalist in exile in New York in the 1880s. Influenced in part by his extensive readings of Emerson, Martí frequently employed the rhetoric of character to articulate the fracturing and unifying forces in Latin American societies at a time of decolonization as well as U.S. imperialism.[20] In such works as "Our America," "The Indians in the United States," "My Race," and "The Truth about the United States," for example, Martí explicitly imagines character as the analytical category that will replace the physiological or biological classifications of race. In "My Race," Martí critiques those forms of social and political affiliation based on the category of race by arguing instead that

> blacks, like whites, can be grouped according to their character—timid or brave, self-abnegating or egotistical—into the diverse parties of mankind. . . . In short, it is the similarity of character—a source of unity far superior to the internal relations of the varying colors of men, whose different shades are sometimes in opposition to each other—that commands and prevails in the formation of parties. An affinity of character is more powerful than an affinity of color.[21]

Martí's substitution of the category of character for that of race, however, also employs a vernacular of class and gender difference. In "My Race," such a vernacular is used to privilege the traits of the peasant class with regard to their "merit" as possessors of character, and in essays such as "Our America," Martí valorizes the masculinity of such a "natural man" who stands in contrast to the feminized figure of the European-identified upper-class "runts" with "their puny arms, with bracelets and painted nails, the arms of Madrid or of Paris."[22]

Pauline Hopkins, in her novel Contending Forces (1900), similarly takes up the rhetoric of character to challenge the representational schemas

through which race is defined and the determinist discourse of racial inheritance from which the cultural meaning of the body was so frequently
derived.[23] But she also seeks to call into question the class and gender presumptions of the rhetoric of character that are so commonly evoked in the
discourse of racial uplift as an alternative to the evolutionary concept of
racial inheritance. Hopkins does this by structuring her novel as an important reflection on, and critique of, the character-building strategies of
the racial-uplift movement itself in the form of its two most representative "characters": Booker T. Washington and W.E.B. Du Bois. Through her
thinly veiled representations of Washington and Du Bois in the characters
of, respectively, Dr. Arthur Lewis and William Smith, Hopkins not only
dramatically restages their famous debate over the form and function of
racial uplift but uses literary strategies of characterization to reconceive in
dramatic form the role of character as itself an instrument of racial uplift
and to recover from the rhetoric of character a concept of historicity detached from the delimiting signifiers of class and gender.

Hopkins tests the limits of the concept of character promoted by these
representative men by making the novel turn on their capacity to recognize one very important signifier of character and story of racial formation, the "story written on the face" of the enigmatic, mixed-race heroine
Sappho Clark. Cast within the narrative confines of the "tragic mulatta"
tale, the story written on the face of Sappho Clark is the story that the
narrative is in a fundamental way designed to tell. That story, however, is
a very complicated one indeed, for it tells not only of the historical origins
of the Smith family in a transnational scene of mercantile capitalism but
also of Sappho's own abduction and rape as a young woman by her white
uncle. Hopkins's mixed-race heroine does not simply signify in her body
the historical legacy of sexual possession under slavery; she is forced to repeat the violence of that legacy as her own sexual violation and social degradation and wear both that violation *and* that history as the enigmatic
"beauty" of that "story written on her face."

But in making Sappho also into a woman of "sterling character," Hopkins measures what her classical recuperation as mother and wife costs as
a historical restitution of slavery's fracturing of African American kinship. In her complicated reworking of the "tragic mulatta" narrative, Hopkins interrogates how indeed that story is recognized as the beauty of the
mixed-race heroine by the two competing male characters, a recognition
that however redoubles the historical injury of race in the name of racial
uplift. Hopkins's innovation in *Contending Forces* is thus to cast these two

representative men as characters in a sentimental romance plot in order to ask how the logic of character they represent might work, as she puts it in her preface, to "raise the stigma of degradation from the race." In framing her own novel as an effort to raise "the stigma of degradation"—a phrase used by Washington and Du Bois to figure the broader effort to challenge degrading racial stereotypes with counterrepresentations of exemplary character—Hopkins thus asks whether the strategies of character building and character representation articulated by Washington and Du Bois can encompass what "raising the stigma of degradation" meant for many African American women writers, namely, making visible the historical legacy and cultural implications of sexual possession and rape under slavery, which renders women's bodies intelligible only under the sign of degradation.[24] Can, in other words, racial uplift's historicizing of race through the concept of character make intelligible the ways that historical formations of race, gender, and class come together to mark women's bodies as degraded? Can racial uplift "expose," as Dana Luciano puts it in her reading of Hopkins's account of racial melancholia in her later work *Of One Blood*, "the psychic impact of American constructions of race on African American subject formation"?[25]

"Lifting While We Climb": Race and the Uplift Ideology

When the National Association of Colored Women, formed in 1896, took as its motto "Lifting While We Climb," it utilized what was perhaps the most powerful figure for African American reform movements throughout the nineteenth century and into the twentieth, the figure of racial uplift.[26] The racial-uplift ideology, as Kevin Gaines has argued in *Uplifting the Race*, was articulated in terms of a narrative of ascent that was both material and spiritual. Late nineteenth-century articulations of racial uplift, Gaines argues, encompassed both a process of economic, political, and social upward mobility and the more personal process of spiritual, moral, and intellectual self-regeneration conceived in terms of the liberation theology of early antislavery folk religious practices.[27] As an ideology of social reform, racial uplift thus entailed two distinct but interdependent processes. Uplift described in the first instance an external process of upward mobility or a rise in economic or social position, but in also evoking the liberation theology of personal transcendence over one's material circumstances, uplift connoted a deeply personal and often arduous process of spiritual self-improvement. More importantly, the racial-uplift ideology articulated the important connections between these two processes by imagining how such an upward mobility was dependent on a process of mental, moral, and even physical self-improvement. In conceiving of upward mobility and self-improvement as highly interdependent processes, the "narratives of ascent," as Henry Louis Gates terms them, that structured the racial-uplift ideology thus put a defining emphasis on the importance of an education in character.[28] As Joseph Gay's "handbook for self-improvement," *Progress and Achievements of the 20th Century Negro* (1913), put it, "here is the keynote to success—character. We do not know what character is, we know only that it accomplishes results."[29] Appropriations of the rhetoric of character by manuals such as Gay's, however, not only emphasize the uplifting effects of character building but also underscore the importance of an education in reading and representing character as necessary to combating the particular obstacles to upward mobility, such as discrimination, disenfranchisement, economic exploitation, and organized violence, that African Americans faced in the post-Reconstruction era. Thus in addition to chapters on "Developing Moral Character," "Physical Training," "The Road to Success," "Opportunity for Business Life," and "The Four 'Learned Professions,'" *Progress and Achievements* offers concrete lessons in "How to Read Character" that incorporate principles of phrenology, palmistry, and anatomy and detailed lessons in etiquette and "impressions made on the eye."

Although a wide range of responses and reformist philosophies emerged in response to the intensified attacks on African American character, civil rights, and bodily welfare in the 1890s, by century's end it was the two competing positions—and public clashes—of Booker T. Washington and W.E.B. Du Bois that came to dominate the discussion of racial uplift in the United States. Ever since professor and political commentator Kelly Miller's characterization of the Washington–Du Bois debate in terms of a conflict between "conservatives" and "radicals" within the racial-uplift movement, scholars have tended to construe the positions of Washington and Du Bois (and their many surrogates) as hypostasized, antithetical inversions of each other and also to represent that antithesis as definitive of, or essential to, the very notion of racial uplift itself.[30] Whereas Washington counsels submission and accommodation to the decline in civil and political rights in the name of a gradual economic rebuilding of the African American community "from the bottom up," Du Bois is said to argue for an assertive and immediate public defense of those rights by a well-educated and professional elite who lift the community "from the top down." Whereas Washington emphasizes an educational regimen of industrial training targeted at the "masses" of African Americans, Du Bois emphasizes a university education for select individuals of "talent and ability."[31]

As Gates and many others have pointed out, most early histories of the period have created an image of an African American community completely divided into "two supposedly irreconcilable camps . . . with Du Bois and Booker T. Washington serving as exemplars and chief spokesmen for these two schools of thought."[32] As Gaines has more critically argued,

> historians have generally framed black thought and leadership narrowly, stressing the opposition between self-help and civil rights agitation, as embodied by Booker T. Washington and W.E.B. Du Bois, respectively. Civil rights liberalism remains the focus of such dichotomous—and masculinist—constructions of black leadership, to the exclusion of more democratic conceptions of uplift.[33]

Indeed, as Hazel Carby has pointed out, even such a critique of the exclusionary aspects of the emphasis on these two "representative men" has itself functioned as the occasion for an ongoing fetishization of their representative status.[34] But a reconsideration of the Washington and Du Bois debate can also reveal the broader tensions produced by the rhetoric of character within the racial-uplift ideology and thus make visible the ways that writers such as Pauline Hopkins were responding not simply to the dominating presence and political strategies of these two representative figures but rather to the limits of their reliance on the rhetoric of character itself.

Booker T. Washington's program of racial uplift draws on the discourse of character building as it was developed particularly in the success and character-building manuals of the postbellum period, but it also adapts that discourse to the more specific problems of racial discrimination by challenging the forms of character representation that sustained those problems. In the collection of lectures Washington published as the book *Character Building,* Washington articulates a model of character building that is, for example, meant "to speak straight to the hearts of our students and teachers and visitors concerning the problems and questions that confront them in the South."[35] Rather than defining character as the product of a cultivating exposure to the high cultural artifacts of civilized society, as Du Bois does, Washington lays claim to an equally entrenched, and at times overlapping, tradition that associated character with commercial and worldly success. Indeed, Washington's own success was often cited as the surest mark not only of his own enterprising character but also of his character-building program.[36] In invoking the ideology of the enterprising, successful character, Washington defends his program of industrial training both as a character-building program and as the means for mobilizing the semiotic power of character within a politics of recognition. Industrial education not only builds the "constructive ability" necessary for economic, social, and political advancement but also creates a class of successful individuals whose property and position will spectacularly attest to the character of the race itself.[37] Thus Washington's famous and highly criticized abdication of "political claims" in the Atlanta compromise was grounded in his confidence that such claims could more surely be advanced through the "slow but sure influences that proceed from the possession of property, intelligence, and high character."[38]

Character is mobilized in the service of racial uplift, on Washington's account, through the formative power of labor in that labor not only builds character but also produces the objects and possessions that will come to "represent" powerfully the virtue and value of that character. Washington's autobiographical *Up from Slavery* not only makes clear the central and formative role of labor in the production of character but also situates his own life story within an entrepreneurial character ideal figured by the narrative arc of a self-reliant rise from rags to riches.[39] The benefits of labor, in other words, derive not simply from the money that it earns but rather from the character that it builds: "At Hampton I not only learned that it was not a disgrace to labour, but learned to love labour, not alone for its financial value, but for labour's own sake and for the independence and self-reliance which the ability to do something which that world wants done brings. . . . At Hampton the student was constantly making the effort through the industries to help himself, and that very effort was of immense value in character-building" (*Up from Slavery*, 48–49, 58).

But the real power of the character produced through labor was, in Washington's view, its ability to secure the very rights of citizenship that Du Bois and others criticize him for forsaking. For character not only had to be formed, but it had also to be made visible in the court of public opinion as the counterfactual challenge to the racist representations of an inherently degraded African American character. And the best way to make character visible was, in Washington's view, by materializing it in "the visible, the tangible" productions of a well-trained industrial and business class:

> My experience is that there is something in human nature which always makes an individual recognize and reward merit, no matter under what colour of skin merit is found. I have found, too, that it is the visible, the tangible, that goes a long ways in softening prejudices. The actual sight of a first-class house that a Negro has built is ten times more potent than pages of discussion about a house that he ought to build, or perhaps could build. (102)

The phenomenological reality of property, in Washington's account, "softens prejudice" because it mobilizes a way of seeing in which "the colour of skin" is eclipsed by the shining value of character itself, a way of seeing in which the merits of character call forth an inevitable and unavoidable recognition *and* reward. Felt as a kind of pleasure and experienced as a duty, the capacity to recognize merit is conceived as a feature of human nature itself, and the task of racial uplift is to appeal directly to this inherent faculty of character recognition. The recognition Washington seeks does not simply see an individual's particular traits of character but rather sees the inherent value of character itself, a value that merits recognition because it embodies value: "the whole future of the Negro rested largely upon the question as to whether or not he should make himself, through his skill, intelligence, and character, of such undeniable value to the community in which he lived that the community could not dispense with his presence" (132–133). More important in the project of racial uplift than the building of character, in other words, is transforming that character into an undeniably tangible and valuable fact of the economic order, a fact that not only testifies to the presence of character but that thereby proves the inalienable right to political and social equality:

> The wisest among my race understand that the agitation of questions of social equality is the extremest folly, and that progress in the enjoyment of all privileges that will come to us must be the result of severe and constant struggle rather than of artificial forcing. No race that has anything to contribute to the markets of the world is long in any degree ostracized, ... while from representations in these buildings of the product of field, of forest, of mine, of factory, letters, and art, much good will come,

yet far above and beyond material benefits will be that higher good, that, let us pray God, will come, in a blotting out of sectional differences and racial animosities and suspicions, in a determination to administer absolute justice, in a willing obedience among all classes to the mandates of law. This, this, coupled with our material prosperity, will bring into our beloved South a new heaven and a new earth. (146)

With the publication of *The Souls of Black Folk* in 1903, the Washington–Du Bois debate broke dramatically onto the public stage. In the chapter "Of Mr. Booker T. Washington and Others," W.E.B. Du Bois directly challenges both Washington's accommodationist stance and the educational philosophy on which it was based. While Du Bois lays out in considerable sociological and historical detail the practical limitations of Washington's "program," however, his ultimate concern is with how this program fails as a method of character building. Nowhere is this more apparent than in Du Bois's critique of Washington's educational agenda. Although Du Bois does recognize the importance of industrial training, particularly for overcoming the feudal peonage of the sharecropping system, the problem with Washington's single-minded emphasis on industrial training, in his view, was that it denied African Americans the specifically character-building effects of a classical, liberal arts education at the college level: "And above all, we daily hear that an education that encourages aspiration, that sets the loftiest of ideals and seeks as an end culture and character rather than bread-winning, is the privilege of white men and the danger and delusion of black."[40] Drawing upon the classically humanist aspirations of training in virtue and character that had long been associated with higher education in the European tradition, Du Bois saw the aim of higher education as not simply to train individuals in a specific set of practical skills but rather to cultivate the entire person and thereby to "humanize" him or her: "The training of the schools we need to-day more than ever,—the training of deft hands, quick eyes and ears, and above all the broader, deeper, higher culture of gifted minds and pure hearts" (11).[41]

While such an education plays a key role in the formation of character, however, Du Bois imagines its effects taking place in a very indirect way. For what he proposes is not universal access to the character-building effects of university training, either as a substitute for or as an added component to vocational training, but rather a hierarchical system of education in which differences of class can finally reflect and be calibrated to differences in the cultivation of character:

[H]ow foolish to ask what is the best education for one or seven or sixty
million souls! shall we teach them trades, or train them in liberal arts? Neither and both: teach the workers to work and the thinkers to think; make
carpenters of carpenters, and philosophers of philosophers, and fops of
fools. Nor can we pause here. We are training not isolated men but a living
group of men,—nay, a group within a group. And the final product of our
training must be neither a psychologist nor a brickmason, but a man. And
to make men, we must have ideals, broad, pure, and inspiring ends of living,—not sordid money-getting, not apples of gold. The worker must work
for the glory of his handiwork, not simply for pay; the thinker must think
for truth, not for fame. (72)

Du Bois's equivocation here on whether education should be geared toward vocational specifics or humanist universals is more telling than it
might otherwise seem. He begins by espousing what might be called a
tautological pedagogy of type: the best education is one that identifies and
then enhances the intellectual and vocational traits of an individual's type.
The pedagogical task is thus not to impose or prescribe an identity on an
individual but rather to identify and realize the identity that an individual
always already contains. But as quickly as Du Bois lays out this pragmati-
cally calibrated and typologically delimited schema of training, he points
the way toward its humanizing, transcendent effects. Although we must
"make carpenters of carpenters, and philosophers of philosophers," in the
end "the final product of our training must be neither a psychologist nor a
brickmason, but a man." In realizing or "educing" the type, education also
transcends that type by making "a man" and makes that "man" through the
ennobling contact with "ideals, broad, pure, and inspiring ends of living"
outside the vocational order, ideals that in the end inspire "him" to realize,
in a platonic calibration of object and ideal, "the glory of his handiwork."[42]
Such a character is thus formed through the aesthetic ability to read in
one's work the expression of one's character.

   This platonic, humanist fantasy through which Du Bois tempers his deterministic pedagogy however, seems to betray the very humanist principles
on which it depends. For while Du Bois clarifies midway through the passage that "[w]e are training not isolated men but a living group of men," he
just as quickly takes it away: "nay," it turns out, we are training not a group
of men but rather "a group within a group." Du Bois's training, it turns out,
has as its end neither particular types of "men" *nor* a fully and broadly hu-
manized "living group of men" but rather a group *within* a group, a group

distinguished by their possession of character. Indeed, the purpose of introducing a liberal arts education is to *select* this group defined by character and distinguish it from the broader group itself: "To-day we have climbed to heights where we would open at least the outer courts of knowledge to all, display its treasures to many, and select the few to whom its mystery of Truth is revealed, not wholly by birth or the accidents of the stock market, but at least in part according to deftness and aim, talent and character" (*Souls of Black Folk,* 77). While Du Bois's "training," it would seem, maximizes the humanity of each "type" of person within his or her destined position on the economic ladder in relation to an aesthetic ideal, its goal is also and more importantly to skim off what he famously calls the "Talented Tenth" (87) of the overall group who are "capable by character and talent to receive that higher training, the end of which is culture" (86).

Du Bois's point here is not to say that Washington's program limits the opportunities of, or fails to recognize, such a talented tenth; his point rather is that the uplifting effects of character on the masses is realized only through the mediated instantiation of character in the talented tenth, not through direct character training. As informed representatives conceived in the liberal mold of John Stuart Mill, the talented tenth form a vanguard of professional men who forcefully represent and defend the interests of African Americans in the public sphere, while also testifying to society at large that character itself is not a property of whiteness alone or even a property of race itself but rather a product of educational accomplishment.[43] Most importantly, the cultivation of a talented tenth is the means through which the resources of character are mobilized for and within the community as a whole. The syntactical position of this "group within a group" between the training of types and the cultivation of "men" in the passage quoted earlier signals this mediating function in that the group within a group is precisely what infuses or communicates the humanizing effects of education to the typologically differentiated masses. The uplifting effects of character are not infused directly into the community as a whole by giving the masses extra courses in character building; the formative effects of character building, rather, must be filtered through the inspirational actions and representative example of a highly cultured and educated elite, or "aristocracy of talent and character," if they are to have their uplifting effect:[44] "Progress in human affairs is more often a pull than a push, surging forward of the exceptional man, and the lifting of his duller brethren slowly and painfully to his vantage-ground" (*Souls of Black Folk,* 79).

Du Bois's emphasis on the character-building effects of higher education was part of a broader Gilded Age suspicion toward the emphasis on
what P.T. Barnum had rather brazenly termed "the art of money getting"
in the popular genre of the success manual, a suspicion that reflects a
growing tension between two different traditions of character building. In
the February 1905 edition of the *Voice of the Negro,* for example, the editors give voice to what was an increasingly vocal attack on the character-
corroding commercialism of the Gilded Age:

> In a commercial age, such as we have fallen upon, he who dares to call at-
> tention to character-building as superior to money-getting, runs the risk
> of being counted out of joint with the times. At the risk of running against
> this mad and merciless saw, the editor declares that the greatest need of the
> hour, is not money, but character. . . . This race must be taught that its chief
> business is not to make money or to try to catch up with any other race.
> Its chief duty is the cultivation of character. Money is not the ruling factor
> of the world. True, it is an essential in life and its possession indicates a
> type of character. But . . . the writer is bold enough to declare that character
> is greater than gold; that our sorest need is that element that eludes troy
> weight and refuses to be measured in the gross scales of avoirdupois and
> scorns the statistical columns of the census report and is too large for a
> banker's vault.[45]

Character is forged, in other words, not within the pursuit of self-interest,
which defined the economic sphere, but rather in the self-perfection at-
tained through the mastery of culture.
    Although Washington and Du Bois both agree that building and dis-
playing character is essential to the project of racial uplift, they ultimately
disagree over both the method of character building and the terms of
character's recognizability as a liberating social fact. And as the editors of
the *Voice of the Negro* make clear in their March 1905 column devoted to
the Washingtonian question "Shall We Materialize the Negro?" the "two
conflicting currents of thought that agitate the market with reference to
the Negro" are distinguished by, on the one hand, a program of "materializing" character and, on the other, a program of "cultivating" character,
programs reflective of a much broader split within the rhetoric of character itself.[46]
    In part, this disagreement over the role of character in racial uplift is a
legacy of both men's appropriation of the philosophy of Frederick Douglass

and his equally conflicted reliance on the uplifting effects of character. Douglass, like Washington, championed industrial training over the limited signifying effects of an elite class of professional men whose "talents can do little to give us character in the eyes of the world."[47] When Harriet Beecher Stowe wrote to Douglass in 1853 asking how she might best put to use the enormous proceeds being generated by *Uncle Tom's Cabin,* he responded that she should fund an industrial college in order better to materialize and make visible the "merits" of African American character: "We must become mechanics; we must build as well as live in houses; we must make as well as use furniture; we must construct bridges as well as pass over them, before we can properly live or be respected by our fellow men."[48] And yet Douglass did not hesitate to premise his own authority on the image of his learned character, and he was equally insistent, like Du Bois, that an aggressive and vocal agitation for civil rights was the vehicle of social and political recognition *because of* the ways that activism itself testified to and garnered respect as the "manliness" of character.

In Douglass's 1848 speech "What Are the Colored People Doing for Themselves?" he most forcefully articulates the role of character in the project of racial uplift:

> What we, the colored people, want, is *character,* and this nobody can give us. It is a thing we must get for ourselves. We must labor for it. It is gained by toil—hard toil. Neither the sympathy nor the generosity of our friends can give it to us. It is attainable—yes, thank God, it is attainable. 'There is gold in the earth, but we must dig it'—so with character. It is attainable; but we must attain it, and attain it each for himself.[49]

But as Douglass goes on to make clear, such an attainment of character is crucial not for its practical effects as a method of self-improvement but rather as challenge to the racialized system of character types, a challenge grounded in the strangely powerful materiality of character:

> Character is the important thing, and without it we must continue to be marked for degradation and stamped with the brand of inferiority. With character, we shall be powerful. Nothing can harm us long when we get character.—There are certain great elements of character in us which may be hated, but never despised. Industry, sobriety, honesty, combined with intelligence and due self-respect, find them where you will, among black or white, must be *looked up to*—can never be *looked down upon.* In their

presence, prejudice is abashed, confused, mortified. Encountering this solid mass of living character, our vile oppressors are ground to atoms. In its presence, the sneers of a caricaturing press, the taunts of natural inferiority, the mischievous assertions of Clay, and fine-spun sophisms of Calhoun, are innoxious, powerless and unavailing. In answer to these men and the sneers of the multitude, there is nothing in the wide world half so effective as the presentation of a character precisely the opposite of all their representations. We have it in our power to convert the weapons intended for our injury into positive blessings. That we may sustain temporary injury from gross and general misrepresentation, is most true; but the injury is but temporary, and must disappear at the approach of light, like mist from the vale. The offensive traits of character imputed to us, can only be injurious while they are true of us. . . . We have the power of making our enemies slanderers, and this we must do by showing ourselves worthy and respectable men.[50]

As Douglass makes clear, acquiring character is essential to racial uplift because it takes possession of and "convert[s] the weapons intended for our injury into positive blessings." The most dangerous weapons, in other words, were the racist representations of African American character circulated in not only the writings and images of "the caricaturing press" but also in the specious racial reasoning of such Southern apologists for slavery as Clay and Calhoun. But in mobilizing the resources of character against the broader rhetoric of character *itself*, Douglass proposes more than simply rewriting the "misrepresentations" of African American character with a set of opposite and ultimately more accurate representations. It is not simply the case that African American character has been misrepresented but rather that it has been construed as reductively representable by typological traits in the first place. The problem, in other words, is that African American character has been construed only as a kind of character type rather than as the type-transcending stuff of character itself.[51]

What Douglass proposes is to unravel and obliterate the typology of character by displaying the sheer value of having character itself. Through such a display of character, the traits conventionally ascribed to "the race" are not so much *re*written as they are *un*written as a locatable object in a racial taxonomy. Having character destroys not just the "marks" and "stamps" of degrading character traits but the possibility of marking and stamping itself. In the face of such a "solid mass of living character, our vile oppressors are ground to atoms" because their "prejudice" no longer can construe character simply as a reductive set of race-specific traits. "[P]rejudice is abashed, confused, mortified" not because it attributed the wrong set of traits but rather because traits can no longer be used to delimit and define racial difference. The only traits that *can* be said to describe such a solid mass of character—"[i]ndustry, sobriety, honesty"—are those that do not delimit its features but rather express the direct and unmediated presence of that substance in the field of action and representation.

Character's power thus lies not in any of the particularly valuable forms it might take but rather in its being the formless, material source of value itself. Like the gold dug from the earth, character's value lies not in its convertibility into a particular material form—a house, a piece of property, a novel, a sociological treatise, or a firm handshake—but rather in its ability to be infinitely convertible into and exchangeable for any form it likes. True character is never reducible to the properties of the forms it takes but rather is the indexical source, like the gold in Fort Knox, of the intrinsic value of those forms, actions, and traits, and its power quite literally lies in what it can get, what it is exchangeable *for,* what it can mobilize the will to acquire and possess. Character is the lost gold of an excessively "gilded" age.

Erasing History, Raising Stigmas

Pauline Hopkins was a prominent writer, editor, and novelist who was also concerned with mobilizing the signifying power of character to challenge prevailing strategies of racial discrimination. As an editor and regular contributor to the *Colored American Magazine* and later the *Voice of the Negro,* publications that were also often dominated by the debate between Washington and Du Bois, Hopkins devoted considerable intellectual energy to this strategy of racial uplift.[52] As Richard Yarborough has pointed out, Hopkins was "the single most productive black woman writer at the turn of the century," having published a diverse body of literary, artistic, and scientific work that included fiction, dramatic plays, biographies, essays, and ethnological studies.[53] Running throughout Hopkins's work in these different areas and disciplines was an interest in their formal and thematic reliance on the rhetoric of character and in particular in the role of character in the racializing discourses common to particular genres of late nineteenth-century literary, scientific, and journalistic discourse. Hopkins's writing thus frequently employs various generic forms associated with the representation and formation of character—particularly drama, biography, ethnology, and temperance fiction—but also critically reappropriates them against their conventional racializing function.[54] She uses, for example, a series of biographies published in the *Colored American Magazine* both to disrupt the conventional associations of the representative character with white masculinity and to discuss the important social issues and political debates normally eclipsed by such representations of the exemplary character. Like Martin Delany and Du Bois before her, Hopkins also published her own ethnological counter-treatise, *The Dark Races of the Twentieth Century* (1905), whose purpose was to turn the racial taxonomies and historical assumptions of ethnology and early anthropology against their traditional hierarchizing function.[55]

But Hopkins also believed in literary fiction as a particularly powerful component of racial uplift because of the opportunities it provided to engage critically the representational forms and reformist aspirations of the rhetoric of character. In her first novel, *Contending Forces* (1900), Hopkins takes up the ideology of racial uplift in the character of its two most prominent advocates, in order to offer a critical reflection on the rhetoric of character on which that ideology relies. In her preface to *Contending Forces,* Hopkins locates the promise of racial uplift not in the signifying capacity of "representative men" but rather in what she refers to as the "simple, homely tale, unassumingly told":

> The colored race has historians, lecturers, ministers, poets, judges and lawyers,—men of brilliant intellects who have arrested the favorable attention of this busy, energetic nation. But, after all, it is the simple, homely tale, unassumingly told, which cements the bond of brotherhood among all classes and all complexions.[56]

While Hopkins recognizes the signifying power of such representative icons, she nonetheless locates in the narrative and representational capacities of literary fiction a greater power to challenge the racializing economies of character types and thus "to raise the stigma of degradation from my race" (13).

Such a power has often been identified with the demystifying power of literary realism as a literary form. Literary realism had been defended by late nineteenth-century writers such as Sui Sin Far, Zitkala Sa, and Charles Chesnutt, for example, because of its capacity to refute reductive cultural stereotypes with realistic, demystifying counterrepresentations of particularized characters. The promise of realist character, in other words, was to dispel the forms of "race libel" that were inherent to, and propagated by, the racializing caricatures of the periodical press, popular theater, and sensational, sentimental, and romance fiction. Charles Chesnutt describes his turn to literary realism, for example, as growing out of his concern that "the Negro in fiction had been standardized, and that there were very few kinds of Negroes" portrayed in fiction. Chesnutt thus developed a realist method of observation and recordation that began with the "record [of his] impressions of men and things, and such incidents or conversations which take place within [his] knowledge," a record that he then put "to future use in literary work": "I shall not record stale negro minstrel jokes or worn out newspaper squibs on the 'man and brother.' I shall leave the realm of fiction, where most of this stuff is manufactured, and come down to hard facts."[57] More recently, critics such as Barbara Christian have similarly celebrated the realism of the novel form for enabling the passage "from stereotype to character," as Christian puts it in the title of her essay, because it is a form in which "stereotyped forms are cracked, new forms are sculpted to become characters who instruct us about their particular lives and therefore about the general themes of the culture."[58]

Realists' efforts to expand and develop the representational means for discerning and displaying in the more subtle marks and manners of the body the real depths of character, however, have also been seen as a literary strategy that transforms their readers into discriminating judges of character, judges who, as Kenneth Warren, Cathy Boeckmann, Henry Louis Gates, Jr., and Nancy Glazener have argued, often reinforced the very system of cultural types they presumed to challenge.[59] As Warren argues, "the efforts by realists to distinguish realistic characterization from sentimental delineations of character also helped, paradoxically, to define social distinctions between the majority of black and white Americans as 'real' and ineffaceable."[60] While Pauline Hopkins celebrates the "simple, homely tale, unassumingly told," she too lodges her reformist hopes not in the discerning eye of realism but rather in the power of the romance form to capture, represent, and record the character of a "people" and also to mobilize the affective and identificatory bonds mediated by literary character:

> Fiction is of great value to any people as a preserver of manners and customs religious, political and social. It is a record of growth and development

from generation to generation. *No one will do this for us; we must ourselves develop the men and women who will faithfully portray the inmost thoughts and feelings of the Negro with all the fire and romance which lie dormant in our history,* and, as yet, unrecognized by writers of the Anglo-Saxon race. (14)

What literature makes possible, on Hopkins's account, is a self-representation of the character of a "people," a self-representation that is distinctly historical as well. Literature "records" the "fire and romance" that would otherwise lie dormant in that history but does so as a historical development measured not in years, eras, or election cycles but by the passage from "generation to generation."

True to her intent, Hopkins offers in *Contending Forces* an incredibly complex, intergenerational tale of "the inmost thoughts and feelings" *and* of the "religious, political, and social condition[s]" in which they form.[61] Indeed, as Ann duCille has argued, "Of the many African American novels written between the publication of *Clotel* in 1853 and the turn of the century, *Contending Forces* arguably offers the most complex (if not complete) representation of the intricacies of black American life in the latter 1800s."[62] Hopkins's novel has frequently been regarded as a rather conventional sentimental romance tale of a mixed-race heroine who, while plagued by a secret and traumatic past, eventually finds solace and recognition in the marriage bond. But as duCille argues, Hopkins's tale "is by no means a little romance."[63] Hopkins not only frames her "little romance" within a complex intergenerational tale of the formation of racialized bodies in the interplay of transnational capitalism and colonial migration, but she also uses her "little romance" to interrogate critically not only the terms of racial uplift but its key representatives as well.[64] Her text thus functions as both a sentimental vehicle of racial uplift and a sustained interrogation of the strategies and figures of the racial-uplift movement. Hopkins has her characters frequently rehearse and debate, often at the expense of dramatic and narrative continuity, many of the central uplift arguments of the day and, more significantly, restages speeches from some of the most recognizable leaders (such as Washington's Atlanta Exposition address) at a meeting of the "American Colored League" in an extended and pivotal scene in the middle of the story. Hopkins even goes so far as to give narrative form, as many scholars have pointed out, to two of the most important proponents of racial uplift of her day, Washington and Du Bois, in the characters of Dr. Arthur Lewis and Will Smith. In taking these two leading and representative men and situating them in a complex intergenerational drama of racial violence, Hopkins interrogates not just these representative characters but also the philosophies of character building they came to represent.

But perhaps the most significant aspect of Hopkins's invocation of the power of literature to challenge the racializing circulation of stereotypes is the way that she refigures the terms though which that literary challenge is posed. The promise of literature in a politics of racial uplift has often been taken to lie in its power to represent the individuating complexity, depth, or "roundedness" of character and thereby to challenge the reductive, cultural stereotypes of racial identity. How the complexity of character is best represented has, of course, been an object of intense debate, and different strategies of characterization have often been used to define and defend the differences between novelistic genres. For literary realists, such a roundedness and plenitude was achieved through practices of representation that eschewed the typologized traits and stock characters of sentimental romance. The danger in Hopkins's utilization of the genre of romance to achieve such a political aim, according to realists and later defenders of the realist form, is that, in mobilizing the sympathetic and identificatory resources of sentimental romance, one risks reproducing the stereotypes that the literary is presumably poised to challenge.[65] Indeed, for scholars such as Christian, the development *away from* the sentimental traffic in stereotypes (with which Hopkins, in Christian's view, would have to be identified) to a literary aesthetics capable of construing the full complexities and realities of character is what defines the formal development and generic progress of black women's writing.[66]

Hopkins, despite her use of the sentimental form, does not so much seek to ground the abstractions of "flat" stereotype in the concrete complexity of a fully "rounded" character as to question literature's reliance on the notion of character itself in the challenge to racial stereotype. Hopkins's novel challenges the theoretical assumptions behind such a story of the political evolution and advancement in literary genre by interrogating what such a representation and recognition of character costs—and occludes.[67] For although an attention to, and representation of, the complexities, contradictions, ambiguities, and impossibilities of what might be called a "rounded" character are indeed a crucial component, in my view, of both good literature *and* good politics, the danger to which Hopkins is calling attention is that this representational ideal of *literary* character is too subsumed within a broader *cultural* discourse of character that ends up prescribing or delimiting yet again the terms through which such a rounded or realized character can be recognized, and it does so in often more covertly racialized terms.

Hopkins makes this case by taking up one of the most stereotyped figures of the Gilded Age, the complex figure of the "tragic mulatta," and asking what it would mean to recognize or reconstrue that figure as "having character."[68] The "mulatto" was a very complex and highly contested figure of racial identity in the Gilded Age. Not only did the fascination with the mulatto figure express broader cultural anxieties over miscegenation and the separation of the races, but the racial "mixing" that the mulatto presumably represented also allegorized for many people the racialized terms through which African American "assimilation" was imagined. And while the mixed-race figure foregrounded what Amy Robinson calls "the false promise of the visible as an epistemological guarantee" of racial identity, the tragic narrative of the mulatto's ultimate inability to "pass" also reiterated the inevitable purchase of the "fictions" of blood and race as determinants of character.[69] Perhaps the most charged aspect of the mulatto figure was the way that, as a figure of "mixed race," the mulatto drew attention to one of the most pernicious aspects of racial subjugation under slavery, namely, the sexual possession of slaves by their masters. A great deal of attention thus fell on the figure of the mixed-race woman because she represented the site of that subjugation and brought into relief the sexual and racial dynamics that structured that subjugation and its ongoing effects and repetitions in the postemancipation era. But in making such a history recognizable, the mixed-race woman also provoked an intense ideological recasting of that history of subjugation by figuratively functioning as a site of the historical disavowal of racial and sexual subjugation. The sexual possession of slaves was recast, in other words, as the seduction of whites by a licentious and uncontained black sexual excess. The mixed-race identity of the mulatto figure, and in particular of the "tragic mulatta," became the bearer of this disavowal and thus a complex site in which the relationships of race, class, and gender and sexuality were negotiated and contested.

The figure of the mixed-race woman, in much of the literature of the postemancipation era, has been construed through a "tragic" plot in which that figure must bear the impossible historical consequences of her mixed-race identity. First, as a figure who bears the history of sexual possession under slavery as the very marks of her mixed-race body, such a narrative goes, the tragic mulatta also traumatically repeats that history by seeking to pass in a white world by forsaking an African American family and community and, in many narratives, by winning the affection of a white suitor. The second tragedy follows from the inevitable disclosure or suspicion of her hidden "racial stain" and subsequent rejection by her white suitor. As Mary Dearborn has put it, "The tragic mulatto trajectory demands that the mulatto woman desire a white lover and either die (often in white-authored versions) or return to the black community."[70]

In *Contending Forces,* Pauline Hopkins shapes her narrative according to many of the conventions of the tragic mulatta tale. At the center of Hopkins's complex intergenerational tale is the story of Sappho Clark, a young stenographer and independent woman who takes up residence as a boarder in the Smith family home.[71] Sappho quickly becomes the figure around whom the romance plot is organized, although she also immediately complicates the gendered positions of such a plot. Sappho earns the affection of the brilliant and Du Bois–like Will Smith, but not before earning (and returning) the enamored affection of Will's younger sister Dora. In the conventional romance plot that takes over, however, Will Smith falls for the somewhat inscrutable Sappho and, much to the chagrin of the villainous John Langley (Will's friend who is also engaged to Dora), pursues her hand in marriage. True to the melodramatic genre, a number of obstacles must be overcome for these lovers and the narrative to find their anticipated resolution within the marriage plot. The most important obstacle is of course Sappho's own "degraded" past—as a young woman Sappho was abducted and raped by her white uncle—and it is this past, along with the son that she bore, that she fears will draw the scorn of her happily bourgeois suitor and his genteel family if revealed. Hopkins's narrative, however, makes the revelation of Sappho's past both the obstacle to the marriage plot and the event that enables its resolution. For when Sappho's past is revealed to John Langley, he attempts to blackmail her into becoming his mistress, to which Sappho responds by reclaiming her son and fleeing back to the South, but not before revealing herself and John's plot to Will, who eventually finds her and "forgives" her tainted past.

In making the domestication of Sappho Clark the narrative fulcrum of the novel, Hopkins invokes and yet transforms many of the dramatic and narrative conventions associated with the tragic mulatta tale. First, Hopkins dramatically restages the logic of "passing" that usually frames the tragic mulatta tale. Unlike her other novels, Hopkins sets most of *Contending Forces* within Boston's African American community, the community in which Sappho passes. The threat that Sappho faces is not the revelation of a hidden racial identity but rather the revelation of a sexual past, a past for which she fears the conventionally smug and genteel Smith family will reject her. The potential obstacle to recognition, in Hopkins's retelling, is not the racial prejudice of a white suitor but rather the sexual mores of a genteel, middle-class family, mores derived from the rhetoric of character. Sappho's "fallen" status, in other words, marks her as lacking the virtue and purity that defines feminine character and that legitimates women's cultural role as the privileged makers, as mothers and wives, of character within the middle-class family. Hopkins's placement of her mixed-race heroine in a black rather than a white community, therefore, does not dissolve the logic of passing but rather reconceives its defining terms: Sappho seeks to pass but not as visibly white but rather as a conventionally bourgeois woman, as an unsullied icon of "true womanhood." And yet although such a shift might be read as a transposition of the passing tale from the logic of race to that of class and gender, Hopkins's tale keeps the racial dimensions of this shift firmly in focus by showing how such a sexual passing is predicated nonetheless on the history of racialization, by binding Sappho's own past with the history of racial violence to which the passing narrative traditionally points.

Second, and relatedly, Hopkins's tragic mulatta seems to escape the tragic fate that her attempts to pass presumably would portend. By novel's end, Sappho is happily reunited with her son, and they are both incorporated into Will Smith's now wealthy family by the marriage bond. Sappho avoids the tragic alternatives not by successfully passing, it would seem, but rather by having her "degraded" past exposed and recuperated through the restoration of a virtuous "feminine character," a character conceived within the prescribed roles of the mother and wife. As Claudia Tate has argued, this use of the ideals of feminine character was a fundamental part of the political aim of the African American domestic novel:

> Whether conservative or liberal, the domestic plots rely on a tradition of politicized motherhood that views mothers and the cultural rhetoric of maternity as instruments of social reform. This tradition held sway from the late eighteenth through most of the nineteenth century, from the ideology of republican motherhood that designated white American mothers responsible for "instructing children in and keeping spouses true to republican principles" to "the cult of true womanhood" that defined white women as the arbiters of moral virtues as well.[72]

The restoration of feminine character was so important in "the ideology of republican motherhood," moreover, precisely because of its role in the formation of character itself. As John Todd argued in his antebellum conduct manual, "Human character, in all its interests and relations and destinies, is committed to woman, and she can make it, shape it, mould it, and stamp it just as she pleases."[73] The "ideal woman" was thus one who aspired not to have character in its generalized form, but rather who in exemplifying the more particularized ideal of feminine character could become the vehicle for the formation of character in her sons and husband.

In *Contending Forces*, however, Hopkins does not simply relegate Sappho to becoming a bearer of restored African American kinship and vehicle of character formation. Throughout the novel, Hopkins identifies Sappho's appeal in terms of her own possession not of a prescribed feminine character but of the "sterling" qualities of character itself. This is what Dora first sees in her, and it is how the narrator ultimately describes her. The question Hopkins poses, in other words, is whether a woman such as Sappho can be recognized not just as an icon of feminine character within the romance narrative but as a resolute and exemplary possessor of character itself. What then does it mean to make the recognition of character the driving element of Hopkins's novel? What would such a recognition of Sappho as a possessor of character entail, and is such a recognition achieved in the otherwise "happy" resolution of the plot in her marriage to Will? Is Hopkins, in making the recognition of Sappho's character that which drives the narrative events of the novel, and also that which, in terms of the tragic mulatta plot, would need to be restored, telling in her seemingly conventional plot a quite radical story of the *costs* of Sappho's restoration within the domestic scene?

From Inheritance to History in Pauline Hopkins's Critique of Racial Character

As Hopkins's narrator makes clear, Sappho Clark is the enigmatic center of *Contending Forces* because of the force of her own resolute and powerful character:

> Sappho possessed a brilliant mind and resolute character. If she had been a religious devotee she would have been as devout and as fervid as a disciple of old. If a sinner, the queen of them all. She had strength of will enough for

a dozen women, which, if ever started on the wrong road, would be difficult
to redirect into the paths of right. (341)

But although Sappho eventually attracts the attention of the many men
in *Contending Forces,* it is the young Dora who first recognizes and is en-
thralled with Sappho's beauty and who, moreover, understands that beauty
as the sign of her powerful character:

> After that evening the two girls were much together. Sappho's beauty ap-
> pealed strongly to Dora's artistic nature; but hidden beneath the classic
> outlines of the face, the graceful symmetry of the form, and the dainty
> coloring of the skin, Dora's shrewd common sense and womanly intuition
> discovered a character of sterling worth—bold, strong and ennobling;
> while in Sappho's lonely self-suppressed life the energetic little Yankee girl
> swept like a healthful, strengthening breeze. (114)

Hopkins describes Dora's attraction here in terms of a complex differen-
tiation and interrelation of her physical "beauty" and her inner, "hidden"
character and the appeal of each of these aspects to different sensibilities of
Dora's. While Dora's "artistic nature" might revel in the formal perfection
of Sappho's face and body, it is her "shrewd common sense and womanly
intuition" that discovers the "character of sterling worth" underneath that
beauty.[74] Dora's recognition of Sappho's sterling character, though difficult
to separate entirely from her strongly appealing beauty, is discovered by
that "shrewd" innate sense for the forms of value that mark Dora as such an
exemplary and "energetic little Yankee girl."

Indeed, the independence and economic self-reliance that initially
mark Sappho as a possessor of character are often the terms through
which Dora's fascination finds expression. In the first mention of Sappho in the prior chapter, the first thing that Dora excitedly says of Sappho
is that "she's got a typewriter, and she says she picks up a good living at
home with it. Talk about your beauties! my, but she's the prettiest creature
I ever saw! I expect all the men in this house will be crazy over her" (89).
And it is Sappho's qualities as a self-possessed woman that allow Dora to
disregard her usual caution against "girl friendships":

> There was a great fascination for her about the quiet, self-possessed
> woman. She did not, as a rule, care much for girl friendships, holding that
> a close intimacy between two of the same sex was more than likely to end

disastrously for one or the other. But Sappho Clark seemed to fill a long-felt want in her life, and she had from the first a perfect trust in the beautiful girl. (97–98)

Sappho and Dora's fondness for each other in this early scene is explained by Hopkins's narrator as a kind of *mutual* recognition of character. Dora's initial fixation on Sappho is addressed to the fact that she is a rare example of a self-employed single women, fashioning her own destiny outside the domestic economy of marriage, whereas "the energetic little Yankee girl" sweeps into Sappho's life because of her enterprising character associated with "New England men."

Indeed, Hopkins situates their mutual recognition as demonstrative of the character-building mechanism of racial uplift itself, as she draws the analogy between their recognition of each other and the Southern black woman's internalization of the traits of the New England "Yankee" character on which the republic was founded:

> [I]n Sappho's lonely self-suppressed life the energetic little Yankee girl swept like a healthful, strengthening breeze. . . . It was the Southern girl's first experience of Northern life. . . . [T]ruth demanded her to recognize the superiority of the vigorous activity in the life all about her. The Negro, while held in contempt by many, yet reflected the spirit of his surroundings in his upright carriage, his fearlessness in advancing his opinions, his self-reliance, his anxiety to obtain paying employment that would give to his family some few of the advantages enjoyed by the more favored classes of citizens, his love of liberty, which in its intensity recalled the memory of New England men who had counted all worldly gain as nothing if demanding the sacrifice of even one of the great principles of freedom. (114–115)

Dora's shrewd common sense recognizes Sappho's character, and in that recognition, Sappho is herself called "to recognize the superiority of the vigorous activity in the life all about her," the life represented by and lived as the energetic little Yankee girl from Boston. And in thus being called to such a recognition by Dora's attentions, Sappho can thereby participate in the spirit of uplift itself—the spirit through which "self-reliant" "Negro men" emulate and exhibit the great traits of "New England men," the irony of course being that, as a self-employed, independent woman, Sappho *already* embodies those values far more than the quite conventional, and betrothed, Dora. More importantly, this recognition of character that initially frames the relationship between Dora and Sappho is explicitly construed in terms of the recognition of the "fallen" women and the role of the restoration of her character in the project of racial uplift:

> "Then you [Dora] are not one of those who think that a woman should be condemned to eternal banishment for the sake of one misstep?" "Not I, indeed; I have always felt a great curiosity to know the reason why each individual woman loses character and standing in the eyes of the world. I believe that we would hang our head in shame at having the temerity to judge a fallen sister, could we but know the circumstances attending many such cases. . . ." "You are a dear little preacher," said Sappho gently, as she looked at Dora from two wet eyes; "and if our race ever amounts to anything in the world, it will be because such women as you are raised up to save us." (100–101)

The appeal of Sappho's sterling character might thus be explained as a consequence of her fallen status, a status that thrusts her into the masculine—and potentially masculinizing—world of self-reliance and labor. Sappho's sterling character, according to such a cultural logic, would thus signify her failure to embody the ideals of feminine character and her masculinization by the world of work and the requirements of self-support. And yet Dora's recognition of Sappho's character is also framed within the terms of the domestic scene as well, and the confusion of desire and identification that the traditional role of the mother as character building entails.

In the scene that follows, Hopkins makes clear that Dora and Sappho's relationship is founded on much more than the abstract recognition of character. The scene opens as Dora and Sappho steal away to Sappho's room during a snowstorm to create their own little world of domestic bliss:

> It was the first great storm Sappho had seen. It was impossible for her to leave home, so she begged Dora to pass the day with her and play "company," like the children. Dora was nothing loathe; and as soon as her morning duties were finished, she told her mother that she was going visiting and would not be at home until tea time. By eleven o'clock they had locked the door of Sappho's room to keep out all intruders, had mended the fire until the little stove gave out a delicious warmth, and had drawn the window curtains close to keep out stray currents of air. Sappho's couch was drawn close beside the stove, while Dora's small person was most cosily bestowed in her favorite rocking-chair. (117)

But as they spend a happily secluded morning together secretly locked away in Sappho's room, Dora and Sappho negotiate the terms of their mutual affection in multiply displaced forms. Referring affectionately to Dora as "her little brownie" and lingering over her "teeth, [her] beautiful white teeth," Sappho's attentions to her friend are frank and rather flirty:[75] "Sappho lay back among her cushions, lazily stretching her little slippered feet toward the warm stove, where the fire burned so cheerily and glowed so invitingly as it shone through the isinglass door. She folded her arms above her head and turned an admiring gaze on the brown face of her friend" (118). While Sappho has her "admiring gaze" trained attentively on her beloved "little brownie," however, Dora sits, with "the usual business-like look upon her face, . . . telling Sappho all about her engagement to John Langley and their plans for the future" (118).

But Dora, who has felt the need to lie to her mother about spending the day with Sappho, is not so distant and distracted as their crossed gazes might suggest. After asking Sappho if she will ever marry, a question that Sappho playfully dodges, the two girls suddenly turn their attentions to the tray of desserts that Dora has made. Sappho, playing on the matrimonial vernacular (and its policing of the body), playfully warns Dora that her love of sweets will scare off her future lovers, at first identified with John but then shifted to Sappho herself:

> That's the fourth time this week, and here it is but Friday. You'll be as fat as a seal, and then John P. won't want you at any price. . . . And your teeth, your beautiful white teeth, where will they be shortly if you persist in eating a pound of bonbons everyday? Think of your fate, Dora, and pause in your reckless career—forty inches about the waist and only scraggy snags to show me when you grin! (120)

Dora, responding instantly to Sappho's suggestive taunts, playfully rejoins by threatening to eat Sappho's slice of pie, after which "there ensued a scramble for the pie, mingled with peals of merry laughter, until all rosy and sparkling, Sappho emerged from the fray with the dish containing her share of the dainty held high in the air" (120). Emerging from this playful struggle, which occurs just out of narrative view, the girls resume "their old positions" and continue to discuss what turns out to be Dora's marital misgivings. After again asking Sappho if she will marry, to which she responds "with a comical twist to her face, 'in the words of Unc' Gulliver, "I mote, an' then agin I moten't"'" (121), Dora confesses to Sappho that what "troubles" her is not so much the idea of marriage itself but rather the trouble of "having a man bothering around." Dora openly admits that she "like[s] John's looks" and in particular the prestige of possessing such a good-looking man, but it is the finality of the marriage contract that she pointedly confesses ultimately "unsexes" her: "That's just what makes me feel so *unsexed,* so to speak; I like John's looks. He's the style of all the girls in our set. I like to know that I can claim him before them all. . . . But for all that, I know I'll get tired of him" (122). Rather than representing the final and culminating realization of her feminine character, the marriage contract is what threatens to "unsex" the "womanhood" that not only would mark Dora's middle-class status but more importantly would mark her legitimate assumption of the maternal role denied under slavery. Or as Sappho tellingly responds, "That's queer talk for an engaged girl, with a fine handsome fellow to court her" (121). But despite the detailed portrait of Dora and Sappho's relationship and their explicit rejections of the heterosexual terms of the marriage contract in it, Dora and Sappho are both ultimately reclaimed by the marriage plot *and* the representative men of the racial-uplift movement, as Dora eventually marries Dr. Arthur Lewis and Sappho marries Will.[76] Sappho's queerness is thus initially positioned as the "inversion" produced by her fall from feminine character into the masculinizing world of work and thus as a product of the rhetoric of character itself. And yet, in establishing Sappho's character as the emulable, character-building object of desire for both Dora and the men, Hopkins also explores the ways that such a queerness lay at the heart of the character-building role assigned to women.

Although it is Dora who discovers in Sappho's beautiful face the "sterling character" hidden beneath, Dora's characterization of that beauty in the discussion with her mother also immediately links it to Sappho's particularly traumatic past: "But really, ma, you won't be able to keep from loving her; she has the sweetest and saddest face I ever saw. I have read of the woman with a story written on her face, but I never believed it anything but a fairly tale. You'll believe me when you see her and talk with her" (89). This "story written on her face" is, as we learn, the story of Sappho's tragic past, and it is the complex task of telling that story, a story identified with the contending forces of the novel's title, that will govern the development of Hopkins's romance plot. In her own reworking of the tragic mulatta plot, Hopkins makes the revelation of Sappho's story the complex and multidimensional motor of the entire novel. First seen but not read by Dora, Sappho's story is first "revealed" in the speech of Luke Sawyer as a polemical rejoinder to the racial-uplift philosophy. But as a story that takes shape as the beauty of Sappho's face, the story also drives the romance plot, as both Will and John are driven by it to possess Sappho, and their desire will be tested by their ability to square that beauty with the story that animates it. It is a story that, most importantly, underlies not only Sappho's beauty but also her character, in that the trials of living both the story and the story's exposure are what have given shape to Sappho's character: "Now she felt that her losses could not be paid, but in the years which followed she learned to value the strong, chastening influence of her present sorrow, and the force of character it developed, fitting her perfectly for the place she was to occupy in carrying comfort and hope to the women of her race" (347). Hopkins thus not only points to how Sappho's story, a story of the sexual subjugation of African American women, is a story that must be "read," but she also portrays the ways that historical story is commonly *mis*read in the many forms of cultural legibility that it takes. Hopkins's novel, in other words, takes measure of the different ways that such a story—and the historical past it represents—achieves its cultural legibility within and as a complex object of desire and identification by making Sappho's face the pivotal site of interpretation and historical understanding for the various characters of the novel.

That story is first presented as the tragic story told by Luke Sawyer of the young Mabelle Beaubean in his speech at the meeting of the American Colored League. Luke's speech is preceded by that of Dr. Arthur Lewis, a speech that Hopkins presents as a kind of caricature of Washington's Atlanta Exposition address:

> [P]olitics is the bane of the Negro's existence. . . . If we are patient, docile, harmless, we may expect to see that prosperity for which we long. . . . We should strive to obtain the education of the industrial school, seeking there our level, content to abide there, leaving to the white man the superiority of brain and intellect which hundreds of years have developed. (250–251)

Luke's speech is also followed by "Will Smith's defense of his race," a speech that invokes the figure and philosophy of W.E.B. Du Bois. Situated between the speeches of Dr. Lewis and Will Smith, Luke's speech is positioned by Hopkins as an important rhetorical intervention in the racial-uplift philosophies of Washington and Du Bois.

Sawyer's entrance on the scene and disruption of this adversarial binary, moreover, is dramatically presented as the challenge of a "representative man" stunningly marked in his physical bearing by the presence of character. Spontaneously responding to the accommodationism of Lewis's speech, Luke, who is not a scheduled speaker, rises from his seat and dramatically lays claim to the stage and speaking position:

> As he passed up the aisle and mounted the steps of the rostrum, the people saw a man of majestic frame, rugged physique and immense muscular development. His face was kindly, but withal bore the marks of superior intelligence, shrewdness and great strength of character. He might have been a Cromwell, a Robespierre, a Lincoln. Men of his physiological development—when white—mould humanity, and leave their own characteristics engraved upon the pages of the history of their times. (255)

Luke too, it seems, has a story written on his face, and he frames his speech as an immediate challenge to the intrinsic elitism of Washington's ostensibly populist rhetoric, a charge frequently applied as well to the elitism of Du Bois's concept of the talented tenth:

> Friends, I am thirty years old and look fifty. I want to tell you why this is so. I want to tell you what brought me *here*. I want to tell the gentlemen who have spoken here tonight that conservatism, lack of brotherly affiliation, lack of energy for the right and the power of the almighty dollar which deadens men's hearts to the sufferings of their brothers, and makes them feel that if only *they* can rise to the top of the ladder may God help the hindmost man, are the forces which are ruining the Negro in this country. It is killing him off by thousands, destroying his self-respect, and degrading him to the level of the brute. *These are the contending forces that are dooming this race to despair!* (255–256)

The story Luke has to tell of the "contending forces that are dooming this race to despair" is a story that "the gentlemen who have spoken here tonight" have failed to tell, and it is a story moreover that *Contending Forces* as a novel is specifically charged in its title to tell. And this story is one that is also written on *Luke's* face. As a man whose sufferings have prematurely aged his thirty-year-old face to look like that of a man of fifty, Luke also appears to have been born twenty years earlier than he actually was. Luke is thus marked as a child raised in the era of slavery rather than in the postemancipation period. The experiences of adversity that he has experienced in the postemancipation era, in other words, have given him the careworn look but also the powerful character produced by the experience of slavery.

The story written on Luke's face consists of two parts. The first is an account of the brutal murder of his entire family, when he was ten, at the hands of a white mob upset at the threat that his father's successful business posed to the local white merchants.[77] The young Luke, who manages to escape into the woods, is found and adopted by a wealthy "colored planter named Beaubean" who raises him with his other children. The second story Luke tells, is that of his beautiful foster sister Mabelle Beaubean, who, at the age of fourteen, is abducted, raped, and left in a New Orleans's brothel, "a poor, ruined, half-crazed creature in whom it was almost impossible to trace a resemblance to the beautiful pet of our household" (260). When Monsieur Beaubean confronts the suspected perpetrator, his own white half-brother and respected state senator, the man baldly admits the crime and moreover details the racist thinking that "justifies" it:

> Crazed with grief, Monsieur Beaubean faced his brother and accused him of his crime. "Well," said he, "whatever damage I have done I am willing to pay for. But your child is no better than her mother or her grandmother. What does a woman of mixed blood, or any Negress, for that matter, know of virtue? It is my belief that they were a direct creation by God to be the pleasant companions of men of my race. Now, I am willing to give you a thousand dollars and call it square." (261)

Beaubean's enraged threats in the face of this stunning revelation, of course, seal his fate, as he is shot that very night by a mob who also burn down his house. Luke, who once again escapes the burning house but this time with Mabelle wrapped in a blanket, takes her to "the colored convent at New Orleans," where she eventually dies, he claims, when "her child was born" (261).

Luke's story is positioned as itself a theoretical intervention in the racial-uplift debate, wherein Hopkins points to the limitations of a reliance on character as the sign of advancement. Luke's speech, in its indictment of the philosophy of racial uplift, aligns the emphasis on the character of exemplary men with the "contending forces," such as "lynching and concubinage," that constitute postemancipation racial domination. But in making the story a crucial turning point in the narrative as well, Hopkins also puts under critique the efficacy of speech making itself as a rhetorical mode by showing its limits as a discloser of the story written on Sappho's face. Luke's story not only has a powerful effect on the "weeping, grief-convulsed audience" (261), but it also has a pronounced effect on one particular member of it: "[A] woman was borne from the auditorium in a fainting condition. John Langley from his seat on the platform leaned over and asked an usher who the lady was. 'Miss Sappho Clark,' was his reply" (262). Sappho's collapse signals to the reader, and more importantly to John Langley, that the story written on Sappho's face is the story of her past as Mabelle Beaubean. This moment of revelation, as Hazel Carby observes, is thus positioned as the "denouement" that sets in motion the narrative resolutions of the rest of the novel.[78] Luke's' revelation is the turning point of the novel not because it "reveals" the story written on Sappho's face but rather because of the way that it compels and motivates alternative ways of reading that story.

Within the frame of the romance plot, Sappho's beauty is positioned as the logical motor of narrative development. Just after Dora's excited declaration of Sappho's beauty, John and Will both come under the influence of that beauty as they meet Sappho for the first time. Introduced to Sappho at a small musical gathering hosted by the Smith family, John and Will are both struck "dumb" by Sappho's stunning beauty and charm:

> John was dumb before so much beauty and wit. Will was so blinded by her charms that he was scarcely conscious of what he was doing; but not a word or movement of hers was lost to him. . . . They were silent for some time, and then Will said: "Miss Clark is a very beautiful woman; don't you think so, John?" "Well," replied John, "beauty is not the word to describe her. She's a stunner, and no mistake," John went to bed; but Will sat by the fire a longer time than usual, thinking thoughts which had never before troubled his young manhood; and unconsciously, one face—the face of Sappho Clark—formed the background of his thoughts. (111–113)

What has never before troubled Will's "young manhood," of course, is the prospect of marriage, and it is the face of Sappho that sets the marriage plot into motion as Will attempts to win over the reluctant Sappho.

But it is the revelation of the story written on Sappho's face as the story of Mabelle Beaubean through the speech of Luke Sawyer that gives John the opening he needs to realize his desire to seduce Sappho as well and thus sets in motion the second complicating narrative of John's deceit. Already betrothed to Dora, John cannot pursue Sappho because to do so would expose him in the eyes of Sappho, as well as everyone else, as the deceitful and unfaithful character that we, the reader, know that he is. But when John learns of Sappho's secret past, he decides to exploit this knowledge by threatening to expose Sappho unless she agrees to become his secret mistress.[79] It is this threat that, in the end, is too much for Sappho to bear and thus what causes her to reclaim her son and flee back to New Orleans and her secret life at the convent where she was originally taken in, but not before exposing John and herself in a confessional letter to Will and Dora. The story written on Sappho's face that sets the conventional marriage plot into motion ends up, through its polemical revelation in Luke's speech, producing the temporary barriers to that plot's resolution that allow for the restoration of the Smith family fortune and the disclosure of their own family's mixed-race story. It is thus the means through which Sappho is revealed as the historical reiteration of the violences that brought the Smith family into existence.

As Hopkins's carefully woven plot thus makes clear, reading the face of her mixed-race heroine is not so much an act of seeing the inherited marks of racial character as it is an exegetical exposure of the historical violences through which race and gender are constituted as social facts. Hopkins makes this clear in her literary exposure, then effacement, of the racial origins of both Will's and John's character. As Hopkins's narrator underscores, Will Smith is the one character in the novel most marked by his possession of character, going so far as to declare, "Emerson's words on character were an apt description of the strong personality of this man: 'A reserved force which acted directly by its presence, and without (apparent) means'" (168). Hopkins's initial depiction of Will takes the form of a racialized account of his own intrinsic and striking beauty:

> Will Smith was tall and finely formed, with features almost perfectly chiseled, and complexion the color of an almond shell. His hair was black and curly, with just a tinge of crispness to denote the existence of Negro blood. His eyes were dark and piercing as an eagle's. Ladies of high position followed his tall form with admiring glances as he moved about his duties at the hotel, and wondered that so much manly beauty should be wasted upon an inferior race. (90)

Just as in the fetishized depiction of Sappho, Will's beauty is construed as the product of a complicated play of racial denotation and connotation. Standing out against a presumably though unmarked connotative field of whiteness, Will's "Negro blood" emerges as the denotative marks of "crispness," "complexion," and dark and piercing eyes. Will's attractiveness, moreover, depends on a fetishizing recognition *and* subsequent disavowal of his racial attributes by the "Ladies of high position" who both are transfixed by Will's racial attributes and lament them at the same time.

In the initial depiction of John Langley that follows, Hopkins again emphasizes the visible manifestations of inherited racial characteristics, but in an unexpectedly different way:

> John Langley, his companion, was shorter in stature and very fair in complexion. His hair was dark and had no indication of Negro blood in its waves; his features were of the Caucasian cut. He possessed a gentle refinement of manner, apt to take well with the opposite sex; but to a reader of character, the strong manhood and honesty of purpose which existed in Will Smith were lacking in John Langley. He was a North Carolinian— a descendant of slaves and southern "crackers." We might call this a bad mixture—the combination of the worst features of a dominant race with an enslaved race; and in some measure John Langley would bear out the unfavorable supposition upon close acquaintance. (90–91).

In Hopkins's depiction of John Langley, she again invokes the notion of racial inheritance as key to defining the character of her main protagonists. The physiological attributes, though lacking the clear "indication of Negro blood," are attractive enough, as Dora had also made clear, to "the opposite sex." But the representational strategy here that appears to reiterate a deterministic logic of racial inheritance, however, ends up substituting class for race as the determinant feature of inherited character. The white "blood" that visually predominates seems at first to be the source, to the "reader of character," of John's flawed character. But John's flawed character is the product not simply of his white blood but of a "bad mixture" and more importantly "the combination of the worst features of a dominant race with an enslaved race." John's flawed character, in other words, is not so much racially defined as it is class defined; it is not the "whiteness" of his blood that determines his character but rather that his "white blood" is that of low-class "crackers" and that it is leavened by the "black blood" of "slaves" rather than free Northern blacks. John's degraded character, in this comparison, also draws attention to how Will's own exemplary character also derives from the class origins of his ancestors: his white blood is that of the wealthy British Montfort family, and his black blood is that of the freeborn and well-traveled Henry Smith.

In making the character of these two men depend on the class position of their ancestors, Hopkins undoes the logic of inherited *racial* character while nonetheless leaving the notion of inheritance itself quite intact. But while Hopkins's uses racial and class origins in order to depict the character of Will and John, the frame tale just as quickly confounds the terms through which that origin can be understood, for Hopkins's invocation of the inheritability of character through lines of "blood" ends up troubling the very logic of inheritance that she seems to be invoking. For the delineation of Will's and John's inherited character ultimately points back not to a line of black and white ancestors but rather to the frame tale of the novel itself, a frame tale that undoes the very notion of race by critically interrogating its historical construction. Hopkins frames the conflict between Will and John over Sappho Clark as a historical repetition and redress of the conflict between Will's and John's great-grandfathers, Charles Montfort and Anson Pollock, a hundred or so years earlier. Hopkins makes the reading of Will's and John's character not a question of identifying how "blood will tell on itself" (108) but rather a question of reading the history through which character is constructed as a reliable indicator of race, class, and gender in the first place. Hopkins's innovation, in other words, is to invoke the logic of inheritance so central to the rhetoric of character not to essentialize the racial and gendered dimensions of character but rather radically to historicize them.

Set a century earlier in the early 1790s, the frame tale that takes up the first quarter of the novel and that is returned to at the novel's end, revolves around the fall of the wealthy British family of the Montforts. Portrayed as its own kind of lynching scene, the murder of Charles Montfort and brutal relegation of his wife and children to slavery is conditioned, on Hopkins's account, by a very complex international clash of colonial and capitalist institutions. Hopkins initially construes Montfort's fall as its own kind of morality play, in that his fall is meted out as a kind of punishment for his privileging of interest over conscience. Charles Montfort moves to North Carolina from Bermuda in order to avoid having to free his slaves because of the new parliamentary bill, passed in 1790, calling for the gradual emancipation of slaves in all the colonies of the British Empire. Montfort's decision to move to the United States of course is driven by the belief that there he can satisfy the dictates of conscience *and* self-interest, for his plan is to build up his wealth to the point where he can free his slaves without great sacrifice and retire comfortably in England as a gentlemen of means. This plan of course is what runs afoul of the North Carolina locals who, suspecting that Montfort intends to free his slaves, plot to prevent him from setting such a dangerous "example." Montfort's "fall" is initially cast within an economy of debt and retribution. Montfort privileges his own self-interest over conscience but ultimately "pays" his debt to conscience and the British crown with his own destruction and the fall of his heirs into slavery.[80]

But Montfort's fall is, on Hopkins's account, also the effect of the transnational movement of Montfort and his family to the United States in his effort to evade emancipation. For what catalyzes the killing of Charles Montfort is the desire of Anson Pollock, a white Southerner whose dispossessed family estate Charles has coincidentally bought, for Charles's beautiful wife, Grace. And like the principal romance narrative of the novel, what drives the seduction narrative here is Grace's questionable racial status—a status that is derived, however, from the legal incongruities between the British and American systems of slavery. Throughout the first chapter the Montforts are portrayed as unproblematic members of the white ruling class in Bermuda, but with their landing in North Carolina, a "shadow" falls across the beautiful Grace Montfort. Described by the narrator in nearly the same terms with which Sappho is initially depicted, Grace appears to some of the "idlers on the wharf" (35) as indelibly marked by the attributes of "color":

> Bill Sampson scratched his head meditatively: "Strikes me, Hank, thet thet ar female's got a black streak in her somewhar." Hank stared at Bill a moment, as though he thought he had suddenly lost his senses; then he burst into a loud guffaw. "You git out, Bill Sampson." "Wall, maybe," said Bill, "maybe so. Thar's too much cream color in the face and too little blud seen under the skin fer a genooine white 'ooman." (41)

The narrator's own depiction of Grace as she steps off the boat onto U.S. soil only further complicates the matter, as Grace is depicted with attributes that are very similar to those of Sappho yet that do not decisively ascribe, as they do with Will and John, a racial origin to her beauty:

> Grace Montfort was a dream of beauty even among beautiful women. Tall and slender; her form was willowy, although perfectly molded. Her complexion was creamy in its whiteness, of the tint of the camellia; her hair, a rich golden brown, fell in rippling masses far below the waist line; brown eyes, large and soft as those seen in the fawn; heavy black eyebrows marking a high white forehead, and features as clearly cut as a cameo, completed a most lovely type of Southern beauty. (40)

Despite the subtly racialized terms of her depiction, however, Hopkins leaves the question of Grace's race fundamentally undetermined just as she calls it into question. And it is a question on which a great deal depends, as many of the critical controversies over the novel make clear. Does the tale of the destruction of the Montfort family and its restoration in the Smith family's reunification with their inheritance and their British cousins at the novel's end, for example, ultimately explain the exemplary character of the Smith family and success of its prodigal son, Will, as a kind of return to the white heritage of which Anson Pollock robbed them one hundred years before, making it, as Houston Baker has argued, ultimately a kind of "white-faced minstrelsy"?[81] Or does the frame tale tell the story of a woman who is forced by the American system to live out the legal consequences of her mixed-race heritage, consequences that are only ultimately rectified in the restoration of the Smith family's inheritance?

Hopkins conspicuously refuses to answer these "questions" by ascribing a racial identity to Grace. Instead of a definitive account of Grace's racial identity, Hopkins instead portrays how Grace's race is itself made into a question and how that *question* is resolved with the determinations of racial character. As Bill Sampson goes on to explain, "You can't tell nothin' 'bout these Britishers; they're allers squeamish 'bout thar nigger brats; yas, sah, very squeamish. I've hern tell that they think nuthin of ejcatin' thar black brats, and freein' 'em, an' makin' 'em rich" (41). Grace's race is called into question, in other words, because of the *failure* of the British system adequately to police the inherited character of racial difference. Unlike the American system, in which a slave's status was determined by the status of his or her mother, within the British colonies the legal status of mixed-race children was not necessarily determined by the presence of "black blood." Because the British system did not organize the distinction between master and slave strictly in terms of a distinction between white and black, *any* British masters could be by law potentially of mixed race. As Hopkins's narrator explains,

> In many cases African blood had become diluted from amalgamation with the higher race, and many of these "colored" people became rich planters or business men (themselves owning slaves) through the favors heaped upon them by their white parents. This being the case, there might even have been a strain of African blood polluting the fair stream of Montfort's vitality, or even his wife's, which fact would not have caused him one instant's uneasiness. (22–23)

Simply as members of the British colonial class, therefore, the "purity" of the Montforts' race cannot be guaranteed and thus remains fundamentally an *indeterminate* feature of their character.

Grace is thus "colored" not by confirmable racial traits or origins but simply by being a member of the British colonial class. It is an institutional *failure* to define and police race that ends up making her into a racialized subject in the United States. Race thus becomes in the frame tale the radically untraceable origin of Will's and John's identity, or rather an origin traceable only as the transnational, historical effect of an institutional failure to determine race. As a British subject within the United States, Grace's race becomes a question and in becoming a question becomes a race. "Colored" by this transnational transposition, Grace's racial identity is more determinately reified, however, by the violence of Anson Pollock. Again, though Hopkins leaves unresolved whether Grace's uncertain racial identity is the condition of Pollock's desire, Pollock nonetheless realizes that desire by defining Grace's race through his very violence against her. After he kills Charles Montfort, Pollock lays claim to Grace and her now "colored" children as his own property, her "blackness" "proven" in a stunning display of the violence of racial property by viciously submitting her to the whip, a spectacle to which Hopkins gives prominent place by illustrating the frontispiece of the novel with an image of this scene.

When Grace kills herself soon after, Pollock takes Lucy, Grace's foster sister and black servant, in her place and enslaves the two young boys, Charles and Jesse. Although the inherited characters of both John Langley and Will Smith are traced to this historical moment, it is also at this moment that the notion of race is completely confounded. In taking Lucy as the racial surrogate for the Grace he could not ultimately possess, Anson Pollock founds the "mixed-race" family from which John (Pollock) Langley will eventually descend. The two young sons, Charles and Jesse, moreover, are both rendered legally black (and slaves) by the fiction of their mother's blackness. Charles is "restored" as white when he is secretly bought by a sympathetic mineralogist and returned to England to reclaim his family's fortune. The younger son, Jesse, however, also eventually escapes to the North, but there, "in his character of a fugitive slave . . . cast[s] his lot with the colored people of the community" (78), eventually marrying the daughter of the family that has taken him in and raising with her a large family: "Thus he was absorbed into that unfortunate race, of whom it is said that a man had better be born dead than to come into the world as part and parcel of it" (79). From this "absorption," of course, the Smith family descends; Ma Smith is Jesse's daughter, and Dora *Grace Montfort* Smith and William *Jesse Montfort* Smith are Jesse's grandchildren. Will Smith's eventual union with Sappho and restoration of the Montfort family inheritance thus marks the symbolic restoration of Charles and Grace and their victory over the Pollock clan. Hopkins's literary delineation of Will's and John's characters thus ends up dissolving the notion of inheritable racial essence and instead demonstrates the radically historical and transnational process through which bodies are marked and unmarked by race and, more importantly, as objects of desire.

But although Sappho's beauty thus becomes the vehicle through which the Smith family's "legacy" is restored, the question still remains, does this mean that the "story written on her face" is ever properly read for the history *it* tells? Hopkins's account of the restoration of the Smith family through the recuperation of Sappho as a model mother and wife suggests that Sappho's story is only partially read. For although Will Smith is able to see in the "character" and beauty of Sappho the "difficult life" that has marked her character and her beauty, his recognition and forgiveness of Sappho are premised on her radical domestication within the role of wife and mother. Sappho's "happy" ending is also the "tragedy" of her own normativization both sexually and professionally. Sappho's beauty makes the bloodlines of Will and John visible as possible bearers of inherited character, but it does not necessarily make visible the complex history of subjugation—a history broader than the sexual possession of slaves by their masters—that forms Sappho's own character.

As the only major character not implicated in the narrative's lines of inheritance, Sappho represents the fact that the fiction of kinship and inherited character can only be maintained at the risk of making visible the complex economic and transnational terms through which it is formed. Although Hopkins's goal of "raising the stigma of degradation" from the race has often been understood as a representational challenge to racial stereotypes, her concern with the "stigma of degradation," it turns out, is a concern with the way that the history of racial and sexual violence has affected the bodies and identities of African American women. Raising the stigma entails, in Hopkins's project of racial uplift, not only being able to read that history but also being able to read the conventions of gender and sexuality that can recognize that history as "degrading" only by normativizing female desire. In her own effort to "raise the stigma of degradation" from the race, Hopkins also challenges the assumptions through which race and gender are written and unwritten as legible social facts. For Hopkins, raising the stigma of degradation involves much more than simply providing powerful counterrepresentations to racial stereotypes or restoring African American kinship through a conventional narrative of normative, heterosexual desire; it involves unearthing the complex historical process through which bodies are marked and experienced as degraded in the first place. Sappho emerges in the novel as a kind of traumatic disruption of the neat representational logic of Washington and Du Bois, both in that her story quite literally is told as a corrective to the Washingtonian and Du Boisian speeches given at the American Colored League and in that the seduction plot mobilized around Sappho's arresting character foregrounds the gender and class foundations of uplift's appeal to character. In Hopkins's attempt to "raise the stigma of degradation" from Sappho's feminine character, in other words, she shows how such a racial resignification must be able to read the history of racial and sexual violence through which the fictions of race's erasure are also maintained. Hopkins's complex interweaving of historical stories as an explanation of her characters' "character" thus seeks to point to the radically historical nature of that character while evacuating the traditional terms through which that "inheritance" is traditionally rendered. Character is for Hopkins the important focus of racial uplift not because it names a radically self-fashioned subject, as Washington would hope, or because it is the cultural expression of innate racial traits, as Du Bois suggests, but rather because it names a complex historical process in which subjects are made and remade by their own attempts to read the past that surrounds them. What Sappho demonstrates is that character names not so much a set of inherited traits but rather the very condition of being historical.

Pauline Hopkins's critique of the dehistoricizing tendencies both of racial science and of the character-building strategies of racial uplift is indicative of a broader critique of the influential role of the rhetoric of character in late nineteenth-century practices of social reform as they were applied in particular to questions of racial integration and, as the next chapter argues, of immigration and assimilation. A key component in the "Americanization" movements that shaped the policies and practices of immigration and naturalization, the rhetoric of character also emerged as an instrument of cultural erasure in the overseas imperialism of America's "civilizing mission" at the turn of the century, a mission that took up and rearticulated the "manifest destiny" of earlier forms of settler colonialism and continental expansion. I thus turn in the next chapter to the work of one of the most influential social reformers and anti-imperial activists of the late nineteenth and early twentieth centuries, Jane Addams, and consider her efforts to reappropriate the traditional character-building function of charity work as a method of historical recovery and cultural preservation within the immigrant neighborhoods of the modern American city. Although Addams often resisted explicitly invoking the rhetoric of character because of the vexed history of its ideological and cultural work, the influential practices of charity work that Addams established in her "settlement house" in the nineteenth ward of Chicago drew extensively on the traditions of building, reading, and representing character. By examining her theoretical and autobiographical writings as well as the practices of the Hull House settlement, the final chapter that follows charts both the impact of the rhetoric of character on the practices of reform that came to define the Progressive era and the naturalization and absorption of the rhetoric of character in some of the most basic understandings of the self and the body in the twentieth century.

5

Character's Conduct

Spaces of Interethnic Emulation in
Jane Addams's "Charitable Effort"

We are now living amid the glories of a new outlook for
woman. . . . She uniformly stamps the coin of character upon life and
conduct on the home and nation, and the home will not suffer because of her zeal to ennoble and purify the body politic.
                                                    —O.P. Furnas, "Our Mothers"[1]

The geography of character is a "branch" sure to be taught some day
in public schools.
                                    —Frances Willard, "Scientific Temperance Instruction
                                                    in the Public Schools"[2]

In 1928, the organizers of the Chicago Association for Child
Study and Parent Education, one of many emerging organizations dedicated to the new science of pedagogy and child rearing, decided to address
its annual conference to one of the most important social-reform projects
in the nineteenth- and early twentieth-century United States, the project
of "Building Character." The "Mid-West Conference on Character Development," as it was called, gathered together a diverse and esteemed group
of clinical psychologists, primary- and secondary-school educators, doctors, social reformers, and university presidents and professors. Some were
noted for their expertise in the scientific study of character development,
others for their practical expertise in the "training of character" as a distinct
method of child rearing. The problems of character and character building were discussed from a number of different disciplinary and theoretical
points of view, with paper sessions and roundtable discussions devoted to

such an array of topics as "Scientific Attitude toward Character Development," "Standards for Character," "Creative Expression and Character Development," "The Use of Leisure Time for Character Development," "Social Attitudes and Character," "Religion and Character," " Building Character through Unified Education," "The Physical Basis of the Child's Emotional Health," "How to Make or Break the Child," "Creative Education and Character," "Ideals and Character," and "Discipline and Character."[3]

In assembling a panel on the topic of "Social Attitudes and Character," the organizers turned to a person who not only was one of the nation's foremost social reformers but who had also made the development of a "social ethic" the central aim of her reformist activities, the social reformer Jane Addams. As cofounder and leading theorist of the Hull House Settlement, established in 1889 in the nineteenth ward of Chicago's West Side tenement district, Jane Addams had become by 1928 perhaps the most famous and influential voice for social justice, poverty relief, and child welfare in the United States.[4] Lauded (and occasionally reviled) as "the conscience of the nation," Addams was ranked, "[i]n every early twentieth century public opinion poll before World War I . . . as the most admired American woman, often as the most admired American," and her work as a social reformer and activist earned her the Nobel Peace Prize in 1931.[5]

Addams had a profound and often direct impact on landmark state and federal legislation of the Progressive era, both through her own direct efforts and through the network of activists and prominent public figures she knew and influenced, including W.E.B. Du Bois, John Dewey, Charlotte Perkins Gilman, Theodore Roosevelt, and Julia Lathrop, who was the first director of the U.S. Children's Bureau. As a time in which explicit, external strategies of social regulation and control became the obsession of both governmental agencies and liberal social thinkers alike, the Progressive era had found a unique and often paradoxical advocate in Jane Addams. Addams envisioned Hull House, the effective platform for her reform work, as a kind of sociological laboratory in which both the working-class, immigrant populations of the tenement district and the middle-class reformers who settled there were together and reciprocally reformed through a communal reworking and readjustment of the performed markers of class, ethnicity, and gender. More important for the conference organizers, Addams had, like many female reformers and charity workers before her, made the study of family and child development central to understanding and ameliorating the effects of urban industrialization on the immigrant working classes and had also made a variety of character-building practices—such as habit training, physical exercise, youth clubs, and elocution and etiquette lessons—central to the work of Hull House.[6]

The brief paper that Addams presented at the conference, titled "Social Attitudes and Character," took up a familiar theme in a familiar style for anyone acquainted with either her extensive writings or her well-publicized work at Hull House.[7] Her anecdotal narrative describes three cases in which she observed the effects of social attitudes on the children of working-class, immigrant families. Addams recounts in particular how the children of recent immigrants negotiate the complex demands of cultural assimilation, demands that often distance them from the character-building traditions of their parents and their country of origin. But what is perhaps most striking about Addams's account of the conflicting demands of these social attitudes is her deep reluctance to invoke the key concept of character in order to describe those demands. Eschewing the kinds of technical or prescriptive accounts of character formation typical of the conference, Addams rarely refers to character at all, making reference to it only at the very end of her talk. And what is most striking about her comments there is that they emphasize not a process of building character through the steady application of parenting or pedagogical methods but rather the emergence of character in situations of intense conflict between distinct cultural traditions.

Why then was Addams so reluctant to evoke the concept of character at this conference explicitly devoted to the study of it? Does this suggest that the project of character building is perhaps an inadequate, even dangerous, response to the complex problems of class mobility and interethnic exchange to which Addams dedicated her life at Hull House? Why does such a prominent social reformer, in an era in which social reform so insistently rallied around the concept of character, resist discussing such a concept in a paper ostensibly devoted to it? Might we understand such a reluctance as itself a statement on the vexed value of the concept of character as an explanatory model for such scenes of cross-cultural contact, and as a statement on its simultaneously promising yet perilous role as an object of social reform? How is Addams redefining here the form and function of social reform by subtly yet insistently calling into question one of its most salient terms and potent strategies?

Taking this reluctance toward the notion of character as a prompt and clue, this chapter examines how Jane Addams's successful and enormously influential model of poverty relief and social reform was founded

less on a project of building character than on a wholesale reconceptualization of the character-building function of the traditional charity
relation, a reconceptualization that reappropriates the "cosmopolitan"
impulse of philanthropy beyond the imperial aspirations that we saw so
carefully delineated in Herman Melville's *The Confidence-Man*. For Addams, as for many other social reformers of her time, the "friendly visit"
of an aid-dispensing, middle-class, and usually female charity worker to
the homes of the poor and often immigrant working classes was the most
important component of professional poverty relief. While the social contact exercised through such a charity relation was very often the means
through which monetary aid was distributed, it was more importantly
the means through which the much more ameliorative "coin" of character
was distributed through the palpable example of the charity worker's own
exemplary middle-class character.

In Addams's account of such a system of character emulation in *Democracy and Social Ethics* (1902) and *Twenty Years at Hull-House* (1910),
however, she critiques the radically disciplinary and ideological function
of the charity relation by demonstrating how it articulates and reinforces
the very class and cultural barriers that it presumes to overcome. The in-
genuity and importance of Addams's argument, however, lies not in its
critique of the rhetoric of character on which charity work had traditionally relied but rather in its simultaneous recuperation of charity work's
potentially democratizing social effects. In her theoretical works, as well
as in her work at Hull House, Addams seeks to reestablish the project of
social reform on the reciprocally beneficial effects of cross-cultural and
interclass identification that are possible in the traditional charity relation. Toward that end, Addams redefines charity work in order to extricate it from the assimilationist imperative of "Americanization" and by
challenging the gendered assumptions of women's work as philanthropic
"stewards of character." By defining character as the complex, incomplete
product of a continual and resolutely social engagement with scenes of
class and cross-cultural contact—and also by continually enabling such
scenes in the parlors, classrooms, workshops, auditoriums, and gymnasi-
ums of Hull House—Addams demonstrates the importance of a properly
intercultural concept of character to the "Progressive" realization of a pluralist, democratic civic sphere.

Stewards of the Nation's Character

Toward the end of the nineteenth century, charity work was essentially defined and motivated by the work of women. As Robyn Muncy has argued, however, the "female dominion in American reform" that emerged by the end of the nineteenth century was a dominion problematically defined by "a combination of autonomy and circumscription."[8] Charity organizations, often staffed, directed, and even funded by women, were one of the few places that women could work outside the home with relative autonomy and in a professional capacity. Charity work was one of the few professional arenas (along with teaching and nursing) in which women could pursue independent careers and, moreover, exert an influence over public policy that was denied to them at the ballot box. This relative autonomy, however, was dearly bought, for it was predicated on both an exclusion from most other professional fields and a highly reductive concept of the essentially benevolent and morally sympathetic feminine character.

Women's circumscription within the profession of charity work was justified by their special suitability for what was perhaps the most important profession of them all: the stewardship of the nation's character. As John Todd had so emphatically put it in his influential manual for young girls, *The Daughter at School,*

> [T]he profession of woman is that of being the educator of the human race, the former of human character. . . . [F]rom her very constitution and nature, from her peculiar sensibilities and tenderness, it seems to me that the great mission of woman is to take the world—the whole world—in its very infancy, when most pliable and most susceptible, and lay the foundations of human character. Human character, in all its interests and relations and destinies, is committed to woman, and she can make it, shape it, mould it, and stamp it just as she pleases. . . . I maintain that we are just what the ladies have made us to be.[9]

While women's charity work was often justified in terms of their role, as Kathleen McCarthy has described it, as the "civic stewards" of the nation's character, this was more specifically conceived as a stewardship of the character they were most immediately in contact with, that is, the character of their children, husbands, and brothers. Women's "professional" role as stewards of character underwrote their advancement into such professions as charity work, teaching, and nursing. As teachers and foreign missionaries, women brought their character-building influences to bear on children outside their own homes, as well as on the "childlike" peoples they were charged with "civilizing." But it was in their capacity as charity workers that women exercised their most pronounced influence over the public sphere. The diverse array of women's voluntary associations that emerged before the Civil War, and the more "scientific" charity organizations that developed after it, could rally their very significant influence over public opinion and government policy on such leading issues as abolition, education reform, and later child labor and factory reform because of their associations with the character-forming capacities of women.

The role of stewards of character that underwrote women's charity work also generated its own unique dilemmas. Women could play an important and very public role in charity work largely because of their position outside of the concerns of the public sphere. Women were reliable guides for the formation and stewardship of character precisely because they were seen to be relatively free from the self-interested and prudential calculations characteristic of masculine agency in the public sphere. The very social role that justified women's increasingly public influence as social reformers also legitimated and presupposed women's exclusion from the professions and enterprises of the public sphere. And by the decades of the 1880s and 1890s, an observation such as Todd's that "we are just what the ladies have made us to be" also became a source of increasing anxiety, as many reformers sought to challenge this "feminization of American culture" with the formation of gender-specific character-building agencies. As we saw in the account of the bad-boy genre's role in the "boyology" institutions discussed in chapter 2, organizations such as the Boy Scouts of America and the Young Men's Christian Association (YMCA), for example, sought to "preserve" the masculine elements of character in the nation's boys by replacing cross-gender character building with same-gender character emulation.[10] Similarly, while women were charged with building character in the youth of the nation (as well as with refining the character of their economically occupied husbands), it was often unclear whether women themselves were taken to have the attributes of character they were entrusted with instilling, since "having character" invariably evoked masculine-coded attributes associated with willing in the public sphere. The sacrificial and sympathetic benevolence that presumably qualified women as stewards of character, in other words, was often difficult to square mimetically with the self-reliant qualities that marked the true possessor of character. What was unclear was how the particular qualities of feminine character could mediate the formation of masculine character, or the putatively universalized character that masculinity was said to secure, and yet could not mediate its own formation as a universalized character as well.

Such a paradox vexed many of the antebellum feminist arguments for improving women's opportunities for education and self-culture, since such arguments relied on women's privileged position as formers, though not necessarily bearers, of public character. As Sarah Edgarton formulated this paradoxical claim, "The most she wants is not a character, a power and independence which erects 'liberty poles,' and shouts 'freedom' from the forum; but the calm, still, holy consciousness of mental and moral power, the elevation and strength which is born of knowledge, of thought, and of self-reliance."[11] Catherine Beecher's famous and influential argument for the establishment of women's colleges and universities made more direct recourse to the domestic ideology of character formation and women's multiple positionalities within the traditional nuclear family:

> The success of democratic institutions, as is conceded by all, depends upon the intellectual and moral character of the mass of the people. . . . It is equally conceded, that the formation of the moral and intellectual character of the young is committed mainly to the female hand. The mother forms the character of the future man; the sister bends the fibres that are hereafter to be the forest tree; the wife sways the heart, whose energies may turn for good or for evil the destinies of a nation. Let the women of a country be made virtuous and intelligent, and the men will certainly be the same. The proper education of a man decides the welfare of an individual; but educate a woman, and the interests of a whole family are secured.[12]

Beecher's argument for enhancing and expanding women's access to higher education was typical in its emphasis on women's role as stewards of character. After the Civil War, such arguments were instrumental in the founding of the first women's colleges and the development of coeducational universities in the late 1860s and 1870s. The pursuit of such educational opportunities, however, in its emphasis on women's traditional role as stewards of character, produced by the late nineteenth century an even greater frustration on the part of women with, on the one hand, their increased access to higher education and yet, on the other hand, a simultaneous lack of a professional venues in which to put that education to work. If women were justified in pursuing such an education in order to enhance their capacities as stewards, such a stewardship all too often demanded that they take their place once again within the confines of the domestic scene.

The Snare of Character

In her semiautobiographical work *Twenty Years at Hull-House,* Jane Addams seems to trace the origins of the Hull House settlement back to just such a set of conflicting gender demands. In her reflections on college life at Rockford Seminary, Addams laments what she calls the "snare of preparation" in higher education. Higher education, she complains, "entangles" the practical energies of students with the "inactivity" of intellectual exercise "at the very period of life when they are longing to construct a world anew and to conform it to their own ideals."[13] More precarious for young women, however, is that this protracted snare of preparation is relieved only by the equally frustrating snare of what she calls the "family claim," which demands that women sacrifice their training to the domestic stewardship of the traditional family. After realizing that her extensive training in social theory, "mental and moral philosophy," literature, and history would find no immediate outlet outside the family claim, Addams turns, like many of her contemporaries, to the otherwise scarce refuge offered by charity work. In describing her inspiration for what would become the Hull House settlement, Addams narrates a typical story of the unique appeal of charity work to the college-educated, middle-class woman:

> I gradually became convinced that it would be a good thing to rent a house in a part of the city where many primitive and actual needs are found, in which young women who had been given over too exclusively to study, might restore a balance of activity along traditional lines and learn of life from life itself; where they might try out some of the things they had been taught and put truth to "the ultimate test of the conduct it dictates or inspires." (61)

But although this famous and often-recounted story of Addams's turn to charity work seems to be yet another example of nineteenth-century women sublimating their character-forming capacities into the legitimate domain of civic stewardship, Addams's full origin story for the founding of Hull House shows that she was also keenly aware of the "snares" that such a conception of charity work also laid for women. Hence while Addams set about founding a social settlement in order to give herself and other women a place to realize their ambitions to participate in the project of civic stewardship, she also founded the settlement in order to eliminate the conditions that put her in the position to need such a project in the first place.

Addams's autobiographical account of the origins of the Hull House settlement is somewhat typical in its derivation of the character of the institution from the autobiographical character of its primary founder.[14] And that story begins not with Addams's postgraduate crisis but rather with the "earliest impressions" described at the beginning of *Twenty Years at Hull-House.* Virtually all of the impressions described in chapter 1 are, Addams readily admits, "directly concerned with my father, although of course I recall many experiences apart from him" (7). As Allen Davis has argued, such an autobiographical beginning to the story of Hull House reiterates familiar patterns in nineteenth-century women's autobiographical writing. The tropes of an "impressive young woman" and the idealized "affection between a tender daughter and a solicitous father," along with tales of overcoming handicaps and childhood plans are, Davis argues, elements that are also "quite common in the autobiographies and the legends of the famous as an explanation for their later acts and deeds of glory."[15] Most readers of *Twenty Years at Hull-House* just as predictably read these opening pages for the information they provide on the influence of this public-spirited and kindhearted father over his daughter's own development as a social reformer.[16] Davis's argument, however, that "Jane Addams was probably not consciously aware that she was patterning her first chapter after the fictions of her day or that she was using a genteel shorthand for a special relationship between father and daughter" belies the ways that Addams makes questioning these autobiographical conventions the very point of the chapter.[17]

Addams's use of the autobiographical mode is distinctive in that serves not just to delineate the formative influences on her young character and therefore on the institution of Hull House but rather to call into question the autobiographical assumptions about character formation on which such an institutional genealogy relies. Addams is careful to reiterate, in the opening lines and first chapter of *Twenty Years at Hull-House,* the theoretical presumptions behind such an autobiographical narrative opening:

> On the theory that our genuine impulses may be connected with our childish experiences, that one's bent may be tracked back to that "No-Man's

Land" where character is formless but nevertheless settling into definite
lines of future development, I begin this record with some impressions of
my childhood. (7)

But though this opening sentence anticipates the autobiographical expectations of her readers, she proceeds through the rest of the chapter to test such
expectations critically through the account of her relationship to her father.

Her father, John H. Addams, was well known as a prototypical self-
made man, who had made his mark first as the founder of flour and tim-
ber mills and other businesses in and around Cedarville, Illinois, and later
as a successful railroad speculator and prominent Illinois state legislator.
Chapter 1 describes the young Jane Addams's close and adulatory relationship with her father in the years between her mother's death when she was
two and a half and her father's second marriage when she was eight years
old. In the account of what she calls the "doglike affection" for her father,
Addams details how that affection expressed itself as a strong desire to
imitate and remake her body in the image of his own. Addams's account
initially describes this imitative desire as a feature of the character-forming influences usually directed toward a mother: "I centered on him all
that careful imitation which a little girl ordinarily gives to her mother's
ways and habits" (12). Her transference of this imitative desire to her father, however, also transforms its basic terms:

> I had a consuming ambition to possess a miller's thumb, and would sit con-
> tentedly for a long time rubbing between my thumb and fingers the ground
> wheat as it fell from between the millstones. . . . I believe I have never since
> wanted anything more desperately than I wanted my right thumb to be
> flattened, as my father's had become, during his earlier years of a miller's
> life. Somewhat discouraged by the slow process of structural modification,
> I also took measures to secure on the backs of my hands the tiny purple and
> red spots which are always found on the hands of the miller who dresses
> millstones. . . . [I] spread out my hands near the millstones in the hope that
> the little hard flints flying from the miller's chisel would light upon their
> backs and make the longed-for marks. (14)

What is striking about her story is that, rather than trying to *imitate* the
professional activities, habits, or persona of her father, the young Addams
tries to *inscribe* the traces of that professional identity onto her own body.
Unlike the imitation of a "mother's ways and habits," Addams replaces

imitation with inscription and recordation through an odd kind of corporeal literalization of his professional habits and in particular their body-modifying effects. She does not cultivate his habits but rather tries to inscribe the residual traces and even wounds of those habits onto, or as the shape of, her own body.

Although Addams initially wonders aloud that "[i]t is hard to account for the manifestations of a child's adoring affection, so emotional, so irrational, so tangled with the affairs of the imagination" (11), by the end of her narration she *is* able to account for these "grotesque attempts to express . . . [her] doglike affection" (12):

> This sincere tribute of imitation, which affection offers to its adored object, had later, I hope, subtler manifestations, but certainly these first ones were altogether genuine. In this case, too, I doubtless contributed my share to that stream of admiration which our generation so generously poured forth for the self-made man. (14)

Addams reproduces the professional marks of her father's body not, according to her own retrospective reading, out of a desire to become her father—to follow in his footsteps as an exemplary model of character—but rather in order to signify and to pay "tribute" to the "adored object" with the gift of imitation. Addams responds to her own feelings for him by wanting to give back to him an image of himself: an image of himself *as* a self-made man. What is most important about this scene is, for Addams, how it is part of the broader "stream of admiration which our generation so generously poured forth for the self-made man." Addams tells this story not simply to describe the features of character that will inform her later work as a social reformer but rather in order to indict retroactively the rhetoric of character that gave shape and expression to her love for her father and to extricate her intensely personal bond with him from the logic of reflective identification. The story's import is thus not as a report on the fatherly influences on her formless character but rather as an autobiographical diagnosis of the cultural elements participating in and governing that formation.

In the subsequent chapter, titled the "Influence of Lincoln," Addams extends this autobiographical critique of childhood influences to call into question more explicitly the cultural iconography and hero worship of the self-made man by analyzing the distinctly cultural dimensions of her own "childish admiration for Lincoln" (24). Like the story of her own father, the

purpose of Addams's account of Abraham Lincoln, whom her father had
known as a young man and had remained friends and correspondent with
throughout his life, is to extricate the real respect and fascination that she
had for "that remarkable personality" from the hero worship of the self-
made man (26). What she claims to have learned is that the "greatness"
of such a man as Lincoln derives not from some self-constituted power
of character but rather from his ability to "draw" on the "capital fund" of
"the people themselves" (29). To misrecognize the political power that is
located in the people, she observes, as a power inhering in Lincoln himself
would be to fall victim to the "political fetishism" of hero worship.[18] What
she learns through the example of Lincoln, a lesson that she will make the
cornerstone of Hull House, is that the rhetoric of character subverts the
capacity to recognize and coordinate the collective powers of a constitu-
ency, a power all too often misrecognized as the sui generis power of the
self-made character. It is thus when she herself witnesses the democratic
possibilities of collective action at the "Old Settler's Day" that she realizes
the distorting effects of the rhetoric of self-made character: "I remember
that I was at that time reading with great enthusiasm Carlyle's 'Heroes and
Hero Worship,' but on the evening of 'Old Settlers' Day,' to my surprise,
I found it difficult to go on. Its sonorous sentences and exaltation of the
man who 'can' suddenly ceased to be convincing" (29). In her delineation
of the events that inspired her to found, with Ellen Gates Starr, the Hull
House settlement, Addams turns the expectations of the autobiographical
mode against themselves. Her narrative tells a story not of the influences
of great men over her still-forming character but rather of her overcoming
of such an ideology of influence and emulation and of how she came to
realize her most basic principles of social reform precisely through that
overcoming.

Charity's Therapy

Although *Twenty Years at Hull-House* is perhaps the most widely read
of Jane Addams's writings today, her earlier work *Democracy and Social
Ethics* gives her most theoretical—and widely read in her own day—account of the mission to which Hull House was dedicated, the mission, as
she describes it at the end of *Twenty Years at Hull-House,* to "socialize democracy": "The educational activities of a Settlement, as well as its philanthropic, civic, and social undertakings, are but differing manifestations of

the attempt to socialize democracy, as is the very existence of the Settlement itself" (290). Her discussion in *Democracy and Social Ethics* collects together the criticisms of the "individualist ethic" scattered throughout *Twenty Years at Hull-House* and develops them into a sustained theoretical critique of the reflective epistemology of character emulation and its role in producing, rather than resolving, what she refers to as the "maladjustments" of Gilded Age society. The term *maladjustment* had emerged toward the end of the Gilded Age as a kind of metonymic shorthand for the systemic and radically dislocating transformations of urban industrialization, mass migration, and commodity culture. Social reform was thus often conceived in the late nineteenth and early twentieth centuries as a technical process of restoring a proper "adjustment" between individuals and their institutional, usually industrial environment. As Scott Nearing, in his 1910 study *Social Adjustment*, puts it: "maladjustment exists in numerous virulent forms, in many parts of the United States. . . . maladjustment is (1) due to economic causes, (2) involving social cost, and (3) remediable through social action."[19]

In *Democracy and Social Ethics*, Jane Addams takes up this common trope of maladjustment as she also diagnoses the social dislocations brought about by the manifold transformations of Gilded Age society. In the ethnographically detailed opening pages of the introduction, Addams seems to evoke a typical scene of working-class discontent:

> All about us are men and women who have become unhappy in regard to their attitude toward the social order itself; toward the dreary round of uninteresting work, the pleasures narrowed down to those of appetite, the declining consciousness of brain power, and the lack of mental food which characterizes the lot of the large proportion of their fellow-citizens. These men and women have caught a moral challenge raised by the exigencies of contemporaneous life; some are bewildered, others who are denied the relief which sturdy action brings are even seeking an escape, but all are increasingly anxious concerning their actual relations to the basic organization of society.[20]

The men and women "unhappy in regard to their attitude toward the social order itself," it would seem, are unhappy because this "social order" so relentlessly "declines" and impoverishes their lives with its "dreary round[s]" of work and "narrowed" pleasures. Addams's account at first glance seems to evoke in familiar terms the "dehumanizing" effects of industrial labor on the working classes. But as the passage develops, what becomes clear is that these unhappy men and women are not the same people as those experiencing these dehumanizing effects of the social order. Toward the end of the passage, the unhappy people are shown to be, oddly enough, not unhappy because of their mind-numbing labor but rather because they are "denied the relief which sturdy action brings." What these people are unhappy about, the passage seems to suggest, is that *someone else* is suffering from such conditions. The unhappy people are unhappy, we realize in returning to the first line, not because of their relation to the social order itself, or in their attitude *toward* the social order itself, but rather "in regard to" that attitude, *because of* that attitude, an attitude apparently unhappily burdened by its awareness of the punishing effects of this social order *on others*. What Addams emphasizes, in this curious transposition of working-class labor onto middle-class anxiety, is that the greatest danger of Gilded Age industrialization is that imposed not on the working classes but rather on a middle class anxiously aware of such an imposition and hence "caught in [its] moral challenge."

Addams evokes the vernacular of maladjustment commonly used to describe the rapid and dislocating transformations in the social, economic, demographic, and urban order of Gilded Age society, yet she does so in order to apply such a concept to the mental and moral travails of those who stand witness to, rather than directly undergo, such transformations. The maladjustment of greatest concern, as she goes on to explain, is the "mental attitude of maladjustment" (*Twenty Years at Hull-House*, 6) or "nervousness" produced by these dislocations in the minds of the middle class. Catherine Beecher made such an argument as early as 1841, when she portended the "difficulties" posed, particularly to "American women," to the nervous system by the "overstimulation" of the nation's quickening "high commercial, political, and religious stimulus."[21] But it was not until the Gilded Age that "American nervousness" became its own distinct, therapeutic vernacular of national self-analysis. George M. Beard's 1881 study *American Nervousness: Its Causes and Consequences* established nervousness as the iconic symptom of modern civilization.[22] But unlike this common association of American nervousness with modernization and urban industrialization, Addams makes the subtle but for her crucial shift of attention from the maladjustments of such an industrial order to the maladjustment produced by an *awareness of* its most pernicious effects. As her argument progresses, it becomes clear that the "dreary round of uninteresting work," narrowed pleasures, and declining consciousness of the unhappy people also describes a middle class becoming all too painfully aware of, in the words of Jacob Riis, "how the other half lives."[23]

Addams describes this maladjustment as a discrepancy between the recognition of a new social ethic and one's ability to apply that ethic to one's own life—a maladjustment, in short, between the consciousness of poverty and the conduct that that awareness demands:

> The stern questions are not in regard to personal and family relations, but did ye visit the poor, the criminal, the sick, and did ye feed the hungry? . . .
> The test they would apply to their conduct is a social test. They fail to be content with the fulfillment of their family and personal obligations, and find themselves striving to respond to a new demand involving a social obligation; they have become conscious of another requirement, and the contribution they would make is toward a code of social ethics. The conception of life which they hold has not yet expressed itself in social changes or legal enactment, but rather in a mental attitude of maladjustment, and in a sense of divergence between their consciences and their conduct. (*Twenty Years at Hull-House*, 6)

The "social ethic" Addams describes is not a philanthropic principle to which she subscribes but rather a sensibility that she sees emerging in middle-class society and that seeks to find expression in the conduct of philanthropic enterprise. This philanthropic sensibility is, in other words, the inexorable and unnerving maladjustment of the Gilded Age. This definitive theoretical text by one of America's foremost social reformers thus makes the quite surprising case that a philanthropic sense of social obligation is not simply a reformist solution to the maladjustments of Gilded Age America but is also in a fundamental way the most pernicious maladjustment of them all. The urgent need of philanthropic reform is not so much to address the needs of the poor but rather to minister to the middle-class anxiety over poverty itself.

Since this consciousness "had not yet expressed itself in social changes or legal enactment" but only "in a mental attitude of maladjustment," however, the charity work that sought such social changes and legal enactments also conveniently offered ready therapy for this anxious state of maladjustment that the philanthropically aware individual experienced. This admission of the therapeutic effects of charity work has been cited by many critics as one of the most compromising aspects of Addams's own reformist work and of nineteenth-century women's charity work more broadly. Jill Conway, for example, argues that "[t]he initial impulse for this kind of feminine migration to the slums was not identification with the working class, as in the European settlement movement, but the recognition that there was a social cure for the neurotic ills of privileged young women in America because their ailments were socially induced."[24] Addams's writings of course provide ample evidence for such a view, since she openly makes such motives elemental to her explanations of the development of Hull House and of social reform more broadly. She not only describes the founding vision of Hull House as conditioned by her own personal "nadir of . . . nervous depression and sense of maladjustment," but the figure of the "anxious," college-educated woman plays a central role in such key essays as "Subjective Necessity for Social Settlements" and "Filial Relations."[25]

But it would be a mistake to take such a story of the "subjective necessity" of the social settlement as also the final statement of its "objective value."[26] Addams's rhetorical grafting of the challenges facing middle-class women onto the travails of working-class poverty is a vexed one, but not therefore a less important one. Addams's situating of the problem of charity work squarely within the psychological dilemmas imposed in particular on middle-class women does not simply reduce poverty relief to a therapeutic hobby of middle-class women. Rather it demonstrates how the social ethic is first experienced by women not because of their innate moral sensibility or benevolent orientation but rather as a product of the restrictive gender roles they must negotiate. Addams is able to show in her subtle transposition how a prototypically feminist challenge, rather than an idealized feminine sympathy, can be the vehicle for a new kind of philanthropically disposed desire for "contact with the moral experiences of the many":

> [Women] desire both a clearer definition of the code of morality adapted to present day demands and a part in its fulfillment, both a creed and a practice of social morality. In the perplexity of this intricate situation at least one thing is becoming clear: if the latter day moral ideal is in reality that of a social morality, it is inevitable that those who desire it must be brought in contact with the moral experiences of the many in order to procure an adequate social motive. (*Twenty Years at Hull-House*, 6)

Addams situates the work of women to realize the social ethic as a final stage of America's developing democracy, for it compels the realization of that democracy not as abstract principles or legal rights (rights that were failing to secure social equality not only in the segregated South but across the United States) but rather as a transformative, engaged, and deeply personal interaction with ethnic, class, and gender alterity:

> We are thus brought to a conception of Democracy not merely as a sentiment which desires the well-being of all men, nor yet as a creed which believes in the essential dignity and equality of all men, but as that which affords a rule of living as well as a test of faith.
>
> We are learning that a standard of social ethics is not attained by traveling a sequestered byway, but by mixing on the thronged and common road where all must turn out for one another, and at least see the size of one another's burdens. To follow the path of social morality results perforce in the temper if not the practice of the democratic spirit, for it implies that diversified human experience and resultant sympathy which are the foundation and guarantee of Democracy. (*Twenty Years at Hull-House*, 7)

In relatively straightforward fashion, Addams's argument for the "mixing on the thronged and common road" seeks to establish the grounds for giving democracy a final, social expression. Addams thus founds her vision of a pluralist or "cosmopolitan" philanthropy as a specifically feminist response to the class inequalities of Gilded Age capitalism. And it was in providing such an arena for engaged, culturally diverse social interactions that Hull House became such an innovative and extraordinarily influential institution of social reform. But what Addams is not altogether clear about is in what does such an "identification with the common lot" (ibid., 9) consist? How does such a proximity to differences of ethnicity, class, and gender produce an identification that recalibrates "maladjustment," and is that adjustment secured only through an erasure of those differences? What do such contacts adjust, and how does that adjustment transform individuals into democratic subjects? And how, finally, is such a scene of interethnic and interclass identification not just a vision of a fully realized democracy but also a powerful tool of social reform?

Character's Coin

Addams elaborates her vision of a democratized social sphere through an analysis of one of the most important, and yet one of the most "maladjusted," of social relations, the charity relation. As her description of the "charitable effort" in chapter 1 of *Twenty Years at Hull-House* insists, one of the most transformative and potentially productive scenes of social contact was the relationship between the charity worker and the charity recipient:

> Probably there is no relation in life which our democracy is changing more rapidly than the charitable relation—that relation which obtains between benefactor and beneficiary; at the same time there is no point of contact in our modern experience which reveals so clearly the lack of that equality which democracy implies. We have reached the moment when democracy has made such inroads upon this relationship, that the complacency of the old-fashioned charitable man is gone forever; while, at the same time, the very need and existence of charity, denies us the consolation and freedom which democracy will at last give. (11)

The "friendly visit" of a charity worker to the home of a "needy" family had long been the bedrock of charity work in the United States. Rooted in the traditional, Protestant duty to visit the poor and less fortunate among one's neighbors, "friendly visiting" was an activity premised on women's role as stewards of character and hence was the central means through which many antebellum benevolence societies distributed aid to the poor. By the 1870s and 1880s, however, the informal and aid-dispensing practices of antebellum friendly visiting had taken a central role in the methods of "scientific charity" developed within the "charity organization movement."

But in so doing, the function of friendly visiting was also dramatically transformed. In efforts to bring organizational efficiency and broad social scope to the problem of poverty relief, the organizers of scientific charity deemphasized the aid-dispensing function of the friendly visit in order to make it into a more scientific tool of information gathering and of cross-class emulation and uplift. As a practical matter, the friendly visit was a means of scrutinizing and assessing the poor. Not only did visitors attempt to distinguish the truly needy from undeserving and self-destructive "failures," they also made a determination of how best to enable a family or individual to help themselves.[27] Charity organizations of the Gilded Age also operated, however, on the assumption that poverty needed to be understood in relation to social factors beyond the individual's control. Hence charity workers attempted in their visit to determine how best to support a family financially not simply by meeting its short-term needs but rather by making a structural change so that the family was no longer dependent on charity aid. Often this meant referring the "worthy case" to an aid-dispensing agency specifically suited to administer to the family's particular need by "providing such services as penny saving banks, coal-saving funds, provident wood-yards, day nurseries for the children of working mothers, and workrooms where women could be trained to become nursemaids, laundresses, or seamstresses."[28] Thus one of the driving goals of scientific charity was, through the study of the conditions of poverty and the scientific application of structural reform, to make charity itself obsolete. As Frank Dekker Watson put it in his early review of the movement, "In this sense it is the purpose of every charity organization society to work for its own extinction."[29]

In addition to assessing the recipient's needs scientifically while cognizant of the "environmental" factors leading to poverty, the friendly visitor also made character reform a central tool of poverty relief. On the one hand, the visitor needed to be a skilled reader of character in order to assess whether the family or its breadwinners had the traits of character that would enable them eventually to triumph over the economic, legal, and social obstacles arrayed against them. The poor were often quite aware of this surveillance function, as Addams points out:

> In moments of indignation the poor have been known to say: "What do you want, anyway? If you have nothing to give us, why not let us alone and stop your questionings and investigations?" "They investigated me for three weeks, and in the end gave me nothing but a black character," a little woman has been heard to assert. (*Democracy and Social Ethics*, 15)

On the other hand, friendly visitors also mobilized their presumed skills as stewards of character in order to uplift the individual by building up his or her capacities for self-determining action and willing. The friendly visit did not just serve, in other words, to distribute aid and gather information; it also functioned to uplift and alleviate the sufferings of the poor through the ameliorative effects of class contact. The aid friendly visitors provided was the example of their own "successful" middle-class character, a character through which the poor, in aspiring to it, would learn what it meant to help themselves.

The "friendliness" of the friendly visit was also a vital instrument of poverty relief. By establishing a "friendly relation" with the poor, visitors not only opened up a sympathetic channel for information gathering but also made their own "superior" and "successful" character an ameliorative force in the lives of the poor. Charity workers often emphasized the *social* importance of the friendly visit as a means of putting the classes in a sympathetic relation to one another, a relation wherein the "silent example" of the visitor could exert its greatest influence. But while workers continually emphasized the friendliness of the friendly visit, that is, the treating of the poor simply as part of their extended circle of friends and social contacts, they were also well aware that to function as examples they needed constantly to distinguish themselves from the poor by exemplifying the traits of their superior class character. The Associated Charities, for example, in a leaflet they issued titled "The Friendly Visitor," at first defends the sincerity of charity workers' friendship with the poor, only to explain that the visitor should *appear* as a friend only in order to exert more effectively the "silent influence" of a social better. The friendly visitor, in other words, should secure the poor's *confidence* in the philanthropic character:

> We are friendly visitors when we call upon our immediate neighbors. . . . We are not to burst upon those of our acquaintance who happen to be poor with advice, moralizing, inquisitiveness or gratuities. When we first meet them we are strangers, and must show the respect due to persons upon whom we have no claim. . . . In any case let us remember that, as nothing springs from nothing, we must ourselves be frank, courteous, patient, sensible, and really friendly, if we are to inspire like qualities in those we seek to influence. Example will do much more than preaching. What we are, and not what we do, counts most.[30]

The "example" had long been preferred to exhortation in the building of character because it enabled individuals to form a self-made character through interpretive emulation rather than by simply having a derivative character "stamped" onto them through the pedagogical application of rules of conduct and moral injunctions. The friendliness of the friendly visit was thus often modeled on the patronizing solicitude of the parent-child relation. As E.E. Kellogg argues in her child-raising guide *Studies in Character Building*, "example counts far more than precept":

> A constant discipline of self on the part of parents is a necessary requisite for effective work in character shaping. They must learn to become good models, for what they *are,* will teach the child far more than what they *say.* What they would build into the child's character they must themselves possess.[31]

The primary goal of friendly visitors was not to advise the poor but rather to offer the better advice in the presentation they made of their own character. The hope of such an ennobling influence was that the poor would inculcate the traits of thrift, self-restraint, and enterprise that were taken to be the vehicles to success. The beneficiary of such a charitable gift of character, however, was put in the position of having to deduce those traits from the manner and conduct of the charity visitor. The decorum of friendly visitors—the cleanliness of their clothes, correctness of speech, deliberateness in conversation, and buoyancy of spirit—had to function as the ambiguous indicators of an otherwise invisible character. How the beneficiary was to deduce from the mannered performances of the visitor the practical traits of character that would uplift them was, of course, left as an uncertain but by no means less necessary feat of interpretation.

The purpose of the friendly visit was not to dictate the terms of character and success that would lift the poor out of their impoverished condition but rather to provide a positive example of successful, middle-class character, in order, if not to lift them out of their condition, at least to assign them responsibility for that condition. Jane Addams's innovations as a reformer and social theorist, however, derive from her ability both to appropriate the power of emulation in class contact and also to extricate it from the individualist rhetoric of self-making for which the process of character formation was commonly mistaken. Addams and Ellen Gates Starr opened Hull House fully prepared to display the ennobling trappings of their class. When they moved into the mansion originally built by Charles J. Hull but later surrounded by the encroaching tenements of a growing Chicago, they sought to restore the house as an emblem of their own class character:

> We furnished the house as we would have furnished it were it in another part of the city, with the photographs and other impedimenta we had collected in Europe. . . . While all the new furniture which was bought was enduring in quality, we were careful to keep it in character with the fine old residence. . . . We believed that the Settlement may logically bring to its aid all those adjuncts which the cultivated man regards as good and suggestive of the best life of the past. (*Twenty Years at Hull-House*, 66)

But while Addams avowed her missionary role as representative of "cultivated man," she also did so by remobilizing the possibilities of reciprocal *exchange* over the top-down *transmission* of culture possible in the performances of class character: "Hull-House was soberly opened on the theory that the dependence of classes on each other is reciprocal; and that the social relation is essentially a reciprocal relation, it gives a form of expression that has peculiar value" (ibid., 64).

In the chapter "Charitable Effort" of *Democracy and Social Ethics,* Addams works through what recognition of such a reciprocal relation of class contact would mean through a detailed analysis of the friendly visit. Addams's account of the corrosive effects of the friendly visit on the poor whom it presumably serves, unlike more contemporary critiques of social welfare, indicts rather than affirms the rhetoric of character that operates through it. For while Addams seizes on the character-forming function of the friendly visit, she also seeks to transform it from an instrument of class and ethnic domination into one of reciprocal recognition. In "Charitable Effort," for example, Addams describes a scene in which the character-building effects of class emulation have gone very much awry. Unlike the hero worship she herself showed as a child to the class position of her father, what confounds the emulatory function of the friendly visit is not only a failure of the beneficiary to imitate and reflect the character of the charity worker but also the more debilitating effects on the charity worker as she discovers that she is a bankrupt spokesperson for the virtues of character she presumably represents:

> The daintily clad charitable visitor who steps into the little house made untidy by the vigorous efforts of her hostess, the washerwoman, is no longer sure of her superiority to the latter; she recognizes that her hostess after all represents social value and industrial use, as over against her parasitic cleanliness and a social standing attained only through status. (*Democracy and Social Ethics,* 12)

Echoing Thornstein Veblen's critique of the empty signs of "leisure class" character, Addams details the ways that emulation breaks down as a mode of poverty relief. The daintily clad "young college woman, well-bred and open-minded" (ibid., 12), who visits the poor family certainly signifies the characteristics of her class, but what thwarts the emulatory function is the emptiness of her signifiers of character as practical guides for the family she visits. The "message" that the charity worker is to send through the example of her own character is the "industrial virtues" that the modern class distinction between "people who work with their hands and those who do not" prevents her from having: "As she daily holds up these standards, it occurs to the mind of the sensitive visitor . . . that she has no right to say these things; that her untrained hands are no more fitted to cope with actual conditions than those of her broken-down family" (ibid., 13).

Not only is the friendly visitor unable to exemplify the "industrial virtues" that would help the family advance to a more secure economic position, but she also fails to exemplify the "successful" character of her own middle-class background. Indeed, what Addams shows is that the emulatory function is fundamentally undercut by the very gesture of charity itself, for the visitor's charity is not representative of the self-interest characteristic of her class: "Success does not ordinarily go, in the minds of the poor, with charity and kind-heartedness, but rather with the opposite qualities. The rich landlord is he who collects with sternness, who accepts no excuse, and will have his own" (ibid., 15). The charity worker's "philanthropy," in other words, occludes the "misanthropy" that should be the indicator of the self-interested, successful character. The charity worker is stuck in a bind of sympathetic identification while also maintaining her role as recriminatory class exemplar. She is drawn into the no man's land of a failed identification with the poor and a failed identification with her own class, a failure signaled by the lack of emulatory "respect":

> The charity visitor, just because she is a person who concerns herself with the poor, receives a certain amount of this good-natured and kindly contempt, sometimes real affection, but little genuine respect. The poor are accustomed to help each other and to respond accordingly to their kindliness; but when it comes to worldly judgment, they use industrial success as the sole standard. In the case of the charity visitor who has neither natural kindness nor dazzling riches, they are deprived of both standards, and they find it of course utterly impossible to judge of the motive of organized charity. (Ibid., 16)

More ominous still, the breakdown of class emulation in the friendly visit transforms it from a vehicle of poverty relief into an instrument of impoverishment. Not only does the friendly visitor assert "industrial virtues" that she herself does not represent, these virtues of industry and self-denial serve to embed her recipients in the conditions of poverty they seek to relieve. The visitor "feels the sordidness of constantly being obliged to urge the industrial view of life" (ibid., 18) because such a view seeks to reconcile and "adjust" the working classes to their industrial lives rather than transforming the "wearing and brutalizing" conditions of their "unceasing bodily toil" (12). The charity relation functions, in its demand for a class mobility that its system of character stewardship actively undermines, as a kind of disciplining technology for maintaining and policing the working classes in their poverty under the pretense of "bettering" them. As Addams says of the "bruised and battered" man "chilled" by his encounter with the friendly visitor, "He does not recognize the disciplinary aspect of the situation" (16).

Addams's critique on the disciplinary aspects of class emulation that operate through the friendly visit should not be taken as a wholesale rejection of the democratic possibilities of character building. Indeed, the rhetoric of character remained central to Addams's conceptualization of progressive reform and played a key role in her delineation of the classic argument for the state's responsibilities toward the social welfare of the nation in *Twenty Years at Hull-House*:

> At such times the residents in various Settlements are driven to a standard of life argument running somewhat in this wise,—that as the very existence of the State depends upon the character of its citizens, therefore if certain industrial conditions are forcing the workers below the standard of decency, it becomes possible to deduce the right of State regulation. (151)

The experiences and exchanges made possible by the social settlement are figured by Addams as not only what bring this "standard of life argument" into perspective but also provide the basis for a broader international coalition of reformers and working-class communities in response to the problems of industrialization as "the residents of an industrial neighborhood gradually comprehend the close connection of their own difficulties with national and even international movements" (ibid.). Addams's goal in charting the failings of the charity relation as a method of poverty relief is thus to reconceive and remobilize the emulatory function of the charity relation in terms of the democratic potentials of interpersonal, cross-cultural contact. As she argues in *Twenty Years at Hull-House*, the immediate and embodied power of character is far more persuasive than the intangible words of reform polemics:

> It is obvious that ideas only operate upon the popular mind through will and character, and must be dramatized before they reach the mass of men. . . . Ethics as well as political opinions may be discussed and disseminated among the sophisticated by lectures and printed pages, but to the

common people they can only come through example—through a personality which seizes the popular imagination. . . . The personal example promptly rouses to emulation. (100–101)

Rather than an emanating source of self-constituted power, however, such an exemplary character is one formed in these very scenes of social contact. Character can serve such a mediating function, in other words, only if it is formed through a "connection with the activity of the many" rather than through the self-interested pursuit of personal achievement:

> When the entire moral energy of an individual goes into the cultivation of personal integrity, we all know how unlovely the result may become; the character is upright, of course, but too coated over with the result of its own endeavor to be attractive. In this effort toward a higher morality in our social relations, we must demand that the individual shall be willing to lose the sense of personal achievement, and shall be content to realize his activity only in connection with the activity of the many. (Ibid., 120)

The democratizing power of character emulation is derailed when it is contained within the narcissistic logic of self-reflection and self-making. What derails the class contact of the charity relation, in other words, is the expectation by the friendly visitor that, in order to steward character, she needs to see herself reflected in the poor that she serves. As the young Addams herself very quickly learned, such "tributes" are exactly what prevent the charity relation from being a truly democratic encounter with the forms of social and cultural difference that form character. Addams founds her model of democracy, in other words, on the recognition that character is a medium of social exchange rather than a measure of social merit.

Practices of Reform, Rhetorics of Character

Jane Addams, in her work at the Hull House settlement and in her theoretical writings, reconceived the disciplinary role women had traditionally played in charity work by turning their constricted role as stewards of character into a sustained critique of the disciplinary function of social reform and its grounding in an individualist ideology of character building. Like other proponents of the settlement house movement, Addams saw in the charity relation not simply an opportunity to "relieve" poverty but rather an opportunity to realize the radically democratic potentials of its cross-cultural exchanges for both the middle-class settlement house workers and the community in which they live. Such an opportunity to rectify the "maladjustments" that structured the class relations and ethnic divisions of the modern city was afforded by the unique space of the settlement house and the opportunities it provided for social contact between individuals from a wide variety of classes, professions, ideological backgrounds, and cultural traditions. Rather than establishing a colonizing foothold among working-class immigrants, as the term *settlement* might suggest, the "typical settlement," as one *Handbook of Settlements* put it, "provides neutral territory traversing all the lines of racial and religious cleavage."[32] By recentering the principle of emulation around a character-building engagement with, and recognition of, various forms of cultural difference, Addams conceives of the settlement house as a place that challenges the conventional logic of emulation, a logic whose social function has often been, as in Twain's *A Connecticut Yankee*, mimetically to reproduce existing social hierarchies. Such an emphasis on the importance of the collective spaces of the settlement house thus challenged the liberal ideology of character formation by underscoring the importance of social interdependency and cross-cultural contact in the constitution and empowerment of character.

Addams's emphasis on the character-building effects of settlement work in what were not simply working-class but also overwhelmingly immigrant neighborhoods seems to evoke the assimilationist practices of "Americanization" that were being promoted by cultural nationalists, government officials, and social scientists at the turn of the century, practices that, as discussed in chapter 2, were frequently organized and legitimated by the discourse of character building.[33] *Americanization* was a term commonly employed to describe a process of cultural assimilation that recent immigrants were presumed to undergo when they arrived in the United States, but it also referred to the institutional practices implemented, for example, on Native American reservations and boarding schools as methods of "civilizing" the savage Indian. As suggested by the famous metaphor of the melting pot that Israel Zangwill coined in 1908, Americanization was understood as a process through which the diverse cultural practices, perspectives, and identifications of "foreigners" were domesticated and erased as they were absorbed into a homogeneously "American" culture. As Theodore Roosevelt put it,

The word "Americanism" may be employed . . . with reference to the Americanizing of the newcomers to our shores. We must Americanize them in every way, in speech, in political ideas and principles, and in their way of looking at the relations between Church and State. We welcome the German or the Irishman who becomes an American. We have no use for the German or Irishman who remains such. We do not wish German-Americans and Irish-Americans who figure as such in our social and political life; we want only Americans, and provided they are such, we do not care whether they are of native or of Irish or of German ancestry.[34]

For educators such as Richard Henry Pratt, founder of the Carlisle Indian School, Americanization was a more intensive, "civilizing" pedagogy of "killing culture" that should be applied to the Native American, as Pratt famously put it, in order to "kill the Indian in him, and save the man."[35] While many citizenship guides, character-building manuals, and sociological and historical studies of Americanization recognized and celebrated the "strength derived from the cosmopolitan character of American citizenship," such a cosmopolitanism was also often conceived as a form of assimilation through which the "nations, creeds and colors, diverse and conglomerate streams of blood [that] have flowed steadily to our shores . . . are lost forever, fused into one distinguished mass called the American people."[36]

In *Twenty Years at Hull-House,* Jane Addams seems to defend such an ideology of Americanization when, for example, she argues that "the public schools in the immigrant colonies deserve all the praise as Americanizing agencies which can be bestowed upon them" (167). But although Addams insists on the character-building opportunities within the working-class immigrant neighborhoods, she does so in order to challenge the nativism and xenophobia that animated the discourse of Americanization and to reclaim a concept of character whose democratizing potential lay in the recognition of its intercultural constitution and transnational origins. The character-building potential of the forms of cultural contact that immigrants experienced and enabled, for Addams, was not grounded in the erasure of cultural origins but rather in its capacity "to preserve and keep whatever of value their past life contained" (ibid., 153) and to preserve, as she puts it in her essay "Americanization," "some sort of a connection with their past history and experiences."[37] Like Pauline Hopkins, Addams thus finds within the rhetoric of character strategies of historical recovery and cultural preservation that make visible the cultural plurality and heterogeneity of national character in the United States. In "Americanization," as well as in such essays as "Recent Immigration—A Field Neglected by the Scholar" and "Recreation as Public Function," Addams more directly challenges xenophobic and nativist practices of Americanization by proposing a "cosmopolitan standard" that recognizes "the future of America must not depend so much upon conformity as upon respect for variety."[38]

Although Addams repudiates in her work the disciplinary practices of the individualist ideology and Americanizing agenda associated with the rhetoric of character, the practices she institutionalized at Hull House nonetheless drew significantly on the many diverse practices of character building explored in the preceding chapters of this book. A brief look at some of the practices instituted at Hull House thus helps to bring into focus the diverse elements of the rhetoric of character surveyed in this book, as well as the ways that the rhetoric of character worked beyond and against the disciplinary forms and individualist ethos with which it has been traditionally associated. Addams's work at Hull House also makes visible the impact of the rhetoric of character on the discourse of progressivism in the early twentieth century and on the legal and political transformations that inaugurated the modern welfare state, and it points to some of the ways that the rhetoric of character continues to shape political discourse, pedagogical theory, and personal practices of self-improvement in the United States today.

The practices that Addams instituted at Hull House, as Louis Menand has argued, were influenced by, but also helped to shape, the broader principles of pragmatist philosophy associated with William James, Charles Sanders Peirce, and particularly John Dewey, Addams's good friend and frequent Hull House visitor.[39] In "A Function of the Social Settlement," for example, Addams distinguishes the principles and mission of settlement house work from that of schools and traditional philanthropy by citing William James's emphasis on practice over the mere accumulation or dissemination of knowledge: "the whole function of thinking is but one step in the production of habits of action. . . . [T]he ultimate test for us of what a truth means is indeed the conduct it dictates or inspires."[40] Addams thus founded Hull House on principles of embodied belief, analysis through application, and deliberative debate whose purpose was not to "teach" knowledge but to "use" it toward the production of new "habits of action" and forms of "conduct." Habits constituted, in other words, the essential material out of which character was socially formed or "settled."

In Addams's efforts to provide such a practical, "socialized education," she instituted at Hull House a wide range of practices, classes, and clubs organized toward practical "training" in domestic tasks such as cooking, dressmaking, and millinery, as well as in a variety of industrial and commercial trades. But as she emphasizes in "A Function of the Social Settlement," Hull House was not simply an industrial or trade school devoted to the integration of bodies into the machinery of industrial capitalism (a charge frequently levied at pragmatists). Repudiating the "money making value" of industrial training, Addams emphasized the more remunerative training in conduct and "habits" that equipped one for the broader "business of living" or in what W.E.B. Du Bois (who lectured at Hull House) referred to as "training men for life."[41] Addams's account of the importance of habit in the formation of character, like those of Twain and the success-manual writers discussed in chapter 2, turns on both the constraints habit imposes and the possibilities it enables. As Shannon Jackson puts it, "before Giddens's theory of practical consciousness, before Bourdieu's theory of the habitus, Jane Addams and her colleagues were theorizing the pivotal role of habitual performance in impeding and facilitating social change."[42] Like Twain, Addams understands habit in terms of the fixed beliefs, behaviors, and modes of interpretation that constitute the material reality of what anthropologists and sociologists of the time were defining by the term *culture*.[43] As Addams puts it in *Democracy and Social Ethics*,

> Our conceptions of morality, as all our other ideas, pass through a course of development; the difficulty comes in adjusting our conduct, which has become hardened into customs and habits, to these changing moral conceptions. When this adjustment is not made, we suffer from the strain and indecision of believing one hypothesis and acting upon another. . . . It is quite obvious that the ethics of none of us are clearly defined, and we are continually obliged to act in circles of habit, based upon convictions that we no longer hold. (11)

Habits, as Addams describes them, are a kind of accumulated or "hardened" disposition that provides one with a practically tested horizon of understandings and interpretative attitudes, a disposition that, however, also lags behind and is in tension with new thoughts, ideas, and "moral conceptions." Thus while Addams proposed that settlement house work required that "all one's habits of living had to be readjusted," it also had to recognize and preserve the cultural history and tested practices that existing habits reflected: "I learned that life cannot be administered by definite rules and regulations; that wisdom to deal with a man's difficulties comes only through some knowledge of his life and habits as a whole" (*Twenty Years at Hull-House*, 100, 110).

It was thus in the disorienting scenes of cross-cultural contact that Addams saw the greatest potential for character building. In the essay "Social Attitudes and Character," with which this chapter began, Addams describes the struggles of the children of immigrants in particular, "who had great difficulty with the social attitude which the people about them . . . took toward the immigrants in general . . . and whose characters have deteriorated under the strain."[44] Indeed, one of the most pronounced "difficulties" faced by immigrants in the nineteenth ward, according to Addams, was that of negotiating the many "differences in social attitudes" they experienced. These young people wrestled with not only the differences between their attitudes and the attitudes of other Americans toward the culture and traditions of their parents but also the differences between the America they knew and the America they saw "depicted on the screen" in "moving pictures," and even the differences between their own attitudes and their parents' attitudes toward their own cultural traditions. But as Addams points out, such "differences in social attitudes work in all kinds of ways" and can even provide an opportunity for character building.[45] Noting that the character of many of the children she had met had been "evolved out of this sense of conflict, if you please, between their background and the contemporaneous society and conditions in which they move," Addams goes on to hypothesize that "to make a synthesis between the difference that confronts you in two given situations is certainly an opportunity for the development of character," a character that she goes on to define as "that tendency of emotional life which, instead of being oppressed by the old loyalties, insists that it shall encompass the new as well."[46]

Hull House facilitated such a formation of character by cultivating the internal conflicts that arise from discrepancies between one's accumulated customs or disposition and the new ideas, judgments, and perspectives that emerge in the new social interactions fostered within the communal spaces of the settlement house. The character-building value of the forms of social contact fostered at Hull House derived from, as Charlene Haddock Seigfried has put it, the "perplexities" they produced.[47] Thus cultivating such scenes of cross-cultural exchange, rupture, and disorientation were essential to the formation of a democratic character both for the middle-class settlement house workers as well as for the immigrant community in which they lived. As an example of one cosmopolitan "citizen of the world" produced this way, Addams tells the story of an Irish American woman who overcame her prejudicial "habits" toward Italians in her neighborhood after participating in one of the many social clubs of Hull House:

> To my mind at that moment the speaker [the woman] had passed from the region of the uncultivated person into the possibilities of the cultivated person. The former is bounded by a narrow outlook on life, unable to overcome differences of dress and habit, and his interests are slowly contracting within a circumscribed area; while the latter constantly tends to be more a citizen of the world because of his growing understanding of all kinds of people with their varying experiences. (*Twenty Years at Hull-House,* 232)

The practices of social reform developed at Hull House were thus founded on a theory of cultural pluralism that, like those of pragmatist philosophers and social theorists such as Alain Locke, Horace Kallen, and Randolph Bourne, challenged the nativist ideology of Americanization with a vision of what Bourne referred to as a "Trans-National America."[48]

Building such a transnational character was something that not only transpired in the intercultural spaces and habit-changing experiences of the settlement house but also in the practices of physical culture that were such a vital part of Hull House. The addition of a gymnasium to the Hull House complex in 1893 grew out of Addams's belief in the power of physical exercise and athletic competition as a form of bodily and mental training:

> Our gymnasium has been filled with large and enthusiastic classes for eighteen years in spite of the popularity of dancing and other possible substitutes, while the Saturday evening athletic contests have become a feature of the neighborhood. The Settlement strives for that type of gymnastics which is at least partly a matter of character, for that training which presupposes abstinence and the curbing of impulse, as well as for those athletic contests in which the mind of the contestant must be vigilant to keep the body closely to the rules of the game. (*Twenty Years at Hull-House,* 284)

Drawing on the discourse of temperance common to many physical-culture organizations, Addams imagines that the benefits of physical exercise, and in particular athletic sports, derive from, in the first instance, the forms of self-discipline that their routinized training frequently required. Not only did athletic competition demand the consistency associated with the well-disciplined character, but it also displaced the habits of drinking, smoking, unhealthy eating, and general torpor to which many people turned for relief from the burdens of labor. Addams also saw the gymnasium as a space where the spectatorial pleasures of team sports could be productively channeled for character building. Like many critics of team sports, Addams was wary of the spectacular, audience-oriented nature of athletic competitions and their tendency to encourage gambling and indulge the savage, spectatorial pleasures of "the fight" and individual self-glory over team success. Addams nonetheless believed the gymnasium could be a vital space for channeling the "sensual and exhausting pleasures" and "all those enthusiasms which are so mysteriously aroused by athletics" into the coordinated interactions and strategic collaborations that led to character building (ibid., 283–284).

But Addams also identifies a range of more subtle benefits from physical exercise that extend beyond its disciplining power. The mental vigilance she describes as necessary for "keep[ing] the body closely to the rules of the game" points not simply to a disciplined capacity for rule following but also to a kind of proprioceptive awareness of one's own body, its distribution and arrangement in space, and its evolving relationship to other bodies in motion. Addams goes on to evoke in the description that follows, for example, an aesthetics of kinesthetic awareness produced by the popular exercise form of calisthenics, a form whose name derived from the Greek word for "beautiful strength":[49]

> As one sees in rhythmic motion the slim bodies of a class of lads, "that scrupulous and uncontaminated purity of form which recommends itself even to the Greeks as befitting messengers from the gods, if such messengers should come," one offers up in awkward prosaic form the very essence of that old prayer, "Grant them with feet so light to pass through life." (*Twenty Years at Hull-House*, 284)

Like William Blaikie and Charlotte Perkins Gilman, Addams thus celebrates the benefits of "a symmetrical muscular development" to the "young people who work long hours at sedentary occupations, factories and offices," not simply because of its restoration of bodily symmetry but "more than anything else" because of the sense of "freedom and ease to be acquired from a symmetrical muscular development" (ibid.)

The Hull House gymnasium was thus a vital space for the cultivation of

Fig. 14. Photograph of an exercise class held in the Hull House gymnasium, c. 1920. (JAMC_0000_0148_0878, Wallace Kirkland, photographer, Jane Addams Memorial Collection Photographs, University of Illinois at Chicago Library)

new forms of "kinesthetic acumen" that also provided, in Addams's view, a performative medium for the social exchanges that constituted Hull House's "immigrant cosmopolitanism."[50] Not only did the excitement of athletic events fuse communities together as undifferentiated cheering throngs, but exercise leaders at Hull House, some trained by Dudley Sargent at Harvard's Hemenway gymnasium, also sought, as Shannon Jackson has argued, "the 'class consciousness' and 'solidarity' that could be achieved when a group of youngsters enacted the same bodily movements in 'rhythmic concord.' They possessed an awareness of how a momentary pause could elicit psychological receptivity and of how attention to rhythm solidified new gestures in developing bodies."[51] Addams's belief in the power of embodied play to transform the material realities and social fabric of the tenement district stemmed from a broader belief in the critical role that public practices of bodily performance played in the formation of character. Drawing on the classical rhetorical tradition, as well the work of influential acting, elocution, and exercise instructor François Delsartre, Addams promoted in the athletic, educational, and industrial classes as well as in the public spaces of Hull House an embodied practice

Fig. 15. Photograph by W.H. Gardiner of the gymnasium stage of Hull House, from Dorothea Moore, "A Day at Hull-House," *American Journal of Sociology* 2 (March 1897): 635.

of "elocution" focused on verbal expression and the coordinated movements and postures of the body as elements of self-expression and character formation. Indeed, the importance of the performative dimensions of athletics and physical culture was most directly recognized by the incorporation of a theater stage into the physical structure of the gymnasium, as well as by the general focus on the gymnasium as a versatile space for public performances and group activities of many kinds (see Figure 15).

The athletic activities of the gymnasium were thus just one part in the broader theatrical space of Hull House, a space organized so that "the daily living practices of its residents—the so-called private realms of experience—were perpetually on display."[52] The activities of the Hull House gymnasium thus make visible the practices of embodied awareness and social performance—or what Jackson has termed "reformance"—to which Hull House was more broadly committed.[53]

Not only did the gymnasium and the public spaces of Hull House in general afford ample opportunities for practices of "reformance," so too was the Hull House theater a place where residents could refine their performative abilities. At Hull House, Addams promoted the theater as a space where "it seems possible to give a training in manners and morals more directly than through any other medium" (*Twenty Years at Hull-House*, 253). As she explains in *The Spirit of Youth and the City Streets*, referring to the statement of an English playwright,

> the theater is literally making the minds of our urban populations today. It is a huge factory of sentiment, of character, of points of honor, of conceptions of conduct, of everything that finally determines the destiny of a nation. The theater is not only a place of amusement, it is a place of culture, a place where people learn how to think, act, and feel.[54]

The theater was also a privileged space in the production and evaluation of knowledge. Addams conceived of the theater not only as a place where one could receive specialized training in the public forms of deportment, gesture, manner, and conduct essential to the formation of character but also as a kind of moral or behavioral laboratory in which different methods of "moral instruction" could be "tested" by performing and evaluating their recommended behaviors: "I have come to believe, however, that the stage may do more than teach, that much of our current moral instruction will not endure the test of being cast into a lifelike mold, and when presented in dramatic form will reveal itself as platitudinous and effete" (*Twenty Years at Hull-House*, 252).

Words as Deeds

Perhaps the best example of Addams's investment in, yet innovations on, the rhetoric of character—and a fitting conclusion for this book—is Addams's own slippage between and conflation of the textual and social dimensions of character throughout her work, but particularly in her first book, *Democracy and Social Ethics*. Katherine Joslin has described *Democracy and Social Ethics* as a book that

> synthesizes masculine and feminine modes of thought and speech, blending rational and intuitive knowledge, intellectual and visceral experience, objective and subjective points of view into patterns of rational and associative logic. In order to discredit what her younger contemporary Mikhail

Bakhtin would call "authoritative discourse"—the inflexible monologic rhetoric of businessmen and pseudoscientists—Addams sets on her stage a polyphony of voices from the Chicago streets, those of charity workers, immigrants, laborers, and tenement dwellers. Her writing, as a result, often has the look and sound of fiction.[55]

The many sketches of striking characters in Addams's books, like the illustrated sketches of people and buildings at Hull House provided for the first edition of *Twenty Years at Hull-House* by Norah Hamilton, are in part examples of Addams's belief in "argument by illustration," her belief, as she puts it in *Democracy and Social Ethics*, "that ideas only operate upon the popular mind through will and character, and must be dramatized before they reach the mass of men."[56] But not only does Addams sketch in her works the theater of urban life around her; she also transforms herself into a quasi-fictional character who takes many fictional forms within her texts: "she crosses the boundaries between classes and genders, casting herself as first one character and then another, transforming the female voice from a private into a public one."[57]

Addams's movements between the positions of author and character in her work, I suggest in closing, provides an important insight into Addams's reconceptualization of the rhetoric of character as a "social ethic," as well as into the interconnections between her written work as a social theorist and her practical work as a social reformer. In the introduction to *Democracy and Social Ethics*, Addams offers an easily overlooked yet informative example of her theory of the social ethic. In the introduction, Addams gives two examples of cultural locations where the social ethic was currently being fostered. The first example is newspapers, which, with their "frank reflection of popular demand" and "omnivorous curiosity equally insistent upon the trivial and the important," makes way in a populist form for "the first dawn of social consciousness" (8). The second example she cites is literature. Literature (or more specifically, the novel) is a vehicle of the social ethic because its presentation of a "wide reading of human life" is "a preparation for better social adjustment—for the remedying of social ills" (8). Literature, she argues, breaks the "insensibility and hardness" of the individualist ethic, an ethic that "is due to the lack of imagination which prevents a realization of the experiences of other people" (8). Literature's staging of scenes of social contact and its evocation of literary character thus make it an imaginative realm generative of the social ethic.

Addams's use of the term *imagination* as the key faculty for apprehending cultural diversity echoes, in a very telling way, another crucial and previously discussed moment of the introduction. When Addams opens the introduction with an account of the "maladjusted" and "unhappy" men and women, her delineation of what plagues them and of what they desire from the social ethic takes place from the comfortable distance of the third-person-narrative perspective. She thus unfolds the tale of their unhappiness from a distant, observational, analytical perspective, noting the causes and conditions of their unhappiness with detachment and professional acumen. She records the facts but, following the common narrative convention, makes herself invisible as a narrating character. All of this changes, however, at the moment when she "imagines" how these men and women might express their own sense of the social ethic:

> These men and women have realized this [the value of "contact with the moral experiences of the many"] and have disclosed the fact in their eagerness for a wider acquaintance with and participation in the life about them. They believe that experience gives the easy and trustworthy impulse toward right action in the broad as well as in the narrow relations. We may indeed imagine many of them saying: "Cast our experiences in a larger mold if our lives are to be animated by the larger social aims. We have met the obligations of family life . . . and we see no other way in which to prepare ourselves for the larger social duties." Such a demand is reasonable, for by our daily experiences we have discovered that we cannot mechanically hold up a moral standard. . . . We are thus brought to a conception of Democracy not merely as a sentiment which desires the well-being of all men, nor yet as a creed which believes in the essential dignity and equality of all men, but as that which affords a rule for living as well as a test of faith. (6–7)

In the overall trajectory of her argument, this moment is a crucial one, as Addams moves from a diagnosis of the concept of "maladjustment" to her thesis that it can be resolved through a democratizing social ethic. More importantly, this moment is also marked by a definitive transition in narrative perspective, as the third-person perspective of her description of "these men and women" and their pursuit of a diverse and broad range of social experiences shifts by the end of the paragraph to the first-person (plural) perspective of a narrating "we." It is a "we," moreover, that remains both the subject and the source of narration for the rest of the introduction.

The introduction of this "we" complicates the argument not only by implicating Addams herself in the actions and realizations of the "men and women" she is describing but also by the same gesture extending that process to include the reader as well. And just in case this shift is mistaken for an arbitrary rhetorical flourish, Addams's brief "Prefatory Note" is clear to underscore the stakes of this narrative development. After explaining that the chapters of *Democracy and Social Ethics* had originally been given as a series of lectures, Addams goes on to note that "[i]n putting them [the lectures] into the form of a book, no attempt has been made to change the somewhat informal style used in speaking. The 'we' and 'us' which originally referred to the speaker and her audience are merely extended to possible readers" (3). It is a strange offer, this "extended" offer of the "we," an offer that virtually no author *explicitly* gives and yet that reading so often assumes. In extending this "we" explicitly to a reader who may or may not feel the interpellative force of the narrative perspective, Addams asserts a kind of textual community with "these men and women," herself, and her "possible readers" modeled on the speech scene of the spoken lecture.

Although this assertion and hailing of the reading subject could be explained as the act of a pragmatist writer concerned that her texts and ideas find their mark in the shared concerns of a "real" audience, Addams's shift does more than simply exemplify pragmatist writing practices. Her shift exemplifies the kind of complex scene of alterity and imagination required of the social ethic, and it does so in two ways. First, Addams's shift from a discussion of "they" to a discussion of "we" demonstrates how the collectivity of such a "we" depends on a retention of the distinctiveness of its members even as they are subsumed by a collective speaking voice. A collective and self-announcing "we," Addams's narrative suggests, finds expression only by imagining what they might be saying ("We may indeed imagine many of them saying . . ."). The narrator who speaks of "them," furthermore, can invoke the "we" only through an imaginative act in which "they" are no longer narratively represented but "imagined" to speak in their own voice. And yet "they," one might be inclined to argue, do not *really* speak, for their speech is being "imagined" by the "we." Yet because "they," in being imagined, thereby become members of the "we," "they" too are "imagining" what "they" are saying, that is, they are "really" speaking. "They" authentically come to speech, in other words, through the collective voice of the "we" but only if they are simultaneously "imagined" as speakers distinct from that "we."

Second, Addams asserts a vision of collectivity composed of a complex amalgam of "real" and "textual" characters. Her "men and women" are textual characters who enable the speaker, Jane Addams, to invoke a "we" in relation to herself and her presumably "real" though no more easily locatable "possible readers." More importantly, in order to legitimate the collective assertion of the book's central claims, Addams must take up a position within the text as a textual character defined in relation to the thoughts and feelings of the text's own "men and women." The "we" that thus dominates and narrates the rest of the introduction ("We are learning . . ."; "We have come . . ."; "We do not believe . . ."; We realize, too . . .") can assert the central theses of the book ("We are thus brought to a conception of Democracy . . .") only by making itself, but not only itself, the object of that narration. Addams can, in other words, assert her textual claims only by herself becoming, in a sense, a textual character who both describes and is being described by the text. Addams thus presents through the narrative development of her "theory" a model of social contact and its complex reorganization of the boundaries and identifications of character. For a theorist whose deeds at Hull House and as a social reformer have garnered vastly more attention than her theoretical writings, such a presentation is an important reminder that words are not simply servants to the deeds of social reform but rather are the necessary social bodies through which such deeds can themselves transpire.

Notes

NOTES TO THE INTRODUCTION

1. Virginia Woolf, "Mr. Bennett and Mrs. Brown," in *The Captain's Deathbed and Other Essays* (New York: Harcourt, 1950), 94–119, reprinted in *Theory of the Novel,* ed. Michael McKeon (Baltimore: Johns Hopkins University Press, 2000), 745–746.

2. W.E.B. Du Bois, *The Autobiography of W.E.B. Du Bois: A Soliloquy on Viewing My Life from the Last Decade of Its First Century* (New York: International Publishers, 1968), 277.

3. Orison Swett Marden, *Character: The Grandest Thing in the World* (New York: Thomas Y. Crowell, 1899).

4. See, for example, Andrew S. Trees, *The Founding Fathers and the Politics of Character* (Princeton, NJ: Princeton University Press, 2004); Cathy Boeckmann, *A Question of Character: Scientific Racism and the Genres of American Fiction, 1892–1912* (Tuscaloosa: University of Alabama Press, 2000), 11–63; Kevin P. Murphy, *Political Manhood: Red Bloods, Mollycoddles, and the Politics of Progressive Era Reform* (New York: Columbia University Press, 2008); David Riesman, *The Lonely Crowd: A Study of the Changing American Character* (1961; repr., New Haven, CT: Yale University Press, 2001). As Cheryl Walker puts it, "American character is a particularly vexed subject, vexed because, on the one hand, we no longer wish to define Americans in terms of certain character traits, modes of behaviour, physical types, and yet, on the other, we have never lost the desire to puzzle over the implications of ideas of the nation for a certain conception of the human being understood to represent those ideas." Cheryl Walker, *Indian Nation: Native American Literature and Nineteenth-Century Nationalisms* (Durham, NC: Duke University Press, 1997), 1. This is not to suggest that character was a term unique to the nationalist discourse of the United States. Indeed, I hope to make clear the importance of the rhetoric of character in the emergence of the concept of the modern nation itself because of the role it played in figuring the unifying ground of the nation in terms of an underlying cultural, ethnic, or racial identity, even if there is not much room for an extensive consideration of other nationalist discourses in this study. See, for example, John Armstrong's argument that "modern nationalist thought, succeeding to an age of cosmopolitanism, has sought permanent 'essences' of national character instead of recognizing the fundamental but shifting significance of boundaries for human identity." John Armstrong, "Nations before Nationalism," *Nationalism,* ed. John Hutchinson and Anthony D. Smith (New York: Oxford University Press, 1994), 141.

5. As Emily Apter has put it, "in the postnational 'beyond,' the category of national character fails to figure prominently, if at all." Emily Apter, *Continental Drift: From National Characters to Virtual Subjects* (Chicago: University of Chicago Press, 1999), 14. See also John Carlos Rowe, "Postnationalism, Globalism, and the New American Studies," in *The Futures of American Studies*, ed. Donald E. Pease and Robyn Wiegman (Durham, NC: Duke University Press, 2002), 178.

6. See, for example, Michael Warner, *The Letters of the Republic: Publication and the Public Sphere in Eighteenth-Century America* (Cambridge, MA: Harvard University Press, 1990), 13–15; Dana Nelson, *National Manhood: Capitalist Citizenship and the Imagined Fraternity of White Men* (Durham, NC: Duke University Press, 1998); Christopher Castiglia, *Interior States: Institutional Consciousness and the Inner Life of Democracy in the Antebellum United States* (Durham, NC: Duke University Press, 2008); David Kazanjian, *The Colonizing Trick: National Culture and Imperial Citizenship in Early America* (Minneapolis: University of Minnesota Press, 2003), 1–34; Eva Cherniavsky, "Body," in *Keywords for American Cultural Studies*, ed. Bruce Burgett and Glenn Hendler (New York: New York University Press, 2007), 28; Robyn Wiegman, "Whiteness Studies and the Paradox of Particularity," in *The Futures of American Studies*, ed. Donald E. Pease and Robyn Wiegman (Durham, NC: Duke University Press, 2002), 269–304; Bruce Burgett, *Sentimental Bodies: Sex, Gender, and Citizenship in the Early Republic* (Princeton, NJ: Princeton University Press, 1998).

7. Warren I. Susman, *Culture as History: The Transformation of American Society in the Twentieth Century* (New York: Pantheon, 1984), 271–285; Karen Halttunen, *Confidence Men and Painted Women: A Study of Middle-Class Culture in America, 1830–1870* (New Haven, CT: Yale University Press, 1982); Richard Wightman Fox, "The Culture of Liberal Protestant Progressivism," *Journal of Interdisciplinary History* 23 (Winter 1993): 639–660; Joan Shelley Rubin, *The Making of Middle-Brow Culture* (Chapel Hill: University of North Carolina Press, 1992). See also Thomas Winter, *Making Men, Making Class: The YMCA and Workingmen, 1877–1920* (Chicago: University of Chicago Press, 2002), 11. In *Democratic Personality*, Nancy Ruttenburg offers an alternate perspective on the history of character that argues the concept of character emerged within liberalism as a containment and domestication of the alternate, competing democratic forms and participatory public voices of a "democratic personality" that had its roots in the confessional discourses and public performances inspired by the Calvinist belief in two spectral worlds of visible and invisible character. Nancy Ruttenburg, *Democratic Personality: Popular Voice and the Trail of American Authorship* (Stanford, CA: Stanford University Press, 1998).

8. Edwin P. Whipple's critique of "Eccentric Character" is just one example of its vexed status within the rhetoric of character. Edwin P. Whipple, *Character and Characteristic Men* (Boston: Ticknor and Fields, 1866), 35–65. See also Gillian Brown's analysis of "odd Americans" in *The Consent of the Governed: The Lockean Legacy in Early American Culture* (Cambridge, MA: Harvard University Press, 2001), 11; and Priscilla Wald's concept of the "uncannily American" in *Constituting Americans: Cultural Anxiety and Narrative Form* (Durham, NC: Duke University Press, 1995), 1–13.

9. William Dean Howells, *Criticism and Fiction* (New York: Harper and Brothers, 1893);

P.T. Barnum, *Dollars and Sense; or, How to Get On: The Whole Secret in a Nutshell* (New York: Henry S. Allen, 1890); Anna Julia Cooper, *A Voice from the South* (New York: Oxford University Press, 1988); Luther Standing Bear, *Land of the Spotted Eagle* (Lincoln: University of Nebraska Press, 2006); W.E.B. Du Bois, *The Souls of Black Folk* (1903; repr., New York: Penguin, 1996); G. Stanley Hall, *Adolescence: Its Psychology and Its Relations to Physiology, Anthropology, Sociology, Sex, Crime, Religion, and Education,* 2 vols. (New York: D. Appleton, 1914); John Dewey, "Character and Conduct," in *Human Nature and Conduct: An Introduction to Social Psychology* (New York: Holt, 1922), 43–58; Theodore Roosevelt, "Character and Success," in *The Strenuous Life: Essays and Addresses* (New York: Century, 1900), 113–124.

10. Guy Debord, *Society of the Spectacle,* trans. Ken Knabb (London: Rebel, 2006).

11. *Liddell and Scott's Greek-English Lexicon,* intermediate abridgment of the 7th ed. (Oxford, UK: Clarendon, 1995), s.v. "χαρακτηρ." Whereas *kharakter* denoted the influence of "impressions" on the substance of the self, the related term *ethos* denoted the expression of these impressions or marks as the ethical orientation, customs, or habits of the individual. Although *ethos* has tended to dominate discussions of character in the classical tradition, and in particular the classical rhetorical tradition that emphasized the proper representation and calibration of one's own character to that of one's audience, the numismatic associations of the term *character* were crucial to the development of the genre of the "literary character" and its depiction of stock literary "types" from Theophrastus up to the development of the modern novel. For a fuller discussion of this tradition, see J.W. Smeed, *The Theophrastan "Character": The History of a Literary Genre* (Oxford, UK: Clarendon, 1985); and James M. May, *The Trials of Character: The Eloquence of Ciceronian Ethos* (Chapel Hill: University of North Carolina Press, 1988).

12. Noah Webster, *American Dictionary of the English Language* (New York: S. Converse, 1828), s.v. "Character."

13. J. Hillis Miller, *Ariadne's Thread: Story Lines* (New Haven, CT: Yale University Press, 1992), 32, 58.

14. John Locke, *An Essay Concerning Human Understanding,* vol. 1 (London: Oxford University Press, 1894), 121.

15. Louisa May Alcott, *Little Women* (1869; repr., New York: Norton, 2004), 358. This version of the alphabet was printed in London by Carrington Bowles in 1782 and was also, according to Patricia Crain, "a popular broadside" in the United States. A chapbook version of *The Comical Hotch-Potch, or The Alphabet Turn'd Posture Master* was also published in Philadelphia in 1814. See Patricia Crain, *The Story of A: The Alphabetization of America from* The New England Primer *to* The Scarlet Letter (Stanford, CA: Stanford University Press, 2000), 89. On the role of alphabets in character building, see Gillian Brown, *The Consent of the Governed: The Lockean Legacy in Early American Culture* (Cambridge, MA: Harvard University Press, 2001), 36–56; Karen Sánchez-Eppler, *Dependent States: The Child's Part in Nineteenth-Century American Culture* (Chicago: University of Chicago Press, 2005), 3–18.

16. American drug companies, interestingly enough, published vividly illustrated alphabet books for children and distributed them in great numbers at the Columbian Exposition so that children might memorize brand names along with ABCs. Alphabets such as

the *Brandreth Columbian ABC for Little Ones* (New York: Benjamin Brandreth, 1893) also incorporated as well many of the racialized images of the midway "types" in their narratives of Columbus's discovery of the New World. See Claire Hoertz Badaracco, *Prescribing Faith: Medicine, Media, and Religion in American Culture* (Waco, TX: Baylor University Press, 2007), 156–158.

17. For an interesting critical discussion of the current status of character as a philosophical and psychological category, see John M. Doris, *Lack of Character: Personality and Moral Behavior* (Cambridge: Cambridge University Press, 2002).

18. William Dean Howells, *A Modern Instance* (New York: Penguin, 1984), 288.

19. Brook Thomas, *American Literary Realism and the Failed Promise of Contract* (Berkeley: University of California Press, 1997), 243.

20. J. Hector St. John de Crèvecoeur, "What Is an American?" in *Letters from an American Farmer* (1782; repr., New York: Penguin, 1981), 66–105; James Fenimore Cooper, *Notions of the Americans Picked Up by a Travelling Bachelor*, 2 vols. (1828; repr., New York: Frederick Ungar, 1963); Sarah Josepha Buell Hale, *Sketches of American Character* (1829; repr., Boston: Freeman Hunt, 1831); Alexis de Tocqueville, *Democracy in America* (1835/1840; repr., New York: HarperPerennial, 1988); Walt Whitman, preface to *Leaves of Grass* (1855; repr., New York: Penguin, 1986), 5–24; Henry James, *The American Scene* (1907; repr., Bloomington: Indiana University Press, 1968), 106, 121.

21. Rupert Wilkinson, *The Pursuit of American Character* (New York: Harper and Row, 1988). Or as Günter Lenz has put it, "American Studies, with its obsessional concern for the character of America, was the original 'identity politics.'" Günter H. Lenz, "Toward a Dialogics of International American Studies," in *The Futures of American Studies*, ed. Donald E. Pease and Robyn Wiegman (Durham, NC: Duke University Press, 2002), 465.

22. Alan Trachtenberg, *The Incorporation of America: Culture and Society in the Gilded Age* (New York: Hill and Wang, 1982), 92.

23. Susman, *Culture as History*, 273.

24. Ibid.

25. Edwin Whipple, *Character and Characteristic Men* (Boston: Ticknor and Fields, 1866), 4.

26. Katherine Blackford and Arthur Newcomb, for example, emphasize perhaps most explicitly among the character manuals the importance of character as a form of rhetorical persuasion, in *Analyzing Character: The New Science of Judging Men; Misfits in Business, the Home and Social Life* (New York: Review of Reviews, 1916), 367–428. See also Jean Ferguson Carr, Stephen L. Carr, and Lucille M. Schultz, *Archives of Instruction: Nineteenth-Century Rhetorics, Readers, and Composition Books in the United States* (Carbondale: Southern Illinois University Press, 2005); Kenneth Cmiel, *Democratic Eloquence: The Fight over Popular Speech in Nineteenth-Century America* (Berkeley: University of California Press, 1990); Thomas W. Benson, ed., *Rhetoric and Political Culture in Nineteenth-Century America* (East Lansing: Michigan State University Press, 1997); Jay Fliegelman, *Declaring Independence: Jefferson, Natural Language, and the Culture of Performance* (Stanford, CA: Stanford University Press, 1993); Thomas Gustafson, *Representative Words: Politics, Literature, and the American*

Language (New York: Cambridge University Press, 1993); and John Bender and David E. Wellbery, eds., *The Ends of Rhetoric: History, Theory, Practice* (Stanford, CA: Stanford University Press, 1990).

27. "Language is indicative of the life and character of a nation. Words, it has been said, are the windows through which we see the soul of a people. The real history of a nation is written in its language, in the very words; frequently it happens that a single word discloses some historical fact not recorded by language itself. Sometimes there is more history in a word than in the written annals." E. Scultz Gerhard, "Word Study—The Value of It," *American Education* 17, no. 8 (April 1914): 462. Raymond Williams, *Keywords: A Vocabulary of Culture and Society* (New York: Oxford University Press, 1983), 23. For a more recent study of keywords in the context of American Studies, see Bruce Burgett and Glenn Hendler, eds., *Keywords for American Cultural Studies* (New York: New York University Press, 2007).

28. Amanda Anderson, *The Way We Argue Now: A Study in the Cultures of Theory* (Princeton, NJ: Princeton University Press, 2006), 131.

29. Brown, *Consent of the Governed*; Karen Sánchez-Eppler, *Dependent States: The Child's Part in Nineteenth-Century American Culture* (Chicago: University of Chicago Press, 2005); Caroline F. Levander, *Cradle of Liberty: Race, the Child, and National Belonging from Thomas Jefferson to W.E.B. Du Bois* (Durham, NC: Duke University Press, 2006). See also Jacqueline S. Reiner, *From Virtue to Character: American Childhood, 1775–1850* (New York: Twayne, 1996).

30. Levander, *Cradle of Liberty*, 7. See also Priscilla Wald, "Naturalization," in *Keywords for American Cultural Studies*, ed. Bruce Burgett and Glenn Hendler (New York: New York University Press, 2007), 171.

31. Homi Bhabha, *The Location of Culture* (New York: Routledge, 2004), 142.

32. Noah Webster, "On the Education of Youth in America," in *Essays on Education in the Early Republic*, ed. Frederick Rudolph (Cambridge, MA: Belknap Press of Harvard University Press, 1965), 43. Webster's desire to compile the unique semantic and orthographic features that distinguish American English in his landmark dictionary was similarly motivated by the belief that such a delineation of the national language would "inspire them [the people of this country] with the pride of national character." Noah Webster, *Dissertations on the English Language* (Boston: Isaiah Thomas, 1789), 397.

33. Lydia Maria Child, *The Mother's Book* (1831; repr., Bedford, MA: Applewood Books, 1992), frontispiece, 1. Fanny Fern, *Ruth Hall: A Domestic Tale of the Present Time* (1855; repr., New York: Penguin, 1997), 25.

34. John Todd, *The Student's Manual: Designed, by Specific Directions, to Aid in Forming and Strengthening the Intellectual and Moral Character and Habits of the Student* (Northampton, MA: J.H. Butler, 1835) and *The Daughter at School* (Northampton, MA: Hopkins, Bridgman, 1854); Amos Bronson Alcott, *Observations on the Principles and Methods of Infant Instruction* (Boston: Carter and Hendee, 1830); Catherine Beecher, *A Treatise on Domestic Economy* (1841; repr., New York: Schocken Books, 1977); Rufus Clark, *Lectures on the Formation of Character* (Boston: John P. Jewett, 1853); Henry Ward Beecher, *Lectures to Young Men, on Various Important Subjects* (New York: M.H. Newman, 1851). I borrow the term

"biopolitical narratives" from Kenneth Kidd, *Making American Boys: Boyology and the Feral Tale* (Minneapolis: University of Minnesota Press, 2004), 16. For a critique of Benedict Anderson's use of "analogy" to describe the relationship between the personal and the national, see Priscilla Wald, *Constituting Americans: Cultural Anxiety and Narrative Form* (Durham, NC: Duke University Press, 1995), 4. See also Judith Butler's argument that "[n]ations are not the same as individual psyches, but both can be described as 'subjects,' albeit of different orders. When the United States acts, it establishes a conception of what it means to act as an American, establishes a norm by which that subject might be known." Judith Butler, *Precarious Life: The Power of Mourning and Violence* (New York: Verso, 2004), 41.

35. Thomas Paine, *Common Sense* (1776; repr., Boston: Bedford/St. Martin's, 2001), 86–95. See also Gillian Brown, "Paine's Vindication of the Rights of Children," in *Consent of the Governed*, 83–106; and Hannah Arendt's discussion of "natality" in Hannah Arendt, *The Human Condition* (Chicago: University of Chicago Press, 1989), 177–178.

36. The Naturalization Act of 1795 slightly modified the wording of the original requirement of "good character" established in the original Naturalization Act of 1790, which specified simply that a person be of "good character." Both explicitly limited naturalization, however, to "free white persons," a stipulation that was eliminated from naturalization law only in 1952. The "good moral character," however, remains fully in force as an explicit requirement of naturalization and immigration, and it is still frequently used to deport or deny citizenship to immigrants.

37. Castiglia, *Interior States*, 6.

38. As Castiglia puts it, the "federalization of affect" that marked "the managed 'character' of sanctioned citizenship" (ibid., 18) was "quickly translated into—and found its broader fulfillment in—the social 'uplift' movements that flourished in the 1820s and 1830s" (21), thus marking "the transition from revolutionary concepts of social liberty to reformist insistence on orderly character" (27). See ibid., 21–34.

39. Walt Whitman, *Franklin Evans, or The Inebriate: A Tale of the Times* (1842; repr., Durham, NC: Duke University Press, 2007). Frank Norris, *Vandover and the Brute* (1914; repr., Lincoln: University of Nebraska Press, 1978). Julia Ward Howe, on the other hand, offers a more positive account, in her originally unpublished novel *The Hermaphrodite*, of the "beauty" inherent to the more "vague and undecided character" of Laurence, the novel's title character, who possesses "a face and form of strange contradictions—the eye and brow command, while the mouth persuades." Julia Ward Howe, *The Hermaphrodite* (1840; repr., Lincoln: University of Nebraska Press, 2004), 16.

40. See Clifford Putney, *Muscular Christianity: Manhood and Sports in Protestant America, 1880–1920* (Cambridge, MA: Harvard University Press, 2001), 3; Donald E. Hall, ed., *Muscular Christianity: Embodying the Victorian Age* (New York: Cambridge University Press, 1994); Thomas Winter, *Making Men, Making Class: The YMCA and Workingmen, 1877–1920* (Chicago: University of Chicago Press, 2002); and Gail Bederman, *Manliness and Civilization: A Cultural History of Gender and Race in the United States, 1880–1917* (Chicago: University of Chicago Press, 1995), 11.

41. "Eleventh Annual Report of the Boy Scouts of America" (Washington, DC:

Government Printing Office, 1922), 1. See also David I. Macleod, *Building Character in the American Boy: The Boy Scouts, YMCA, and Their Forerunners, 1870–1920* (Madison: University of Wisconsin Press, 1983). The Roosevelt quote is from the inscription titled "Youth" in the Rotunda of the American Museum of Natural History, New York City, New York.

42. Slavoj Žižek, *The Parallax View* (Cambridge, MA: MIT Press, 2006), 60.

43. William Wells Brown, *Clotel; or, The President's Daughter* (1853; repr., New York: Modern Library, 2000), 48; Scott Sandage, *Born Losers: A History of Failure in America* (Cambridge, MA: Harvard University Press, 2005), 142, 164, 184.

44. See, for example, Benjamin Franklin's linking of "credit and character" in *The Autobiography* (1818; repr., New York: Vintage Books, 1990), 59, 65. Horatio Alger described his novels as "designed to illustrate the truth that a manly spirit is better than the gifts of fortune. Early trial and struggle, as the history of the majority of our successful men abundantly attests, tend to strengthen and invigorate the character." Horatio Alger, preface to *Luck and Pluck; or, John Oakley's Inheritance* (Boston: Loring, 1869), v. Literalizing the connection of character and capital, the publishers of Barnum's success manual *Dollars and Sense* appended to it an actual economic treatise on money and banking by Henry M. Hunt titled *Money! Where It Comes From and Where It Goes To: Being a Concise History of Money, Banks and Banking.* P.T. Barnum, *Dollars and Sense; or, How to Get On: The Whole Secret in a Nutshell* (New York: Henry S. Allen, 1890). See also Booker T. Washington, *Character Building* (1903; repr., Amsterdam: Fredonia Books, 2002); and Julia E. M'Conaughy, *Capital for Working Boys: Chapters in Character Building* (London: Hodder and Stoughton, 1884). For a historical overview of the success manual, see Judy Hilkey, *Character Is Capital: Success Manuals and Manhood in Gilded Age America* (Chapel Hill: University of North Carolina Press, 1997).

45. Joel Hawes, *Lectures to Young Men on the Formation of Character* (Boston: Congregational Board of Publication, 1856), 102.

46. "The final product of our training must be neither a psychologist nor a brickmason, but a man. And to make men, we must have ideals, broad, pure, and inspiring ends of living,—not sordid money-getting, not apples of gold." W.E.B. Du Bois, *The Souls of Black Folk* (1903; repr., New York: Penguin, 1996), 72.

47. See Luther Standing Bear, "What the Indian Means to America," in *Land of the Spotted Eagle* (1933; repr., Lincoln: University of Nebraska Press, 2006), 247–260; José Martí, "My Race" (1893), in *Selected Writings*, ed. and trans. Esther Allen (New York: Penguin, 2002), 318–321; and Charles Chesnutt, "Wife of His Youth," in *The Wife of His Youth and Other Stories* (1899; repr., Ann Arbor: University of Michigan Press, 1968).

48. Frederick Douglass, "What Are the Colored People Doing for Themselves?" in *Negro Social and Political Thought,* ed. Howard Brotz (New York: Basic Books, 1966), 207.

49. Noah Webster, *American Dictionary of the English Language* (New York: S. Converse, 1828), s.v. "Reputation."

50. As Thomas Haskell argues, the "Age of Contract" is defined by "a growing reliance on mutual promises, or contractual relations, in lieu of relations based on status, custom, or traditional authority [and] comes very close to the heart of what we mean by 'the rise of capitalism.'" Thomas Haskell, "Capitalism and the Origins of the Humanitarian Sensibility, Part

2," *American Historical Review* 2 (June 1985): 553. See also Brook Thomas, *American Literary Realism and the Failed Promise of Contract* (Berkeley: University of California Press, 1997), 2.

51. For a broader account of the emergence of character as a "progressive" ideal in seventeenth- and eighteenth-century England, and of the role of narrative in its constitution, see Michael McKeon, "Generic Transformation and Social Change: Rethinking the Rise of the Novel," in *Theory of the Novel: A Historical Approach*, ed. Michael McKeon (Baltimore: Johns Hopkins University Press, 2000), 382–397.

52. Nancy Ruttenburg, *Democratic Personality: Popular Voice and the Trial of American Authorship* (Stanford, CA: Stanford University Press, 1998), 37–43.

53. Anthony Gross, ed. and comp., *Lincoln's Own Stories* (New York: Harper and Brothers, 1912), 109.

54. Walter Benjamin, "Fate and Character," in *Reflections*, ed. Peter Demetz, trans. Edmund Jephcott (New York: Schocken Books, 1986), 304.

55. John Stuart Mill, *On Liberty* (1859; repr., Indianapolis: Hackett, 1978), 57.

56. Noah Webster, *American Dictionary of the English Language* (New York: S. Converse, 1828), s.v. "Character."

57. Warner, *Letters of the Republic*, xiii.

58. Ibid., 42.

59. See Jun Xing, *Asian America through the Lens: History, Representations, and Identity* (Lanham, MD: AltaMira, 1998); Henry Louis Gates, *The Signifying Monkey: A Theory of African-American Literary Criticism* (New York: Oxford University Press, 1988); and Halttunen, *Confidence Men and Painted Women*.

60. Noah Webster, *American Dictionary of the English Language* (New York: S. Converse, 1828), s.v. "Reputation"; E.L. Godkin, "The Rights of the Citizen to His Own Reputation," *Scribner's Magazine* 8, no. 1 (July 1890): 58–67.

61. See Jane Gaines, *Contested Culture: The Image, the Voice, and the Law* (Chapel Hill: University of North Carolina Press, 1991), 211–213.

62. See Samuel D. Warren and Louis D. Brandeis, "The Right to Privacy," *Harvard Law Review* 4, no. 5 (December 1890); Robert C. Post, "Rereading Warren and Brandeis: Privacy, Property, and Appropriation," *Case Western Reserve Law Review* 41 (1991): 647.

63. Clyde Peirce, *The Roosevelt Panama Libel Cases* (New York: Greenwich, 1959), 87. See also Norman Rosenberg, *Protecting the Best Men: An Interpretive History of the Law of Libel* (Chapel Hill: University of North Carolina Press, 1986), 4.

64. Cheryl Harris, "Whiteness as Property," in *Critical Race Theory: The Key Writings That Formed the Movement*, ed. Kimberlé Crenshaw, Neil Gotanda, Gary Peller, and Kendall Thomas (New York: New Press, 1995), 282.

65. Bruce Burgett, *Sentimental Bodies: Sex, Gender, and Citizenship in the Early Republic* (Princeton, NJ: Princeton University Press, 1998), 13.

66. Karen Sánchez-Eppler, *Touching Liberty: Abolition, Feminism, and the Politics of the Body* (Berkeley: University of California Press, 1997), 1, cited in Burgett, *Sentimental Bodies*, 15.

67. Jürgen Habermas, "The Transformation of the Public Sphere's Political Function," in *The Structural Transformation of the Public Sphere: An Inquiry into a Category of Bourgeois*

Society, trans. Thomas Buger (Cambridge, MA: MIT Press, 1994), 181–235. Warren Susman identifies these transformations as beginning in the 1880s and culminating in the first decade of the twentieth century but goes on to note, "There is general agreement among historians that some significant material change occurred in the period we are considering. Whether it is a change from a producer to a consumer society, an order of economic accumulation to one of disaccumulation, industrial capitalism to finance capitalism, scarcity to abundance, disorganization to high organization—however that change is defined, it is clear that a new social order was emerging." Susman, *Culture as History,* 275. Karen Halttunen identifies this shift more with the "aesthetics of personal style" that emerged in the late 1840s and 1850s and the "worldly acceptance of self-display, social formalism, and ceremonial ritual as appropriate expressions of middle-class position." Halttunen, *Confidence Men,* 153.

68. Halttunen, *Confidence Men,* 206.

69. David Riesman, *The Lonely Crowd: A Study of the Changing American Character* (New Haven, CT: Yale University Press, 2001). As David Lloyd and Paul Thomas have put it, "It has become a virtual commonplace of postmodernity that we inhabit a society of the spectacle. But . . . it is important not to forget the extent to which the figure of the spectator has historically been the exemplary, even heroic, type of political subjectivity." David Lloyd and Paul Thomas, *Culture and the State* (New York: Routledge, 1998), 31. See also Kathy Peiss, "Making Up, Making Over: Cosmetics, Consumer Culture, and Women's Identity," in *The Sex of Things: Gender and Consumption in Historical Perspective,* ed. Victoria de Grazia (Berkeley: University of California Press, 1996), 312; and Jackson Lears, "Beyond Veblen: Rethinking Consumer Culture in America," in *Consuming Visions: Accumulation and Display of Goods in America, 1880–1920,* ed. Simon J. Bronner (New York: Norton, 1989), 76–77.

70. See, for example, Frederick Douglass, "A Slaveholder's Character" (chapter 5) and "Characteristics of Overseers" (chapter 8), in *Life and Times of Frederick Douglass, Written by Himself* (1893), in *Frederick Douglass: Autobiographies* (New York: Library of America, 1994).

71. Douglass, *Life and Times of Frederick Douglass,* 935. Harriet Beecher Stowe invokes this common trope of character-building adversity in her argument that great characters have come only from conditions of great impoverishment, struggle, and difficulty in *The Lives and Deeds of Our Self-Made Men* (Hartford, CT: Worthington, Dustin, 1872), vi–viii. For later character builders such as Theodore Roosevelt, adversity was not simply a condition that builds character as one passes through it but rather should be maintained as a permanent state of imminent failure, strife, or "strenuosity." See Theodore Roosevelt, "The Strenuous Life," in *The Strenuous Life: Essays and Addresses* (New York: Century, 1900), 1–24.

72. Hilkey, *Character Is Capital,* 129.

73. Helen H. Jun, "Black Orientalism: Nineteenth-Century Narratives of Race and U.S. Citizenship," *American Quarterly* 58, no. 4 (December 2006): 1050.

74. Todd, *The Daughter at School,* 207.

75. Richard Brodhead, *Cultures of Letters: Scenes of Reading and Writing in Nineteenth-Century America* (Chicago: University of Chicago Press, 1993), 17–27.

76. Margaret Fuller, *Woman in the Nineteenth Century* (1845; repr., New York: Norton, 1998), 45.

77. Ibid., 77, 79.

78. Michael Paul Rogin, *Subversive Genealogy: The Politics and Art of Herman Melville* (Berkeley: University of California Press, 1985), 239.

79. As Fowler put it, "This science of mind not only teaches us our characters, but also, what is infinitely more important, how to IMPROVE them. It shows us in what perfection consists, and how to form character and mould mind in accordance with its conditions." O.S. Fowler, *Self-Culture, and Perfection of Character: Including the Management of Youth* (1847; repr., New York: Samuel R. Wells, 1868), v. For a comprehensive background on the rise of phrenology in the United States, see John D. Davies, *Phrenology, Fad and Science: A 19th-Century American Crusade* (New Haven, CT: Yale University Press, 1955).

80. Newell Dwight Hillis, *A Man's Value to Society: Studies in Self-Culture and Character* (Chicago: Fleming H. Revell, 1896), 283.

81. Louis Althusser, "Ideology and Ideological State Apparatuses," in *Lenin and Philosophy and Other Essays* (New York: Monthly Review Press, 1971), 168.

82. Samuel R. Wells, *New Physiognomy, or Signs of Character as Manifested through Temperament and External Forms and Especially in the Human Face Divine* (New York: Fowler and Wells, 1876), 582. Wells, for example, spends an entire chapter on "Exercises in Expression," a chapter that specifies how to make facial expressions of astonishment, curiosity, wonder, credulity, contempt, and so on, in order to "imprint" the trait represented by such an expression onto one's character. Amateur detective Auguste Dupin puts such a performative capacity to a more innovative use in Edgar Allan Poe's "The Purloined Letter": "When I wish to find out how wise, or how stupid, or how good, or how wicked is any one, or what are his thoughts at the moment, I fashion the expression of my face, as accurately as possible, in accordance with the expression of his, and then wait to see what thoughts or sentiments arise in my mind or heart, as if to match or correspond with the expression." Edgar Allan Poe, "The Purloined Letter," in *Complete Tales and Poems of Edgar Allan Poe* (New York: Vintage Books, 1975), 215–216.

83. John Locke, *Some Thoughts Concerning Education* (1693; repr., Indianapolis: Hackett, 1996), 36–39. See also G. Brown, *Consent of the Governed*, 30–35.

84. As Chief Justice Roger B. Taney put it, "But if he ranks as a citizen in the State to which he belongs, within the meaning of the Constitution of the United States, then, whenever he goes into another State, the Constitution clothes him, as to the rights of person, with all the privileges and immunities which belong to citizens of the State." See also the Treaty of Guadalupe Hidalgo that ended the U.S.-Mexico War of 1848, which similarly describes the taking on and off of the "character of the citizen."

85. Nelson Sizer, *How to Study Strangers by Temperament, Face and Head* (New York: Fowler and Wells, 1895); Katherine M. H. Blackford, *Character Analysis by the Observational Method* (New York: Independent Corporation, 1920); David V. Bush and W. Waugh, *Character Analysis: How to Read People at Sight* (Chicago: Huron, 1923); Edgar Pierce, *The Philosophy of Character* (Cambridge, MA: Harvard University Press, 1924); William McDougall, *Character and the Conduct of Life: Practical Psychology for Everyman* (New York: G.P. Putnam's Sons, 1927); Ernst Kretschmer, *Physique and Temperament: An Investigation of the*

Nature of Constitution and of the Theory of Temperament, trans. W.J.H Sprott (1925; repr., New York: Humanities Press, 1951).

86. See Shawn Michelle Smith, *American Archives: Gender, Race, and Class in Visual Culture* (Princeton, NJ: Princeton University Press, 1999), 113–135; and Karen Sánchez-Eppler, "Then When We Clutch Hardest: On the Death of a Child and the Replication of an Image," in *Sentimental Men: Masculinity and the Politics of Affect in American Culture,* ed. Mary Chapman and Glenn Hendler (Berkeley: University of California Press, 1999), 64–88.

87. Boeckmann, *A Question of Character,* 3. For Michel Foucault, character was a concept foundational to the classical episteme of "natural science" itself: "Natural history must provide, simultaneously, a certain *designation* and a controlled *derivation.* And just as the theory of structure superimposed articulation and the proposition so that they became one and the same, so the theory of *character* must identify the values that designate and the area in which they are derived. . . . The structure selected to be the locus of pertinent identities and differences is what is termed the *character.*" Michel Foucault, "Character," in *The Order of Things: An Archaeology of the Human Sciences* (New York: Vintage, 1973), 138–140.

88. Boeckmann, *A Question of Character,* 11–62. See also Robert W. Rydell, *All the World's a Fair: Visions of Empire at American International Expositions, 1876–1916* (Chicago: University of Chicago Press, 1984); and Linda Frost, *Never One Nation: Freaks, Savages, and Whiteness in U.S. Popular Culture, 1850–1877* (Minneapolis: University of Minnesota Press, 2005).

89. Michel Foucault, *Discipline and Punish: The Birth of the Prison* (New York: Vintage Books, 1995); Jonathan Crary, *Techniques of the Observer: On Vision and Modernity in 19th Century America* (Cambridge, MA: MIT Press, 1992); Allan Sekula, "The Body and the Archive," *October* 39 (Winter 1986): 3–64. See also Smith, *American Archives.*

90. Jane Tompkins, *Sensational Designs: The Cultural Work of American Fiction, 1790–1860* (New York: Oxford University Press, 1985), xvii. See also Cathy Davidson, *Revolution and the Word: The Rise of the Novel in America* (New York: Oxford University Press, 1988), 55–82.

91. Glenn Hendler, *Public Sentiments: Structures of Feeling in Nineteenth-Century American Literature* (Chapel Hill: University of North Carolina Press, 2001), 1.

92. Ian Watt, *The Rise of the Novel* (Berkeley: University of California Press, 1957).

93. As Habermas puts it, "The empathetic reader repeated within himself the private relationships displayed before him in literature; from his experience of real familiarity, he gave life to the fictional one, and in the latter he prepared himself for the former." Habermas, *Structural Transformation,* 50–51. Benedict Anderson, *Imagined Communities: Reflections on the Origin and Spread of Nationalism* (New York: Verso, 1995). Works that take up or critically engage Habermas and/or Anderson include Warner, *Letters of the Republic*; Hendler, *Public Sentiments*; Lauren Berlant, *The Anatomy of National Fantasy: Hawthorne, Utopia, and Everyday Life* (Chicago: University of Chicago Press, 1991); Linda Kerber, *Women of the Republic: Intellect and Ideology in Revolutionary America* (Chapel Hill: University of North Carolina Press, 1997); and Elizabeth Maddock Dillon, *The Gender of Freedom: Fictions of Liberalism and the Literary Public Sphere* (Stanford, CA: Stanford University Press, 2004). For a more critical perspective on the influence of Anderson, see Sara Castro-Klarén and

Notes

John Charles Chasteen, eds., *Beyond Imagined Communities: Reading and Writing the Nation in Nineteenth-Century Latin America* (Baltimore: Johns Hopkins University Press, 2003). For a more comprehensive critique of the influence of the discourse of liberalism on literary history, see Nancy Ruttenburg, *Democratic Personality: Popular Voice and the Trial of American Authorship* (Stanford, CA: Stanford University Press, 1998).

94. Alcott, *Little Women*, 271.

95. As J. Hillis Miller puts it, "the assumption that the primary function of novels is to present characters is a red thread running through reigning assumptions about what is important in realistic fictions and about what procedures should be used in interpreting it." Miller, *Ariadne's Thread*, 29. Watt, for example, argues that "the novel is surely distinguished from other genres and from previous forms of fiction by the amount of attention it habitually accords both to the individualization of its characters and to the detailed presentation of their environment." Watt, *The Rise of the Novel*, 17–18.

96. See Deidre Shauna Lynch, *The Economy of Character: Novels, Market Culture, and the Business of Inner Meaning* (Chicago: University of Chicago Press, 1998), 4. See also Kristie Hamilton, *America's Sketchbook: The Cultural Life of a Nineteenth-Century Literary Genre* (Athens: Ohio University Press, 1998); Smeed, *The Theophrastan "Character"*; and David A. Brewer, *The Afterlife of Character, 1726–1825* (Philadelphia: University of Pennsylvania Press, 2005).

97. Lynch, *Economy of Character*, 10. The terms "flat" and "round," of course, originate in E.M. Forster, *Aspects of the Novel* (New York: Harvest Books, 1956), 67–82.

98. See, for example, F.O. Matthiessen, *American Renaissance: Art and Expression in the Age of Emerson and Whitman* (New York: Oxford University Press, 1968), 351–368.

99. Amy Kaplan, *The Social Construction of American Realism* (Chicago: University of Chicago Press, 1988), 24. Richard Chase similarly distinguishes the novel from the romance by the former's emphasis on character over plot. Romantic characters are inferior to the "realistic" characters of the novel because they are "two-dimensional types . . . not complexly related to each other or to society or to the past." Richard Chase, *The American Novel and Its Tradition* (Garden City, NY: Doubleday/Anchor Books, 1957), 13. See also Thomas Peyser, *Utopia and Cosmopolis: Globalization in the Era of American Literary Realism* (Durham, NC: Duke University Press, 1998), 100–101. More symptomatic of the significance of character within realism is the abundance of realist novels titled by their principal character, such as *Annie Kilburn, Ethan Frome, Martin Eden, Sister Carrie, Jennie Gerhardt, McTeague, Maggie*, or the more schematic *Twelve Men*.

100. See, for example, Nancy Glazener, *Reading for Realism: The History of a U.S. Literary Institution, 1850–1910* (Durham, NC: Duke University Press, 1997); Michael A. Elliot, *The Culture Concept: Writing and Difference in the Age of Realism* (Minneapolis: University of Minnesota Press, 2002), 40; Brook Thomas, *American Literary Realism*, 10; and Kaplan, *Social Construction*, 13. For a defense of the complex narrative and cultural function performed by the sentimental type, see Tompkins, *Sensational Designs*, xvi–xvii, 134–136, 175.

101. William Dean Howells, *Criticism and Fiction* (New York: Harper and Brothers, 1893), 115.

102. Henry James, *Portrait of a Lady* (New York: Viking, 1996), 255. Howells, *Criticism and Fiction*, 15–16. Although realism's concern with "detail" is often associated with the documentary mechanics of photography, James, like Howells, made clear that "the virtues of detail" might indeed be "the virtues of the photograph," but "the photograph lacks the supreme virtue of possessing a character." Henry James, "Miss Mackenzie," in *Notes and Reviews* (Cambridge, MA: University Press, 1921), 74.

103. Glazener, *Reading for Realism*, 95.

104. Lynch, *Economy of Character*, 15.

105. A. Anderson, *Way We Argue Now*, 135. Character has remained an important category of analysis however, among more narratological approaches. See, for example, Alan Palmer, *Fictional Minds* (Lincoln: University of Nebraska Press, 2004); James Phelan, *Living to Tell about It: A Rhetoric and Ethics of Character Narration* (Ithaca, NY: Cornell University Press, 2005); Thomas F. Petruso, *Life Made Real: Characterization in the Novel since Proust and Joyce* (Ann Arbor: University of Michigan Press, 1991).

106. Ibid.

107. Edward Bellamy, "To Whom This May Come," in *"The Blindman's World" and Other Stories* (Boston: Houghton Mifflin, 1898), 7, quoted in Stacey Margolis, *The Public Life of Privacy in Nineteenth-Century American Literature* (Durham, NC: Duke University Press, 2005), 2.

108. Margolis, *Public Life of Privacy*, 3.

109. S. Weir Mitchell, *Characteristics* (New York: Century, 1902), 10.

NOTES TO CHAPTER 1

1. David Hume, *A Treatise on Human Nature* (Oxford, UK: Clarendon, 1965), 159–160.

2. J. Hillis Miller, *Ariadne's Thread: Story Lines* (New Haven, CT: Yale University Press, 1992), 58.

3. Karen Halttunen, *Confidence Men and Painted Women: A Study of Middle-Class Culture in America, 1830–1870* (New Haven, CT: Yale University Press, 1982); Susan Kuhlmann, *Knave, Fool, and Genius: The Confidence Man as He Appears in Nineteenth-Century American Fiction* (Chapel Hill: University of North Carolina Press, 1973); Gary Lindberg, *The Confidence-Man in American Literature* (New York: Oxford University Press, 1982); Warwick Wadlington, *The Confidence Game in American Literature* (Princeton, NJ: Princeton University Press, 1975).

4. Herman Melville, *The Confidence-Man: His Masquerade*, ed. Harrison Hayford, Hershel Parker, and G. Thomas Tanselle (1857; repr., Evanston and Chicago: Northwestern University Press and The Newberry Library, 1984), 8. Further references to the novel are to this edition and are cited parenthetically in the text.

5. Michael Paul Rogin, *Subversive Genealogy: The Politics and Art of Herman Melville* (Berkeley: University of California Press, 1985), 239.

6. For J. Hillis Miller, such a tension between the novel's production and effacement of

such a fantasy of selfhood is essential to the very function of the novel form: "The function of the novel in the economy of modern bourgeois society, I suggest, has been the paradoxical one of reinforcing, to some degree even creating, the linguistic error of a belief in unitary selfhood, while at the same time putting that belief in question, demystifying in one way or another the error." Miller, *Ariadne's Thread*, 34.

7. Wadlington, *Confidence Game*, 9.

8. See Kristie Hamilton, *America's Sketchbook: The Cultural Life of a Nineteenth-Century Literary Genre* (Athens: Ohio University Press, 1998).

9. David Kazanjian, *The Colonizing Trick: National Culture and Imperial Citizenship in Early America* (Minneapolis: University of Minnesota Press, 2003), 4.

10. As Robyn Wiegman notes, "Herman Melville has been perceived as *the* American master of male bonding narratives, a writer obsessively devoted to sentimental renderings of life among men." Robyn Wiegman, "Melville's Geography of Gender," in *Herman Melville: A Collection of Critical Essays*, ed. Myra Jehlen (Englewood Cliffs, NJ: Prentice Hall, 1994), 187.

11. See Elizabeth Renker, "'A——!': Unreadability in *The Confidence-Man*," in *The Cambridge Companion to Herman Melville*, ed. Robert S. Levine (New York: Cambridge University Press, 1998), 129.

12. For a succinct yet comprehensive overview of approaches to the Indian-hater story, see John Bryant, "*The Confidence-Man*; Melville's Problem Novel," in *A Companion to Melville Studies*, ed. John Bryant (New York: Greenwood, 1986), 315–350.

13. For a critique of the depoliticizing effects of such approaches, see Stephen Matterson, "Indian-Hater, Wild Man: Melville's *Confidence-Man*," *Arizona Quarterly* 52, no. 2 (Summer 1996): 22.

14. William M. Ramsey, "The Moot Points of Melville's Indian-Hating," *American Literature* 52, no. 2 (May 1980): 224–235.

15. See Watson G. Branch, "The Mute as 'Metaphysical Scamp,'" in Herman Melville, *The Confidence-Man: His Masquerade*, ed. Hershel Parker (New York: Norton, 1971), 316–319.

16. "Arrest of the Confidence Man," *New York Herald*, July 8, 1849, reprinted in Herman Melville, *The Confidence-Man: His Masquerade*, ed. Hershel Parker (New York: Norton, 1971), 227. For a full discussion of the historical figure of the confidence man, see Tom Quirk, *Melville's Confidence Man: From Knave to Knight* (Columbia: University of Missouri Press, 1982), 19–46.

17. On the confidence man's cosmopolitanism, see Sheila Post-Lauria, *Correspondent Colorings: Melville in the Marketplace* (Amherst: University of Massachusetts Press, 1996), 223; Quirk, *Melville's Confidence Man*, 16–17; and John Bryant, *Melville and Repose: The Rhetoric of Humor in the American Renaissance* (New York: Oxford University Press, 1993), 109–128, 244–264.

18. Michael Banton, "The Idiom of Race," in *Theories of Race and Racism*, ed. Les Back and John Solomos (New York: Routledge, 2000), 52–58.

19. In his later, unfinished novel *Billy Budd, Sailor*, Melville again invokes this dependence of character on a kind of civilized "taste": "The character marked by such qualities has to an initiated taste an untampered-with flavor like that of berries, while the man thoroughly

civilized, even in a fair specimen of the breed, has to the same moral palate a questionable smack as of a compounded wine." Herman Melville, *Billy Budd, Sailor,* in *Billy Budd, Sailor and Other Stories* (New York: Penguin, 1986), 301–302.

20. Thank you to David Lloyd for this point.

21. Alan Trachtenberg, *The Incorporation of America: Culture and Society in the Gilded Age* (New York: Hill and Wang, 1982), 3–7. On the "federalization of affect," see Christopher Castiglia, *Interior States: Institutional Consciousness and the Inner Life of Democracy in the Antebellum United States* (Durham, NC: Duke University Press, 2008), 18.

22. Elizabeth Renker's formulation perhaps comes closest to the analysis here: "One of the Confidence-Man's techniques is to authenticate his own future incarnations by recommending them in advance of their appearance, a tautological method of establishing credit." Renker, "A——!" 41.

23. The necessity of such a referential circulation of black reputation through white character was most prominent in the prefatory attestations by white abolitionist editors of the veracity of published slave narratives. And as W.E.B. Du Bois points out in his landmark work *The Souls of Black Folk,* such a system of "character reference" was a common and often required practice even in the postbellum South: "Similar to such measures is the unwritten law of the back districts and small towns of the South, that the character of all Negroes unknown to the mass of the community must be vouched for by some white man." W.E.B. Du Bois, *The Souls of Black Folk* (1903; repr., New York: Penguin, 1996), 125.

24. An early review of the novel shows how this renaturalization can take place as the gesture of criticism itself: "The principal characters in the book are—1. The "Confidence-Man" himself, . . . 2. A lame black man (we are sure there is a lame black man . . . for we still maintain he was lame in spite of the assertions of the white man with the wooden leg)." *London Illustrated Times,* April 25, 1857, reprinted in Herman Melville, *The Confidence-Man: His Masquerade,* ed. Hershel Parker (New York: Norton, 1971), 277. See also Christopher Looby, "'As Thoroughly Black as the Most Faithful Philanthropist Could Desire,'" in *Race and the Subject of Masculinities,* ed. Harry Stecopoulos and Michael Uebel (Durham, NC: Duke University Press, 1997), 71–115.

25. See also Bryant, "*The Confidence-Man,*" 316.

26. Dow's dialogue opens with the sociably inquisitive "Curious Character" bombarding his laconically pious "Friend Singular" with questions about the "singularity" of his "singular character" and eventually turns to the question of whether Jesus Christ could have been a confidence man. Lorenzo Dow, *Cosmopolite Interrogated: or, A Dialogue between the Curious and Singular!* (New York: John C. Totten, 1813).

27. Ralph Waldo Emerson, "Self-Reliance," in *Ralph Waldo Emerson: Essays and Lectures* (New York: Library of America, 1983), 265.

28. Toni Morrison, *The Bluest Eye* (New York: Vintage, 1970), 164.

29. For an excellent account of Melville's nuanced approach to questions of racial representation, see Samuel Otter, "'Race' in *Typee* and *White-Jacket,*" in *The Cambridge Companion to Herman Melville,* ed. Robert S. Levine (New York: Cambridge University Press, 1998) 12; and Samuel Otter, *Melville's Anatomies* (Berkeley: University of California Press, 1999).

30. Elizabeth Foster, introduction to *The Confidence-Man: His Masquerade,* by Herman Melville (New York: Hendricks House, 1954), lxvii.

31. Helen Hunt Jackson, *Ramona* (1884; repr., New York: Signet, 2002), 346.

32. The irony here is that Melville is retelling a story that itself had a very large role in propagating such stereotypes and recasting it as a subtle genealogy of the formation of stereotypes. See Jonathan A. Cook, *Satirical Apocalypse: An Anatomy of Melville's* The Confidence-Man (Westport, CT: Greenwood, 1996), 184.

33. Frederick Jackson Turner, "The Significance of the Frontier in American History," in *Frederick Jackson Turner: Wisconsin's Historian of the Frontier,* ed. Martin Ridge (Madison: State Historical Society of Wisconsin, 1993), 26–47; William Graham Sumner, "Sociology," in *Collected Essays in Political and Social Science* (New York: Holt, 1885), 95–96.

34. Wai-chee Dimock, *Empire for Liberty* (Princeton, NJ: Princeton University Press, 1989).

35. As Toni Morrison puts it, "we can consider the possibility that Melville's 'truth' was his recognition of the moment in America when whiteness became ideology." Toni Morrison, "Unspeakable Things Unspoken: The Afro-American Presence in American Literature," *Michigan Quarterly Review* (Winter 1989): 1.

36. Homi Bhabha, "Introduction: Narrating the Nation," in *Nation and Narration,* ed. Homi Bhabha (New York: Routledge, 1994), 1.

37. Warren I. Susman, *Culture as History: The Transformation of American Society in the Twentieth Century* (New York: Pantheon, 1984), 271–286. Early examples of such a perspective include Richard Chase, "Melville's Confidence Man," *Kenyon Review* 11 (Winter 1949): 136; and Neil Harris, *Humbug: The Art of P.T. Barnum* (Chicago: University of Chicago Press, 1973), 221–223. See also David Sewell, "Mercantile Philosophy and the Dialectics of Confidence: Another Perspective on *The Confidence-Man,*" *ESQ* 30 (2nd Quarter 1984): 99–110.

38. Halttunen, *Confidence Men,* 206, 153–190.

39. Ibid., 207.

40. Ibid., 25.

41. Ibid., 49.

42. Ibid., 50.

43. Ralph Waldo Emerson, "Character," in *Ralph Waldo Emerson: Essays and Lectures* (New York: Library of America, 1983), 498, 495.

44. Ibid., 505, 503, 498.

45. Rufus W. Clark, *Lectures on the Formation of Character: Temptations and Mission of Young Men* (Boston: John P. Jewett, 1853), 213, 326, 350.

46. P.T. Barnum, *Dollars and Sense; or, How to Get On: The Whole Secret in a Nutshell* (New York: Henry S. Allen, 1890), 17.

47. Booker T. Washington, *Character Building* (1903; repr., Amsterdam: Fredonia Books, 2002), 3.

48. Edwin Whipple, *Character and Characteristic Men* (Boston: Ticknor and Fields, 1866), 159.

49. This federating capacity is of course a very loaded one at the time of the novel, on the

eve of the Civil War and its challenge to the federating capacity of the Union government. The Asylum agent more openly raises this looming "federal" question when he justifies the value of his worldwide federation of charities: "Indeed, such a confederation might, perhaps, be attended with as happy results as politically attended that of the states" (38). See also Castiglia on "federal affect" in *Interior States*, 17–59.

NOTES TO CHAPTER 2

1. Frances Willard, *What Frances E. Willard Said,* ed. Anna A. Gordon (New York: Fleming H. Revell Company, 1905), 105.

2. Thornstein Veblen, *The Theory of the Leisure Class* (1899; repr., New York: Dover, 1994), 136.

3. John Quincy Adams and Charles Francis Adams, *The Life of John Adams,* vol. 2 (Philadelphia: Lippincott, 1871), 376. In all fairness, it should be noted that the Adams family was not very well disposed toward the memory of Jefferson, given his role in the libelous attack on John Adams as a "hermaphroditical character" during Adams's presidency.

4. Gordon Wood, *Revolutionary Characters: What Made the Founders Different* (New York: Penguin, 2006), 36.

5. F.O. Matthiessen, *American Renaissance: Art and Expression in the Age of Emerson and Whitman* (New York: Oxford University Press, 1941), 105.

6. Sheila Post-Lauria, *Correspondent Colorings: Melville in the Marketplace* (Amherst: University of Massachusetts Press, 1996), 223. Karen Halttunen, *Confidence Men and Painted Women: A Study of Middle-Class Culture in America, 1830–1870* (New Haven, CT: Yale University Press, 1982), 31.

7. Everett Carter, in his oft-cited essay on the novel, famously divides readers into "'hard' critics who have seen the book as an attack on sentimentalism about the past" and "'soft' critics who have read it as either ambivalent or as an attack on technology and the American faith in material progress." Everett Carter, "The Meaning of *A Connecticut Yankee,*" *American Literature* 50, no. 3 (November 1978): 418.

8. William Dean Howells, *My Mark Twain: Reminiscences and Criticisms* (1910; repr., Kingsport: Louisiana State University Press, 1967). John Carlos Rowe, "How the Boss Played the Game: Twain's Critique of Imperialism in *A Connecticut Yankee in King Arthur's Court,*" in *The Cambridge Companion to Mark Twain,* ed. Forrest G. Robinson (New York: Cambridge University Press, 1995), 175–192.

9. Mark Twain, *A Connecticut Yankee in King Arthur's Court* (1889; repr., Berkeley: University of California Press, 1984), 67. Further references to the novel are to this edition and are cited parenthetically in the text.

10. Michael Davitt Bell, *The Problem of American Realism: Studies in the Cultural History of a Literary Idea* (Chicago: University of Chicago Press, 1993), 58.

11. James L. Johnson, *Mark Twain and the Limits of Power* (Knoxville: University of Tennessee Press, 1982). As Joe Fulton notes, critics who focus on the novel's shifting perspective on the modern technology of Twain's day invariably see a kind of autobiographical statement

of Twain's own frustrations with technology in the aftermath of his failed investment in the impossibly complex mechanism of the Paige Compositor, which not only brought Twain and his publishing house to bankruptcy but also inaugurated, in many critics' view, the pessimistic perspective of Twain's later writings. Joe B. Fulton, *Mark Twain's Ethical Realism: The Aesthetics of Race, Class, and Gender* (Columbia: University of Missouri Press, 1997).

12. Bill Brown, *The Material Unconscious: American Amusement, Stephen Crane, and the Economies of Play* (Cambridge, MA: Harvard University Press, 1996), 173.

13. Kenneth Kidd, *Making American Boys: Boyology and the Feral Tale* (Minneapolis: University of Minnesota Press, 2005), 50.

14. T.J. Jackson Lears, *No Place of Grace: Antimodernism and the Transformation of American Culture, 1880–1920* (Chicago: University of Chicago Press, 1994), 146; see also Caroline F. Levander, *Cradle of Liberty: Race, the Child, and National Belonging from Thomas Jefferson to W.E.B. Du Bois* (Durham, NC: Duke University Press, 2006), 9.

15. Roberta Trites, *Twain, Alcott, and the Birth of the Adolescent Reform Novel* (Iowa City: University of Iowa Press, 2007), 76.

16. Mark Twain, *The American Claimant* (1892; repr., New York: Oxford University Press, 1996), 217.

17. Richard S. Lowry, *"Littery Man": Mark Twain and Modern Authorship* (New York: Oxford University Press, 1996), 95–98.

18. Mark Twain, *Mark Twain's Book for Bad Boys and Girls,* ed. R. Kent Rasmussen (Chicago: Contemporary Books, 1995); Mark Twain, *Mark Twain's Helpful Hints for Good Living: A Handbook for the Damned Human Race,* ed. Lin Salamo, Victor Fischer, and Michael B. Frank (Berkeley: University of California Press, 2004).

19. Mark Twain, *Mark Twain's Notebooks and Journals,* vol. 1, ed. Frederick Anderson (Berkeley: University of California Press, 1975), 398.

20. Mark Twain, "Advice to Youth" (1882), in Salamo, Fischer, and Frank, *Mark Twain's Helpful Hints,* 137.

21. See Cathy Boeckmann, *A Question of Character: Scientific Racism and the Genres of American Fiction, 1892–1912* (Tuscaloosa: University of Alabama Press, 2000), 101–107.

22. Ibid., 103; Alan Gribben, "Mark Twain, Phrenology and the 'Temperaments': A Study of Pseudoscientific Influence," *American Quarterly* 24, no. 1 (March 1972): 45–68.

23. For background on the bad-boy genre, see Glenn Hendler, *Public Sentiments: Structures of Feeling in Nineteenth-Century American Literature* (Chapel Hill: University of North Carolina Press, 2001), 184–211; Kidd, *Making American Boys*; and Marcia Jacobson, *Being a Boy Again: Autobiography and the American Boy Book* (Tuscaloosa: University of Alabama Press, 1994).

24. Thomas Bailey Aldrich, *The Story of a Bad Boy* (1869; repr., Hanover: University of New Hampshire Press, 1990); Charles Dudley Warner, *Being a Boy* (1877; repr., Boston: Houghton, Mifflin, 1897); William Dean Howells, *A Boy's Town* (1890), in *Selected Writings of William Dean Howells,* ed. Henry Steele Commager (New York: Random House, 1950).

25. Aldrich, *Story of a Bad Boy,* v–vi.

26. As Aldrich puts it, "This is the story of a bad boy. Well, not such a very bad, but a

pretty bad boy; and I ought to know, for I am, or rather I was, that boy myself" (ibid., 1). Although bad-boy authors did not always identify their stories as strict autobiographies in the ways that, for example, Aldrich and Howells did, they did celebrate the realist fidelity of their account because of its grounding in their "insider" knowledge as former or "ex"-boys. As Warner puts it in his preface to *Being a Boy*: "While the book . . . was not consciously biographical, it was of necessity written out of a personal knowledge. . . . I was dealing with a young life of the past, I tried to be faithful to it, strictly so, and to import into it nothing of later experience, either in feeling or performance." Warner, *Being a Boy*, viii–ix.

27. Howells, *Boy's Town*, 732.

28. Brown, *Material Unconscious*, 176.

29. Hendler, *Public Sentiments*,186–187.

30. Ibid., 186.

31. Ibid., 187.

32. David I. Macleod, *Building Character in the American Boy: The Boy Scouts, YMCA, and Their Forerunners, 1870–1920* (Madison: University of Wisconsin Press, 1983), 55.

33. Warner, *Being a Boy*, 150.

34. Gail Bederman, *Manliness and Civilization: A Cultural History of Gender and Race in the United States, 1880–1917* (Chicago: University of Chicago Press, 1995).

35. Frank Norris, "Child Stories for Adults," in *The Responsibilities of the Novelist and Other Literary Essays* (New York: Doubleday, Page, 1903), 114.

36. Howells, *Boy's Town*, 765.

37. For an excellent account of the impact of fetishism on the development of nineteenth-century cultural theory, see Peter Logan, *Victorian Fetishism: Intellectuals and Primitives* (Albany: State University of New York Press, 2009).

38. Aldrich, *Story of a Bad Boy*, 38.

39. Warner, *Being a Boy*, 151, 153.

40. Hendler, *Public Sentiments*, 198.

41. Howells, *Boy's Town*, 828.

42. Martha Banta, "The Boys and the Bosses: Twain's Double Take on Work, Play, and the Democratic Ideal," *American Literary History* 3. no. 3 (Fall 1991): 497, 489.

43. William Byron Forbush, *The Boy Problem: A Study in Social Pedagogy* (Boston: Pilgrim, 1901). Girls were also identified as a "problem" by authors such as Mary Moxcey, who notes in *Girlhood and Character*, "The fact that you have opened this book shows that you have something to do with girls. And if you have, you doubtless have some 'girl problem.'" Mary E. Moxcey, *Girlhood and Character* (New York: Abingdon, 1916), 17. See also Phyllis Blanchard, *The Adolescent Girl: A Study from the Psychoanalytic Viewpoint* (New York: Moffat, Yard, 1920).

44. Edwin Puller, "The Eternal Boy Problem," in *Your Boy and His Training: A Practical Treatise on Boy Training* (New York: D. Appleton, 1916), 1.

45. Ernest Thompson Seton, *Boy Scouts of America: A Handbook of Woodcraft, Scouting, and Life-Craft* (New York: Doubleday, Page, 1910), xi–xii, reprinted in *The Call of the Wild: 1900–1916*, ed. Roderick Nash (New York: George Braziller, 1970), 19–20.

46. Ralph Waldo Emerson, "Self-Reliance," in *Ralph Waldo Emerson: Essays and Lectures* (New York: Library of America, 1983), 261.

47. Joseph Kett, *Rites of Passage: Adolescence in America 1790 to the Present* (New York: Basic Books, 1978), 133–134; Lears, *No Place of Grace*, 141–182.

48. Perry Edwards Powell, *The Knights of the Holy Grail: A Solution of the Boy Problem* (Cincinnati: Press of Jennings & Graham, 1906); William Byron Forbush, *The Boys' Round Table: A Manual of Boys' Clubs Explaining the Order of the Knights of King Arthur* (Albany, NY: Brandow, 1907); Boy Scouts of America, *Boy Scouts Handbook* (1911; repr., Mineola, NY: Dover, 2005), 237–254.

49. Amy Kaplan and Donald E. Pease, eds., *Cultures of United States Imperialism* (Durham, NC: Duke University Press, 1994). See John Carlos Rowe, "How the Boss Played the Game: Twain's Critique of Imperialism in *A Connecticut Yankee in King Arthur's Court*," in *The Cambridge Companion to Mark Twain*, ed. Forrest G. Robinson (New York: Cambridge University Press, 1995), 186.

50. As Randall Knoper puts it, "Mystification and demystification make each other possible; they are among the basic innovations that Hank brings to Arthur's court." Randall Knoper, *Acting Naturally: Mark Twain in the Culture of Performance* (Berkeley: University of California Press, 1995), 143.

51. See Cindy Weinstein, *The Literature of Labor and the Labor of Literature: Allegory in Nineteenth-Century American Fiction* (New York: Cambridge University Press, 2008), 129–169.

52. Kidd, *Making American Boys*, 19.

53. See ibid., 67; Mark Seltzer, *Bodies and Machines* (New York: Routledge, 1992), 149–172; Brown, *Material Unconscious*, 171.

54. Henry William Gibson, *Boyology; or, Boy Analysis* (New York: Association Press, 1922).

55. Kidd, *Making American Boys*, 69.

56. Edward Sisson, *The Essentials of Character: A Practical Study of the Aim of Moral Education* (New York: Macmillan, 1915), 184. See also Newell Dwight Hillis, *The Contagion of Character: Studies in Culture and Success* (New York: Fleming H. Revell, 1911).

57. Seltzer, *Bodies and Machines*, 153; Michael Rosenthal, *The Character Factory: Baden-Powell and the Origins of the Boy Scout Movement* (New York: Pantheon Books, 1986). See also Walter Benn Michaels, "Armies and Factories: *A Connecticut Yankee*," in *Mark Twain: A Collection of Critical Essays*, ed. Eric J. Sundquist (Englewood Cliffs, NJ: Prentice Hall, 1994), 129.

58. Robert Baden-Powell, *Headquarter's Gazette* 5 (November 1911), 2, quoted in Rosenthal, *Character Factory*, 6, and in Seltzer, *Bodies and Machines*, 153.

59. Rosenthal, *Character Factory*, 284.

60. Marian M. George, *Character Building* (Chicago: A. Flanagan, 1909), 2, 10, 91.

61. George Propheter, "The Habits of Habits," *Health* 55, no. 11 (November 1905): 369. See also Henry Park Schauffler, *Adventures in Habit-Craft: Character in the Making* (New York: Macmillan, 1927).

62. Veblen, *The Theory of the Leisure Class*, 136.

63. Charles Chauncy, *Seasonable Thoughts on the State of Religion in New-England* (Boston, 1742), 6.

64. John Locke, *Some Thoughts Concerning Education* (1693; repr. Indianapolis: Hackett, 1996), 41. For an analysis of the tension between this definition of character and Locke's empiricist definition of the mind as a blank slate or "white page," see Ala A. Alryyes, *Original Subjects: The Child, the Novel, and the Nation* (Cambridge, MA: Harvard University Press, 2001), 38.

65. *Liddell and Scott's Greek-English Lexicon*, intermediate abridgment of the 7th ed. (Oxford, UK: Clarendon, 1995), s.v. "Kharakter."

66. Benjamin Franklin, *The Autobiography* (1818; repr., New York: Vintage Books, 1990), 81, 85.

67. Rufus W. Clark, *Lectures on the Formation of Character: Temptations and Mission of Young Men* (Boston: John P. Jewett, 1853), 28 (emphasis added).

68. John Todd, *The Student's Manual: Designed, by Specific Directions, to Aid in Forming and Strengthening the Intellectual and Moral Character and Habits of the Student* (Northampton, MA: J.H. Butler, 1835), 47.

69. Judy Hilkey, *Character Is Capital: Success Manuals and Manhood in Gilded Age America* (Chapel Hill: University of North Carolina Press, 1997).

70. Ibid., 20–22.

71. See Alan Gribben, *Mark Twain's Library: A Reconstruction*, vol. 2 (Boston: G.K. Hall, 1980).

72. Mark Twain, *A Connecticut Yankee in King Arthur's Court* (New York: Charles L. Webster, 1889).

73. Hilkey, *Character Is Capital*, 21.

74. William Mathews, *Getting On in the World; or, Hints on Success in Life* (Chicago: S.C. Griggs, 1877), 164.

75. Samuel Smiles, *Character* (New York: A.L. Burt, 1872), 166.

76. Clark, *Lectures on the Formation of Character*, 35, 36.

77. Smiles, *Character*, 75. See Hilkey, *Character Is Capital*, 21.

78. Smiles, *Character*, 165.

79. Mathews, *Getting On in the World*, 160–161.

80. Ibid., 160.

81. Ibid.

82. Walter Benjamin, "Fate and Character," in *Reflections*, ed. Peter Demetz (New York: Schocken Books, 1986), 306.

83. In early manuals by Rufus Clark and George Peck, for example, the "energy of character" was already an established trope for understanding the "force" accumulated as character's second nature. As Peck puts it, "It is the want of *energy of character* [in youth] that makes them the victims of foreign influences." George Peck, *Formation of a Manly Character* (New York: Nelson and Phillips, 1853), 113. See also "Energy of Character," in Clark, *Lectures on the Formation of Character*, 44–46.

84. Helen Keller, *The Open Door* (New York: Doubleday, 1957), 30.

85. William James, *The Principles of Psychology*, vol. 1 (1890; repr., New York: Dover, 1950).
86. Ibid., 125.
87. Alexander Hamilton, James Madison, and John Jay, *The Federalist Papers* (New York: New American Library, 1999), 351; Friedrich Nietzsche, *On the Genealogy of Morals*, trans. Walter Kaufman (New York: Vintage Books, 1989), 57–65.
88. From the abridged version of the *Principles* published in 1892 as *Psychology: Briefer Course*, reprinted in *The Writings of William James: A Comprehensive Edition*, ed. John McDermott (Chicago: University of Chicago Press, 1977), 9.
89. Allison Winter, *Mesmerism: Powers of Mind in Victorian Britain* (Chicago: University of Chicago Press, 1998), 308.
90. James, *Principles of Psychology*, 105, 120, 127. Edgar Pierce opens his treatise *Philosophy of Character* by noting the incompleteness of James's approach to what he calls "the problem of the relation of purpose to bodily movements" (v), but he goes on to echo James's concern that "[i]f philosophy and psychology are more than mere pernicious pastimes, they must aid in the building of this new society, they must furnish the fundamentals for a sound theory of character, for on the development of character all else depends." Edgar Pierce, *The Philosophy of Character* (Cambridge, MA: Harvard University Press, 1924), 3.
91. James, *Principles of Psychology*, 127.
92. Ibid., 122 (original emphasis).
93. Ibid., 121 (emphasis mine).
94. Ibid.
95. Thomas Winter, *Making Men, Making Class: The YMCA and Workingmen, 1877–1920* (Chicago: University of Chicago Press, 2002), 12–13.
96. Ibid., 12.
97. Hilkey, *Character Is Capital*, 133; David Roediger, *The Wages of Whiteness: Race and the Making of the American Working Class* (New York: Verso, 2007).
98. Washington Irving, "Philip of Pokanoket," in *The Sketch Book of Geoffrey Crayon, Gent.* (1819–20; repr., New York: E.P. Dutton, 1922), 283. See also Irving's "Traits of Indian Character," in *The Sketch Book*, James Fenimore Cooper's *Last of the Mohicans*, Lydia Maria Child's *Hobomok*, and Catherine Sedgwick's *Hope Leslie*.
99. Ernest Thompson Seton and Julia Seton, *The Gospel of the Redman: A Way of Life* (Santa Fe, NM: Seton Village, 1966); Ernest Thompson Seton, *Two Little Savages: Being the Adventures of Two Boys Who Live as Indians and What They Learned* (1903; repr., New York: Dover, 1962).
100. Charles A. Eastman, "Training for Service," in *Indian Scout Craft and Lore* (1914; repr., New York: Dover, 1974), 190; Charles Alexander Eastman, "An Indian Boy's Training," in *Indian Boyhood* (1902; repr., Boston: Little, Brown, 1922), 52. See also Luther Standing Bear, *Land of the Spotted Eagle* (1933; repr., Lincoln: University of Nebraska Press, 1978).
101. Cindy Weinstein, *The Literature of Labor and the Labors of Literature: Allegory in Nineteenth-Century American Fiction* (New York: Cambridge University Press, 1995), 129–73.
102. See also Seltzer, *Bodies and Machines*, 7–9.
103. Daniel Carter Beard, *Hardly a Man Is Now Alive* (New York: Doubleday, Doran, 1939), 338.

104. Henry Nash Smith, *Mark Twain's Fable of Progress: Political and Economic Ideas in "A Connecticut Yankee"* (New Brunswick, NJ: Rutgers University Press, 1964), 76.

105. See Bernard L. Stein, "Explanatory Notes," in Mark Twain, *A Connecticut Yankee In King Arthur's Court* (Berkeley: University of California Press, 1983), 458; and Beverly R. David, "The Unexpurgated *A Connecticut Yankee*: Mark Twain and His Illustrator, Daniel Carter Beard," *Prospects* 1 (1975): 101.

NOTES TO CHAPTER 3

1. Newell Hillis, *A Man's Value to Society: Studies in Self-Culture and Character* (Chicago: Fleming H. Revell, 1897), 92.

2. F.D. Gage, "Sojourner Truth," *The Independent . . . Devoted to the Consideration of Politics, Social and Economic Tendencies, History, Literature, and the Arts,* April 23, 1863, 1.

3. Effie J Squier, "Sojourner Truth," *Zion's Herald,* December 12, 1883, 1.

4. Notice from the *Fall River Papers,* reprinted in "Book of Life," in *Narrative of Sojourner Truth* (New York: Penguin, 1998), 135; Anna Julia Cooper, *A Voice from the South* (New York: Oxford University Press, 1988), 141.

5. Karen Sánchez-Eppler, *Touching Liberty: Abolition, Feminism, and the Politics of the Body* (Berkeley: University of California Press, 1993), 20.

6. For an overview of the publication history of the *Narrative of Sojourner Truth* and the controversies surrounding it, see Nell Irvin Painter, *Sojourner Truth: A Life, A Symbol* (New York: Norton, 1996), 103–112; and Erlene Stetson and Linda David, *Glorying in Tribulation: The Lifework of Sojourner Truth* (East Lansing: Michigan State University Press, 1994), 13–24.

7. Of the accounts published shortly after the Akron meeting, Marius Robinson's in the *Anti-Slavery Bugle* was perhaps the fullest as well as the most reliable. Although Robinson similarly cites Truth's claim to "have as much muscle as any man," he makes no mention of Truth's arm-bearing performance and presents Truth's words in standard English. As Nell Irving Painter points out, however, all these versions—including those by feminist historians that attempt to retranslate the dialect of Gage's version back into a more neutral language—remain fictional reconstructions of the "real" and by all accounts rhetorically innovative Sojourner Truth. My focus on and citation of Gage's dialect version derives from my interest in charting the role it played in constructing the fictional Sojourner Truth that came to dominate historical accounts of the late nineteenth and early twentieth centuries. See Painter, *Sojourner Truth,* 98, 121–131, 258–273; Stetson and David, *Glorifying in Tribulation,* 110–120; and Carleton Mabee, *Sojourner Truth: Slave, Prophet, Legend* (New York: New York University Press, 1993), 67–82.

8. When Frances Titus edited and republished Oliver Gilbert's original edition of Truth's autobiography in 1875, she appended to it a "Book of Life," which, along with Stowe's article, also included Gage's rendition of the 1851 speech. It was with the republication of Gage's version in the 1881 edition of *History of Woman Suffrage,* however, that the predominance of Gage's reconstruction of the symbolic Sojourner Truth was firmly

established both in popular culture and in feminist historiography. See Painter, *Sojourner Truth*, 259.

9. Daphne Brooks, *Bodies in Dissent: Spectacular Performances of Race and Freedom, 1850–1910* (Durham, NC: Duke University Press, 2006), 158. See also Jacqueline E. Brady, "Pumping Iron with Resistance: Carla Dunlap's Victorious Body," in *Recovering the Black Female Body*, ed. Michael Bennett and Vanessa D. Dickerson (New Brunswick, NJ: Rutgers University Press, 2000), 253–254; and Stetson and David, *Glorifying in Tribulation*, 115.

10. Brooks, *Bodies in Dissent*, 158–159.

11. Theodore Roosevelt, "The Strenuous Life," in *The Strenuous Life: Essays and Addresses* (New York: Century, 1900); Josiah Strong, *Our Country: Its Possible Future and Its Present Crisis* (New York: Baker and Taylor, 1891); George Beard, *American Nervousness: Its Causes and Consequences* (New York: G.P. Putnam's Sons, 1881); S. Weir Mitchell, *Wear and Tear, or Hints for the Overworked* (Philadelphia: J.B. Lippincott, 1897), and *Characteristics* (1891; repr., New York: Century, 1913); G. Stanley Hall, *Adolescence: Its Psychology and Its Relations to Physiology, Anthropology, Sociology, Sex, Crime, Religion, and Education*, 2 vols. (New York: D. Appleton, 1914).

12. Amy Kaplan, *The Anarchy of Empire in the Making of U.S. Culture* (Cambridge, MA: Harvard University Press, 2002), 121–145.

13. James Fenimore Cooper, *Last of the Mohicans* (New York: Penguin, 1986), 29; Gail Bederman, *Manliness and Civilization: A Cultural History of Gender and Race in the United States, 1880–1917* (Chicago: University of Chicago Press, 1995), 15.

14. Edgar Rice Burroughs, *Tarzan of the Apes* (1914; repr., New York: Penguin, 1990).

15. Kaplan, *Anarchy of Empire*, 97. See also Bederman, *Manliness and Civilization*, 170–216; John F. Kasson, *Houdini, Tarzan, and the Perfect Man: The White Male Body and the Challenge of Modernity in America* (New York: Hill and Wang, 2001), 10.

16. Theodore Roosevelt, "The American Boy," in *The Strenuous Life: Essays and Addresses* (New York: Century, 1900), 156. See also Theodore Roosevelt, "Character and Success," in ibid., 118.

17. "Muscle-Training," *The Youth's Companion* 78, no. 3 (January 21, 1904): 40.

18. M.V. O'Shea, "Physical Training in the Public Schools," *Atlantic Monthly* 75, no. 448 (February 1895): 254.

19. Arthur Conan Doyle, foreword to *The Construction and Reconstruction of the Human Body: A Manual of the Therapeutics of Exercise*, by Eugene Sandow (London: John Bale, Sons and Danielsson, 1907), x.

20. See Bederman, *Manliness and Civilization*, 10–20; Kasson, *Houdini, Tarzan, and the Perfect Man*; and Michael Kimmel, *Manhood in America: A Cultural History* (New York: Free Press, 1996).

21. John Todd, *The Student's Manual: Designed, by Specific Directions, to Aid in Forming and Strengthening the Intellectual and Moral Character and Habits of the Student* (Northampton, MA: J.H. Butler, 1835), 260–292; Rufus Clark, *Lectures on the Formation of Character: Temptations and Mission of Young Men* (Boston: John P. Jewett, 1853), 31. See in particular

Frederick A. Atkins, *Moral Muscle, and How to Use It: A Brotherly Chat with Young Men* (Chicago: Fleming H. Revell, 1890).

22. John O'Reilly, *Athletics and Manly Sports* (1890), quoted in Roberta J. Park, "Muscles, Symmetry and Action: 'Do You Measure Up?': Defining Masculinity in Britain and American from the 1860s to the Early 1900s," *International Journal of the History of Sport* 23, no. 2 (May 2005): 376.

23. Todd, *Student's Manual*, 260–292.

24. [William Russell], "Prospectus," *American Journal of Education* 1 (1826): 2–3, quoted in Roberta J. Park, "Healthy, Moral and Strong: Educational Views of Exercise and Athletics in Nineteenth-Century America," in *Fitness in American Culture: Images of Health, Sport, and the Body, 1830–1940*, ed. Kathryn Grover (Amherst: University of Massachusetts Press, 1989), 135.

25. "Muscles and Brains," *Saturday Evening Post*, September 3, 1870, 4; "Mr. Slim's Developments in Physical Culture," *Ballou's Dollar Monthly Magazine* 15, no. 5 (May 1862): 499.

26. John DeMotte, *The Secret of Character Building* (Chicago: S.C. Griggs, 1894), 61.

27. G. Stanley Hall, "Educational Needs," *North American Review* 136 (March 1883): 284. See also Charles H. Parkhurst, "Character and Muscle," *Congregationalist* 84, no. 7 (February 16, 1899): 227.

28. "The Muscle Question," *Circular*, August 12, 1858, 114. See, for example, "Muscle and Womanhood," *Herald of Health*, December 2, 1867, 267; "Men and Muscle," *The Independent . . . Devoted to the Consideration of Politics, Social and Economic Tendencies, History, Literature, and the Arts*, August 31, 1871, 1; "Muscle Will Tell," *Massachusetts Ploughman and New England Journal of Agriculture*, August. 5, 1871, 1; "Mind and Muscle," *Ballou's Monthly Magazine*, July 1, 1867, 80; and "A Hit at the Muscle Mania," *Saturday Evening Post*, April 12, 1862, 8.

29. For background on the rise of phrenology in the United States, see John D. Davies, *Phrenology, Fad and Science: A 19th-Century American Crusade* (New Haven, CT: Yale University Press, 1955). See also Cathy Boeckmann, *A Question of Character: Scientific Racism and the Genres of American Fiction, 1892–1912* (Tuscaloosa: University of Alabama Press, 2000), 44–49; and Christopher Castiglia, *Interior States: Institutional Consciousness and the Inner Life of Democracy in the Antebellum United States* (Durham, NC: Duke University Press, 2008), 172–189.

30. Jan Todd, *Physical Culture and the Body Beautiful: Purposive Exercise in the Lives of American Women, 1800–1870* (Macon, GA: Mercer University Press, 1998), 175.

31. Ibid., 176; O.S. Fowler, *Self-Culture and Perfection of Character Including the Management of Youth* (New York: Samuel R. Wells, 1847), 88.

32. Hillis, *A Man's Value to Society*, 92.

33. See Boeckmann, *A Question of Character*, 11–63.

34. See Clifford Putney, *Muscular Christianity: Manhood and Sports in Protestant America, 1880–1920* (Cambridge, MA: Harvard University Press, 2001), 3; and Donald E. Hall, ed., *Muscular Christianity: Embodying the Victorian Age* (New York: Cambridge University Press, 1994).

35. As Pamela Moore has put it, the muscles built by bodybuilding "are the ultimate expression of a postmodern belief in corporeal malleability." Pamela Moore, introduction to *Building Bodies*, ed. Pamela Moore (New Brunswick, NJ: Rutgers University Press, 1997), 2.

36. Michael Anton Budd, *The Sculpture Machine: Physical Culture and Body Politics in the Age of Empire* (New York: New York University Press, 1997), 82.

37. The *National Police Gazette* was founded in 1845 by journalist George Wilkes and only finally ceased publication some 137 years later—after undergoing many reincarnations as sporting magazine, celebrity tabloid, and pornographic "girlie" magazine—in 1982. See Guy Reel, *The* National Police Gazette *and the Making of the Modern American Man, 1876–1906* (New York: Palgrave Macmillan, 2006).

38. Shelley Streeby, *American Sensations: Class, Empire, and the Production of Popular Culture* (Berkeley: University of California Press, 2002), 258.

39. Quoted in Edward Van Every, *Sins of New York, as "Exposed" by the Police Gazette* (1930; repr., New York: Benjamin Blom, 1972), 9.

40. Reel, National Police Gazette *and the Making of the Modern American Man*, 28.

41. Michel Foucault, *Discipline and Punish: The Birth of the Prison* (New York: Vintage Books, 1995), 251.

42. See Allan Sekula, "The Body and the Archive," *October* 39 (Winter 1986): 3–64; and Shawn Michelle Smith, *American Archives: Gender, Race, and Class in Visual Culture* (Princeton, NJ: Princeton University Press, 1999), 65–93.

43. Sekula, "The Body and the Archive," 15–16; Smith, *American Archives*, 71.

44. Sekula, "The Body and the Archive," 10.

45. Reel, National Police Gazette *and the Making of the Modern American Man*, 4.

46. "This Is The Greatest of All Contests: The Diamond Medal Isn't Won Yet, So There Is a Chance for You, If You Have Muscles," *National Police Gazette* 80, no. 1205 (June 14, 1902): 7.

47. Reel, National Police Gazette *and the Making of the Modern American Man*, 103.

48. Tom Sharkey, "Be a Strong Man, Not a Caricature," *National Police Gazette* 86, no. 1438 (March 4, 1905): 7.

49. Streeby, *American Sensations*, 28, 27.

50. See David L. Chapman, *Sandow the Magnificent: Eugene Sandow and the Beginnings of Bodybuilding* (Urbana: University of Illinois Press, 2006).

51. So visually captivating were Sandow's muscular displays that he quickly became a sensation in New York while also capturing the attention of Thomas Edison, who filmed Sandow's muscle dance in order to showcase the subtle visualizing power of his new moving picture technology. Ibid., 76–77, 97–98. Kasson, *Houdini, Tarzan, and the Perfect Man*, 73–74.

52. "The Ladies Idolize Sandow," *National Police Gazette* 63, no. 856 (January 27, 1894): 6. For Sandow's own account of these backstage performances, see Eugene Sandow, *Strength and How to Obtain It* (London: Gale and Polden, 1897), 125. See also Kasson, *Houdini, Tarzan, and the Perfect Man*, 56–60.

53. "The Ladies Idolize Sandow," 6, emphasis mine.

54. Sandow's "Great Competition" was held in London's Royal Albert Hall in September 1901. See Chapman, *Sandow the Magnificent*, 129–136. Macfadden held his first contest

two years later in New York's Madison Square Garden. See Mark Adams, *Mr. America: How Muscular Millionaire Bernarr Macfadden Transformed the Nation through Sex, Salad, and the Ultimate Starvation Diet* (New York: HarperCollins, 2009), 50–57.

55. "So-Called Beauty Contest," *New York Times,* October 2, 1905, 5.

56. Thomas Waugh, *Hard to Imagine: Gay Male Eroticism in Photography and Film from Their Beginnings to Stonewall* (New York: Columbia University Press, 1996), 184.

57. Ibid., 183. See also Kasson, *Houdini, Tarzan, and the Perfect Man,* 67.

58. Quoted in Waugh, *Hard to Imagine,* 185.

59. Bernarr Macfadden, *Superb Virility of Manhood: Giving the Causes and Simple Home Methods of Curing the Weaknesses of Men* (New York: Physical Culture, 1904), 175–176. See also Graham Robb, *Strangers: Homosexual Love in the Nineteenth Century* (New York: Norton, 2004), 134.

60. See R. Marie Griffith, "Apostles of Abstinence: Fasting and Masculinity during the Progressive Era," *American Quarterly* 52, no. 4 (December 2000): 609. For an account of the role of fasting in modern bodybuilding, see Ann Bolin, "Flex Appeal, Food, and Fat: Competitive Bodybuilding, Gender, and Diet," in Moore, *Building Bodies,* 184–208. Special thanks to Fred Rogers for first introducing me to Macfadden's character-building obsessions.

61. Moore, *Building Bodies,* 76–77.

62. Julia Seton, *The Short Cut: Regeneration through Fasting* (1928; repr., New York: Cosimo, 2006), 14.

63. Leslie Heywood, "Masculinity Vanishing: Bodybuilding and Contemporary Culture," in Moore, *Building Bodies,* 171, 174.

64. On women's muscle building in contemporary culture, see Laurie Schulze, "On the Muscle," in Moore, *Building Bodies,* 9–30.

65. See, for example, "Female Sandbaggers," *National Police Gazette* 4, no. 638 (November 30, 1889): 1; "Chased by a Pretty Girl," *National Police Gazette* 55, no. 652 (March 8, 1890): 1; and "The Gutters Full of Jag Juice," *National Police Gazette* 55, no. 653 (March 1, 1890): 1.

66. "On Her Muscle," *National Police Gazette* 65, no. 907 (January 19, 1895): 7; "She Resented an Insult," *National Police Gazette* 63 (February 24, 1894): 3.

67. "A Boston Husband's Punishment," *National Police Gazette* 78, no. 1245 (June 29, 1901): 8.

68. "Shoots When Pressed," *National Police Gazette* 63, no. 856 (January 27, 1894), 6.

69. See Kasson, *Houdini, Tarzan, and the Perfect Man,* 46–49.

70. "Vassar Vengeance," *National Police Gazette* 36, no. 152 (August 21, 1880): 6.

71. "Belles of Comic Opera Who Will Spend the Summer Developing Muscles," *National Police Gazette* 81, no. 1300 (July 19, 1902): 2.

72. See Laura Mulvey, "Visual Pleasure and Narrative Cinema," *Screen* 16, no. 3 (1975): 6–18; Mikhail Bakhtin, *Rabelais and His World,* trans. Helene Iswolsky (Bloomington: Indiana University Press, 1984). In Freud's analysis of fetishism, on which accounts such as Mulvey's rely, such a fetishization of phallic femininity would mark not the reconsolidation of heterosexual desire but rather a kind of queer sexuality that wards off both the overt homosexuality suggested by such a need for a "penis-substitute" in women and the heterosexuality that would embrace the

anatomical terms of sexual difference. As Freud explains it, three possibilities arise from the male's recognition of the anatomical terms of sexual difference: "some of them become homosexual in consequence of this experience, others ward it off by creating a fetish, and the great majority overcome it." Sigmund Freud, "Fetishism," in *Sexuality and the Psychology of Love* (New York: Collier Books, 1963), 216. See also Chris Holmlund, "Visible Difference and Flex Appeal: The Body, Sex, Sexuality, and Race in the *Pumping Iron* Films," in Moore, *Building Bodies*, 87–102.

73. Judith Halberstam, *Female Masculinity* (Durham, NC: Duke University Press, 1998), 46.

74. "Here's a Handsome Girl Who Can Box and Tend Bar," *National Police Gazette* 76, no. 1192 (June 23, 1900): 6.

75. Judith Butler, "Imitation and Gender Insubordination," in *Inside/Out: Lesbian Theories, Gay Theories*, ed. Diana Fuss (New York: Routledge, 1991), 13–31.

76. "Although the gay male world of the prewar years was remarkably visible and integrated into the straight world, it was . . . a world very different from our own. Above all, it was not a world in which men were divided into 'homosexuals' and 'heterosexuals.'" George Chauncey, *Gay New York: Gender, Urban Culture, and the Making of the Gay Male World, 1890–1940* (New York: Basic Books, 1994), 12.

77. "Such a Dilemma," *National Police Gazette* 32, no. 37 (June 8, 1878): 3; "Pretty Female Tramp," *National Police Gazette* 63, no. 853 (March 17, 1894): 2.

78. "They Could Take Care of Themselves," *National Police Gazette* 39, no. 230 (April 1, 1882): 10.

79. "A Female Romeo; Her Terrible Love for a Chosen Friend of Her Own Alleged Sex Assumes a Passionate Character," *National Police Gazette* 34, no. 89 (June 7, 1879): 6. See also Lisa Duggan, *Saphic Slashers: Sex, Violence, and American Modernity* (Durham, NC: Duke University Press, 2000).

80. Charlotte Perkins Gilman, *The Living of Charlotte Perkins Gilman* (New York: Arno, 1972), 29. Of the very few, sustained considerations of Gilman's interest in physical culture is Jane Lancaster's "'I Could Easily Have Been an Acrobat': Charlotte Perkins Gilman and the Providence Ladies' Sanitary Gymnasium," *American Transcendental Quarterly (ATQ)* 8, no. 1 (March 1994): 33–52.

81. Gilman, *Living*, 73, 35.

82. Ibid., 56.

83. Ibid., 58. See also Ann J. Lane, *To Herland and Beyond: The Life and Work of Charlotte Perkins Gilman* (New York: Pantheon Books, 1990), 57.

84. Charlotte Perkins Gilman, *The Diaries of Charlotte Perkins Gilman*, vol. 1, *1879–87*, ed. Denise D. Knight (Charlottesville: University of Virginia Press, 1994), 6.

85. Gilman, *Living*, 32–33, 56.

86. Ibid., 66; Lancaster, "I Could Easily Have Been an Acrobat."

87. Quoted in Patricia Vertinsky, *The Eternally Wounded Woman: Women, Doctors and Exercise in the Late Nineteenth Century* (New York: Manchester University Press, 1990), 207.

88. William Blaikie, *How to Get Strong and How to Stay So* (1879; repr., New York: Harper and Brothers, 1902). Blaikie also published a popular exercise manual designed more specifically for children, *Sound Bodies of Our Boys and Girls* (1883; repr., New York: Harper and Brothers, 1890). Although he differed in philosophy from his mentor, Harvard

physical-culture professor Dudley Sargent, Blaikie based many of his methods as well as his many weightlifting machines on those invented by Sargent.

89. Blaikie, *How to Get Strong*, 12–24. Or as Eugene Sandow described it, the white middle class was in danger of becoming "a race of people whose sole physical exertion will [soon] consist in pressing buttons and turning levers." Eugene Sandow, *The Gospel of Strength, According to Sandow* (Melbourne: T. Shaw Fitchett, 1902), 29.

90. Blaikie, *How to Get Strong*, 3–4.

91. This critique of the unbalanced muscular effects of athletics was echoed by a number of professional strongmen and physical-culture advocates, particularly Eugene Sandow and Max Unger (who went on to become better known by his professional name, Lionel Strongfort). See Sandow, *Gospel of Strength*, 60; and Max Unger, *Intelligence in Physical Culture* (New York: Max Unger's Health and Strength Institute, 1910), 7.

92. Carolyn Thomas De La Peña, *The Body Electric: How Strange Machines Built the Modern American* (New York: New York University Press, 2003), 54.

93. John Harvey Kellogg, *Life, Its Mysteries and Miracles: A Manual of Health Principles* (Battle Creek, MI: Modern Medicine, 1910), 363.

94. "What I did determine on and largely secure was the development of a fine physique. Blaikie's *How to Get Strong and How to Stay So* was a great help. Early country life gave a good start, and housework kept some muscles in use, the best of it is scrubbing the floor." Gilman, *Living*, 64.

95. Blaikie, *How to Get Strong*, 32.

96. Ibid., 33–34 (original emphasis).

97. Catherine Beecher, *Physiology and Calisthenics for Schools and Families* (New York: Harper and Bros., 1856). See also Todd, *Physical Culture and the Body Beautiful*, 24.

98. See Todd, *Physical Culture and the Body Beautiful*, 12.

99. Ibid., 89. See also Martha H. Verbrugge, *Able-Bodied Womanhood: Personal Health and Social Change in Nineteenth-Century Boston* (New York: Oxford University Press, 1988), 136.

100. Vertinsky, *Eternally Wounded Woman*, 217. The account in the *San Francisco Examiner* goes on to identify such muscularity as an indictment of Stetson's masculinity as well: "He said she followed gymnastics until she became very muscular. G. Walt is not a muscular man, and somewhat undersized, so his complaint seemed to hint that his wife was rather the head of the household before she picked up her dress reform duds, her Bellamy writings and her muscular development and put off for California." Quoted in Mary A. Hill, *Charlotte Perkins Gilman: The Making of a Radical Feminist, 1860–1896* (Philadelphia: Temple University Press, 1980), 197.

101. Charlotte Perkins Gilman, "If I Were a Man," *Physical Culture*, July 1914, 31–34, reprinted in *The Charlotte Perkins Gilman Reader*, ed. Ann J. Lane (New York: Pantheon Books, 1980), 32–38. See also Janet Beer and Ann Heilmann, "'If I Were a Man': Charlotte Perkins Gilman, Sarah Grand and the Sexual Education of Girls," in *Special Relationships: Anglo-American Affinities and Antagonisms, 1854–1936*, ed. Janet Beer and Bridget Bennett (Manchester: Manchester University Press, 2002), 178–201.

102. Charlotte Perkins Gilman, "If I Were a Woman," *Physical Culture,* August 1914, 152–156.

103. Gilman, "If I Were a Man," 32–33.

104. This model of modern liberal citizenship, as David Kazanjian has put it, "presumes to ignore all the myriad, particularistic differences among subjects—trade, heritage, wealth, race, gender, religion, the list is supposedly infinite—in order to apprehend each subject equally." David Kazanjian, *The Colonizing Trick: National Culture and Imperial Citizenship in Early America* (Minneapolis: University of Minnesota Press, 2003), 2.

105. Gilman, "If I Were a Man," 37.

106. Ibid., 33.

107. Charlotte Perkins Gilman, *Women and Economics* (Boston: Small, Maynard, 1900), 33.

108. Ibid., 339.

109. See Alys Eve Weinbaum, *Wayward Reproductions: Genealogies of Race and Nation in Transatlantic Modern Thought* (Durham, NC: Duke University Press, 2004), 93–95.

110. While the recovery and republication of much of Gilman's work since the 1970s has largely turned on the importance of her feminist critique within the history of feminism in the United States, it is only recently that the racial and nationalist dimensions of Gilman's feminist politics have begun to be rigorously examined. See Bederman, *Manliness and Civilization,* 121–169; and Weinbaum, *Wayward Reproductions,* 61–105.

111. Charlotte Perkins Gilman, *What Diantha Did* (Durham, NC: Duke University Press, 2005). On the autobiographical resonances of these early narratives, see Jennifer S. Tuttle, "Rewriting the West Cure: Charlotte Perkins Gilman, Owen Wister, and the Sexual Politics of Neurasthenia," in *The Mixed Legacy of Charlotte Perkins Gilman,* ed. Catherine J. Golden and Joanna Schneider Zangrando (Newark: University of Delaware Press, 2000), 103–121.

112. Gilman, *What Diantha Did,* 142–143.

113. Ibid., 185–186. Although Ross's argument seems to be a reactionary defense of Lamarck's recently disproven theory of acquired characteristics, his experiments in fact reveal the ways that the Lamarckian thesis was being translated into a theory of culture by the language of muscle and character. As Ross explains, "An acquired trait is one gained by exercise; it modifies the whole organism. It must have an effect on the race. We expect the sons of a line of soldiers to inherit their father's courage—perhaps his habit of obedience—but not his wooden leg" (185).

114. Charlotte Perkins Gilman, *The Crux* (1910; repr., Durham, NC: Duke University Press, 2003).

115. Ibid., 109, 122, 140.

116. Ibid., 152.

117. Ibid., 154, 156.

118. Ibid., 156.

119. Ibid., 147.

120. Ibid.

121. Charlotte Perkins Gilman, *Herland, The Yellow Wall-Paper, and Selected Writings* (New York: Penguin, 1999).

122. Ibid., 88.

123. Ibid., 57.

124. Ibid., 88.

125. See Weinbaum, *Wayward Reproductions,* 145–186; and Bederman, *Manliness and Civilization,* 121–169.

126. Pauline Hopkins, *Of One Blood; or, The Hidden Self,* in *The Magazine Novels of Pauline Hopkins* (New York: Oxford University Press, 1988), 441–621.

127. Gilman, *Herland,* 130, 44, 21–22.

128. Ibid., 131, 67.

129. Ibid., 55.

130. Ibid., 129.

131. Frantz Fanon, *Black Skin, White Masks,* trans. Richard Philcox (New York: Grove, 2008), 92.

132. Frederick Douglass, *The Heroic Slave* (1853), in *Frederick Douglass: Selected Speeches and Writings,* ed. Philip S. Foner (Chicago: Lawrence Hill Books, 1999), 220, 222.

133. As Mrs. Bellmont says of young Frado in Harriet Wilson's *Our Nig,* "If she wasn't tough she would have been killed long ago." Harriet E. Wilson, *Our Nig; or, Sketches from the Life of a Free Black* (New York: Penguin, 2009), 89; Frederick Douglass, *Life and Times of Frederick Douglass, Written by Himself* (1893), in *Frederick Douglass: Autobiographies* (New York: Library of America, 1994), 865–866. See also Du Bois's comments on the global implications of such a logic of labor and muscle in *Darkwater:* "Who does the physical work of the world, those whose muscles need the exercise or those whose souls and minds are stupefied with manual toil?" W.E.B. Du Bois, *Darkwater: Voices from within the Veil* (New York: Washington Square, 2004), 163.

NOTES TO CHAPTER 4

1. Michel Foucault, "Character," in *The Order of Things: An Archaeology of the Human Sciences* (New York: Vintage Books, 1973), 138–140.

2. Walter Benjamin, "Fate and Character," in *Reflections,* ed. Peter Demetz, trans. Edmund Jephcott (New York: Schocken Books, 1986), 309.

3. [J. Max Barber], "Our Symposium," *Voice of the Negro* 2, no. 1 (January 1905): 670.

4. H.S. Bradley, "The Opportunity for an Object Lesson," *Voice of the Negro* 2, no. 1 (January 1905): 674.

5. William Hayes Ward, "A Northern Man's Message," *Voice of the Negro* 2, no. 1 (January 1905): 676 (original emphasis).

6. William H. Council, "A Message to the Negro Race of the Twentieth Century," *Voice of the Negro* 2, no. 1 (January 1905): 682.

7. Kelly Miller, "A Word to the Twentieth Century Negro," *Voice of the Negro* 2, no. 1 (January 1905): 678.

8. I am following Kevin Gaines in using the shorthand "racial uplift" to describe collectively a broad array of reform movements in the post-Reconstruction period. My interest

in using the term is that it was important to those writers for whom character's intrinsic association with a civilizing process is central to their articulations of racial uplift. The danger of applying this term in such a general way is that it can occlude the ways in which the evolutionary hierarchies—and assimilationist logic—that such a notion of "uplift" frequently entailed were rejected by many writers and reformers. Kevin K. Gaines, *Uplifting the Race: Black Leadership, Politics, and Culture in the Twentieth Century* (Chapel Hill: University of North Carolina Press, 1996).

9. As Kevin Gaines observes, "Reconstruction advocates of uplift transformed the race's collective historical struggles against the slave system and the planter class into a self-appointed personal duty to reform the character and manage the behavior of blacks themselves" (ibid., 20). Gaines's recognition of the importance of character building, however, is typically fleeting in that it explains away the emphasis on character as simply a turn to the self-help ideology of "American individualism" when in fact it was frequently mobilized to address the problems of such an approach.

10. Though Du Bois and Washington were both asked for contributions, their positions ended up being mostly represented by surrogates such as William Council, the head of a prominent Southern industrial school, and Kelly Miller, the respected Howard University professor. Du Bois's own submission did not so much offer a message as it did launch an attack on Washington for his censoring of critics within the African American press. And although Washington had also promised a submission, it never arrived in time for publication.

11. Booker T. Washington, *Character Building* (1903; repr., Amsterdam: Fredonia Books, 2002), 91.

12. W.E.B. Du Bois, *The Souls of Black Folk* (1903; repr., New York: Penguin, 1996), 79.

13. Joseph R. Gay, *Progress and Achievements of the 20th Century Negro: A Handbook for Self-Improvement Which Leads to Greater Success* (New York: Western W. Wilson, 1913); Elias M. Woods, *The Negro in Etiquette: A Novelty* (St. Louis: Buxton and Skinner, 1899); Silas X. Floyd, *Floyd's Flowers, or Duty and Beauty for Colored Children* (Atlanta: Hertel, Jenkins, 1905); Emma Azalia Hackley, *The Colored Girl Beautiful* (Kansas City, MO: Burton, 1916); Sarah Estelle Haskin, *The Handicapped Winners* (Nashville, TN: Publishing House of the M.E. Church, 1922). See also Katherine Capshaw Smith, "Childhood, the Body, and Race Performance: Early 20th-Century Etiquette Books for Black Children," *African American Review* 40, no. 4 (Winter 2006): 795–812.

14. Cathy Boeckmann, *A Question of Character: Scientific Racism and the Genres of American Fiction, 1892–1912* (Tuscaloosa: University of Alabama Press, 2000), 16.

15. Ibid., 4.

16. On the historical collapse of Lamarckian theories of racial recapitulation, see Gail Bederman, *Manliness and Civilization: A Cultural History of Gender and Race in the United States, 1880–1917* (Chicago: University of Chicago Press, 1995), 109.

17. Boeckmann, *A Question of Character,* 19. For a historical overview of the debates over monogenism and polygenism in the European philosophical tradition, see Robert Ber-

nasconi and Tommy L. Lott, "Introduction" in *The Idea of Race*, ed. Robert Bernasconi and Tommy L. Lott (Indianapolis: Hackett, 2000); and Boeckmann, *A Question of Character*, 19.

18. Boeckmann, *A Question of Character*, 20.

19. Joseph Le Conte, *The Race Problem in the South* (1892; repr., Miami: Mnemosyne, 1969), 366.

20. See Anne Fountain, *José Martí and U.S. Writers* (Gainesville: University Press of Florida, 2003), 27–46; and José Martí, "Emerson," *The America of José Martí*, trans. Juan de Onís (New York: Noonday, 1953), 216–238.

21. José Martí, "My Race" (1893), in *José Martí: Selected Writings*, ed. and trans. Esther Allen (New York: Penguin, 2002), 319–320.

22. José Martí, "Our America" (1891), in Allen, *José Martí*, 289.

23. Hopkins interrogates, in other words, the tension between what Werner Sollors refers to as the concepts of "consent" and "descent." See Werner Sollors, *Beyond Ethnicity: Consent and Descent in American Culture* (New York: Oxford University Press, 1987).

24. See Jennifer Putzi, "'Raising the Stigma': Black Womanhood and the Marked Body in Pauline Hopkins's *Contending Forces*," *College Literature* 31, no. 2 (Spring 2004): 1–21.

25. Dana Luciano, "Passing Shadows: Melancholic Nationality and Black Critical Publicity in Pauline E. Hopkins's *Of One Blood*," in *Loss: The Politics of Mourning*, ed. David L. Eng and David Kazanjian (Berkeley: University of California Press, 2003), 162.

26. Cited in Jonathan Scott Holloway, "Racial Conferrals and Claims: The Politics of Race Leadership in the Early Twentieth Century," review essay, *American Quarterly* 50, no. 2 (1998): 415–423.

27. Kevin Gaines, *Uplifting the Race: Black Leadership, Politics, and Culture in the Twentieth Century* (Chapel Hill: University of North Carolina Press, 1996), 1–18.

28. "Blacks are wedded to narratives of ascent . . . and we have made the compounded preposition 'up from' our own: up from slavery, up from Piedmont, up from the Bronx, always up. But narratives of ascent, whether or not we like to admit it, are also narratives of alienation, of loss." Henry Louis Gates, Jr., "Parable of the Talents," in *The Future of the Race*, by Henry Louis Gates, Jr., and Cornel West (New York: Knopf, 1996) 3.

29. Joseph R. Gay, *Progress and Achievements of the 20th Century Negro: A Handbook for Self-Improvement Which Leads to Greater Success* (New York: Western W. Wilson, 1913), 127.

30. Kelly Miller, *Race Adjustment* (New York: Neale, 1908), reprinted as *Radicals and Conservatives* (New York: Schocken Books, 1968).

31. When the Marxist historian Cedric Robinson, for example, argues that "[b]y the second half of the nineteenth century, two alternative Black political cultures had arisen," he invokes the conceptual binary most commonly associated with Washington and Du Bois, that of "elite" and "masses." Cedric J. Robinson, *Black Movements in America* (New York: Routledge, 1997), 96–97. Alternate renditions of this binary have also been offered by Ross Posnock, who sees a contrast between Washington's "racial authenticity" and Du Bois's "racial cosmopolitanism," and Dana Luciano, who, sympathetic to Washington, sees a contrast between "the passive consumption that constitutes participation in the print public sphere" and

the "active participation in the face-to-face democratic community." Ross Posnock, "How It Feels to Be a Problem: Du Bois, Fanon, and the 'Impossible Life' of the Black Intellectual," *Critical Inquiry* 23, no. 2 (Winter 1997): 323–349; Luciano, "Passing Shadows," 151.

32. Gates, "Parable of the Talents," 33. See also Jacqueline M. Moore, *Booker T. Washington, W.E.B. Du Bois, and the Struggle for Racial Uplift* (Wilmington, DE: Scholarly Resources, 2003), xv.

33. Gaines, *Uplifting the Race*, 2. Most conspicuously left out of this picture of racial uplift, as Gaines and many others have pointed out, is the early migration movement led by Benjamin "Pap" Singleton, A.A. Bradley, and Richard H. Cain and culminating in Marcus Garvey's Back-to-Africa movement, as well as the black women's club movement, led by Ida B. Wells, which was one of the most effective political organizations of the time. See Cornel West, "Black Strivings in a Twilight Civilization," in Gates and West, *Future of the Race*, 67–68. As Hazel Carby has put it, "though Afro-American cultural and literary history commonly regards the late nineteenth and early twentieth centuries in terms of great men, as the Age of Washington and Du Bois, marginalizing the political contributions of black women, these were the years of the first flowering of black women's autonomous organizations and a period of intense intellectual activity and productivity." Hazel Carby, *Reconstructing Womanhood: The Emergence of the Afro-American Woman Novelist* (New York: Oxford University Press, 1987), 6–7.

34. Hazel Carby, "The Souls of Black Men," in *Race Men* (Cambridge, MA: Harvard University Press, 1998), 21.

35. Washington, preface to *Character Building*.

36. Frederick Drinker, for example, describes Washington as having a "character worth emulating." Frederick Drinker, *Booker T. Washington: The Master Mind of a Child of Slavery* (New York: Negro Universities Press, 1915), 211. And yet the danger of this form of recognition can be seen in William Dean Howells's suggestion that such an exemplarity renders Washington an object of utility: "we may safely recognize in Booker T. Washington an Afro-American of unsurpassed usefulness and an exemplary citizen." William Dean Howells, "An Exemplary Citizen," *North American Review*, September 1901, 288.

37. "By constructive ability or constructive genius we mean the ability to form, devise and build. How many of us are in possession of this faculty? How many of us can formulate plans to meet emergencies? How many of us in time of necessity can come forward with arrangements and connections for which posterity will bless us?" Booker T. Washington, "Constructive Ability," *Voice of the Negro* 2, no. 9 (September 1905): 648.

38. Booker T. Washington, *Up from Slavery: An Autobiography* (New York: Modern Library, 1999), 153. Further references to this source are to this edition and are cited parenthetically in the text.

39. As Sidonie Smith puts it, "Booker T. Washington was probably the first well-known black Horatio Alger." Sidonie Smith, *Where I'm Bound: Patterns of Slavery and Freedom in Black American Autobiography* (Westport, CT: Greenwood, 1974), 30, 32.

40. W.E.B. Du Bois, *The Souls of Black Folk* (1903; repr., New York: Penguin Books, 1996),

79. Further references to this source are to this edition and are cited parenthetically in the text.

41. See also Thomas Augst, *The Clerk's Tale: Young Men and Moral Life in Nineteenth-Century America* (Chicago: University of Chicago Press, 2003), 24–26.

42. I borrow the term "educing" from David Lloyd and Paul Thomas, "Educing the Citizen," in *Culture and the State* (New York: Routledge, 1998), 115–125.

43. See John Stuart Mill, *Considerations on Representative Government* (New York: Liberal Arts Press, 1958), 24–25, 47–53, 111.

44. Willard B. Gatewood, *Aristocrats of Color: The Black Elite, 1880–1920* (Bloomington: Indiana University Press, 1990). While Cornel West holds that "Du Bois is the brook of fire through which we all must pass in order to gain access to the intellectual and political weaponry needed to sustain the radical democratic tradition in our time," he also identifies Du Bois's notion of the talented tenth as the Achilles heel that reveals the "philosophic inadequacy" of his "interpretation of the human condition." West, "Black Strivings in a Twilight Civilization," 55–56.

45. "Character-Training," *Voice of the Negro* 2, no. 2 (February 1905): 126.

46. "Shall We Materialize the Negro?" *Voice of the Negro* 2 (March 1905): 194. The "two conflicting currents of thought" identified and articulated in "Shall We Materialize the Negro?" as Cynthia Schrager has argued, are thus representative of a broader "border dispute being waged in late-nineteenth-century western culture between science and religion, between the material and the spiritual—a split that William James characterized in terms of an antipathy between the 'scientific-academic' and the 'feminine-mystical minds.'" Cynthia D. Schrager, "Both Sides of the Veil: Race, Science, and Mysticism in W.E.B. Du Bois," *American Quarterly* 48, no. 4 (1996): 552.

47. Frederick Douglass, "What Are the Colored People Doing for Themselves?" (1848), in *Negro Social and Political Thought,* ed. Howard Brotz (New York: Basic Books, 1966), 207.

48. Frederick Douglass, "Letter to Harriet Beecher Stowe" (1853), in *Frederick Douglass: Selected Speeches and Writings* (abridged), ed. Philip S. Foner (Chicago: Lawrence Hill Books, 1999), 217.

49. Douglass, "What Are the Colored People Doing for Themselves?" 207.

50. Ibid.

51. The power of the rhetoric of character to define what counts as the representational indicators of personal identity and to reform a set of institutions geared toward the formation and building of character might thus be understood as an intervention in what Michael Omi and Howard Winant refer to as the "racial formation" of the late nineteenth century. Michael Omi and Howard Winant, *Racial Formation in the United States* (New York: Routledge, 1994), 56.

52. Hopkins began a successful career at the *Colored American Magazine* both as editor and as a contributor of both serialized novels and sociological essays. Hopkins's successful tenure, however, was cut short in 1904, when the *Colored American Magazine* was taken over by Fred R. Moore, who was financially backed by Booker T. Washington and who presumably forced Hopkins out because, as Du Bois put it, "her attitude was not conciliatory

enough" to the Washington agenda. [W.E.B. Du Bois], "The Colored American Magazine in America," *Crisis* 5 (November 1912): 33, quoted and discussed in Richard Yarborough, introduction to *Contending Forces,* by Pauline Hopkins (New York: Oxford University Press, 1988), xliii. This story of Hopkins's move to the *Voice of the Negro,* however, has more recently been disputed. See Gaines, *Uplifting the Race,* 44. See also Alisha R. Knight, "Furnace Blasts for the Tuskegee Wizard: Revisiting Pauline Elizabeth Hopkins, Booker T. Washington and the Colored American Magazine," *American Periodicals: A Journal of History, Criticism, and Bibliography* 17, no. 1 (2007): 41–64; and Penelope L. Bullock, *The Afro-American Periodical Press, 1838–1909* (Baton Rouge: Louisiana State University Press, 1981), 107–110.

53. Yarborough, introduction to *Contending Forces,* xxviii. For a full bibliography of Hopkins's work, see Malin LaVon Walther, "Works by and about Pauline Hopkins," in *The Unruly Voice: Rediscovering Pauline Elizabeth Hopkins,* ed. John Cullen Gruesser (Urbana: University of Illinois Press, 1996), 221–224.

54. See, for example, "The Evils of Intemperance and Their Remedy," *Famous Men of the Negro Race* and *Famous Women of the Negro Race,* and *The Dark Races of the Twentieth Century,* which were recently reprinted in *Daughter of the Revolution: The Major Nonfiction Works of Pauline E. Hopkins,* ed. Ira Dworkin (New Brunswick, NJ: Rutgers University Press, 2007).

55. See, for example, Martin Robinson Delany, *The Condition, Elevation, Emigration, and Destiny of the Colored People of the United States* (1852; repr., Baltimore: Black Classic Press, 1993); and W.E.B. Du Bois, *The Health and Physique of the Negro American* (Atlanta: Atlanta University Press, 1906).

56. Pauline Hopkins, *Contending Forces: A Romance Illustrative of Negro Life North and South* (1900; repr., New York: Oxford University Press, 1988), 13. Further references to the novel are to this edition and are cited parenthetically in the text.

57. Charles Chesnutt, *Essays and Speeches,* ed. Joseph R. McElrath, Jr., Robert C. Leitz, III, and Jesse S. Crisler (Stanford, CA: Stanford University Press, 1999), 513; Charles Chesnutt, *The Journals of Charles W. Chesnutt,* ed. Richard H. Brodhead (Durham, NC: Duke University Press, 1993), 126.

58. Barbara Christian, "Images of Black Women in Afro-American Literature: From Stereotype to Character," in *Black Feminist Criticism: Perspectives on Black Women Writers* (New York: Pergamon, 1985), 19.

59. As Glazener succinctly puts it, "The same penchant for classification that marked such sinister intellectual enterprises as racial anthropology, sexology, and phrenology flourished in U.S. literary culture during the latter half of the nineteenth century." Nancy Glazener, *Reading for Realism: The History of a U.S. Literary Institution, 1850–1910* (Durham, NC: Duke University Press, 1997), 1. See also Kenneth Warren, *Black and White Strangers: Race and American Literary Realism* (Chicago: University of Chicago Press, 1993), 6–9; Boeckmann, *A Question of Character,* 8; and Henry Louis Gates, Jr., *Figures in Black: Words, Signs, and the Racial Self* (New York: Oxford University Press, 1987), 22–23.

60. Warren, *Black and White Strangers,* 15.

61. The latter formulation comes from the advertised prospectus for *Contending Forces*

published in the *Colored American Magazine,* which drew heavily and often verbatim from the preface although with some subtle, and very telling, modifications. "Prospectus of the New Romance of Colored Life, 'Contending Forces,'" *Colored American Magazine,* September 1900, 195. Hazel Carby has also noted this important historical aim of Hopkins's work: "her use of history to rewrite an American heritage and question the boundaries of inheritance was important in her fiction and shaped her political perception." Carby, *Reconstructing Womanhood,* 128.

62. Ann duCille, *The Coupling Convention: Sex, Text, and the Tradition in Black Women's Fiction* (New York: Oxford University Press, 1993), 38.

63. Ibid., 36.

64. See Colleen C. O'Brien, "'Blacks in All Quarters of the Globe': Anti-Imperialism, Insurgent Cosmopolitanism, and International Labor in Pauline Hopkins's Literary Journalism," *American Quarterly* 61, no. 2 (June 2009): 245–270.

65. Susan Gilman cites from Robert A. Bone's *The Negro Novel in America* (New Haven, CT: Yale University Press, 1965) as one example of such an perspective: "It has been said, for example, that the early black novelist was so 'caught between the anti-Negro stereotypes and his own counter stereotypes . . . [that] in the end he avoided the problem by seeking refuge in the flat static characters of conventional melodrama." Susan Gilman, "The Mulatto, Tragic or Triumphant? The Nineteenth-Century American Race Melodrama," *The Culture of Sentimentality in Nineteenth-Century America,* ed. Shirley Samuels (New York: Oxford University Press, 1992), 224.

66. Christian, "Images of Black Women in Afro-American Literature," 19. For Christian, this evolution, which begins with the work of Zora Neale Hurston and culminates with Toni Morrison, is intimately tied to the development of genre and in particular to the capacities of realism and modernism to represent what E.M. Forster might term the "rounded" character. For a more focused analysis of the role of character and characterization in the aims and development of black women's writing, see Deborah E. McDowell, who takes as her starting point the fact that "imagining the black woman as a 'whole' character or 'self' has been a consistent preoccupation of black female novelists throughout their literary history." Deborah E. McDowell, "'The Changing Same': Generational Connections and Black Women Novelists," *New Literary History* 18, no. 2 (Winter 1987): 283.

67. Hazel Carby similarly argues that "it is necessary to confront Christian's assertions that the prime motivation for nineteenth- and early twentieth-century black writers was to confront the negative images of blacks held by whites and to dispute the simplistic model of the literary development of African American women writers indicated by such titles as 'From Stereotype to Character.'" Carby, *Reconstructing Womanhood,* 14.

68. See Eve Allegra Raimon, *The "Tragic Mulatta" Revisited: Race and Nationalism in Nineteenth-Century Antislavery Fiction* (New Brunswick, NJ: Rutgers University Press, 2004).

69. Amy Robinson, "It Takes One to Know One: Passing and Communities of Common Interest, *Critical Inquiry* 20 (1994): 716.

70. Mary Dearborn, *Pocahontas's Daughters: Gender and Ethnicity in American Culture* (New York: Oxford University Press, 1978), 74.

71. Hopkins was able to pursue a literary career largely because she also supported herself as a stenographer.

72. Claudia Tate, *Domestic Allegories of Political Desire: The Black Heroine's Text at the Turn of the Century* (New York: Oxford University Press, 1992), 14.

73. John Todd, *The Daughter at School* (Northampton, MA: Hopkins, Bridgman, 1854), 207.

74. By describing that character as "sterling," of course, Dora smuggles back in the notion of feminine purity that such a recognition would presumably escape, for "sterling" not only denotes the "other" precious metal on which the monetary system was standardized but also is a term for the purest form of such a metal. For an account of the debates over the gold and silver standards that were raging at the time, see Walter Benn Michaels, *The Gold Standard and the Logic of Naturalism* (Berkeley: University of California Press, 1987).

75. For a concise overview of the developing meaning of Sappho as both a historical figure and as an archetype of lesbian desire in the Gilded Age, see Siobhan B. Somerville, "Inverting the Tragic Mulatta Tradition: Race and Homosexuality in Pauline E. Hopkins's Fiction," in *Queering the Color Line: Race and the Invention of Homosexuality in American Culture* (Durham, NC: Duke University Press, 2000). Sappho, the ancient Greek poet, was taken in the earlier part of the nineteenth century to represent either female licentiousness or desexualized abstract love, but by century's end, Somerville argues, "a different sexualized narrative increasingly circulated around the figure of Sappho, who became enmeshed in emerging understandings of female inversion and homosexuality. Sappho, in fact, came to symbolize the manifestation of this 'new' sexuality in women, as evidenced by the terms used to label it by literary and medical men alike: 'sapphism' and 'lesbianism'" (ibid., 85–86). What is perhaps most significant about the name Sappho in the context of *Contending Forces*, however, is that it is the name that "Mabelle ("my beauty") Beaubean" *chooses* for herself in order, the narrative suggests, to leave her past behind, or at least the past represented by that name. As Somerville also points out, "it is remarkable that critical discussions of Hopkins have tended to avoid the name's obvious cultural associations with lesbian desire" (ibid., 85). Elizabeth Ammons is typical in this regard, when she ascribes Sappho's name to her namesake's own fragmentary historical presence and literary talent: "Sappho survives barely, like her namesake whose verse we have only in fragments." Elizabeth Ammons, *Conflicting Stories: American Women Writers at the Turn into the Twentieth Century* (New York: Oxford University Press, 1991), 78.

76. As Siobhan Somerville puts it, "Despite Hopkins's use of the conventional marriage plot in the conclusion of *Contending Forces*, scenes of female homoeroticism structure the narrative in important ways. Hopkins portrays couples as potential sites for the expression of desire and identification, at the same time that she mitigates their threat to the narrative's overall heterosexual trajectory." Somerville, *Queering the Color Line*, 99.

77. Hopkins seems to be drawing here on a well-known story that was frequently cited in Ida B. Wells's antilynching campaign. See duCille, *Coupling Convention*, 37; and Shawn Michelle Smith, *American Archives: Gender, Race, and Class in Visual Culture* (Princeton, NJ: Princeton University Press, 1999), 145.

78. "In preparation for the denouement which linked the personal history of Sappho to the history of black persecution in the South, Hopkins assembled all her characters for a meeting

of the American Colored League, called in response to the increased number of lynchings in the South." Carby, *Reconstructing Womanhood,* 137.

79. John's threat nonetheless makes clear the real risk that Sappho faces in being exposed, the risk that her rape will not even be legible in terms of consent: "'I was a victim! an innocent child!' moaned [Sappho]. 'I know,' said John, 'but girls of fourteen are frequently wives in our Southern climes, where women mature early. A man as supercilious as Will in his pride of Northern birth would take no excuse, and would never forgive'" (319). For an account of the confounding of consent and the intelligibility of rape under slavery, see Saidiya V. Hartman, "Seduction and the Ruses of Power," in *Scenes of Subjection: Terror, Slavery, and Self-Making in Nineteenth-Century America* (New York: Oxford University Press, 1997), 79–112.

80. As Carby puts it, "Commercial interest and a desire for profit motivated Montfort to keep his slaves and move to the United States. The consequence in Hopkins's fictional world was that a debt needed to be paid on two levels: the debt that accrued within the family history of the Montforts and, by implication, a debt that was owed to the whole black community from the profits of the slave trade." Carby, *Reconstructing Womanhood,* 136.

81. Houston Baker, *Workings of the Spirit: The Poetics of Afro-American Women's Writing* (Chicago: University of Chicago Press, 1991), 26.

NOTES TO CHAPTER 5

1. O.P. Furnas, "Our Mothers," *Herald of Gospel Liberty* 112, no. 19 (May 6, 1920): 441.

2. Frances Willard, "Scientific Temperance Instruction in the Public Schools," *Arena* 12, no. 64 (March 1895): 10.

3. The Chicago Association for Child Study and Parent Education, *Building Character: Proceedings of the Mid-West Conference on Character Development, February, 1928* (Chicago: University of Chicago Press, 1928), v–vi.

4. For a comprehensive but relatively concise overview of Addams's diverse body of work as a social reformer, see Robyn Muncy, *Creating a Female Dominion in American Reform: 1890–1935* (New York: Oxford University Press, 1991), 3–37. See also Louise W. Knight, *Citizen: Jane Addams and the Struggle for Democracy* (Chicago: University of Chicago Press, 2005); and Jean Bethke Elshtain, *Jane Addams and the Dream of American Democracy: A Life* (New York: Basic Books, 2002).

5. Kathleen D. McCarthy, *Noblesse Oblige: Charity and Cultural Philanthropy in Chicago, 1849–1929* (Chicago: University of Chicago Press, 1982), 109; Michael B. Katz, *In the Shadow of the Poorhouse: A Social History of Welfare in America* (New York: Basic Books, 1986), 162.

6. For a more detailed account of Addams's impact specifically on women's and children's policy issues, see Molly Ladd-Taylor, "Hull House Goes to Washington: Women and the Children's Bureau," in *Gender, Class, Race, and Reform in the Progressive Era,* ed. Noralee Frankel and Nancy S. Dye (Lexington: University Press of Kentucky, 1991), 110–126.

7. Jane Addams, "Social Attitudes and Character," in *Building Character: Proceedings of the Mid-West Conference on Character Development, February, 1928,* The Chicago Association for Child Study and Parent Education (Chicago: University of Chicago Press, 1928), 294–295.

8. Muncy, *Creating a Female Dominion*, xii.

9. John Todd, *The Daughter at School* (Northampton, MA: Hopkins, Bridgman, 1854), 207, 208.

10. David I. Macleod, *Building Character in the American Boy: The Boy Scouts, YMCA, and Their Forerunners, 1870–1920* (Madison: University of Wisconsin Press, 1983), 44–59.

11. Sarah C. Edgarton, "Female Culture," *Mother's Assistant* 3 (1843): 94–95, reprinted in *Antebellum American Culture*, ed. David Brion Davis (University Park: Pennsylvania State University Press, 1979), 77.

12. Catherine Beecher, *A Treatise on Domestic Economy* (1841; repr., New York: Schocken Books, 1977), 13.

13. Jane Addams, *Twenty Years at Hull-House* (1910; repr., New York: Penguin Books, 1998), 61. Further references to this work are to this edition and are cited parenthetically in the text.

14. Booker T. Washington, for example, similarly inscribed the origins of the Tuskegee Institute within his autobiography in term of his own Horatio Alger–like rise from rags to riches in *Up from Slavery* (1901).

15. Allen F. Davis, *American Heroine: The Life and Legend of Jane Addams* (Chicago: Ivan R. Dee, 2000), 160, 162.

16. Jean Bethke Elshtain, for example, begins her own account of Addams's life and work with just such an autobiographical reiteration: "John Addams's deep civic involvement clearly influenced his daughter's development. . . . To his precocious, civic-minded daughter, he was a figure to admire and to emulate." Elshtain, *Jane Addams and the Dream*, 2.

17. Davis, *American Heroine*, 161.

18. Pierre Bourdieu, "Delegation and Political Fetishism," in *Language and Symbolic Power*, trans. Gino Raymond and Matthew Adamson (Cambridge, MA: Harvard University Press, 1994), 203–219.

19. Scott Nearing, *Social Adjustment* (New York: Macmillan, 1910), vii.

20. Jane Addams, *Democracy and Social Ethics* (Urbana: University of Illinois Press, 2002), 6. Further references to this work are to this edition and are cited parenthetically in the text.

21. Beecher, *Treatise on Domestic Economy*, 20.

22. George M. Beard, *American Nervousness: Its Causes and Consequences* (New York, 1881).

23. Jacob A. Riis, *How the Other Half Lives: Studies among the Tenements of New York* (1890; repr., New York: Dover, 1971). See also Robert H. Bremner on what he refers to as "the discovery of poverty" by the middle class, in *From the Depths: The Discovery of Poverty in the United States* (New York: New York University Press, 1956).

24. Jill Conway, "Women Reformers and American Culture, 1870–1930," *Journal of Social History* 5, no. 2 (Winter 1971–1972): 170–171. Toynbee Hall, the settlement in England on which Hull House and other settlements were modeled, was much more explicitly founded on the aesthetic and civilizing promise of class contact. The group of middle-class men who decided to live among the poor in London's East End made it their mission to expose the poor to the art, literature, and philosophy presumably denied to them by their class position: "The poor need more than food; they need also the knowledge, the character, the happiness which are

the gifts of God to this Age." Samuel Barnett, "Twenty-One Years of University Settlements," in *Practicable Socialism* (London, 1915), 165.

25. Addams, *Twenty Years at Hull-House,* 55. "Subjective Necessity for Social Settlements" was a lecture republished as chapter 6 in *Twenty Years at Hull-House,* and "Filial Relations" appears as chapter 2 in *Democracy and Social Ethics.*

26. See Jane Addams, "The Objective Value of a Social Settlement," originally published with "Subjective Necessity" in *Philanthropy and Social Progress,* ed. Henry C. Adams (New York: Thomas Y. Crowell, 1893), reprinted in *The Jane Addams Reader,* ed. Jean Bethke Elshtain (New York: Basic Books, 2002), 29–45.

27. Robert H. Bremner, *American Philanthropy* (Chicago: University of Chicago Press, 1988), 95.

28. Ibid.

29. Frank Dekker Watson, *The Charity Organization Movement in the United States: A Study in American Philanthropy* (New York: Macmillan, 1922), 101.

30. The Associated Charities, "The Friendly Visitor," quoted in Watson, *Charity Organization Movement,* 150.

31. E.E. Kellogg, *Studies in Character Building: A Book for Parents* (Battle Creek, MI: Good Health, 1905), 112, 23.

32. Robert A. Woods and Albert J. Kennedy, preface to *Handbook of Settlements,* ed. Robert A. Woods and Albert J. Kennedy (New York: Charities Publication Committee, 1911), v.

33. When Addams and Starr established Hull House, Chicago was a city whose population had just doubled in the preceding ten years and in which 78 percent of the city residents were either immigrants or the children of immigrants. Muncy, *Creating a Female Dominion,* 11.

34. Theodore Roosevelt, "True Americanism," in *American Ideals* (New York: G.P. Putnam's Sons, 1920), 25–26.

35. Richard Henry Pratt, "The Advantages of Mingling Indians with Whites," in *Americanizing the American Indians: Writings by the "Friends of the Indian," 1880–1900,* ed. Francis Paul Prucha (Cambridge, MA: Harvard University Press, 1973), 260.

36. John B. Torbert, "The Meaning of Our Flag," in *Americanization: Principles of Americanism, Essentials of Americanization, Technic of Race-Assimilation,* ed. Winthrop Talbot and Julia E. Johnson (New York: H.W. Wilson, 1920), 66–67.

37. Jane Addams, "Americanization," *Publications* (American Sociological Society) 14 (1919), reprinted in Elshtain, *Jane Addams Reader,* 244.

38. Quoted in Shannon Jackson, *Lines of Activity: Performance, Historiography, Hull-House Domesticity* (Ann Arbor: University of Michigan Press, 2000), 224, 226.

39. Louis Menand, introduction to *Pragmatism: A Reader,* ed. Louis Menand (New York: Vintage Books, 1997).

40. Jane Addams, "A Function of the Social Settlement" (1899), in *Pragmatism: A Reader,* ed. Louis Menand (New York: Vintage Books, 1997), 274–275. See also John Dewey, "The Place of Habit in Conduct," in *Human Nature and Conduct: An Introduction to Social Psychology* (New York: Holt, 1922), 13–88; and John Dewey, "Habits as Expressions of Growth,"

in *Democracy and Education: An Introduction to the Philosophy of Education* (New York: Macmillan, 1916), 54–62.

41. Ibid., 277, 283, 168; W.E.B. Du Bois, *Souls of Black Folk* (1903; repr., New York: Penguin, 1996), 1.

42. Jackson, *Lines of Activity*, 27.

43. See Michael A. Elliot, *The Culture Concept: Writing and Difference in the Age of Realism* (Minneapolis: University of Minnesota Press, 2002); and Brad Evans, *Before Cultures: The Ethnographic Imagination in American Literature, 1865–1920* (Chicago: University of Chicago Press, 2005).

44. Addams, "Social Attitudes and Character," 291.

45. Ibid., 293.

46. Ibid., 295.

47. Charlene Haddock Seigfried, introduction to *Democracy and Social Ethics*, by Jane Addams (Chicago: University of Illinois Press, 2002), xxiii.

48. Alain Locke, "The Concept of Race as Applied to Culture" (1924), in *The Idea of Race*, ed. Robert Bernasconi and Tommy L. Lott (Indianapolis: Hackett, 2000), 89–99; Horace Kallen, "Democracy *versus* the Melting Pot," in *Reading in Social Problems,* ed. Albert Benedict Wolfe (Boston: Ginn, 1916), 344–371; Randolph Bourne, "Trans-National America" (1916), in *The American Idea: The Best of the Atlantic Monthly,* ed. Robert Vare (New York: Broadway Books, 2007), 576–583. See also Menand, *Pragmatism*, xxvii. For a broader consideration of the politics of race in the settlement house movement, see Elisabeth Lasch-Quinn, *Black Neighbors: Race and the Limits of Reform in the American Settlement House Movement, 1890–1945* (Chapel Hill: University of North Carolina Press, 1993).

49. Jackson, *Lines of Activity*, 111.

50. Ibid., 116.

51. Ibid.

52. Ibid., 152.

53. "Sharing an etymological root that means 'to bring into being' or 'to furnish,' *performance* underscores the material acts of construction implicit in the term *reform,* elements that are often obscured when the Reform Period is wholly equated with a series of legislative and policy changes. . . . Intervening in abstracted narratives of the settlement's 'results,' performance complicates mystified assumptions about how these reform endeavors worked in daily life. . . . The emphasis now is not on the product made by the settlement artist as much as on the activity of making, where the significance of that activity cannot be measured in terms of what it completes." Ibid., 9, 11.

54. Jane Addams, *The Spirit of Youth and the City Streets* (New York: Macmillan, 1921), 83–84.

55. Katherine Joslin, *Jane Addams: A Writer's Life* (Urbana: University of Illinois Press, 2004), 61.

56. Addams, *Democracy and Social Ethics*, 100. See also Joslin, *Jane Addams,* 15.

57. Joslin, *Jane Addams,* 61.

Index

Page numbers in italics refer to illustrations.

of Judging Men (Blackford and
Newcomb), 246n26
Anderson, Amanda, 12, 31
Anderson, Benedict, 28
"An Exemplary Citizen" (Howells), 276n36
antislavery movement. *See* abolitionists
Apter, Emily, 244n5
Arendt, Hannah, 248n35
Ariadne's Thread (Miller), 36
Armstrong, John, 243n4
"Athletes Trained for the Diamond
Trophy" (in *National Police Gazette*),
128
Athletics and Manly Sport (O'Reilly),
267n22
Autobiography (Franklin), 63, 87–88
The Autobiography of W.E.B. Du Bois (Du
Bois), 1

"bad boy" figure: as character ideal, 72–73;
masculinity restored by, 68, 73–74, 80,
111; in realist fiction, 66–67, 71–76; and
romance, 75–76; and "savagery," 74–76,
99–102; Twain's critique of, 76–77,
78–81
Baden-Powell, Robert, 86
Baker, Houston, 199
Bakhtin, Mikhail, 239, 269n72
Banta, Martha, 77
Barnum, P.T., 16, 58–59
Baumfree, Isabella (Sojouner Truth),
112–116, 155
Beard, Daniel Carter: as Boy Scout
founder, 105, 109; illustrations of
Clarence, *104, 106*; promotion of *A
Connecticut Yankee,* 109; use of Sarah
Bernhardt as model, 109, *110*
Beard, George M., 117, 217, 282n22
Bederman, Gail, 117
Beecher, Catherine: and character-
building manuals, 13–14; on modern
anxiety, 217; on women as stewards of

character, 210; and women's exercise,
145
Beecher, Henry Ward, 14, 247n34
Being a Boy (Warner), 74, 260–261n26
Bell, Michael Davitt, 66
Bellamy, Edward, 255n107
Benjamin, Walter, 18, 92, 157
Berlant, Lauren, 253n93
Bernhardt, Sarah, 109, *110*
Bertillon, Alphonse, 125
Bhabha, Homi, 13, 56
The Bigelow Papers (Lowell), 64
Billy Budd, Sailor (Melville), 256–257n19
Blaikie, William, 46, 270–271n88
The Bluest Eye (Morrison), 52
bodybuilding. *See* physical culture
movement
Boeckmann, Cathy: on racial science, 161;
on realist characterization, 179; on
Twain and phrenology, 71
Bourdieu, Pierre, 282n18
boyology: and *A Connecticut Yankee,*
68–69, 80–83; and character-building
agencies, 81–82; and "chumship," 82;
role of "bad-boy" figure in, 81–82
Boyology; or. Boy Analysis (Gibson), 262n54
"boy problem," 77–78
Boys' Brigade, 81
Boy Scouts of America: and chivalric
code, 80; as "citizen-making factory,"
86; "Eleventh Annual Report," 248–
249n41; features of, 69, 82; founding
of, 9, 81; idealization of Native
American, 99, 101; and preservation of
"masculine" character, 209
The Boys' Round Table (Forbush), 262n48
Brandeis, Louis, 20, 250n62
Brodhead, Richard, 23
Brooks, Daphne, 115
Brown, Bill, 69, 73
Brown, Gillian, 244n8, 245n15
Brown, William Wells, 16, 69, 73, 249n43

Bryant, John, 256n12
Budd, Michael, 123
Building Character: Proceedings of the Mid-West Conference on Character Development, February, 1928, 204, 281n3
Burgett, Bruce, 244n6, 247n27
Burroughs, Edgar Rice, 118
Butler, Judith, 140, 247–248n34

Camp Fire Girls, 99
Capital for Working Boys: Chapters in Character Building (M'Conaughy), 249n44
Carby, Hazel, 168, 276n33, 278–279n61
Castiglia, Christopher, 15, 257n21
character: as alphabetic element, 5–8, 87, *104*, 108, 245nn15-16; as capital, 15–17, 95–96, 98–99, 249n44; conceived as interiority, 3, 25–26, 28–31, 49–50, 76; conceived as social ethic, 218–220, 238–242; dialectical concept of, 42–43, 50–51, 57–62; double meaning of, 10–12; and ethos, 11, 31, 245n11; etymology of, 5, 245n11; historicity of, 35, 156, 164–165, 180, 195–202, 230; identified with masculinity, 4, 21, 68, 74, 78, 80, 92–93; as inscription, 5, 7, 87–88, 213–214, 245n11; interdependence with personality, 57–62; as legal object, 20–21; linked with citizenship, 14–15, 26, 86, 169–170, 248n36; and literary realism, 28–32, 102–103, 177–179, 181, 254n95, 254n99; and the novel form, 27–32; perceived decline, 3–4, 9, 57–58, 78; as physiological reflex, 94–96; rearticulated as habit, 87–90; unverifiability of, 18, 48–50; as will, 92–93; women as stewards of, 208–211. *See also* character building; character representation; rhetoric of character
Character and Characteristic Men (Whipple), 59

"Character and Conduct" (Dewey), 244–245n9
"Character and Muscle" (Parkhurst), 267n27
"Character and Success" (Roosevelt), 244–245n9, 266n16
character building: and adversity, 23, 92–93, 251n71; "bad boy" as model, 70–76; factory as model, 85–86; habit as primary instrument of, 87–90; as historical process, 35, 156, 164–165, 180, 195–202, 230; idealization of "savagery," 74–76, 99–102; imperialism disguised as, 45, 67, 69, 81, 82–83; legitimated by character representation, 17–19; muscle building as, 15, 119–123, 142–143; and nationalist discourse, 13–15; novel as agent of, 27–30, 67, 70–76, 181–182, 239, 254n95; and racial uplift ideology, 157–159, 168–174; relationship to classical rhetorical tradition, 10–12; as restoration of masculinity, 68, 74, 78, 80; role of women in, 23–24, 136–141, 208–211, 221; social hierarchies reinforced by, 4, 15, 19–20, 96–99; through class emulation, 97–98, 221–227; through cross-cultural exchange, 207, 224–225, 228–229, 233–234; Twain's critical interrogation of, 65, 67–69, 81. *See also* character; character representation; rhetoric of character
character-building agencies: and "bad boy" figure, 81–82; as "character factories," 85–86; chivalric code invoked by, 80; development of, 81–82; features of, 69, 82; idealization of Native American, 99–102; and same-gender emulation, 209; social hierarchies reinforced by, 98–99
character-building manuals: as "biopolitical narratives," 13–14;

embodiment of character: implications reassessed, 3–4, 31; as instrument of discrimination, 7–8, 22; as instrument of reform, 7, 21–27
Emerson, Ralph Waldo, 58, 78
Emile (Rousseau), 145
emulation: as cross-cultural reciprocal act, 207, 224–225, 228–229, 233–234; of middle class character, 221, 222–227; same-gender, 209
The Essentials of Character (Sisson), 262n56
ethos, 11, 31, 245n11
evolutionary theory, and racial science, 161–164
exercise. *See* muscle building
expressivist theory of self, 18

Fanon, Frantz, 154
"Fate and Character" (Benjamin), 157
Federalist Papers, No.63 (Madison), 93
"Female Culture" (Edgarton), 282n11
"female masculinity," 136–141
feminine ideal: Blaikie's redefinition of, 145; in *Contending Forces,* 183–184; in *National Police Gazette,* 127, 129; and Sojourner Truth, 112–116
feminism, and Sojourner Truth, 112–116
feminists: appropriation of rhetoric of character, 21–22; and paradox of women as stewards of character, 209–210; and Sojourner Truth, 112–116, 265n7. *See also* Addams, Jane; Gilman, Charlotte Perkins
Fern, Fanny, 13
fetishism: character as challenge to, 8, 84, 115; character as product of, 64-5, 74-75, 196; Freud on, 269n72; and the naturalization of race, 46-7, 49, 61; role in rhetoric of character, 9, 16-17, 139-140, 215
Floyd, Silas X., 161

Floyd's Flowers (Floyd), 274n13
Forerunner (Gilman), 146
Formation of a Manly Character (Peck), 263n83
Forster, E.M., 254n97, 279n66
Foster, Elizabeth, 40, 53
Foucault, Michel, 27, 125, 157, 253n87
Fowler, Orson Squire, 25, 121, 252n79, 267n31
Fox, Richard K., 127
Franklin, Benjamin: "Art of Virtue," 142; and character-as-capital, 16, 249n44; as character builder, 63; on habit, 87–88
Franklin Evans, or The Inebriate (Whitman), 15
Freud, Sigmund, 1, 94, 269–270n72
friendly visit: Addams critique of, 225–227; class emulation as goal of, 222–224; functions of, 221–222; as reciprocal exchange, 224–225. *See also* charity relation; philanthropy
Fuller, Margaret, 24
Furnas, O.P., 204

Gage, Frances, 112–116, 265nn7-8
Gaines, Kevin, 166, 168, 276n33
Galton, Francis, 26, 125, 159
Garvey, Marcus, 276n33
Gates, Henry Louis, Jr.: and literary realism, 179; on racial uplift ideology, 167; on Washington-Du Bois debate, 168
Gay, Joseph, 161, 167
gender difference: destabilized in physical culture movement, 15, 131–135, 136–141; Gilman's critique of, 146–149; and muscular body rhetoric, 117–118, 123; as premise of racial uplift ideology, 164–166; and rhetoric of character, 4, 15, 19–20; and Sojourner Truth, 112–116
Genealogy of Morals (Nietzsche), 93

George, Marian M., 86, 262n60

Getting On in the World; or, Hints on Success in Life (Mathews), 90

Gibson, Henry William, 81

Gilbert, Olive, 114, 265n6

The Gilded Age: A Tale of Today (Twain and Warner), 64

Gilman, Charlotte Perkins: adoption of Blaikie's weightlifting program, 143–146; critique of gender distinctions, 146–149; and gender implications of muscle building, 15, 146–147; as physical culture advocate, 116, 142–143; and physical culture as eugenic mechanism, 147–151, 272n110, 272n113; refiguring of women's civilizing mission, 152–154. See also *The Crux*; *Forerunner*; *Herland*; "If I Were a Man"; "If I Were a Woman"; *What Diantha Did*

Girl Scouts of America, 99

Glazener, Nancy, 30, 179

Gneiting, Teona, 109

Godkin, E.L., 20, 250n60

Goodrich, Samuel, 72

The Gospel of Strength (Sandow), 271n89, 271n91

The Gospel of the Redman (Seton), 101

Habermas, Jürgen, 22, 28

habit: Addams's concept of, 231–232; and danger of addictive repetition, 89–91; ethical implications of, 94–95; as expression of fixed character, 87; paradoxical role in character building, 85–86, 94; as pervasive concept, 85–86; as physiological inscription, 94–95; as primary instrument of character building, 87–90; and problem of agency, 95–96; racialized discourse of, 90–91; as repetition of unpleasant acts, 91; second nature created by, 91–92; social hierarchies reinforced by, 96–99

"Habits as Expressions of Growth" (Dewey), 284n40

"The Habits of Habits" (Propheter), 262n61

Hackley, Emma Azalia, 161

Halberstam, Judith, 140

Hale, Sarah Josepha Buell, 9, 246n20

Hall, G. Stanley, 5, 117, 120

Hall, James, 53

Halttunen, Karen, 10, 22, 57–58, 250–251n67

Handbook of Settlements (ed. Woods and Kennedy), 283n32

The Handicapped Winners (Haskin), 274n13

Hardly a Man is Now Alive (Beard), 109

Harris, Cheryl, 21

Haskin, Sarah Estelle, 161

Health and Physique of the Negro American (Du Bois), 159, 160

Hendler, Glenn, 28, 73, 74, 75, 247n27

Herland (Gilman), 151–154

The Hermaphrodite (Howe), 248n39

The Heroic Slave (Douglass), 155

Heywood, Leslie, 136

Hilkey, Judy, 88, 89, 98

Hillis, Newell Dwight, 112, 121–122, 262n56

Hopkins, Pauline: and character as historical process, 35, 156, 164–165, 180, 195–202; critique of racial uplift ideology, 164–166; as editor and writer, 177–178, 277n52; treatment of literary character, 180–182. See also *Contending Forces*

Howe, Julia Ward, 248n39

Howells, William Dean: advice to Mark Twain, 71, 73; as "bad boy" author, 66, 72, 74, 75, 76; on Booker T. Washington, 276n36; as realist, 29

How the Other Half Lives (Riis), 282n23

How to Get Strong and How to Stay So (Blaikie), 143

How to Study Strangers by Temperament, Face and Head (Sizer), 252n85
Hull House: compared with Toynbee Hall, 282–283n24; physical culture at, 234–237; practices employed at, 231–232; role of theater at, 237–238; as venue for cross-cultural exchange, 205, 224–225, 233–234
Hume, David, 36

"If I Were a Man" (Gilman), 146–147
"If I Were a Woman" (Gilman), 146
imperialism: disguised as character building, 45, 67, 69, 81, 82–83; as national muscle building, 118–119; self-reliance as fiction of, 53–56, 60
Indian Boyhood (Eastman), 264n100
Indian Nation: Native American Literature and Nineteenth-Century Nationalisms (Walker), 243n4
Indian Scout Craft and Lore (Eastman), 264n100
industrial training: in *A Connecticut Yankee,* 85–86, 99; Addams concept of, 232; as central to Washington's character building, 168, 169; critiqued by Du Bois, 171; Douglass as advocate of, 175
inheritance: and habit as corrective mechanism, 83–85, 87; and historicity of character, 35, 156, 164–165, 195–197, 201–202; and physical culture as eugenic mechanism, 147–151; and racial science, 161–163
Intelligence in Physical Culture (Unger), 271n91
Irving, Washington, 101, 264n98

Jackson, Helen Hunt, 53
Jackson, Shannon, 232, 236, 237
James, Henry, 16, 29, 255n102
James, William, 93–95, 231

Jefferson, Thomas, 63–64
Joslin, Katherine, 238–239
Jun, Helen H., 23

Kaplan, Amy, 29, 118
Kazanjian, David, 40, 272n104
Keller, Helen, 92–93
Kellogg, E.E., 223
Kellogg, John Harvey, 144
Kett, Joseph, 79
Kidd, Kenneth, 81, 82
The Knights of the Holy Grail: A Solution of the Boy Problem (Powell), 80, 262n48

"The Ladies Idolize Sandow" (*National Police Gazette*), 130
Lamarck, Jean-Baptiste: influence on character builders, 88; theory applied to cultural evolution, 161–162; theory "proved" in *What Diantha Did* (Gilman), 149, 272n113
law: and concept of will, 93–94; and reputation, 20–21
Lears, T.J. Jackson, 70
Le Conte, Joseph, 163
Lectures on Mental Science According to the Philosophy of Phrenology (Weaver), 71
Lectures to Young Men, on Various Important Subjects (Henry Ward Beecher), 247n34
Lectures to Young Men on the Formation of Character (Hawes), 249n45
Levander, Caroline, 13
liberalism: and American character, 38; challenged by Addams's social ethic concept, 229; character as central concept in, 2, 3, 14, 18–19; and concept of will, 93–94
Life, Its Mysteries and Miracles (Kellogg), 271n93
Life and Times of Frederick Douglass (Douglass), 155

About the Author

James B. Salazar is an assistant professor of English at Temple University, where he teaches courses in nineteenth-century U.S. literature and culture.